"Kevin Diller's study offers a courageous and provocative invitation to reconsider what he calls the 'epistemological dilemma' of Christian theology. Committed to ultimate trust in its subject-matter, the reality of the triune God in his trinitarian self-revelation, it may not give in to relativizing suspicions of the human capacities of knowledge, but is called to embrace a commitment to the *logos* of theology, the capacities of human rationality, created, fallible, fallen, and yet destined to participate in the truth that God is and gracefully discloses to his created images. Starting from a concise analysis of Barth's theology of revelation and its 'theo-foundational' epistemology, Diller engages Alvin Plantinga's reformed epistemology, carefully reconstructed and defended against its philosophical critics, in a sustained conversation. The outcome is the proposal of a 'unified response' to the epistemological dilemma, drawing on the intellectual resources of both enterprises, rather than constructing a master theory which transcends them both. Blowing like a fresh wind through prejudices and complacencies that have haunted the relationship between philosophy and theology in modern times, Diller's argument explores with philosophical precision and theological depth the possibilities of a Christian epistemology, where neither philosophy nor theology lose their intellectual integrity or Christian commitment. Reading this book is a liberating experience because it encourages its readers to engage theology philosophically and philosophy theologically, both critically and constructively, in the expectation that they both have much to gain from an exchange that is no longer tied to preconceived but often poorly grounded rules of engagement."

Christoph Schwöbel, University of Tübingen

"In this groundbreaking study, Kevin Diller addresses a fundamental challenge for the Christian faith, namely, how one can affirm the knowability, universality and warrant of its theological claims while simultaneously recognizing the frailty and fallibility of those who hold them. Drawing on the complementary insights of Karl Barth and Alvin Plantinga, whose approaches are so often mistakenly assumed to be in tension, Diller provides an original, rigorously argued and deeply convincing response to the epistemological grounding problem. This field-changing volume exemplifies analytic theology at its finest. More significantly it defines the way forward for any theology that seeks to be true to the trinitarian and incarnational core of the Christian gospel. This is not only inspirational but obligatory reading for academics, students and intellectually engaged Christians alike."

Alan J. Torrance, University of St Andrews

"In this thorough and rigorously argued volume, Kevin Diller propounds an astonishing thesis. He contends that Karl Barth and Alvin Plantinga are in fundamental convergence with regard to human knowledge of God. Conversant with a wide range of scholarship on both Barth and Plantinga, Diller admirably answers their critics, clarifies their ambiguities and limitations, and shows that their remaining differences are smaller than previously assumed. This is a groundbreaking work of major proportions that will need to be reckoned with by theologians and philosophers alike for years to come."

George Hunsinger, Princeton Theological Seminary

"Bridging the divide between an analytic philosophy like Plantinga's and a Christologically-based account of theological knowledge like Barth's will seem counterintuitive to many. But given the rancorous, often divisive character of so much theological debate these days, it is much needed. Beginning with the observation that neither Plantinga nor Barth is a 'non-foundationalist'—that both are, in fact, 'theo-foundationalists' who ground knowledge of God in a trinitarian conception of revelation—Diller goes on to argue that Barth's theological epistemology, while not dependent upon any general theory, is at least compatible with Plantinga's. The results are intriguing and give promise of opening a conversation between the followers of these two great Reformed thinkers."

Bruce L. McCormack, Princeton Theological Seminary

"Christians today are faced with epistemological challenges all the time: How can I know that this is the truth? What warrant do I have for my beliefs? Is the Bible trustworthy? Can I know that there is a God? The list goes on. The great Swiss theologian Karl Barth gave certain answers to these worries. In a different context, philosopher Alvin Plantinga has spent much of his career tackling such issues. However, these two thinkers are often regarded as providing quite different answers to these questions. In this book, Kevin Diller gives an account of Barth and Plantinga that shows a deep consonance between them and their respective attempts to address the epistemological troubles we face. This is an outstanding work that repays careful study. All those who care about the future of Christian theology and philosophy, and the conversation between the two disciplines, ought to read it."

Oliver Crisp, Fuller Theological Seminary

"This excellent book is a welcome and significant contribution to the growing body of work in analytic theology generally and to the literature on the epistemology of theology in particular. Kevin Diller argues persuasively for a very unexpected conclusion—that the theological-epistemological views of Karl Barth and Alvin Plantinga are complementary rather than conflicting. Theologians and philosophers alike will profit from Diller's clear, careful and insightful exposition of these two towering figures. Diller helps to put the relationship between contemporary theology and analytic philosophy in new perspective and represents an important further step in building bridges between the two disciplines."

Michael Rea, University of Notre Dame

"In this work, Kevin Diller attempts to show that Alvin Plantinga's religious epistemology and Karl Barth's theology of revelation are not only consistent, but mutually supportive. Many will initially find this conclusion surprising and perhaps downright implausible, but Diller's arguments for his claim are careful and clear and show a deep understanding of both Barth and Plantinga. Many theologians who know Barth well know little about contemporary Christian philosophy in general and very little about Plantinga. Many Christian philosophers have only a superficial understanding of Barth's theology. This book will be profoundly helpful to both groups."

C. Stephen Evans, Baylor University

STRATEGIC INITIATIVES IN EVANGELICAL THEOLOGY

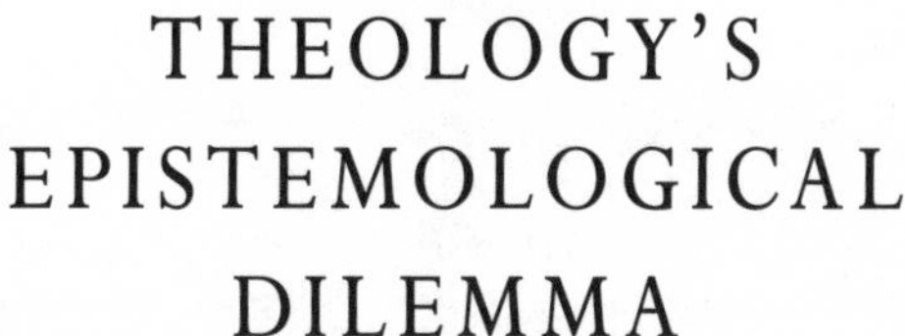

THEOLOGY'S EPISTEMOLOGICAL DILEMMA

HOW KARL BARTH AND ALVIN PLANTINGA PROVIDE A UNIFIED RESPONSE

KEVIN DILLER

FOREWORD BY ALVIN PLANTINGA

◆

An imprint of InterVarsity Press
Downers Grove, Illinois

InterVarsity Press
P.O. Box 1400, Downers Grove, IL 60515-1426
www.ivpress.com
email@ivpress.com

InterVarsity Press® is the book-publishing division of InterVarsity Christian Fellowship/USA®, a movement of students and faculty active on campus at hundreds of universities, colleges and schools of nursing in the United States of America, and a member movement of the International Fellowship of Evangelical Students. For information about local and regional activities, write Public Relations Dept., InterVarsity Christian Fellowship/USA, 6400 Schroeder Rd., P.O. Box 7895, Madison, WI 53707-7895, or visit the IVCF website at www.intervarsity.org.

Cover design: Cindy Kiple
Interior design: Beth McGill
Images: photo of Alvin Plantinga: Photo by Matt Cashore / University of Notre Dame
Karl Barth: © STR/Keystone/Corbis

ISBN 978-0-8308-3906-3 (print)
ISBN 978-0-8308-9699-8 (digital)

Printed in the United States of America ♾

As a member of the Green Press Initiative, InterVarsity Press is committed to protecting the environment and to the responsible use of natural resources. To learn more, visit greenpressinitiative.org.

Library of Congress Cataloging-in-Publication Data

Diller, Kevin, 1971-
Theology's epistemological dilemma : how Karl Barth and Alvin Plantinga provide a unified response / Kevin Diller.
pages cm
Includes bibliographical references and index.
ISBN 978-0-8308-3906-3 (pbk. : alk. paper)
1. Philosophical theology. 2. Philosophy and religion. 3. Knowledge, Theory of (Religion) 4. Christian philosophy. 5. Barth, Karl, 1886-1968. 6. Plantinga, Alvin. I. Title.
BT40.D55 2014
230.01--dc22

2014033401

P 23 22 21 20 19 18 17 16 15 14 13 12 11 10 9 8 7 6 5 4 3 2 1
Y 33 32 31 30 29 28 27 26 25 24 23 22 21 20 19 18 17 16 15 14

To Gwenael

whose creative spark is the consistent instrument

of divine renewal in our life together

CONTENTS

◆

FOREWORD

◆

It's a real pleasure to add my bit to Kevin Diller's excellent book, and I'm delighted to be bracketed with Karl Barth, the premier twentieth-century theologian. Diller's claim here is something of a surprise; the worlds of theology and philosophy are, if not mutually exclusive, at any rate a bit standoffish. But Diller makes a very good case. Barth rejects the fundamental claims of the Enlightenment; I agree. Barth rejects any attempt to come to knowledge of God "from below"; I agree. Barth argues that serious Christian believers should not be apologetic (they have nothing for which to apologize); again, I agree.

I learned a great deal about Barth from Diller's book. I also learned a good deal about my own work, and I very much appreciated his thoughtful replies to my critics. Let me say again how pleased I am to learn from Diller's book how close Barth and I really are.

Alvin Plantinga

ACKNOWLEDGMENTS

◆

A number of people deserve recognition for providing the support, illumination and encouragement that have made this project possible. It began as a PhD thesis at the University of St Andrews under the phenomenal care and brilliant direction of Professor Alan Torrance, in whose debt I will ever remain for his trenchant theological insight, tenacious encouragement and unflagging demonstration of the most profound courage, charity and generosity in the face of tremendous adversity.

St Andrews provided an idyllic setting for thinking theologically about and engaging philosophically with the gift of Christian faith. And the St Mary's postgraduate community sustained our family with an extraordinarily supportive and intellectually vibrant Christian environment. Special thanks to all those in the Roundel and at the pubs who sparked my thinking, cheered my heart and encouraged my faith, most significantly Drs. Aaron Kuecker, Luke Tallon, Kelly Liebengood, Josh Moon, Daniel Driver, Marc Cortez, Jeremy Gabrielson, Jason Goroncy, R. J. Matava and Matt Farlow.

This project was enabled by funding, support and research leave that came from several generous sources. These include the Ogilvys and the Rawlinsons for the St Mary's postgraduate research building (the Roundel) and the use of Wester Coates house in the East Neuk of Fife; Rev. Rory McLeod and the Parish Church of the Holy Trinity in St Andrews; Michael Rea and the Center for Philosophy of Religion at the University of Notre Dame; the Center for Barth Studies at Princeton Theological Seminary and the Karl Barth Research Collection at Luce Library; and the Taylor University Bedi Center for Teaching and Learning Excellence.

Colleagues, mentors and friends who have sustained us through this work are too numerous to list. Of those who have had a particular impact on this book, some require special acknowledgment. In addition to Professor Alan Torrance, these include Alvin Plantinga, Bruce McCormack, Gary Deddo and Oliver Crisp. I deeply appreciate those who read and gave comments on earlier drafts: Andrew Torrance, Matthew Graham and especially David Congdon, along with a number of blind reviewers and editors who gave invaluable feedback. The significance of the inspiration and friendship of Mike Hammond, along with the rest of the so-called Round Table, cannot be understated. Finally, my students and colleagues at Taylor University have been immensely encouraging of this project and determined that it be given careful attention. I have particularly benefited from the encouragement of Jim Spiegel, Brad Seeman, Greg MaGee, Faye Checkowich, Matt DeLong, Drew Moser, Steve Morley, Steve Austin, Ryan James, Tim Herrmann, Jeff Cramer and Scott Moeschberger.

The most personal and most important acknowledgment must go to my blessed family, through whom I am constantly nourished and renewed. My parents and Gwen's parents have been extremely supportive. Sophia, Naomi, Andrew and Isaac have contributed in ways they do not yet fully understand. And I am convinced that any depth of insight the book may achieve is in large measure parallel to depths of growth that Gwen and I have experienced together during this period of our lives. I am extremely thankful for her insights and the steadfastness of her love and encouragement.

ABBREVIATIONS

Karl Barth:

BHet H. Martin Rumscheidt, ed., *Revelation and Theology: An Analysis of the Barth-Harnack Correspondence of 1923* (Cambridge: Cambridge University Press, 1972), pp. 29-53.

CD *Church Dogmatics*, trans. Geoffrey W. Bromiley, ed. Geoffrey W. Bromiley and Thomas F. Torrance, 4 vols. (Edinburgh: T & T Clark, 1956–1975).

DHet "The Principles of Dogmatics According to Wilhelm Herrmann," in *Theology and Church: Shorter Writings, 1920–1928,* trans. Louise Pettibone Smith (New York: Harper & Row, 1962), pp. 238-71.

Eet *Ethics,* ed. Dietrich Braun, trans. Geoffrey W. Bromiley (Edinburgh: T & T Clark, 1981).

EI *Ethik I: Vorlesung Münster, Sommersemester 1928,* ed. Dietrich Braun, complete works 2, part 2 (Zurich: Theologischer Verlag, 1973).

GD *The Göttingen Dogmatics: Instruction in the Christian Religion,* vol. 1, ed. Hannelotte Reiffen, trans. Geoffrey W. Bromiley (Grand Rapids: Eerdmans, 1991).

KD *Die kirchliche Dogmatik* (Munich: Kaiser, 1932–1967).

PT "Philosophie und Theologie," in *Philosophie und Christliche Existenz: Festschrift für Heinrich Barth,* ed. Gerhard Huber (Basel: Helbing & Lichtenhahn, 1960), pp. 93-106.

PTet "Philosophy and Theology," in *The Way of Theology in Karl Barth: Essays and Comments,* ed. H. Martin Rumscheidt (Allison Park, PA: Pickwick, 1986), pp. 79-95.

SITet "Fate and Idea in Theology," trans. George Hunsinger, in *The Way of Theology in Karl Barth: Essays and Comments,* ed. H. Martin Rumscheidt (Allison Park, PA: Pickwick, 1986), pp. 25-61.

Alvin Plantinga:

GOM *God and Other Minds: A Study of the Rational Justification of Belief in God,* Contemporary Philosophy (Ithaca, NY: Cornell University Press, 1967).

RBG "Reason and Belief in God," in *Faith and Rationality: Reason and Belief in God,* ed. Alvin Plantinga and Nicholas Wolterstorff (Notre Dame, IN: University of Notre Dame Press, 1983), pp. 16-93.

WCB *Warranted Christian Belief* (Oxford: Oxford University Press, 2000).

WCD *Warrant: The Current Debate* (Oxford: Oxford University Press, 1993).

WPF *Warrant and Proper Function* (Oxford: Oxford University Press, 1993).

INTRODUCTION

◆

More often than not, the difficult conversations I find myself in these days stem from some kind of challenge to the credibility, reliability or relevance of Christian theology. These challenges are pointed, have serious consequences and influence theology at every interface—public, academic and ecclesial. At their root is the epistemological dilemma created by two indispensable but conflicting affirmations. Christian theologians are required to adopt a high view of theological knowledge while also maintaining a low view of the unaided capacities of the human knower to secure such knowledge. To use the biblical imagery, Christian theology must acknowledge itself an impoverished earthen vessel while daring not to diminish the value of the treasure it confesses.

More than occasionally, attempts to respond to this dilemma champion one of these affirmations at the cost of excluding the other. Consider the impact of relaxing one's commitment to either of these competing assertions. If we abandon conviction in the knowability, universality and warrant of theological truth claims, then theology becomes impotent and largely irrelevant. To some degree, this has happened in the academy, where Christian theology often persists by cultural inertia or morphs into something altogether different. On the other hand, if we relinquish affirmation of the weakness, inadequacy and fallibility of the Christian theologian, we violate our own theological principles, prove ourselves intellectually naive and—most seriously—threaten to abandon and distort the very object of theology. And, despite how well-intentioned, desperate attempts to demonstrate the credibility, reliability and relevance of Christian theology are perhaps the surest way to undermine it.

The point of this book is to promote a constructive though not desperate response that addresses and reframes this fundamental epistemological question confronting not only Christian theology but also Christian belief universally. In this introduction, I consider some of the difficulties that attend this question and give the aims and structure of this book's response to them.

ADDRESSING THE EPISTEMIC PROBLEMS FOR CHRISTIAN FAITH

In many ways, epistemology is the chief stumbling block for Christian theology and, for that matter, for any revelation-based faith. At every turn, faith is challenged to produce its credentials, to justify its claims, to "put up or shut up." And, given the practical import of the various historical, ethical and metaphysical commitments of faith, prudence requires subjecting them to critical scrutiny. In an age where technological advances make it ever easier for the few to destroy the many, and where some religious beliefs are taken to endorse violence,[1] who could deny the urgency of requiring that such beliefs be carefully examined? Examination, however, requires principles, methods, criteria, recognized authorities and a bevy of other epistemological considerations. Epistemological issues are difficult within any discipline, but the issues become seemingly impenetrable for theology, where the very claims in question affect how those claims ought properly to be evaluated.

It's worth noting that the epistemic problems for Christian theology are not isolated to explicit discussions of the relationship between faith and reason but are in fact at the heart of nearly every serious contemporary challenge to theology. From the questions of theology's standing with respect to other academic disciplines,[2] to the questions of competing reli-

[1]While it is commonly voiced that religious belief has the propensity to promote violence and is perhaps inherently dangerous because this propensity is insulated from the check of reason, the connections between religious belief and violence are much more complex than is often suggested. See William T. Cavanaugh, *The Myth of Religious Violence: Secular Ideology and the Roots of Modern Conflict* (Oxford: Oxford University Press, 2009).

[2]Theology's standing as an academic (theoretical) discipline has been controversial since medieval scholasticism because of its drift from serving the practical needs of the church, but the debate for at least the last century within the broader academy has to do with whether Christian theology as an academic discipline can be properly conducted from a position of committed belief. This is

gious traditions,[3] to the questions of the sources of revelation and their correct interpretation,[4] to the very practical questions of just how and what can be preached in a church—all of these debates hinge at a fundamental level on the nature and possibility of revealed knowledge. And the epistemic problems aren't just a concern for theologians and church leaders. Every believer is confronted with the challenge of balancing the convictions of belief with a proper kind of epistemic humility. How should we think about the knowledge of faith? Does it give us confidence in and certainty about the *truth*? Is believing with certainty a virtue or a vice?

Epistemic problems are nothing new, of course, at least since the Enlightenment, when a search began in earnest to show why a reasonable person should be expected to accept the normativity of theological claims—or claims of any kind for that matter. As the pursuit of knowledge segmented into more specialized and formalized disciplines, it remained universal that each discipline must face critical scrutiny about the epistemological legitimacy of its claims. No discipline—whether philosophy, history, mathematics or physics—was able to find entirely self-secure and noncircular defenses, but accepting assertions simply on the basis of their alleged origins in divine revelation seemed a particularly unreliable way of arriving at *true* beliefs. Centuries later, despite several important shifts in the philosophical jet stream, the problems of epistemological grounding have remained the same. We may have lost our early Enlightenment optimism and naiveté, but in significant ways this is still the Age of Reason.

---

certainly a live debate today within the American Academy of Religion, where many argue that detachment and neutrality must be maintained for theological scholarship to be worthy of the name. As Ronald S. Hendel writes, "facts are facts, and faith has no business dealing in the world of facts" (Hendel, "Biblical Views: Farewell to SBL; Faith and Reason in Biblical Studies," *Biblical Archaeology Review* 36, no. 4 [2010]: 28, 74).

[3]The trend in the twentieth century, emblemized by the work of John Hick, that argued for an essential agreement in the core values of the world's religions has given way to a more realistic recognition of the stubborn incompatibility of their central motivating affirmations (e.g., Stephen Prothero, *God Is Not One: The Eight Rival Religions That Run the World—and Why Their Differences Matter* [New York: HarperCollins, 2010]).

[4]Questions of authority are at the heart of the major divisions in the Christian church and persist to this day as a primary impediment to reconciliation. Christian Smith presses the authority issue further by suggesting that an authority claim is defeated if it cannot yield interpretive agreement and consistency among those acknowledging that authority (Smith, *The Bible Made Impossible: Why Biblicism Is Not a Truly Evangelical Reading of Scripture* [Grand Rapids: Brazos Press, 2011]).

It's no wonder that the greatest figures in contemporary Christian theology and philosophy have made wrestling with these problems a key feature of their work. But are we willing to embrace their solutions? Have we even understood their proposals? Or should we assume that the epistemological conundrums are insoluble and resign ourselves to accept the epistemic problems in theology as fundamentally unresolvable?

Certain ways of dealing with the question of epistemological grounding have proven to fail, though failure has not diminished their popularity. They essentially amount to attempts, on the one hand, to respond directly to the question and attempts, on the other, to avoid or transcend the question altogether. Attempts to respond directly to the question and accept the terms of the question come in two kinds. There are ambitious attempts to render revelation irrelevant by providing a more solid, independent basis for, and thereby a confirmation of, its claims. There are the perhaps just slightly less ambitious attempts to secure the sources of revelation by providing an independent accreditation of their authority. And there are combinations of these two strategies. On the other hand, attempts to avoid the question take many forms, some more promising than others. To the extent that they fail, they fail to take the question seriously or to provide reasons for thinking that the terms of the question are wrongheaded. In general, failed responses will either be unconvincing or they will ignore or trivialize the epistemological issues.

THE PRIMARY AIM: ELUCIDATING A COMBINED BARTH/PLANTINGA RESPONSE

In my view, however, there is more heartening news. There are more cogent and helpful Christian responses to the epistemological grounding problem, though perhaps they have lacked the purchase or clear articulation necessary to saturate the general thinking of the church. The aim of this book is to attempt to address this deficiency by mining two of the most penetrating responses in recent Christian intellectual history—Karl Barth's theology of revelation and Alvin Plantinga's epistemology of Christian belief. Barth is one of the twentieth century's most accomplished theologians. Plantinga is one of the most influential figures in contemporary Anglo-American analytic philosophy. But the work of these eminent thinkers on the epistemological questions has remained, for many, rather opaque if not wholly misunderstood. The average seminary introduction to their thought would leave many seeing them as altogether unlikely associates, and even those with a clearer understanding of their work may not have grasped the possibilities for a robust, combined, interdisciplinary vision. In the investigation of their thought that follows, it will become clear not only that each provides a deeply cogent and theologically faithful response to the epistemological grounding problem in their respective disciplines but also that their responses are compatible and complementary.

Barth's theology and Plantinga's philosophy have already had a massive impact on the shape of contemporary Christian thought—the number of translations of their works alone attests to this. However, their solutions to Christian theology's fundamental epistemological vexation have yet to resound either in proportion to their strength or in proportion to their need. Yet, few issues are of greater consequence for contemporary Christian belief and practice. And so, by clarifying and combining the resources of these two profound Christian thinkers, I hope to suggest a lucid, sensible and thoroughly Christian response to the basic epistemological questions facing Christian theology today.

In chapter one, I begin by honing what I take to be the basic epistemological issue facing Christian theology. The result will be a clarified statement of the core difficulty and the principal assumptions that typically govern it. With respect to this general question, there is no attempt made to give a synopsis of current research or rehearse the history of the debates surrounding it. It is sufficient to have in hand an expression of the main concerns for dialogue with Barth and Plantinga.

Chapters two and three are aimed at elucidating the central features of Barth's theology of revelation and clarifying his attitude toward the place of epistemology in theology. Barth's commitment to theological realism and the divinely enabled possibility of a concrete knowledge of God is often obscured by his interlocutors. I attempt to clarify Barth's view, noting his affirmation that human knowledge of God is objective, personal, cognitive knowing, enabled by the Spirit's transforming gift of participation in revelation. I also attempt to dispel the common notion that Barth is hostile to epistemology in particular and philosophy in general, and chart the boundaries he gives for its interface with theology. Together, these two chapters provide us with the essential elements of Barth's response to the core epistemological issues.

In chapters four and five, I turn to Plantinga's Christian epistemology of warranted belief, presenting it in conversation with Barth's theology of revelation. I highlight and defend the general concord in their shared inductive approach and agreed rejection of the necessity and sufficiency of human arguments for warranted Christian belief. Their contributions are complementary—Barth providing what Plantinga lacks in theological depth and Plantinga providing what Barth lacks in philosophical clarity and defense. By the conclusion of chapter five we have the main lines of a theological epistemology mutually informed by Barth and Plantinga, which is briefly summarized into an emerging proposal in chapter six.

Chapters seven through nine test, elucidate and strengthen the combined Barth/Plantinga epistemological proposal by examining its fruitfulness for contributing to three areas of theological debate and considering the objections that emerge from them. Chapter seven tackles the question of the possibility and place of natural theology. Chapter eight looks at the nature of faith, fideism and the constitution of a genuine human knowledge of God. Chapter nine investigates the function of scripture as a source of revelation and theology's distinctive norm. Much of our discussion aims at elucidating the combined and compatible responses of Barth and Plantinga, which in each instance provides a helpfully constructive response.

The book concludes with an attempt to bring together the insights of the Barth/Plantinga proposal as refined by the exchange in chapters seven through nine, while briefly considering other areas of interest in contemporary theology where the thesis moves us past the inevitable stalemates. I contend that the mutually informed Barth/Plantinga theological epistemology provides a cogent, sustainable and philosophically nuanced solution to the core epistemological issues identified in chapter one. If this is true, and sufficiently straightforward, then perhaps it need no longer be the case that epistemological tripwires continue to stifle movement in theology. Moreover, we will have some helpful guidance for sorting out the kinds of dispositions we ought to have toward our faith-enabled beliefs.

A SECONDARY AIM: ANALYTIC THEOLOGY AND THE INCOMPATIBILITY OF BARTH AND PLANTINGA

A secondary goal of this work is to make a contribution in alignment with the aspirations of the recent analytic theology initiative[5]—enlivening exchange between Christian theologians and Christian analytic philosophy. Barth and Plantinga make an excellent test case for the potential fruitfulness of such an exchange, particularly because, as noted above, they are often viewed more as opponents than colleagues. There is a certain kind of pleasant disappointment that comes when, upon finally meeting a long-standing and deeply respected opponent head to head, a much anticipated fight evaporates into essential agreement. In my view, this is what we find with Plantinga and Barth. There are those who would generally prefer a fight rather than peace. We can, after all, so cherish the principle at stake in the fight that we begin mistakenly to associate the fight with that principle itself. The advantage, however, of a fighting impulse is that it prevents an easy concord—an all too quick and simple resolution that, for its failure to trouble the heart of the matter, turns true enemies into false friends and invites them to tea. As we look closely at their proposals, I will attempt to ask the tough questions and keep the real differences between Barth and Plantinga in mind.

Biographically speaking, Karl Barth and Alvin Plantinga are neither long-standing opponents nor close comrades. They are, in fact, rarely brought into dialogue at all. The surface picture for the prospect of fruitful exchange is doubtful. There is the obvious separation of more than a generation. Barth was forty-six years old and had just finished his first volume of the *Church Dogmatics* when Plantinga was born. At the time of Barth's death in 1968, Plantinga was thirty-six years old and had

[5]See Oliver D. Crisp and Michael C. Rea, eds., *Analytic Theology: New Essays in the Philosophy of Theology* (Oxford: Oxford University Press, 2009).

only just published his first major work, *God and Other Minds*. Plantinga confirms that he never met Barth in person.[6]

Contextual and disciplinary distinctions also seem to place Karl Barth and Alvin Plantinga worlds apart—absorbed in different questions, using different methods and addressing different audiences. Barth, as a theologian with particular philosophical concerns, addresses himself to theology, with the audience of philosophical theologians and philosophers of religion being only a distant second.[7] Plantinga's audience is not as clear cut. He is a philosopher with particular theological concerns addressing himself to philosophical theology and atheology. What may seem a chasm between the disciplines of philosophy and theology for Barth can appear almost transparent for Plantinga. Barth's core objective, it will be argued, is to challenge perspectives on theological epistemology predominantly and uncritically accepted in nineteenth- and twentieth-century theology. Plantinga's work, on the other hand, is to a large degree aimed at challenging philosophical arguments against Christian belief on philosophy's own terms.

Disciplinary differences, however, have never stopped theologians from doing philosophy or philosophers from doing theology. The real reason for our restrained expectations is that Barth is often understood to have denounced quite explicitly the possibility of a fruitful dialogue with philosophy. Nicholas Wolterstorff, Plantinga's closest philosophical compatriot,[8] seems to have once held this common view: "Barth has little direct influence on philosophy. There is, in that, a certain historical justice: Barth made clear that in his theology he had little use for philosophy. He regarded philosophical theology as idolatrous; and as to

[6]It would seem that Plantinga's best opportunity to have met Karl Barth would have been on Barth's 1962 US lecture tour while Plantinga was teaching philosophy at Wayne State University. That same year Plantinga attended a colloquium of philosophers and theologians at Princeton Seminary, where Barth's views were at the center of debate. See Brand Blanshard, "Critical Reflections on Karl Barth," in *Faith and the Philosophers*, ed. John Hick (London: Macmillan, 1964), pp. 159-200.

[7]In an article written in honor of his brother, a philosopher, Barth describes the chasm separating theology from philosophy but cautions that "the philosopher and the theologian will surely before everything else not permit themselves to be farther apart than within earshot or to lose sight of each other." PTet, p. 90 (PT, p. 102).

[8]Alvin Plantinga, "Self-Profile," in *Alvin Plantinga*, ed. James E. Tomberlin and Peter van Inwagen (Dordrecht: D. Reidel, 1985), p. 31.

philosophy of religion, he insisted that Christianity is not a religion."[9] The common view is that, in his zeal to preserve the character and freedom of theology, Barth utters a resounding "No!" to any role for philosophy.[10] This injunction is taken to be an absolute parting of ways, where philosophy is "excommunicated as not merely an alien but an enemy."[11] Brian Hebblethwaite blames Karl Barth for the persisting divide between Christian philosophers and theologians, claiming that Barth rejected "any 'points of connection' between theology and philosophy." He contends that Barthianism takes the "extreme position" that theology has its own philosophically inaccessible, internal logic and is, therefore, "protected from debate and criticism."[12] This presents a daunting initial picture of incompatibility between Plantinga and Barth.

One conclusion of the research conducted in this book is that there is very little warrant for the initial supposition of incompatibility and far greater support for a positive assessment of the compatibility and com-

---

[9]Nicholas Wolterstorff, "The Reformed Tradition," in *A Companion to Philosophy of Religion*, ed. Philip L. Quinn and Charles Taliaferro, Blackwell Companions to Philosophy 8 (Cambridge, MA: Blackwell, 1997), p. 166.

[10]Barth has clearly and famously said a resounding "No!" to natural theology in his response to Emil Brunner (Barth, *Nein! Antwort an Emil Brunner* [Munich: Kaiser, 1934]). This denouncing of natural theology is misunderstood by some to be an embargo on all philosophy. It is common, particularly of philosophers, to suggest that Barth's approach is "anti-philosophical" (John Edwin Smith, "Experience and Its Religious Dimension: Response to Vincent G. Potter," in *Reason, Experience, and God: John E. Smith in Dialogue*, ed. Vincent Michael Colapietro [New York: Fordham University Press, 1997], pp. 93, 98); posits an "inherent opposition between faith and reason" (Dewey J. Hoitenga, *Faith and Reason from Plato to Plantinga: An Introduction to Reformed Epistemology* [Albany: State University of New York Press, 1991], p. 238); "allow[s] very little place to reason" (John Macquarrie, *Principles of Christian Theology*, 2nd ed. [New York: Scribner, 1977], p. 16); "has had the courage to break with philosophy frankly and thoroughly" (Blanshard, "Critical Reflections on Karl Barth," p. 159); recommends "theology should not touch philosophy with a barge pole" (Aidan Nichols, *The Shape of Catholic Theology: An Introduction to Its Sources, Principles, and History* [Collegeville, MN: Liturgical Press, 1991], p. 43); and "rejects philosophy as the work of the devil" (Kevin Hart, "The Experience of God," in *The Religious*, ed. John D. Caputo [Malden, MA: Blackwell, 2002], p. 161).

[11]Herbert Stewart, "The 'Reverent Agnosticism' of Karl Barth," *Harvard Theological Review* 43, no. 3 (1950): 231.

[12]Brian Hebblethwaite, *Philosophical Theology and Christian Doctrine* (Oxford: Blackwell, 2005), p. 5. Hebblethwaite singles out Thomas F. Torrance as a prime exemplar of this noetically insular Barthian theological position. The reference Hebblethwaite offers, however, refutes his own claim. Torrance is clear and emphatic that "the interior or material logic of theological knowledge does not allow us to neglect the external or formal logic of our human modes of thought and speech" (*Theological Science* [London: Oxford University Press, 1969], p. 219). One aim of the second chapter will be to show that just as Hebblethwaite is wrong about Torrance, he is also wrong about Barth.

plementarity of Barth's theology of revelation and Plantinga's epistemology of Christian belief. Barth's chief concern can be expressed negatively, though incompletely, as a denial of the possibility of a theological epistemology from below. In similar terms, Plantinga's project can be summarized as a denial of the impossibility of a theological epistemology from above. This is not to suggest that the relationship between their thought can simply be construed as two sides of the same coin. Not settling for an easy peace, we will have to consider several points of conflict and divergence along the way before arriving at what will turn out to be a qualified but overwhelmingly positive assessment.

So, as far as the secondary goal of this work goes, a strong case is made for the fruitfulness of enlivening the exchange between Christian theologians and Christian analytic philosophy. Rusty Reno has perceptively highlighted a perplexing cleavage that exists between contemporary Christian theology and contemporary Christian analytic philosophy. Reno expresses lament over the fact that theology has largely ignored philosophical partners who exhibit particular promise for assisting with theology's postmodern challenges. "Catholic or not, in the main [theology] cannot see the apparent renewal of philosophy in the English-speaking world. Alvin Plantinga, Peter van Inwagen, William Alston, and the rest of the Society of Christian Philosophers can meet for twenty years, but theology remains blind."[13] By focusing on a question of central importance, in light of the thought of two intellectual giants who have, to a great degree, shaped the landscapes of these disciplines, this study may be seen both as an attempt to overcome the divide between Christian theology and Christian analytic philosophy and as a case study to support Reno's intuition that a significant compatibility exists between at least some of those inhabiting these disciplines at the level of fundamental commitments. It is hoped, furthermore, that enlivening dialogue in the area of theological epistemology with a view to clarifying core concerns, terms and the implications of positions will help to correct misconceptions that may have discouraged exchange in the past and in so doing contribute to a revival of constructive collaboration.

---

[13]R. R. Reno, "Theology's Continental Captivity," *First Things* 162 (2006): 29.

PART ONE

◆

Prospects for a Combined Barth/Plantinga Approach to Christian Theological Epistemology

1

WHAT IS THE EPISTEMIC PROBLEM?

◆

If one finds oneself already well aware of the long-standing epistemological difficulties facing theology, one may want simply to scan the conclusion of this chapter and move on to the next. To a large extent, the observations I make here have been noted by countless philosophers and theoreticians in ages past. After all, though theology has some unique challenges, the epistemological difficulties facing theology are, to a great degree, no different from the epistemological difficulties that have always faced any pursuit of knowledge. In this chapter, I observe that at the root of these difficulties is the circularity generated by the humanly unattainable requirement that we certify the reliability of our own noetic resources independently by means of those same resources. In subsequent chapters we will go into greater detail in several areas that are only here quickly referenced.

THE VALUE OF SKEPTICISM

At the outset, let me make an observation that will serve as both an introduction and a disclaimer. Though I teach philosophy, I have encountered students who seem as if they were better off remaining naive about epistemological difficulties. On a first encounter with skeptical arguments against the possibility of knowledge, for instance, some students begin to doubt the most obvious and mundane beliefs about themselves and the world. There are those who would argue that this is altogether positive. Some pedagogues appeal to Socrates and contend that emptying oneself of knowledge is the beginning of wisdom.[1] I am not convinced that such extremes do much more than exhaust friends and family.[2] To be sure, exposing one's assumptions to criticism is a healthy and necessary discipline. But often, rather than arriving at a fair examination of assumptions, unconsciously held intuitions about knowledge are tacitly leveraged by skeptical arguments to the effect of confusing one's most elemental beliefs. When the broader gamut of our assumptions about knowledge are fairly examined, skeptical arguments can serve helpfully to highlight conflicts between them. In what follows, I suggest that we can take skepticism seriously as an avenue for getting at the key epistemological issues, but I argue that we need not take seriously its radical conclusions.[3] A brief elaboration on this theme will allow us to place one stake in the ground and then begin to make headway on the question at hand.

It is debatable whether skepticism, in its purest forms, is a tenable philosophical position.[4] Skepticism to the extreme is complete withholding—that is, withholding of all assent, all belief. The oft-noted, and perhaps glaringly obvious, problem it faces is that it either remains mute or is self-defeating. This problem, however, was not generally the issue that the so-called common-sense philosophers raised against skepticism. Their argument was that the clarity of the conviction that we do in fact know some things outweighs the other considerations.[5] If a conflict

---

[1]It is often held that Socrates taught this, though what he means by his claim to have no knowledge is usually taken to be a pedagogical ploy; see Gregory Vlastos, "Socrates' Disavowal of Knowledge," *Philosophical Quarterly* 35, no. 138 (1985): 1-31. Friedrich Nietzsche says with ironic twist, "Nihilism, as the denial of a truthful world, of being, might be *a divine way of thinking*" (*Will to Power*, trans. Walter Kaufmann and R. J. Hollingdale [New York: Random House, 1967], p. 15, emphasis original).

[2]Though epistemic kenosis is perhaps the path Descartes chose, this is notably not what the scripture writers thought about the path to wisdom (Ps 111:10; Prov 1:7; 9:10; 15:33). Robert Audi bucks the trend in his introduction to epistemology, where he neither initiates nor confines epistemology to a dialogue with skepticism; see *Epistemology: A Contemporary Introduction to the Theory of Knowledge*, 3rd ed. (New York: Routledge, 2010), p. xv.

[3]We can think of skepticism as analogous to theological heresy, which Barth appreciated for its awakening force, opening our eyes and ears, providing "a chance to learn something positive" (*Karl Barth's Table Talk*, rec. and ed. John D. Godsey [Edinburgh: Oliver & Boyd, 1963], p. 50).

[4]There are, of course, a number of different positions that fall under the designation of skepticism. Perhaps the purest form is the Pyrrhonian version, which attempts to make no claims whatsoever.

[5]G. E. Moore's classic response to Hume on the existence of the objects of sense perception follows this exactly. Rather than attempt an independent verification, he simply holds up his hands and

exists, in most cases the more strongly attested assumption should be the *last* to be jettisoned. It is far more likely that a presupposition attending the skeptical argument (about the criteria for or nature of knowledge) should be subjected to doubt than that we should conclude that knowledge is impossible. That an independent, noncircular argument cannot be marshaled to prove that knowledge is possible is not a liability. The strongest demonstration that knowledge is possible comes with the very act of knowing and our second-order reflections on it.[6] In other words, before we even launch into our epistemological reflections, we already have the incorrigible sense that we have some knowledge. We may recognize that our experiences of knowing are imperfect, fuzzy or incomplete, but we cannot dismiss the clarity of the sense of knowing or the conviction that we possess knowledge to some limited degree. And, without any clearer grounds from which to build an argument against the reliability of this sense of knowing, we are left with the clearest datum in epistemology: knowledge is a human possibility. We are, therefore, entitled to take the possibility of knowledge as a rightful presumption, one that skeptical arguments cannot assail since their conclusions are always weaker by comparison.

So, most thoughtful human beings—and even a few philosophers and theologians—will, I think, agree with this first stake in the ground: that knowledge for human beings, though perhaps weak and impartial, is self-evidently a possibility. The epistemic problem we are seeking to identify is not the challenge to develop an independent, noncircular, rational argument against radical skepticism.[7] The epistemic problem is not that knowledge might not be possible. The epistemic problem that plagues theology has to do with the criteria, conditions, content and

---

says, "Here is one hand, and here is another" (Moore, *Philosophical Papers* [New York: Collier Books, 1967], pp. 144-48).

[6]This approach to epistemology is often known as particularism and is distinguished from methodism. We will see that both Barth and Plantinga adopt a particularist approach, beginning with particular, paradigmatic acts of knowledge.

[7]There are, of course, many different kinds of skepticism and many helpful philosophical treatments of it. In contrast to the position of this book is J. L. Schellenberg's trilogy. In his final volume, *Will to Imagine: A Justification of Skeptical Religion* (Ithaca, NY: Cornell University Press, 2009), p. 1, Schellenberg argues that while religious belief is not justified, it is reasonable to take a stance of faith toward the notion that "there is a metaphysically and axiologically ultimate reality."

nature of something that *is* a real possibility. Nevertheless, the rejection of the skeptical conclusion does not render skepticism unuseful. It can still serve us as a tool for exposing core epistemological concerns—to which we now turn.

WHAT IS KNOWLEDGE? AND WHAT DOES IT REQUIRE?

Sparing the historical recapitulations, at the heart of the matter for most skeptics is a worry that the requirements for knowledge cannot be achieved humanly.[8] This worry has fundamentally two components. The first is a supposition about the nature of knowledge.[9] The second is a determination about the requirements necessary to attain it, in other words, to know something means *x* and therefore requires *y*. The skeptic usually reasons that since *y* (whatever is required to have knowledge) cannot be attained, we cannot have knowledge. Given that knowledge is possible (our stake in the ground: we do know things), there are naturally two kinds of responses: (1) responses that adjust our understanding of what it is to know and (2) responses that adjust the requirements for knowledge. It is difficult, however, to adjust one and not the other. Like hitting a target with a ball, an adjustment in angle requires a change in velocity and vice versa.

The typical skeptic has an unattainably high view of knowledge. It notoriously features the ideal of certainty[10] and roughly requires that one be in a position vis-à-vis what is known such that one could not fail to be correct.[11] However, not only must we be in this position; but we must also somehow see that we are in this position. Sometimes it is said that there must be no reason to doubt the possibility of our being correct about the things we know. In whatever form, the requirement for the impossibility of failure is patently unrealistic. To err is human, and there are many ways humanly to err.

---

[8]We will see that the Barth/Plantinga proposal agrees that the knowledge of God cannot be achieved humanly.

[9]In this discussion we are mostly dealing with propositional knowledge—sometimes referred to as declarative or indicative knowledge, or knowledge that some proposition *x* is true.

[10]The notion of certainty, as with most important philosophical terms, has proven impressively contentious. See, for instance, Peter D. Klein, *Certainty: A Refutation of Scepticism* (Minneapolis: University of Minnesota Press, 1981), pp. 117-36.

[11]Much more will be said about this in chapter 4 when we engage Plantinga's epistemology.

In what follows, I will briefly entertain four important areas of ineliminable, potential human epistemic failure. Each is a facet of the general epistemic problem we are seeking to identify. Each is broadly recognized as an aspect of our human noetic limitations. To flesh these out, it will be helpful to work with an example—a common uncontroversial instance of human knowing with which all readers would be familiar. Consider your knowledge of your own name. This proposition is usually expressed in the first-person form, e.g., "my name is Kevin." Most of us are fairly confident about what our name is most of the time, but we must acknowledge that we cannot rule out several possible avenues of epistemic failure.

1. Small-scale failures. Beginning with what might be called small-scale failures, I have in mind things like the possibility that you misremember your name, that your parents deceived you about your name or that the people you think are your parents are not your parents at all. I am drawing an admittedly artificial distinction between these kinds of failures and large-scale failures that involve more invasive kinds of error. The potential for small-scale failure stems from our basic inability to grasp correctly all the relevant facts. Like other kinds of potential failure, it is a feature of our basic human epistemic limitations. The larger-scale potentials for failure are more systemic, and, for sake of presentation, I divide them into failures of interpretive framework, semantic failures and second-order epistemic failures.

2. Failures of interpretive framework. We need not clarify the boundary between small- and large-scale failure. All failures can be construed as failures to grasp correctly the relevant facts though, of course, the very notion of facts becomes controversial. This second class of potential failure is the possibility that we are gravely mistaken about salient features in our general understanding of the nature of reality. I have in mind larger-scale deceptions like the possibility that you are a brain in a vat (BIV) hooked up to the "matrix," that your memories have just been uploaded from another human being, or that you are not in fact human but are a single molecule of carbon dioxide.[12] These possibilities

[12]That I may be under the illusion of an evil spirit, suggested in René Descartes's first meditation, is a paradigmatic example for Western epistemologists (Descartes, *Meditations on First Philosophy*, trans. John Cottingham, rev. ed. [Cambridge: Cambridge University Press, 1996], p. 15).

are simultaneously ridiculous and impossible to disprove. They are the kinds of fanciful scenarios that give philosophers a bad reputation with "normal" people. They involve massive distortions in our view of reality. Nevertheless, there is no way to discount the potential for large-scale failure in our interpretive frameworks.

It is extremely significant that our primary means of growing in knowledge is inductive. It involves trial and error and the formation of functional generalizations, and it assumes the relative regularity of our environment and consistency of our experience. The provisional assumptions we make may only be tested for consistency with experience. This leaves open two significant avenues for epistemic failure, both of which are well known in the epistemology of science. The first has to do with the untestability of the assumption that the world is regular.[13] The second has to do with the possibility of generating multiple internally consistent though mutually exclusive interpretive frameworks.[14] In both cases there is no epistemically neutral human point of view from which an evaluation can be made.[15] We cannot transcend our own interpretive frameworks; therefore, we cannot provide ourselves assurance of their accuracy or their superiority to competing internally consistent frameworks.[16] The impossibility of providing a self-guarantee of our frameworks for understanding and interpreting reality is an unavoidable human epistemic limitation that provides truly large-scale potential for epistemic failure.

This is a profound and perhaps profoundly unsettling realization that is worth pausing briefly to absorb—we have *no way* to prove to ourselves or anyone else that we are not under massive epistemic delusion. This

[13]This is often referred to as the problem of induction and is often associated with Hume. See, for example, Karl Popper, *Conjectures and Refutations: The Growth of Scientific Knowledge* (New York: Harper & Row, 1962), p. 56.

[14]This is the problem of the underdetermination of theory by data. See Pierre Duhem's classic, *The Aim and Structure of Physical Theory* (Princeton, NJ: Princeton University Press, 1954), p. 258, where he writes, "No isolated hypothesis and no group of hypotheses separated from the rest of physics is capable of an absolutely autonomous experimental verification."

[15]Nietzsche hastily concludes that "the world with which we are concerned is false" (*Will to Power*, p. 330).

[16]Thomas Kuhn noted that, for this reason, paradigm shifts in science do not result from hypotheses gradually evolving from one to the next but are utterly revolutionary in nature (Kuhn, *The Structure of Scientific Revolutions* [Chicago: University of Chicago Press, 1962], p. 10).

gives us a healthy degree of epistemic humility. An awareness of our humble estate is important; however, it is also important to see that this in no way requires that we suspend our deeply held convictions that we are not in fact massively deluded.

*3. **Semantic failures.*** We are also open to epistemic failures at the level of the expressions by means of which we articulate the propositions we think we know. The English expression we were considering is "my name is *x*." To what extent are we dependent on the capacity to formulate an expression of a proposition in human language in order for it to be an article of knowledge? Regardless of the answer, it would seem that for all effable knowledge we are susceptible to epistemic failures caused at the level of semantic reference. One might protest that this is not really a problem for knowledge as much as it is a problem for the effability of knowledge. But, if an encoding of some kind is necessary for the acquisition and retrieval of knowledge—whether or not expressed—then semantic failures are a potential problem for knowledge in general. We will return to this issue in chapter eight, even there only scratching the surface.[17] Suffice it here to observe that in the expression we are considering, "my name is *x*," there is a variety of potential semantic difficulties. For each term there is the impossibility of ensuring idealized referential success and idealized success of predication. Terms could always be more precise. What ensures the proper mapping of concepts to the terms and to the realities? How do I know that I know what I mean by this expression? Qualifications could be added, but this would simply multiply the difficulties.

*4. **Second-order epistemic failures.*** Finally, there are large-scale, second-order or metaepistemic possibilities for failure. Perhaps I think I know what my name is, but I am wrong about the requirements for knowledge. Or, perhaps the noetic equipment that I trust to deliver true beliefs about my name is untrustworthy, broken or designed for some other purpose entirely. Perhaps all that strong phenomenology around the experience that I have when I consider what my name is—that makes me so con-

[17]Recognition of the difficulties of the linguistic expression of propositions generated a movement in twentieth-century Western analytic philosophy known as the "linguistic turn." See Ludwig Wittgenstein's classic, *Tractatus Logico-Philosophicus* (New York: Harcourt, Brace, 1922).

vinced that I really do know my name—is misleading. This kind of potential for epistemic failure takes us to the heart of our human epistemic predicament. In the vain quest for epistemic certainty of the impossible-to-fail kind, we are dependent on our thinking equipment to assure ourselves of failure-proof thought. We simply cannot certify the reliability of our own noetic resources independently by means of those same resources.[18]

TRUE BELIEF

Where does this leave us? Returning to our stake in the ground, the epistemic problem we are after is not the seeming impossibility of knowledge. We accept that knowledge is a human possibility. The skeptic's requirements for knowledge are unattainable. The skeptic's requirements are motivated by an idealized conception of the nature of knowledge. It would seem, therefore, that the problem is with the skeptic's conception of the nature of knowledge. Indeed, rejecting the skeptic's view of what constitutes knowledge has been the most popular response to the skeptic's dilemma.

When philosophers of knowledge refer to modernism, they typically have in mind an enterprise that accepted the skeptic's gauntlet and was optimistic about the possibilities of providing a reasoned solution. Postmodernism in epistemology has generally seen a rejection of the skeptic's terms in search of a more open view of knowledge. Obtaining this more open view, however, has involved making adjustments to the most fundamental notion in all of philosophy: the notion of truth—more specifically, what it means to believe the truth.

For a belief to constitute a genuine act of knowing, it has long been thought that what is believed must be true and that its being true must motivate the believing of it in some nonaccidental way that entitles the believing. We will look at this entitlement condition more closely in chapter four when we investigate Plantinga's thoughts on

[18]Attempting to do so could also ensnare us in a repeating loop of certification. This is Michael Bergmann's conclusion in "A Dilemma for Internalism," in *Knowledge and Reality: Essays in Honor of Alvin Plantinga,* ed. Thomas M. Crisp, Matthew Davidson and David Vander Laan (Dordrecht: Kluwer Academic, 2006), pp. 137-77.

justification and warrant. For now, let us consider problems for the notion of true belief.

Generally speaking, the theory of truth that skepticism assumed is referred to as a simple or modest correspondence view of truth—roughly, that a true belief stands in a relationship of rightly corresponding with the realities affirmed in the belief. It is worth noting at this point that correspondence theories of truth come in many different varieties and have an elaborate and controversial history. I'm trying, if possible, to avoid the controversy by leaving unspecified the precise nature of the correspondence relation and any specific attending metaphysical commitments.[19] My interest in suggesting the most modest kind of correspondence lies in its unavoidable connection to the notion of a single, coherent external reality. If one believes, as many of us do, that there is an external reality that exists in large part independently of our thoughts, opinions and preferences, then it is very difficult to have anything like a standard view of knowledge and not hold to some minimal kind of correspondence view of true belief.[20] On this view, the truth or falsity of a belief depends in some fundamental way on what is true ontologically—that is, in reality.

Postmodern responses to skepticism have often adjusted the theory of truth by retreating from a strict ontological requirement. For this reason, their theories of truth are often referred to as epistemic or prag-

---

[19]I want to avoid getting bogged down here in a quagmire of alternatives and distinctions. I speak here of a correspondence *view,* not an explanatory hypothesis or detailed correspondence *theory.* A correspondence view is sometimes quickly dismissed after being associated with one articulation—e.g., Aquinas's articulation of truth as "the conformity or equation of thing and intellect" (*De Veritate,* I.1; *Truth,* vol. 1, trans. Robert W. Mulligan [Indianapolis: Hackett, 1994], p. 6). We can steer clear of an elaborate explanation of the mechanics of the correspondence between that which is believed and the realities affirmed in the belief. In other words, we do not need an explanation of the how in order to see that, as Kant puts it, truth is "the agreement of knowledge with its object" (1781, A58; Immanuel Kant, *Critique of Pure Reason,* trans. Norman Kemp Smith, rev. 2nd ed. [New York: Palgrave Macmillan, 2003], p. 97).

[20]It is also possible for a correspondence view of truth to be naively oversimplistic. This is particularly the case, as Janet Martin Soskice points out, if we adopt a strictly representational epistemology, "wherein the knowing agent is somehow set apart from, maybe outside of, the world that is known" (Soskice, "The Ends of Man and the Future of God," in *The End of the World and the Ends of God: Science and Theology on Eschatology,* ed. John Polkinghorne and Michael Welker [Harrisburg, PA: Trinity Press International, 2000], p. 84). Soskice is discussing concerns raised by Charles Taylor in "Overcoming Epistemology," in *After Philosophy: End or Transformation?* ed. Kenneth Baynes, James Bohman and Thomas McCarthy (Cambridge, MA: MIT Press, 1987), pp. 464-88.

matic. They attempt to protect the notions of knowledge, meaning and truth from skepticism by indexing truth in some way to the human knower.[21] The impossibility of a safeguarded human objectivity is not a problem if one abandons commitment to an independent reality—at least as regards its connection to true belief.[22] The skeptical requirement that beliefs must certifiably correspond to the way things really are seems to be undermined if there is no intelligibility to the idea that there is a way things really are. This solution, however, pays a high price by fairly radically modifying the general conception of knowledge—removing what many of us would take to be an essential component: that to know involves believing something about the way things really are. That there is a coherent, external, independent reality seems to be one of our most unshakably tenacious assumptions. While some philosophers of religion argue against this assumption,[23] I will take it as a given for the purposes of our discussion here that, for Christian theology, this commitment is nonnegotiable.[24] To be sure, there are many ways in which theology can fruitfully adapt and adopt postmodern insights, but commitment to a way things really are imposes a limit.

---

[21]It is worth noting that some philosophers think that attempting to establish a theory of truth is foolhardy. They suggest that the notion of truth is so basic that it is unanalyzable (see G. E. Moore, *Some Main Problems of Philosophy* [New York: Humanities Press, 1953], p. 261). Donald Davidson makes a compelling case for this in his brilliant essay, "Truth Rehabilitated," in *Rorty and His Critics,* ed. Robert Brandom (Oxford: Blackwell, 2000), pp. 65-74. Davidson comments instructively on the relative virtues of the competing theories of truth: "Correspondence, while it is empty as a definition, does capture the thought that truth depends on how the world is, and this should be enough to discredit most epistemic and pragmatic theories. Epistemic and pragmatic theories, on the other hand, have the merit of relating the concept of truth to human concerns, like language, belief, thought and intentional action, and it is these connections which make truth the key to how mind apprehends the world" (ibid., pp. 72-73).

[22]In Jean-François Lyotard's classic treatment of the "postmodern turn," he charts the epistemological crisis for scientific knowledge (*The Postmodern Condition: A Report on Knowledge* [Minneapolis: University of Minnesota Press, 1979], p. xi).

[23]Don Cupitt suggests that most Continental theologians—including Bonhoeffer!—are anti-realists, meaning that God "is real only to his followers and within their perspective" (Cupitt, "Anti-Realist Faith," in *Is God Real?* ed. Joseph Runzo [London: Palgrave Macmillan, 1993], p. 52). See also Karin Johannesson, who argues that "metaphysical realism does not provide us with a perspective we can imagine and is therefore not useful to us" (Johannesson, *God Pro Nobis: On Non-Metaphysical Realism and the Philosophy of Religion,* trans. Marie Taaqvist [Leuven: Peeters, 2007], p. 245).

[24]Central to our epistemic problem, as Christopher J. Insole points out, is that taking the ontologically realist view forces one to face the possibility that one's beliefs about reality could be false. See Insole, *The Realist Hope: A Critique of Anti-Realist Approaches in Contemporary Philosophical Theology* (Aldershot, UK: Ashgate, 2006), p. 10.

This brings us to the end of another road and a second stake in the ground. Just as we cannot produce a noncircular argument to demonstrate that knowledge is possible, so also we cannot demonstrate that there is in fact an independent reality. It is axiomatic, however, for Christian theology as traditionally conceived that there is an independent reality. Given that our concern is to identify the fundamental epistemic problem for Christian theology, we can take it as given that the question has to do neither with the possibility of knowledge nor with the possibility of an independent reality. Mutatis mutandis, Christian theology assumes some minimal correspondence view of truth.[25] If Anselm is correct, Christian theology is "faith seeking understanding." It begins with a self-revealed, objectively real, divine being, the knowledge of whom is said either to be or to come by means of faith.

The epistemic problem for contemporary Christian theology is that it cannot follow either of the paths we have treated here generally as skepticism and postmodernism. It is forced to sit uncomfortably with a high view of knowledge and a low view of the unaided capacities of the human knower to self-secure such knowledge. This is the dilemma that generates particular difficulties for its task.

PARTICULAR EPISTEMIC ISSUES FOR CHRISTIAN THEOLOGY

Stemming from the epistemic problem we have identified, the underlying epistemological issues facing Christian theology are not new, and neither are the material issues behind the main contemporary difficulties. What is the nature of theological knowledge? Is there such a thing? (As is always the case, the questions of epistemology and ontology, while distinct, go hand in hand.) Does theology have a unique way of knowing? Does it have defensible regulative criteria and norms? Does it require specific approaches or methods? The practical driver for many of these questions has to do with the relevance of theology, in both public and

[25]Christian theology is in no way obligated to one particular fleshing out of the correspondence view, and may be well advised to avoid further elaboration. An excellent discussion of this is found in Louis Dupré's essay "Reflections on the Truth of Religion," *Faith and Philosophy* 6, no. 3 (1989): 260-74, where he argues for the helpfulness of aspects of correspondence, coherence and disclosure models of truth.

academic spheres as well as within the life of the church. Why think it should have any relevance at all? Does theology have a voice or is it—following Jeffrey Stout's well-known figure—unable to advance beyond throat clearing?[26]

In this book, after developing a constructive response to what we have in this chapter identified as the epistemic problem for theology, we will grapple with issues of nature, ground, authorization, criteria, method and relevance by focusing our attention on three interrelated debates. We begin, in chapter seven, addressing the question of theology's relationship to the canons of reason and the concern for publicly available evidence. In keeping with Barth's and Plantinga's own discussions, we will address this as the question of the possibility and place of natural theology. In chapter eight we extend the discussion of the relationship between theology and reason to the classic concern about the relationship between reason and faith. Here we address the question of theology's way of knowing and examine faith as a particular mode of theological knowing. Then, in chapter nine, we confront the question of the criteria and norm for Christian theology. With what qualifications can scripture serve this function given the frailties of human knowing and the limitations of human language? Finally, in the concluding postscript, we take the Barth/Plantinga proposal as clarified and extended by these interrelated debates and return once again to the epistemological dilemma identified above as the main question of this book. In what ways can and should theology maintain a commitment to truth alongside an awareness of fallibility?

If we consider for a moment George A. Lindbeck's widely discussed *The Nature of Doctrine,* we find an attempt to wrestle with the problems highlighted in this chapter. Lindbeck's own conclusion is to declare a preference for his famous "cultural-linguistic" approach. The criteria he identifies to conduct his assessment of the competing approaches fall

---

[26]"Preoccupation with method is like clearing your throat: it can go on for only so long before you lose your audience. Theologians who dwell too long on matters of method can easily suffer both kinds of alienation they fear. They become increasingly isolated from the churches as well as from cultural forums such as the academy and the leading nonsectarian journals of opinion" (Stout, *Ethics After Babel: The Languages of Morals and Their Discontents* [Princeton, NJ: Princeton University Press, 1988], p. 163).

under the rubrics of faithfulness, applicability and intelligibility. Lindbeck, however, recognizes that his assessment faces the basic problem that "each type of theology is embedded in a conceptual framework so comprehensive that it shapes its own criteria of adequacy."[27] He recognizes, as we discussed earlier, that this enabling feature of human knowledge also eliminates the possibility of an objectively neutral assessment or defense. But how does Lindbeck's approach address the hopes and intentions of theology, despite real human epistemic limitations, to confess what is true about the realities of God and the world—truths that, while they cannot be *confessed* independently of cultural and linguistic frameworks, *are* independent of and prior to those frameworks? Here Lindbeck's preferred approach offers little assistance.[28] His own view is set as a via media between two ostensive extremes. In the experiential-expressive model, theology uses prevailing cultural conceptualities as a vehicle for the expression of religious experience. The cognitivist approach, on the other hand, is precritical. It fails to appreciate the impact of cultural and linguistic frameworks, thinking instead naively in terms of timeless propositions. Lindbeck's own view, it seems to me, attempts to bridge the cognitivist desire to anchor theology in a deposit of truth with the experientialist desire to anchor theology in a given religious experience. The result, however, appears to be a bridge suspended in midair. Given human epistemic realities, Lindbeck seems to think that this is "the most that can be done."[29]

Following the work of Karl Barth and Alvin Plantinga, chapters two through five of this book attempt to develop a constructive response to the epistemic problem facing Christian theology. The proposal will agree with Lindbeck about the limitations of human knowing while at-

---

[27]George A. Lindbeck, *The Nature of Doctrine: Religion and Theology in a Postliberal Age* (Philadelphia: Westminster, 1984), p. 113.

[28]Lindbeck, nevertheless, acknowledges the importance of this when, stressing the primacy of the "cultural-linguistic" approach, he states, "while a religion's truth claims are often of the utmost importance to it (as in the case of Christianity), it is, nevertheless, the conceptual vocabulary and the syntax or inner logic which determine the kind of truth claims the religion can make" (ibid., p. 35). At another point he says, "Antifoundationalism, however, is not to be equated with irrationalism. The issue is not whether there are universal norms of reasonableness, but whether these can be formulated in some neutral, framework-independent language" (ibid., p. 130).

[29]Ibid., p. 113.

tempting to say something more positive about what authorizes fallible attempts to grasp and express propositions that intend truthfully to refer to the realities of Creator and creation. In so doing, I will describe a philosophically critical, theologically motivated response in continuity with Miroslav Volf's critique of Lindbeck, in which Volf contends for a public theology, which, "looking through the spectacles of its own culture, . . . sees the city whose builder and architect is God."[30] The result will not be a triumphalist removal of human weakness. Neither will it be a folding into antifoundationalism. Instead, following Barth and Plantinga, I will argue for a properly critical theo-foundational view of theology's epistemic warrant.

To reiterate, the epistemic problem for Christian theology identified in this chapter is the seemingly unavoidable tension between a properly high view of theological knowledge and yet a low view of the independent capacities of human theologians. This problem generates a number of epistemological issues and questions widely debated today. For some, there is a degree of frustration with a preoccupation with these questions. This is the case partly because it has been going on for so long without a clear resolution and partly because it is counted a distraction from genuinely constructive theology. Others of us find that the very legitimacy of moving forward with work on the other side of these questions is threatened without an adequate, if provisional, response to them. The approach of the rest of this book will, to some degree, do both at the same time. As we will find, particularly in our engagement with Karl Barth, an adequate response to these fundamental questions is not possible prior to our finding ourselves to be those addressed by God. The pre-engagement of God's self-revelation ultimately forms the basis for any positive response to the seemingly insurmountable epistemic problem facing Christian theology.

---

[30]Volf, "Theology, Meaning, and Power," in *The Future of Theology: Essays in Honor of Jürgen Moltmann*, ed. Miroslav Volf, Carmen Krieg and Thomas Kucharz (Grand Rapids: Eerdmans, 1996), p. 113. Volf's critiques of Lindbeck are incisive and helpful, especially in Volf's reticence to minimize the propositional aspects of theology.

2

BARTH'S THEOLOGY OF REVELATION

For Us and for Our Salvation

◆

The intent of this chapter and the next is to explore Barth's theological epistemology along with his safeguards against the usurpations of philosophy. I will endeavor to show that Barth's attitude toward epistemology is understood best in the light of commitments that stem from his theology of revelation, centered on the saving and self-revealing action of God in Christ by the Spirit. I will begin in this chapter with an analysis of the salient implications of his theology of revelation for theological knowing. The next chapter will look at how these implications shape Barth's understanding of the role of philosophy in theology. I will attempt to elucidate Barth's central concerns and their implications for the relationship between faith and philosophy, charting what I take to be Barth's notion of philosophy's proper function. In chapters four and five I will bring Plantinga into dialogue with Barth's concerns, arguing that where those concerns overlap, Plantinga's epistemology agrees and helpfully extends Barth's theological epistemology, just as Barth's theology of revelation helpfully extends Plantinga's epistemology of Christian belief.

Let me be clear that I am not attempting to contribute a new insight about Barth to the field of Barth studies. I do hope to make Barth more comprehensible for some of those outside that field, but I will not be advancing a new theory or engaging deeply in the many exciting and fascinating subtleties of the work done on the development of Barth's thought over his career. I take it that, at least from the *Church Dogmatics* onward, Barth's central views on theological epistemology do not change. Barth's emphases may change, but his core views do not.

In the first volume of the *Dogmatics* Barth attempts to elucidate and defend the "way of knowledge" followed in theology. In part two of volume one Barth gives an extended treatment of revelation, and in part one of volume two his concern is the "knowledge of God." It is legitimate to refer to this as Barth's theological epistemology, the concerns of which are never far from view throughout the *Dogmatics*. His theological epistemology is distinguished from a general theory of knowledge.[1] It is *theological* epistemology and as such exclusively focused on the knowledge of God as the gift of God. It therefore diverges in both scope and direction from general epistemologies. Nevertheless, Barth addresses the chief questions posed by any theory of knowledge, including the nature, object, subject, source, direction and criteria of theological knowing. Critical in Barth's account is the inseparable nature of revelation and God's saving, reconciling and redeeming action. "Revelation is reconciliation, as certainly as it is God himself: God with us, God beside us, and chiefly and decisively God for us."[2]

A brief exposition and clarification of Barth's theology of revelation will allow us to draw the following conclusions about Barth's theological epistemology: (1) the principles of theological knowing are known in reflection on the gift of the knowledge of God; (2) knowing God is personal, cognitive, participative knowing; (3) knowing God is divinely initiated, self-attesting grace; and (4) knowing God is personal transformation and reconciliation with God. Once this groundwork is established, we will move on in chapter three to discuss the implications for Barth's view of the relationship between philosophy and theology.

KNOWING IN REFLECTION ON REVELATION

The key move in any theory of knowing is the first move, or the logically

---

[1]Some comments on human cognition in general can be found in *CD* II/1, §27, "The Limits of the Knowledge of God." See Andrew McFarlane, "Sense and Spontaneity: A Critical Study of Barth's Kantian Model of Human Cognition in *CD* II/1," paper presented at the Scottish Barth Colloquium, St Andrews University, St Mary's College, 2006.

[2]Karl Barth, *God in Action: Theological Addresses* (New York: Round Table Press, 1936), p. 17.

primary move. How does an epistemology get off the groun primal glue holds it together? In the case of theological epis we are particularly concerned with what basis is given for the possibility of knowing God. In order to understand Barth's distinctive theological epistemology, therefore, it is important to pay close attention to how it emerges. Barth suggests, at one point, that his comments on knowing God are simply an "analysis of the biblical concept of revelation."[3] As even an expeditious stroll through the *Church Dogmatics* will attest, at every turn Barth defends the legitimacy of his position by appeal to scripture. Scripture as the written word of God has "supremacy."[4] It would be a mistake, however, to conclude that either the Bible or a biblically informed theory of revelation is for Barth the foundation of a theological system of knowing. Here enters Barth's famous qualification that scripture is not revelation in and of itself, but a means[5] used by God to "bear witness to revelation."[6] The initiating move in Barth's theological epistemology is not the claim that the Bible by itself, or the Bible read in the light of human reason, is the foundation or source of knowledge. Barth believes that the real initiating move is not a claim we make but a claim made on us. The initial move is made by God himself.[7] God wills to be known because and by means of his will to be with us.[8] Knowledge of God is initiated and enabled by the covenantal love of God, who establishes communion with us by "bringing us to participate in the love in which the Father loves the Son and as Son the Father."[9] In the light of this initiating self-revelation, we see that God is not re-

---

[3]*CD* I/1, p. 359.

[4]Holy scripture is supreme over proclamation; *CD* I/1, p. 102.

[5]By referring to scripture as a medium, means, instrument or form, Barth is emphatic that scripture is useless on its own. Compare these statements: "Thus God does reveal Himself in statements, through the medium [*Mittel*] of speech, and indeed of human speech" (*CD* I/1, pp. 137-38; *KD* I/1, p. 142). "The fact that God takes form does not give rise to a medium [*kein Medium*], a third thing between God and man, a reality distinct from God that is as such the subject of revelation" (*CD* I/1, p. 321; *KD* I/1, p. 339).

[6]*CD* I/1, p. 111. This is explored further in chapters 8 and 9.

[7]As Barth put it at the beginning of his first cycle of dogmatics in Göttingen in 1924, the basis for any human speech about God is that God has spoken, *Deus dixit;* see *GD*, pp. 10-14, 45-68.

[8]"He wills to be ours, and He wills that we should be His. . . . He does not will to be Himself in any other way than He is in this relationship. . . . This is God's conduct towards us in virtue of His revelation" (*CD* II/1, p. 274).

[9]*CD* IV/2, pp. 778-79.

vealed by us or the Bible, or by anything other than God himself. The basis for the possibility of knowing God is "God's action on man."[10] "The possibility of the knowledge of God springs from God, in that He is Himself the truth and He gives Himself to man in His Word by the Holy Spirit to be known as truth."[11]

In Barth's view, therefore, there are no first principles to establish or appeal to. God has taken the initiating action, such that "already on the way, we give an account of the way which we tread."[12] What is taken as the a priori ground of knowing in Barth's theological epistemology is the effectual self-revealing action of God making himself known to us prior to any philosophical reflection. We cannot ground the actual knowledge of God in a theoretical epistemological account. There is no source that we can appeal to other than the actual knowledge of God, so we must begin our theoretical epistemological account from the fact of the actual knowledge of God.[13] This is why Barth insists that the path of knowing is "from above to below" (*von oben nach unten*).[14] It is common for commentators well versed in the philosophical debates in epistemology to struggle to grasp this theo-foundationalism[15] in Barth. In order to make sense of Barth, often an expedition is launched to unearth a basic principle that is motivating his thought—the *real* foundation or

---

[10]*CD* I/1, p. 110 (*KD* I/1, p. 113, "Handeln Gottes am Menschen"). Note that I have not endeavored to update the translations with gender-inclusive language. All of Barth's references to *Mensch(en)*, translated "man" or "men," should be understood to be gender inclusive.

[11]*CD* II/1, p. 63.

[12]*CD* I/1, p. 43.

[13]"The type of thinking that wants to begin with the question of the knowability of God and then to pass on from that point to the question of the fulfillment of the knowledge of God is not grateful but grasping, not obedient but self-autonomous" (*CD* II/1, p. 63).

[14]Barth uses the expression "von unten nach oben" to describe the wrong way to ground theological knowing and to distinguish from the only proper and indeed possible orientation for theology "von oben nach unten" (*KD* I/1, pp. 135, 178, 179, 189, 255, 440). This does not mean that the medium of revelation is not of the *unten*. The incarnation is a historical, this-worldly and indeed empirical reality; nevertheless, the *Ursprung* is *von oben* and therefore the way of revelation, the way we come to know God "von oben nach unten führt" (*KD* I/1, p. 440; *CD* I/1, p. 419).

[15]In adopting the term *theo-foundationalism* to apply to Barth's theological epistemology I do not intend to suggest that Barth has committed himself to a general foundationalism. Other metaphors could be substituted so long as they affirm that the ground for the knowledge of God is not only given by God but, as we shall discuss next, *is* God in his self-revelation. The distinction between classical foundationalism and what I am calling Barth's theo-foundationalism will be clarified in the next chapter.

source.[16] Barth insists, however, that his theological reflections (whether they be on the wholly otherness of God, the freedom of God or the fallenness of humans) are not the basis of his view of revelation but really are reflections based on the revelation given.[17] What may seem confusing is that at no point does Barth offer an argument to ground this supposition. He urges instead that all theology should be done as an attempt to think correctly from this a priori.[18]

Barth's view of theological knowledge is theo-foundational. Knowledge is anchored and initiated from above. Our analysis of the way of knowing is in light of the gift of knowing. This should be sufficient to establish a first proposition about Barth's theological epistemology: *(1) The principles of theological knowing are known in reflection on the gift of the knowledge of God.*

GOD AS OBJECT AND SUBJECT OF HIS PERSONAL, COGNITIVE REVELATION

It is Barth's radical reorientation of the starting point and direction of theological knowing that explains his assertion that the primary question in theological reflection is not "how do we know God?" but rather "who is our God?"[19] The how question only becomes the initial question if we are starting from outside the fact of the reality of given revelation. Theology, as a second-order reflection on a firsthand personal revelation, seeks to clarify its understanding of who this revealed God is. This is just what Barth attempts to do in his theology of revelation. God is none

[16]Both Helm and Wolterstorff determine that what motivates Barth's theology of revelation is his notion of the sovereign freedom of God. See Paul Helm, *The Divine Revelation: The Basic Issues,* Foundations for Faith (Westchester, IL: Crossway, 1982), pp. 40-41; and Nicholas Wolterstorff, *Divine Discourse: Philosophical Reflections on the Claim That God Speaks* (Cambridge: Cambridge University Press, 1995), pp. 73-74. Looking for a hidden motivator for Barth's theological epistemology is an academically legitimate pursuit. It must, however, be recognized that Barth believed that the ground for knowing God really is laid and occupied a priori by God himself.

[17]As Alan Torrance observes, "our very conceptions of divine freedom are themselves freely conditioned by God" (Torrance, *Persons in Communion: An Essay on Trinitarian Description and Human Participation, with Special Reference to Volume One of Karl Barth's Church Dogmatics* [Edinburgh: T & T Clark, 1996], p. 49).

[18]"All its knowledge, even its knowledge of the correctness of its knowledge, can only be an event, and cannot therefore be guaranteed as correct knowledge from any place apart from or above this event" (*CD* I/1, p. 42).

[19]*CD* I/1, p. 301.

other than who he, through himself, reveals himself to be in his revelation. The nature of the knowledge of God is the *self-revealing* revelation of God.[20]

To grasp properly what Barth is saying, it may be helpful to distinguish, as Barth does, three components of the act of revelation, which correspond to the persons of the Trinity. There is the revealer, the act of revealing, and the consequence or effect of the act of revealing (which Barth calls the "revealedness"). Barth maps these to the persons of the Trinity, united yet distinct as the Revealer, Revelation and Revealedness. He contends that this is what "distinguishes the Christian concept of revelation as Christian."[21] Revelation (*Offenbarung*) has an objective and a subjective sense. We use it to refer either to the objective action and content being revealed or to the subjective appropriation that results from being revealed to. In Barth's notion of revelation, these two senses are united, though distinct. In the act of revelation, the revealer is united to the content and reception of revelation. Revelation is the address of God. Revelation "is itself the Word of God." Jesus Christ is the Revelation of God. God is his revelation.[22] "He is also His self-revealing."[23] The effect of revelation in us is the gift of the Spirit.[24] In this way, God remains "indissolubly subject, in His revelation."[25]

Many clear-headed individuals in the English-speaking world, and especially those with a background in analytic philosophy, will find the sentences of the preceding paragraph highly perplexing, if not nonsensical.[26] For some, such Barthianisms are evidence of Barth's antirational tendencies. After all, if revelation is interlaced with the mystery of the Trinity, what hope is there of understanding it? Some Barth interpreters suggest that Barth's dialectical method is intended to involve

---

[20]See *CD* II/1, pp. 31-62.

[21]*CD* I/1, p. 301.

[22]*CD* I/1, p. 118.

[23]CD I/1, p. 299.

[24]See CD I/2, pp. 203-79, for Barth's much fuller exposition of the Holy Spirit as the subjective reality and subjective possibility of revelation.

[25]*CD* I/1, p. 382.

[26]Adolf von Harnack apparently found such constructions in Barth totally "obscure" ("An Open Letter to Professor Karl Barth," in *The Beginnings of Dialectic Theology*, ed. James McConkey Robinson and Jürgen Moltmann [Richmond: John Knox, 1968]). Referenced in George Hunsinger, *Disruptive Grace: Studies in the Theology of Karl Barth* (Grand Rapids: Eerdmans, 2000), p. 333.

confusions and contradictions. It is not that Barth's theology is anti-rational but that it confronts and is confronted by the crisis of human language and fallen reason. On this view, we will reach a point in Barth's writing where rational tensions cannot and should not be resolved; furthermore, retaining unresolved confusion is what it means really to *get* Barth. Stephen H. Webb expresses this view when he writes, "It is possible that more sense can be made from Barth's position than I have allowed here, but really to read Barth is to refuse to resist his endless perplexities and contradictions."[27]

This is a misunderstanding of Barth's dialectical method. In the present case, applying this principle would be doubly confusing: in a way we cannot humanly conceive of, God gives us a knowledge of God that we cannot know. What is at issue here is at the heart of our main concern about Barth's attitude toward reason and philosophy, and the prospects of constructive response to theology's epistemological dilemma. The contention we face here is that Barth is finally and only an apophatic theologian. He may appear to be making positive theological claims, but he then expunges any meaning associated with those claims so that they are ultimately negations and not claims at all. If it is actually the case that Barth is merely an apophatic theologian, then it is hard to see how there can be positive, cognitive Christian belief—much less a discussion about its warrant. Moreover, by radically undercutting reason and language, such a position, appealing to reason and expressed in language, is patently self-defeating.

Surely the mere apophatic Barth is an option we can quickly dismiss. On the one hand, Barth does commonly use dialectic negatively, to cut through a false synthesis.[28] This negative action, however, is almost always part of a positive theological declaration. Barth is clearly not saying that God in God's self-revealing revelation remains unrevealed.[29]

---

[27]Stephen H. Webb, *Re-Figuring Theology: The Rhetoric of Karl Barth,* SUNY Series in Rhetoric and Theology (Albany: State University of New York Press, 1991), p. 74.

[28]Barth reflects on how this featured especially in his earlier writing: "How things were cleared away there and almost only cleared away!" (*The Humanity of God* [London: Westminster John Knox, 1960], p. 43). See also Paul Brazier, "Barth's First Commentary on Romans (1919): An Exercise in Apophatic Theology?" *International Journal of Systematic Theology* 6, no. 4 (2004): 387-403.

[29]Barth does affirm that in the mediation itself, God remains hidden (*CD* I/1, pp. 175-79, 320-24). This will be discussed further in chapter 8. It is sufficient here to affirm that, though God is unveiled through a veil, God is really revealed.

Barth is making a concrete cognitive claim: "God is objective and therefore He can be truly known."[30] He is even willing to declare that it is possible for a human knowledge of God to be "a clear and certain knowledge, not equal but at least similar to the clarity and certainty with which God knows Himself in His Word."[31] Interpreting Barth as merely apophatic undermines Barth's central thesis about revelation—namely, that revelation is the effectual self-revealing of God. The crisis of human language and the problem of fallen reason are neither the first nor the final word. God in Christ miraculously overcomes these humanly insurmountable barriers to make himself known by the power of the Spirit. And if these considerations are not enough, Barth explicitly condemns apophatism as a way to God.[32] "Even knowledge of the impossibility of knowledge of the Word of God outside its reality is possible only on the presupposition of this real knowledge."[33] An apophatic way to God, as a negative human word, might suggest a means of arriving at the destination by human steam.[34] Barth's theology of revelation may strike some as initially obscure, but there is no reason to think that by it Barth merely intends to be obscurant. To be sure, revelation is for Barth both a miracle and mystery,[35] but it would be neither if it were not a real revealing.

Returning then to Barth's core claim about revelation—that "God the Revealer, is identical with His act in revelation and also identical with its effect"[36]—it may be possible to clarify what Barth means by looking more closely at what seems so perplexing about it. One challenge is to understand how both identity and distinction can be maintained among

---

[30]*CD* II/1, p. 32. "We have made a positive assertion, pronouncing a definite Yes to the knowability of the Word of God" (*CD* I/1, p. 196).

[31]*CD* I/1, p. 243.

[32]"An indication of the limits of our conceiving . . . must not be allowed to condense into a negative proof" (*CD* I/1, p. 164).

[33]*CD* I/1, p. 197.

[34]As Colin E. Gunton has noted, "The apparent modesty and humility of the negative way masks quite a different movement, a movement for unity with God which operates apart from that communion mediated through Jesus" (Gunton, *Act and Being: Towards a Theology of the Divine Attributes* [Grand Rapids: Eerdmans, 2003], p. 63). Of course, apophaticism does not require this assumed independent movement.

[35]*CD* II/1, pp. 181, 283-84; *CD* I/1, p. 331.

[36]*CD* I/1, p. 296.

the subject, act and effect in revelation. What does Barth mean by identifying God with action and effects? And, could this not lead to untoward theological consequences?[37] Indeed, the theological consequences could be disastrous if we begin with an abstract notion of any of the three. We might, for instance, start with an abstract notion of action and propose that the revealing subject in identity with the act of revealing should be understood in terms of this notion of action. This kind of essentialist actualism could easily reduce God to a totemic principle or an impersonal force. In the same way, equating God with an abstract notion of the effect of revelation has radical implications. This approach reduces God to a way of speaking about subjective transformation or enlightenment. These paths are out of bounds for Barth, who with traditional Christian orthodoxy would reject affirmations that identify God with anything that is not the objective, personal and concrete God who acts in history in the person of Christ.[38] In order to come to grips with Barth's notion of revelation, therefore, we must heed his words that "the Bible always understands what it calls revelation as a concrete relation to concrete men."[39] Barth's identification of subject, act and being is not the fruit of reflection on general philosophical notions of being and act or cause and effect. As before, these notions also are intended to be the fruit of reflection on the gift of the knowledge of God. Barth's theology of revelation will remain unintelligible as long as general philosophical presumptions are assumed to be the key either to understanding its motivation or to unlocking its interpretation.

Barth contests that he is attempting to be faithful to the concrete God of the Bible who is revealed as Father, Son and Holy Spirit. That the

---

[37]It is my intent here to clarify Barth's notion of revelation, not to defend Barth's doctrine of the Trinity. Along these lines, Barth has been critiqued as flirting with modalism (Jürgen Moltmann, *The Trinity and the Kingdom: The Doctrine of God* [San Francisco: Harper & Row, 1981], pp. 139-44) and de-emphasizing intra-trinitarian communion and consequently human participation in it (Alan Torrance, *Persons in Communion,* 103-7), as well as deriving the doctrine of the Trinity analytically from a theory of revelation (William J. Abraham, *Canon and Criterion in Christian Theology: From the Fathers to Feminism* [Oxford: Oxford University Press, 1998], p. 388).

[38]"In God's revelation, which is the content of His Word, we have in fact to do with His act. . . . What is concerned is always the birth, death and resurrection of Jesus Christ, always His justification of faith, always His lordship in the Church, always His coming again, and therefore Himself as our hope" (*CD* II/1, p. 262; cf. *CD* IV/2, p. 300).

[39]*CD* I/1, p. 325.

revealing Father is one with his act of revelation is nothing more than the confession of John 1:1: "the Word was God." Since the Word of God is the speech of God, and because "we shall have to regard God's speech as also God's act,"[40] Jesus Christ, therefore, is God's self-revealing act. The same concrete biblical analysis shapes Barth's conclusion that the Spirit of God is the revealedness of God. That the Revealer and revealing act are one with the effect of that act is the confession that in revelation we are given the Spirit of truth. It is the fellowship of the Spirit that unites us to Christ. This union in the Spirit is the subjective impartation of the revelation of God. The Spirit guarantees for us "personal participation in revelation."[41] Christ is the objective revelation of God, and the Spirit is the gift of the subjective realization of that revelation in us: the gift of "faith, knowledge and obedience."[42] The ministry of the Spirit enables a participation in Christ's human knowing of the Father. The gift of the effect of revelation is the gift of God giving himself. "In His revelation [the love of God] seeks and creates fellowship where there is no fellowship and no capacity for it."[43]

Barth's theology of revelation is plainly at odds with some assumptions that accompany a general philosophical or history-of-religions approach to the question of revelation. It is dissonance with these background assumptions that obscures Barth's position. In the vernacular or "plain sense," *revelation* has to do with bringing to light heretofore hidden information.[44] In its traditionally distinguished forms, special and general, revelation is typically imagined to be a deposit of information or traces of God left for humans to discover and decipher, e.g., what Paul Helm calls the "disclosure of truths" in the form of a "straight propositional account."[45] Barth stresses, on the other hand, that reve-

---

[40]*CD* I/1, p. 133.

[41]*CD* I/1, p. 453.

[42]Ibid.

[43]*CD* II/1, p. 278.

[44]See Alan Torrance's penetrating analysis of this in which he notes that importing a general model of revelation "can lead one to postulate a distinction (which too easily becomes a disjunction) between the being of S^r [the divine subject] and the being and nature of x [what is revealed]" (*Persons in Communion,* p. 66).

[45]Helm, *Divine Revelation,* p. 35.

lation is fundamentally personal[46]—the person of Jesus Christ is God's revelation. Revelation is never merely a description or an idea; it is "God's speaking person."[47] A strictly or fundamentally propositional view of Christian revelation would replace intimate, personal knowing with a theoretical, depersonalized abstraction.[48] "For the point of God's speech is not to occasion specific thoughts or a specific attitude but through the clarity which God gives us, and which induces both these in us, to bind us to Himself."[49]

Some who are familiar with Barth's affirmation of revelation as fundamentally personal draw the drastically mistaken conclusion that, for Barth, revelation is thereby seen as emptied of "objective truth."[50] The fact, however, that revelation is personal and relational does not mean that it is a strictly noumenal, suprarational and extramental experience with no impact on our minds. "The supremely real and determinative entry of the Word of God into the reality of man"[51] induces and encompasses "specific thoughts." The personal nature of revelation does not "impl[y] its irrationality."[52] In the gift of hearing God's speaking, we are said to be given "very distinct and in themselves clear thoughts regarding what is said to us."[53] Barth affirms that personal revelation remains ra-

---

[46]Barth grants that in revelation we may have to do with facts, but these are not isolated propositions, they are facts that are "created and presented by a person" (*CD* I/1, p. 205).

[47]*CD* I/1, pp. 136-37.

[48]"But will the truth of revelation submit to such materialisation and depersonalisation? Can one have it in abstraction from the person of Him who reveals it and from the revelatory act of this person in which it is given to other persons to perceive?" (*CD* I/1, p. 270). See also the priority of the question "Who is God in His Revelation?" (*CD* I/1, pp. 297-301). In chapter 8 we will take a closer look at the distinction between personal and propositional knowing, including the objections of Helm and Wolterstorff.

[49]*CD* I/1, p. 175.

[50]See for instance Roger E. Olson's comments in this regard contrasting Alister McGrath and Kenneth Collins with Barth, whom he lumps together with Brunner, in Olson, *Reformed and Always Reforming* (Grand Rapids: Baker Academic, 2007), p. 157.

[51]*CD* I/1, p. 193.

[52]*CD* I/1, p. 138. This affirmation is missed by those who assume that Barth is advocating "irrationalism," famously by Brand Blanshard at a 1962 gathering of philosophers and theologians at Princeton Seminary and the philosophers in agreement who were noted to have "cheered on so enthusiastically" (Blanshard, "Critical Reflections on Karl Barth," in *Faith and the Philosophers*, ed. John Hick [London: Macmillan, 1964], pp. 159-200; Dennis O'Brien, "On the Limitations of Reason," in *Faith and the Philosophers*, pp. 232-34). The thirty-year-old Alvin Plantinga was included in this auspicious gathering, though his recorded contribution makes no comment on the debate over Barth.

[53]*CD* I/1, p. 174.

tional, verbal and cognitive.[54] In fact, Barth believes that personal communication is fundamentally rational. "Speech, including God's speech, is the form in which reason communicates with reason and person with person."[55] Barth will grant to the common notion of revelation that revelation is indeed intellectually engaging, but not that it is a mere transmission of propositional statements.[56] God makes himself personally known to us in relationship with us by the gift of communion with the Spirit, who is the subject of the knowing relation.[57] It is in this participative communion only, however, that information about God is personally and cognitively enjoyed and properly known.[58]

These comments on the nature of the knowledge of God serve to support the second claim about Barth's theological epistemology: *(2) Knowing God is personal, cognitive, participative knowing.* This statement affirms both the objective revelation of God's address to us in Christ and the subjective response of our participation in that knowing by the gift of the Spirit. We have not, however, in these few words removed the mystery of the miracle of revelation; nor, on Barth's view, is it ever possible on our side of the relation to unravel the mystery.

THE HIDDENNESS OF GOD IN REVELATION

Some of what Barth has to say about revelation appears to temper, if not contradict, his positive affirmations on the possibility for humans to know God. Although Barth affirms that the speech of God is rational, cognitive and verbal, it is nevertheless indirect and, therefore, in its crea-

---

[54]The personal character of God's Word is not, then, to be played off against its verbal or spiritual character (*CD* I/1, p. 138).

[55]*CD* I/1, p. 135.

[56]Barth warns against thinking that "propositions or principles are certain in themselves like the supposed axioms of the mathematicians and physicists, and are not rather related to their theme and content, which alone are certain, which they cannot master, by which they must be mastered if they are not to be mere soap-bubbles" (*CD* I/1, p. 165).

[57]"The Holy Spirit is God Himself in His freedom exercised in revelation to be present to His creature, even to dwell in him personally, and thereby to achieve his meeting with Himself in His Word and by this achievement to make it possible" (*CD* I/2, p. 198; cf. *CD* II/1, p. 181).

[58]"God knows Himself; the Father knows the Son and the Son the Father in the unity of the Holy Spirit. This occurrence in God Himself is the essence and strength of our knowledge of God. . . . [I]t is an occurrence in which man as such is not a participant, but in which he becomes a participant through God's revelation" (*CD* II/1, p. 49).

turely, secular form, leaves God hidden.[59] Barth claims not only that for us the speech of God remains shrouded in mystery but also that this is necessarily so. The notion that God is necessarily hidden in his revelation seems flatly self-contradictory. Given our concern to understand Barth's theological epistemology, it is vital for us to get clear about the way in which he understands God to be both hidden and yet revealed. If Barth is affirming the necessary and absolute unrevealedness of God, then his thoughts will not combine well with Plantinga's or offer much by way of a constructive theological epistemology. We have already seen, however, that Barth promotes revelation as a real revealing.[60] It would be wrong, therefore, to view Barth's constructive approach to revelation as simply a sleight-of-hand skepticism. How then are we to resolve this pointed confrontation between revelation and mystery?

One possibility is that in God's revelation God is only partially revealed and therefore only partially hidden. We can safely rule this out as an option for Barth. On the contrary, Barth actually seems to assert both that our knowledge of God is "similar to the clarity and certainty with which God knows Himself"[61] and yet that God remains completely hidden behind an "untearably thick veil."[62] God is "fully revealed and fully concealed in His self-disclosure."[63] Barth really is affirming both hiddenness and revealedness to be absolutely and simultaneously true. There is a key difference, however, in the perspective from which both of these claims can be simultaneously made. From above or inside the knowing relation, God is really revealed, but from below or outside the knowing relation, God is utterly hidden. The stark opposition between these perspectives must be emphasized in

[59]There is the potential for some confusion here in what we mean by God's hiddenness in this discussion. Philosophers of religion talk about the experience of divine hiddenness, when God seems silent or without witness. This is often discussed as a problem for belief in God. As we will see, this is not what Barth means by God's hiddenness in revelation. Revelation means God is *not* silent. That is not to say that Barth would not agree with Paul K. Moser's thesis that God may withhold revelation for gracious purposes (see Moser, *The Elusive God* [New York: Cambridge University Press, 2008]).

[60]Cf. Alan Torrance's rebuttal of Battista Mondin's charge that Barth's form-content distinction "is heading in the direction of a *credo quia absurdum*" (Torrance, *Persons in Communion,* pp. 168-76).

[61]*CD* I/1, p. 243.

[62]*CD* I/1, p. 168; cf. *CD* II/1, pp. 341-43.

[63]*CD* II/1, p. 341.

order to maintain a narrow path that runs between two lethal theological tripwires. On one side is the error of divinizing the creaturely; on the other side is the error of secularizing the divine. On a third side, which actually connects the other two, is the consequence of negating real divine-to-human revelation.

For Barth, affirming God's hiddenness is affirming that human language, conceptuality and noetic equipment are insufficient for arriving at a knowledge of God on their own.[64] Knowing that we lack this independent capacity for knowing God is something we know in the hindsight of receiving the grace of actually knowing God. In the hindsight of faith, we know God to be the holy, infinite, independent Creator fully distinct from his fallen, finite, dependent creatures. As creatures, we must receive knowledge in creaturely form. But the knowledge of God has no human analogy by which it could come to us directly in creaturely form.[65] The divine content of revelation must therefore be communicated indirectly through a creaturely form,[66] but in such a way that the divine content does not become the creaturely form. This means that in terms of the creaturely form alone, God is hidden behind a "wall of secularity."[67] From outside, this wall is unscalable. This does not mean that the form of the creaturely form is unimportant, only that the nature of its reference to God is such that "the power of this reference does not lie in itself; it lies in that to which it refers."[68] The creaturely form is a means by which God chooses to break through to us.

The origination of revelation is, however, unidirectional;[69] we cannot

---

[64]See esp. *CD* II/1, pp. 179-204.

[65]In chapter 8 we will discuss Barth's rejection of the *analogia entis* in a more detailed discussion of the nature of human knowledge of God.

[66]Barth's point here is both more severe and yet more optimistic than Calvin's notion of accommodation. In the famous passage in the *Institutes* (1.13.1), Calvin explains that, accommodating to our feebleness (*tenuitati*), God in a certain way lisps (*quodammodo balbutire*) to give us a knowledge of him by stooping down to our level (*longe infra eius altitudinem descendere*). For Barth the creaturely form on its own is not an accommodated, lesser form of revelation; it is utter hiddenness—nonrevelation. As an instrument in the hands of the self-revealing action of God, however, this creaturely form becomes the place of the real revelation of God at his full height.

[67]*CD* I/1, p. 165.

[68]*CD* I/1, p. 197.

[69]Referring to revelation as *unidirectional* means that only by God are we drawn into the knowledge of God; it does not mean that knowing God is somehow *unilateral*—that it fails somehow to be genuine human knowing with genuine human reciprocation.

use the means to break through to God. God gives himself *in and through* the creaturely form, not *as* the creaturely form. The creaturely form, although it is only form and not content, is nevertheless indispensable because of our creatureliness. "The secular form without the divine content is not the Word of God and the divine content without the secular form is also not the Word of God."[70] The "united but not confused" Chalcedonic formula fits exactly.[71] Incarnation is revelation. The creaturely form, or human nature, of Christ is united with the divine nature in the person of the Logos. This revelation is established by God uniting himself to an anhypostatic creaturely nature. The human does not become the divine. The creaturely form has no personhood of its own. It is not, on its own, revelation. Outside of the gift of faith, the creaturely form only hides God. This hiddenness is graciously overcome in the miracle of revelation, whereby God, who remains a mystery in a creaturely form, lifts people up by means of the creaturely form in faith to participate in the knowing relation in which God knows himself.[72]

The possibility of the personal and cognitive revelation of God is, next to all other acts of human knowing, unreservedly sui generis.[73] In every other instance, the object and subject in the knowing relation are both created. Human knowledge of God is necessarily indirect and therefore cannot be penetrated from below.[74] Because God does not become transparently visible in the creaturely form, God's taking on creaturely form is insufficient for revelation. There are two reasons for this opacity: our fallenness and our finitude.[75] Our fallenness means the

---

[70]*CD* I/1, p. 175.

[71]Bruce L. McCormack writes, "The central thrust of the ancient dogma was that the Logos (the second Person of the Holy Trinity) took to Himself human flesh (i.e. a human 'nature,' complete, whole, and entire) and lived a human life in and through it. The proximity to Barth's dialectic of veiling and unveiling was obvious. In that God takes to God's Self a human nature, God veils God's Self in a creaturely medium" (McCormack, *Karl Barth's Critically Realistic Dialectical Theology: Its Genesis and Development, 1909–1936* [Oxford: Oxford University Press, 1995], p. 327). See also Trevor Hart, *Regarding Karl Barth: Essays Toward a Reading of His Theology* (Carlisle, UK: Paternoster, 1999), pp. 14-17.

[72]*CD* II/1, p. 51.

[73]*CD* I/1, p. 164.

[74]On the limitations of our knowledge of God, see *CD* II/1, pp. 57-61.

[75]*CD* I/1, pp. 167-68.

of our knowledge structures and language for grasping truth. Our finitude means the lack of any capacity for, or bridge of analogy to, God. Both of these keep us from seeing God through the veil of the creaturely form. In the gracious miracle of revelation, both of these problems are overcome.[76] We are given the eyes of faith to see despite the brokenness of our knowledge structures and language, and we are borne across the gulf that separates Creator and creature through a participation by the Spirit in the Son's knowledge of the Father. Only God could make God known.[77]

The miracle of revelation raises one significant question: is the miracle of revelation a perpetual reality or not? Barth is clear that we cannot assume that it is. Revelation cannot be presupposed, even as a present fulfillment.[78] Barth warns that we do not have at our disposal a "constantly available relationship between God and man."[79] That is to say not that God does not draw us into ongoing relationship but that the relationship is not made available to us in such a way that it is in our control. This is, for Barth, another affirmation of the hiddenness of God from outside the unidirectional movement from God to us in revelation. We are never left with a capacity that would reverse this direction. This is what Barth is most intent on guarding against. Not even on the basis of the move having already been made from above to below do we have an assurance of our own grasp. The past experience of revelation cannot be allowed to become a postulate in a system whereby we build back to a demonstration of the knowledge of God. Barth rejects the idea of the perpetual availability of revelation because we are never brought into a

[76]It is astonishing how many theologians dismiss Barth because of his strong denial of an independent human capacity for revelation, never hearing his clear positive declaration made in passages like the following: "The saying *finitum non capax infiniti* cannot really prove what has to be proved at this point. If the real experience of the man addressed by God's Word is against this saying, then the saying must go, as every philosophical statement in theology that is in contradiction with this experience must go" (*CD* I/1, p. 220). Rolfe King makes this mistake and documents a number who have somehow concluded that Barth denies the possibility of revelation (King, *Obstacles to Divine Revelation: God and the Reorientation of Human Reason* [New York: Continuum, 2008], pp. 22-24).

[77]"God can be known only by God. At this very point, in faith itself, we know God in utter dependence, in pure discipleship and gratitude" (*CD* II/1, p. 183).

[78]*CD* I/1, p. 261.

[79]Barth argues that to view revelation as a "constantly available relationship" reduces grace to nature (*CD* I/1, p. 41).

state where we have hold of the ground of grace. In fact, it is the other way around: the ground of grace has hold of us. We confess and know God on the basis of the gift of this grace alone. We cannot show how we know in some way independent from our connection to that ground. And so, a perpetual revelation, outside of our being in Christ, is not possible. Barth's comments on this are geared toward obliterating any confidence that could be placed on our *independent* perpetual experience, understanding, appropriation, translation or communication of revelation.

This brings us to an important observation regarding the freedom of God in his revelation. The gift of the knowledge of God is given to us with assurance in the knowing relation, but we are not also given any means whereby we could demonstrate either to ourselves or to others that we have been given this knowledge. The question might be put this way: can we know that we have true knowledge of God? But stating the question like this might result in a misleading answer from Barth. We have already established that the experience of the Word of God is cognitive. One implication of this is that when we are addressed by God in his revelation, we are cognizant of what is happening. In the gift of knowing God, we are aware that it is God we are knowing. In other words, in God's self-disclosure, we know that we truly know God. Knowing that we truly know is part of the gift of participating in Christ's knowledge of the Father. The question is misleading, however, because it is assumed that in order to know that we know, we must have some reason to justify our knowledge claim. A justifying reason in the form of some tangible evidence or argument we are not given, according to Barth. The only justification we have is the event of revelation itself.[80] What justifies our knowing that we know God is the fact that God has made himself known and nothing else.[81] All we have to point to as a

[80]Calvin, similarly, says that revelation in scripture is self-attesting (αὐτοπίστον); it is not subject to rational demonstration but is confirmed by the testimony of the Spirit (*neque demonstrationi et rationibus subiici eam fas esse: quam tamen meretur apud nos certitudinem, Spiritus testimonio consequi, Institutes,* 1.7.5). He also observes here the human form serving the disclosure of the divine content (*hominum ministerio, ab ipsissimo Dei ore ad nos fluxisse*).

[81]Barth argues that "self-certainty" must be based only on the "certainty of God" (*CD* I/1, p. 196). Barth affirms the same when he writes, "In faith man has and knows and affirms only this possibility of knowledge of God's Word, the possibility which lies in the Word of God itself, has come to him in the Word, and is present to him in the Word" (*CD* I/1, p. 224).

basis for our knowledge of God is the gift of grace. But this basis, precisely because it is divinely given and "thus withdrawn from our grasp,"[82] is therefore "an assurance with a metal that makes it superior to every other assurance."[83]

This brings us to the third conclusion about Barth's theological epistemology: *(3) Knowing God is divinely initiated, self-attesting grace.* The grace of revelation is God's overcoming our fallenness and finitude. It is initiated from the object of revelation—from above to below. From the outside we cannot break through the creaturely form to see God directly; nor do we have in our being a capacity or analogy for spanning the gulf. Revelation always requires God's action. God's action in the grace of faith attests to the truth of the knowledge of God and allows us to know God through the creaturely form. So God's hiddenness and revealedness are not in contradiction. In fact, if God did not take the creaturely form that hides him, there would be no means for revealing himself either. "What seems in the first instance an absurd obstacle that God Himself has put in the way is in fact His real way to us."[84] And if our assurance were grounded in anything other than the self-attesting grace of revelation, it would be built only on sinking sand.

REVELATION AS WHOLE-PERSON TRANSFORMATION

We have covered the features of Barth's theology of revelation that are salient for clarifying his from-above, theo-foundational, theological epistemology. But before we begin to investigate the implications of these features for the epistemological issues raised earlier, we should first take note of the inseparability of revelation and the personal transformation it requires and effects. Just as the way of knowing God is fundamentally different from the way we know other objects of knowledge, so too is the nature of the knowing itself unlike any other knowledge.[85] We

[82]*CD* I/1, p. 226.

[83]Ibid.

[84]*CD* I/1, p. 168.

[85]Knowledge of God is like other knowledge in its objectivity, but unlike other knowledge in that "its object is the living Lord of the knowing [man]" (*CD* II/1, p. 21). Barth is emphatic that we do not know God by the same capacity that we know other things: "God is known only by God" (*CD* II/1, pp. 182, 183).

have already touched on this uniqueness when we looked at Barth's claim that God is not just the object; he is also, particularly as the Spirit, the subject of the knowing.[86] For theological knowledge to be possible, according to Barth, we must be drawn up, by the gift of the Spirit, to participate in the knowing by which God knows himself. In Barth's view, revelation is bound up with soteriology. Revelation is for us and for our salvation. "The place of divine revelation is also and in itself the place of divine reconciliation."[87] Revelation and reconciliation are effected together by the Word made flesh.[88] As way, truth and life, Christ by the Spirit enables all aspects of our reconciliation with God, including the reconciliation of our minds.[89]

God cannot properly be known from a distance. Theological knowing requires that God establish fellowship with us, a relationship that cannot but be not only cognitively illuminating but also personally transformative. We must be given the eyes to see and ears to hear.[90] For this reason Barth speaks of God's address as "the transposing of man into the wholly new state."[91] The knowledge of any object has far-reaching and determinative consequences for the knower. We exist in relationship with, though distinct from, the objects of our knowledge both past and present. Barth provisionally defines knowledge as "the confirmation of human acquaintance with an object whereby its truth becomes a determination of the existence of the man who has the knowledge."[92] If this is so for ordinary objects, then how much more significant (and radically different) must the determination of the existence of the knower be in the human acquaintance with God.

---

[86]"In the work of the Holy Spirit . . . the light of the crucified and risen and living Jesus Christ does not merely shine objectively, but shines subjectively into fully human eyes and is seen by them" (*CD* IV/3, p. 761).

[87]*CD* II/1, p. 547.

[88]*CD* I/2, p. 214.

[89]As Colin Gunton writes, "It is preferable to say that revelation is first of all a function of that divine action by which the redemption of the creation is achieved in such a way that human blindness and ignorance are also removed" (Gunton, *A Brief Theology of Revelation* [Edinburgh: T & T Clark, 1995], p. 111).

[90]"We acquire eyes and ears for God in the Holy Spirit" (*CD* I/2, p. 248).

[91]*CD* I/1, p. 152.

[92]*CD* I/1, p. 198. Barth is clear that no general definition of knowledge can be imposed or presumed. Definitions must be left open to correction "in the light of the object concerned" (*CD* I/1, p. 190).

The impact of the Word of God is on all human faculties, not "intellect alone, yet at any rate the intellect also and not last of all."[93] Revelation never fails to be cognitive, but "the determination of human existence by God's Word can be understood just as much as a determination of feeling, will, or intellect."[94] "Πίστις says more than γνῶσις, but in all circumstances it says γνῶσις too."[95] It is therefore the whole person who is affected by this revelation. In fact, the transformation is so comprehensive that we become new creatures by participation in Christ. Sanctification is "an event of revelation in virtue of the enlightening work of the Holy Spirit."[96]

We have already established that the barrier of our fallenness is overcome in revelation. The impact on the whole person in the experience of knowing God is a turning of our rebellion against God and a being brought into conformity with God. "To have experience of God's Word is to yield to its supremacy."[97] "It comes . . . in such a way as to bend man, and indeed his conscience and will no less than his intellect and feeling. It does not break him; it really bends him, brings him into conformity with itself."[98] Every aspect of who we are is touched by revelation. Revelation is made possible by the gift of faith, which is required for those without eyes to be able to see God.[99] But this gift and the seeing imply a reconstitution of our minds, the submission of our wills and the transformation of our being. "Knowledge in the biblical sense directly includes, indeed, it is itself at root, μετάνοια, conversion, the transformation of the νοῦς, and therefore the whole man, in accordance with the One known by him."[100]

We must be cautious, nevertheless, about the conclusions drawn

---

[93]*CD* I/1, p. 205.

[94]*CD* I/1, p. 204.

[95]*CD* I/1, p. 229.

[96]*CD* IV/2, pp. 581-82. Barth's massive volume 4 of the *Church Dogmatics* is explicitly devoted to the doctrine of reconciliation, but because of the inseparability of reconciliation from the knowledge of God, revelation remains a constant theme.

[97]*CD* I/1, p. 206.

[98]Ibid.

[99]*CD* I/1, p. 223; *CD* I/2, p. 248.

[100]*CD* IV/3, p. 185. Barth understands the New Testament notion of repentance (μετανοεῖν) to refer not only to a transformation of the mind but more comprehensively to death and rebirth (*CD* I/1, p. 387; *CD* IV/2, p. 563).

from the insistence that revelation involves whole-person transformation. There are a least three faulty inferences that must be avoided: First, the consequence of personal transformation must never be read backward as a condition of revelation. Repentance and obedience are given with the gift of faith; they are not a prerequisite for revelation. Barth leaves no doubt that, in his view, the Word of God is spoken in "unconditional freedom."[101] Second, following from the first, God is free to reveal himself by the Spirit in Christ to all people. The free revelatory work of the Spirit is not confined to the institutional church or only to those who have "professed Christ." Third, following from the second, the personal transformation involved in revelation does not create a privileged class of God-knowers. The transformation that comes with revelation neither revives nor implants an *independent* capacity for knowing God.[102] While it is true that "a new, regenerate man will arise," it is also true that he "does not possess this regenerate man."[103] There is no sense in which one is transformed to stand as a new creature on one's own, as if it were possible to have direct access to the knowledge of God outside of communion with God freely established by God.[104] Barth seems most anxious to dispel this erroneous conclusion because of its seductive appeal in the history of theology.[105] To grant that there could be a human faculty that enables independent knowing of God is to ignore all that Barth believes we discover about the nature of revelation in the gift of revelation.[106] Our dependence on God's breaking through from above to below is removed if there is another more direct channel of knowing that is

---

[101] *CD* I/1, p. 157.

[102] *CD* II/1, p. 66.

[103] *CD* I/1, p. 222.

[104] Ronald F. Thiemann argues in *Revelation and Theology: The Gospel as Narrated Promise* (Notre Dame, IN: University of Notre Dame Press, 1985), pp. 42-43, that Barth "denies us our humanity" by stipulating that God is only known when the human subject is given a participation in God's self-knowing. He suggests that the human subject is discounted because the human is not the one doing the knowing in that relation. Thiemann fails to consider the possibility of a real human participation in Christ's human knowing of the Father. This charge ignores Barth's strong affirmation of humanity inherent in the participation by which the human subject genuinely, humanly knows God.

[105] We will meet these concerns particularly in chapter 7, where we look at what room Barth and Plantinga make for natural theology.

[106] *CD* II/1, p. 194.

under our control. For Barth, the God we know to be God in his revelation could not be known in any other way.[107] Moreover, it is impossible to have any assurance in a knowledge of God delivered by a human faculty. This move would attempt to ground faith in a human source, thus dangling it over the abyss of uncertainty and opening the door to the diabolical illusion of a way of theological knowing from below to above.

The personal, cognitive, self-attesting, divinely initiated knowledge of God can never be conceived of as anything other than gift freely given. Barth strictly maintains that nothing could merit or deliver independent access to the knowledge of God. Nevertheless, revelation could not involve a person's participation by the Spirit in Jesus Christ, the Word of God, without also transforming that person. This transformation involves the reconstitution of mind and will such that the knower is brought into conformity with God, a transformation that is maintained only in the knowing relation effected by the Spirit in the gift of faith. "Communion with God . . . is realized in the revelation of God."[108] This is, of course, not to say that personal transformation is comprehensive and instantaneous, though the ultimate goal of reconciliation is the regeneration of the whole person. It is with these provisos that the fourth observation about Karl Barth's theological epistemology should be understood: *(4) Knowing God is personal transformation and reconciliation with God.*

CONCLUSION

I have sought here to clarify the most important implications of Barth's theology of revelation for understanding his theological epistemology—summarizing them into four statements that address his understanding of the order, nature, direction and impact of theological knowing. With this positive groundwork laid, we are now ready to investigate how Barth's uncompromising from-above theo-foundationalism shapes his view of the relationship between philosophy and theology. The common

---

[107]"The revelation attested in [scripture] refuses to be understood as any sort of revelation alongside which there are or may be others" (*CD* I/1, p. 295).

[108]*CD* I/2, p. 257.

assumption of a general antithesis between Barth's theology and philosophy is an obstacle to hopes of finding in Barth an open dialogue with the likes of Alvin Plantinga and a constructive response to epistemological questions.

3

BARTH'S ENGAGEMENT WITH PHILOSOPHY

A Theo-foundational Epistemology

◆

While the conclusions of Barth's theology of revelation do indeed curtail the free rein of philosophy over theology, they hardly amount to an all-out ban. The intent of this chapter is to determine what Karl Barth understands to be the primary theological boundaries for properly functioning philosophy in the service of theology, and thereby to correct the misunderstanding that Barth's position is one of blanket interdiction and isolation. We will explore the implications of Barth's theological epistemology to grasp his primary concerns with what he takes to be the inevitable use of philosophy in the theological task. In so doing, I will defend the aptness of Barth's theology of revelation for constructive dialogue with analytic epistemology and its promise for responding to and reframing theology's epistemological difficulties.

My approach will focus on a selection of Barth's work where he comments extensively on the relationship between philosophy and theology.[1] With the exception of an essay penned for his brother Heinrich's seventieth-birthday Festschrift in 1960, the material we will consider is taken primarily from the *Church Dogmatics* and from Barth's publications in the time just prior, while he was living in Göttingen and

[1]In Kenneth Oakes's masterful study, he notes that Barth nowhere gives a full and precise account of the relationship between philosophy and theology; however, that does not deter Oakes from identifying, as I will do here, some of Barth's distinct thoughts about that relationship. See Oakes, *Karl Barth on Theology and Philosophy* [Oxford: Oxford University Press, 2012], pp. 245, 264-65.

Münster. In this period, Barth clarifies theology's independent starting point and the proper relationship of philosophical assumptions and methods to the theological task.[2] We will begin with a consideration of some explicit statements Barth makes concerning philosophy and how it differs from theology. This discussion will establish that it is not philosophy per se that Barth rejects but the way in which philosophy typically operates. Then we will look at Barth's censure of the uncritical acceptance in theology of modernist philosophical presuppositions. Here I will detail Barth's response to a collection of philosophical assumptions that are rarely distinguished in theological literature. Finally, I will highlight a representative instance of Barth's reflections on philosophy in relationship to theology. This will enable us to see that the criterion for evaluating the usefulness of philosophical assumptions and methods in the service of theology is the same criterion by which theology itself is evaluated, namely, the revelation of God. My modest goal is to understand how Barth's convictions about the givenness of divine self-revelation sets the priorities for constructive theological engagement with philosophy.

WHY THEOLOGY IS NOT PHILOSOPHY

The suggestion that Barth's theology has "little use for philosophy" is in most respects untenable. From the 1920s onward, Barth's position did not change.[3] Theology cannot avoid philosophy because theology is done in philosophy's own arena. "If we open our mouths, we find our-

[2]The dubious suggestion of Hans Urs von Balthasar that Barth's "final emancipation from the shackles of philosophy" did not come until 1930 after "a struggle, that lasted nearly ten years," should not deter us from concluding that the positions Barth enunciates during the Göttingen and Münster years constitute his mature position. The material from 1932 and 1960 diverges in no way from the earlier material we will discuss. The English translation of Balthasar here tries to soften the claim by opting for "final emancipation" and mysteriously inserting "a gradual process, indeed a struggle." Referring to what he finds to be Barth's second turning point, Balthasar writes, "Der zweite [Wendepunkt] ist der Endpunkt der Befreiung aus den Schlacken der Philosophie, um zu einer echten, selbständigen Theologie zu gelangen; er liegt, nach einem fast zehnjährigen Ringen um diese Befreiung, ungefähr 1930" (Balthasar, *Karl Barth: Darstellung und Deutung seiner Theologie* [Cologne: J. Hegner, 1951], p. 101; translated by Edward T. Oakes as *The Theology of Karl Barth: Exposition and Interpretation* [San Francisco: Ignatius Press, 1992], p. 93).

[3]As Kenneth Oakes argues, "Barth's later thoughts concerning theology and philosophy are similar to those he had already established in the middle of the 1920s" (Oakes, *Karl Barth on Theology and Philosophy*, p. 224).

selves in the province of philosophy."[4] In fact, Barth begins his *Church Dogmatics* with the observation that there is only a pragmatic justification for distinguishing theology from philosophy. Philosophy is not *necessarily* "secular or pagan." "There might be such a thing as *philosophia christiana*."[5] He later expands on this suggestion by proposing the possibility of a Christian philosopher who is in fact a "Krypto-Theologe."[6] These and other positive statements about philosophy and its relationship to theology require that any explanation of Barth's much-vaunted aversion to philosophy must retain for philosophy some rightful place. It must be stressed that Barth's strict cautions about philosophy are not aimed at philosophy "in principle"[7] but only at the non-Christian stance that philosophy has in fact adopted. There is no reason why there could not be a Christian philosophy, but the fact is "there never has actually been a *philosophia christiana,* for if it was *philosophia* it was not *christiana,* and if it was *christiana* it was not *philosophia*."[8] It is philosophy's abandoning of the theological task and way of knowing that has occasioned the need for theology as a stopgap measure.[9]

Both theology and philosophy, and the other sciences for that matter, are human attempts to know the truth that theology knows to be the Truth that has made itself known as the ground of all other being and truth. As fellow human beings engaged in this enterprise, the philosopher and theologian are companions. Barth says they face "common difficult tasks."[10] But it is exactly this commonality that gives rise to a turf-war-like confrontation. It is the *way* in which philosophy approaches the Truth that has provoked theology to take its artificially

[4]From a lecture Barth gave at the University of Utrecht in 1935, *Credo: A Presentation of the Chief Problems of Dogmatics with Reference to the Apostles' Creed,* trans. J. Strathearn McNab (London: Hodder & Stoughton, 1936), p. 183. Similarly, in 1928, Barth says that theology is done in the domain of philosophical reflection (*Eet,* p. 21). In 1929, Barth writes that theology works within the framework of philosophy (SITet, p. 27). And, in 1960, Barth places theologians and philosophers in the same sphere confronted by common problems, taking different paths (PTet, p. 80).

[5]*CD* I/1, p. 5.

[6]PT, pp. 98-99 (PTet, pp. 85-86).

[7]*CD* I/1, p. 5.

[8]*CD* I/1, p. 6.

[9]It is "unfortunate that the question of the truth of talk about God should be handled as a question apart by a special faculty" (*CD* I/1, p. 5).

[10]PTet, p. 80.

independent stand. The theological way of knowing is "motivated wholly by the power of the primordial movement from above to below. The theologian stands and falls with this sequence, in fact, with its irreversibility."[11] It is significant to note that Barth sees the movement from below to above as legitimate and important, but only as a secondary movement from the first movement that is irreversibly from above to below.[12] The faux pas of philosophy has been to reverse this order, believing that it has started from below with creation and the light of independent human reason. If indeed there is any consideration for the Creator, it is made in philosophy on the basis of the creation. In so doing, philosophy judges according to "alien principles"[13] rather than theology's first and final criterion, Jesus Christ, the revelation of God.

The distinction between philosophy and theology, therefore, must be carefully drawn. Barth identifies two strategies that must be rejected. The first is to distinguish theology as a special offshoot of philosophy submitting to the same general criteria of evaluation. This is the strategy of apologetics, as Barth uses the term—"the attempt to establish and justify theological thinking in the context of philosophical, or, more generally and precisely, nontheological thinking."[14] The second strategy, connected to the first, is "the method of isolation."[15] Theology is distinguished as the enlightened and now independent philosophy. There are, however, two reasons why theology cannot assert a special superiority to philosophy. First, Barth stresses that "just as well and just as badly as philosophy, theology is a human science."[16] It has no special superhuman access to the Truth by which to demonstrate its truth. Second, "all truth is enclosed in God's Word."[17] There is no special preserve of theological truth that is by nature hidden from philosophy. In fact, a philosophy that "has the hearing of the Word of God as its presuppo-

---

[11]PTet, pp. 84-85.

[12]Barth even suggests that the priority and attention philosophy gives to creation could serve to remind theology of the importance of humanity and the world, which, being relegated to a secondary concern, are actually thereby exalted (PTet, pp. 84, 92-93).

[13]*CD* I/1, p. 6.

[14]*Eet,* p. 21.

[15]Ibid., p. 24.

[16]Ibid., p. 34.

[17]Ibid., p. 27.

sition" would be an "equal partner" to theology.[18] Philosophy may be Christian philosophy and theology Christian theology to the extent that each is aligned with the Truth. Such philosophy would "speak very differently but will not in fact have anything different to say."[19] For this reason, any distinction between philosophy and theology is "only a relative and methodological but not material antithesis."[20]

Barth's aversion to philosophy is not, therefore, an interdiction on the language, conceptions or questions of philosophy; these are all fair game for the theologian and part of what it means that theology is inevitably done in the overlapping *Raum der Philosophie*. The difference is that theology stands in an orientation acknowledging the primacy of God's self-revelation for the understanding and appropriation of everything with which it and philosophy share an interest. It is not the realm of philosophy that Barth objects to; that would be to cut theology off from its own turf. It is the anti-theological orientation of philosophy that requires vigorous resistance. Bruce McCormack speaks to this difference when he clarifies what it means for Barth to be "anti-metaphysical." What Barth objects to is the "order of knowing" in classical metaphysics from below, "extrapolating from observed phenomena." But this rejection of the metaphysical *way* "does not entail the bracketing-off of particular regions of discourse from discussion in an a priori fashion."[21] The proposal that Barth has "little use for philosophy" is only accurate if applied to the historical neglect philosophy has shown for the theological task and way of knowing. This neglect has created the need for "the separate existence of theology" as an "emergency measure."[22]

The charge that Barth's theological epistemology is finally anti-philosophical and possibly even irrational[23] is one that Barth himself addressed. This critique has often come packaged with the "neo-orthodox"

---

[18]Ibid., p. 23.

[19]Ibid., p. 33.

[20]Ibid., p. 30. There is a significant translation error here where "theological" stands in place of the original "philosophischen," obscuring entirely the point of this sentence (*EI*, p. 47).

[21]Bruce McCormack, *Karl Barth's Critically Realistic Dialectical Theology: Its Genesis and Development, 1909–1936* (Oxford: Oxford University Press, 1995), p. 246.

[22]*CD* I/1, p. 7.

[23]Pope Benedict XVI has called Barth's position the "amputation of reason" (Joseph Ratzinger, *Introduction to Christianity* [San Francisco: Ignatius Press, 2004], p. 139).

designation.[24] The implication is that Barth champions a return to a premodern, precritical era of positive orthodoxy, choosing to remain naive by ignoring the epistemological questions raised by modernity. The notion that Barth was advocating a premodern or prescientific theology began several years before the first volume of the *Church Dogmatics* and is addressed directly by Barth in correspondence with Adolf von Harnack.[25] Barth had challenged what Harnack would call "contemporary scientific theology,"[26] which marked its origins from the Enlightenment.[27] Harnack was clear that to abandon this Enlightenment project was, in his view, to abandon "the only possible way of grasping the object epistemologically."[28] He advanced the notion that "historical knowledge and critical reflection" were the conduits for a proper human reception of revelation.[29] In response, Barth catalogs and rejects those human grounds that had been proposed to fulfill the Enlightenment's foundationalist requirements. He rejects those subjective grounds that Harnack also rejects, as well as those foundations sacred to Harnack.[30] Barth, however, protests Harnack's conclusion that Barth is, on this account, a despiser of reason and science. In a move that only serves to confirm Harnack's suspicions, Barth appeals to Luther and Paul.[31] This leads Harnack to suspect that Barth simply wishes to recast an uncritical, premodern theology. However, and this is the salient point, Barth categorically rejects any simple "repristination" of classical or pre-Enlightenment theology. He sees the value of reclaiming for theology the "idea of a determinative *object*" unconstrained by "the determinate character of the

[24]Often the two are conflated, as in "Karl Barth's anti-philosophical neo-orthodoxy" (Herbert Spiegelberg with Karl Schuhmann, *The Phenomenological Movement: A Historical Introduction,* 3rd rev. ed. [The Hague: Nijhoff, 1982], p. 430). Bruce McCormack challenges the Balthasarian thesis of a later non-dialectical Barth that may have bolstered the "neo-orthodox" reading of Barth, which "remains the predominant one in the English-speaking world" (McCormack, *Karl Barth's Critically Realistic Dialectical Theology,* pp. 24-25).

[25]Harnack addressed his original grievances to "the despisers of scientific theology," of which Barth was foremost in his estimation (BHet, p. 29).

[26]Ibid., p. 36.

[27]Ibid., p. 31.

[28]Ibid., p. 36.

[29]Ibid., p. 29.

[30]"'Inner openness, heuristic knowledge, experience, heart' and the like on the one hand and 'historical knowledge and critical reflection' on the other" (ibid., p. 32).

[31]Ibid., p. 38.

method."[32] But he is resolute in the face of the question of "repristinating a classical theological train of thought" that, as theologians, "we must-think *in* our time *for* our time."[33] The idea that Barth advocates at any stage a positive neo-orthodoxy that is uncritical with respect to epistemological problems is indefensible even on a surface reading. Barth recognizes that a theology that thinks in and for its time would have to take seriously the question of theology's way and ground of knowledge, and he does just that by giving this very question pride of place in *CD* I/1. Despite Barth's clear display of critical appreciation for the question, Harnack still only sees in Barth an unscientific notion of revelation teetering "between absolute religious scepticism and naive biblicism."[34] Harnack cannot fathom the validity of a starting point that grasps the knower but is not grasped *by* the knower independent of the given knowing relation. Harnack's commitment to the exclusive rationality of the way of knowing from below to above forces his conclusion that Barth is rejecting critical thought en masse.

Harnack's difficulties with Barth are similar to those of Wolfhart Pannenberg. Like Harnack, Pannenberg determines that Barth's rejection of an earthbound scientific epistemology must leave Barth hopelessly mired in subjectivism.[35] Pannenberg believes that if human reason and experience are subjugated, only two options remain: subjectivism and fideism. In explicit agreement with the Enlightenment, Pannenberg states that "a 'positive' theology of revelation which does not depend on rational argument can rely only on a subjective act of will or an irrational venture of faith."[36] It is clear, moreover, that for Pannenberg these two alternatives collapse into each other. Both are an indication of a wholly arbitrary and irrational positivism that stifles intersubjective dialogue.[37] Neither Pannenberg nor Harnack can understand Barth's "from above" as anything other than making an arbitrary human start. For this reason,

[32]Ibid., pp. 41-42, emphasis original.

[33]Ibid., emphasis original.

[34]Ibid., p. 53.

[35]Harnack assumes that if the ground is not "historical knowledge," then the basis must be in the individual's "subjective experience" (ibid., p. 29).

[36]Wolfhart Pannenberg, *Theology and the Philosophy of Science* (Philadelphia: Westminster, 1976), p. 273.

[37]Ibid., p. 274.

Pannenberg sees rejecting Barth's "from above" as crucial for theology "if it does not want to fall into the hopeless and, what is more, self-inflicted isolation of a higher *glossolalia,* and lead the whole church into this blind alley."[38] But this conclusion only follows if one rules out a priori that God has acted to give himself in Jesus Christ by the Spirit as the ground of theological knowing. This a priori ban on the givenness of divine self-revelation is the arbitrary assumption driving Pannenberg's conclusions. He writes, "Barth's apparently so lofty objectivity about God and God's word turns out to rest on no more than the irrational subjectivity of a venture of faith with no justification outside itself."[39] But dependence on faith becomes fideistic in Pannenberg's sense only if that faith is an arbitrary human choice. The tables turn dramatically if that faith is the gift of divine self-revelation. Barth would agree that it has no justification outside itself. But what justification could be more secure than God's own self-attestation? Far from fideistic, this alternative, invisible to Pannenberg and Harnack, offers what Barth would see as the only escape possible from the ghettos of human reason.[40]

For those who would presume that cognitive human knowledge of God could not be given from above, Barth's rejection of the from-below way of philosophical knowing is patently irrational, and amounts to an uncritical and naive wholesale rejection of philosophical thought. For Barth, however, the distinction between philosophy and theology is only necessary to preserve (against this mindset) a from-above, theo-foundational way of knowing. In no way does this require a retreat on the part of theology from the realm of philosophy. On the contrary, it is this order of knowing that motivates a critical awareness of and response to the language, concepts and questions raised by philosophy.[41]

---

[38]Pannenberg, *Basic Questions in Theology: Collected Essays* (Philadelphia: Fortress, 1971), 2:189-90.

[39]Pannenberg, *Theology and the Philosophy of Science,* p. 273.

[40]I take a closer look at whether and in what sense Barth may be considered a fideist in Kevin Diller, "Does Contemporary Theology Require a Postfoundationalist Way of Knowing?" *Scottish Journal of Theology* 60, no. 3 (2007): 16-19.

[41]Barth even grants that "it is quite right . . . that an education in the arts and a familiarity with the thinking of the philosopher, psychologist, historian, aesthetician, etc., should be demanded of the dogmatician or the theologian" (*CD* I/1, p. 283)—though this familiarity is not what makes one a theologian.

CONTESTING THE ONTOLOGICAL PRESUPPOSITION OF THE ENLIGHTENMENT

Our focus thus far on Barth's theological epistemology recognizes that the first volume of the *Church Dogmatics* is, above all else, Barth's attempt to elucidate and defend the way of knowledge followed in theology. He famously renounces traditional post-Enlightenment prolegomena, operating as a philosophic preamble to theology, undertaken in an attempt to establish the noetic grounds, scientific character and academic legitimacy of theology.[42] In so doing, Barth is making a break with core epistemological assumptions of modernity's Enlightenment project. The question could be raised whether the reading of Barth being advanced here is at odds with the received opinion that Barth stands the Enlightenment on its head by reversing the priorities of epistemology and ontology that were themselves reversed by Descartes.[43] Is not Barth's real priority ontology rather than epistemology? Though my focus has been on understanding Barth's theological epistemology, we have already seen that God in God's self-revealing action precedes ontologically and makes possible theological knowing. Conceding priority to the question of theology's way and ground of knowledge does not mean that Barth allows the traditional, post-Enlightenment, epistemological assumptions to go unquestioned. Conceding priority to the question does not mean that Barth allows the question itself to establish the terms of the debate or condition its

---

[42]As Eberhard Busch notes: "The dogmatics of the 19th century understood the 'prolegomena' with which it began as a preamble addressing the general human and human-religious presuppositions which would make a 'doctrine of faith' *possible*" (Busch, *The Great Passion: An Introduction to Karl Barth's Theology,* ed. Darrell L. Guder and Judith J. Guder, trans. Geoffrey W. Bromiley [Grand Rapids: Eerdmans, 2004], p. 42, emphasis original). For Barth "the prefix *pro* in prolegomena is to be understood loosely to signify the first part of dogmatics rather than that which is prior to it" (*CD* I/1, p. 42). Nancey Murphy provides a concise overview of the way in which theology after Descartes, both conservative and liberal, acquiesced to the general philosophical requirements of foundationalism (Murphy, *Beyond Liberalism and Fundamentalism: How Modern and Postmodern Philosophy Set the Theological Agenda,* Rockwell Lecture Series [Valley Forge, PA: Trinity Press International, 1996], pp. 11-35).

[43]E.g., "what characterizes the modernity which is the target of Barth's critique? The first is the inversion of the order of being and knowing, of ontology or metaphysics and epistemology. In pre-modern times, the question of the being (or essence) of something had primacy over the question of how it can be known" (Christoph Schwöbel, "Theology," in *The Cambridge Companion to Karl Barth,* ed. John B. Webster [Cambridge: Cambridge University Press, 2000], p. 29).

outcome. It is in fact the ontological priority of the object of theological knowing that provides the epistemic basis for theology.

Barth saw that, despite all appearances, Enlightenment modernism begins with its own ungrounded ontological assumption.[44] This presumption is an optimism about the constitution and capacity of unassisted human reason that provides the basis for knowing God from below. What follows here is an analysis of how Barth's insistence on the priority of God's self-revelation leads to his dismantling of the Enlightenment assumptions. The question, as Barth puts it in *CD* I/1, is, what is the "particular way of knowledge taken in dogmatics"?[45] Originating with Descartes, and extending through Locke, Kant, Schleiermacher, Harnack and many others, this question comes packaged with at least three constraining assumptions about its answer:

1. *The obligation assumption:* An explanation or an account of the way of theological knowledge is an obligation on which the legitimacy of the theological-knowledge claim rests.
2. *The general starting-point assumption:* An account of the way of theological knowing must stem from a general epistemology that grounds all knowing or all metaphysical claims.
3. *The access-foundationalist assumption:* The way of theological knowledge must be anchored in trustworthy and readily accessible grounds.

These three assumptions are related and given in order of increasing specificity. The first assumes an obligation to give an account; the second defines the direction that must be taken in fulfilling that obligation; and the third stipulates the rules that must be obeyed while following the defined direction in fulfillment of the obligation.[46] Barth was not willing to give any of these attending assumptions a free pass.

The obligation assumption. First, Barth rejects the notion that the-

[44]"This nexus of problems, however, is that of an ontology, and since Descartes . . ." (*CD* I/1, p. 36).

[45]*CD* I/1, p. 25.

[46]This parsing of the assumptions of Enlightenment modernism can be mapped to the elements of Plantinga's "classical package" (*WCB*, p. 82). The obligation assumption corresponds to the duty of classical deontologism; the general starting-point assumption is implied in most versions of classical foundationalism and the access-foundationalist assumption corresponds to both classical evidentialism *and* classical foundationalism.

ology is obligated to give a reckoning of its particular theological way of knowing. In fact, he does not grant, as an initial assumption, that giving such an account is even possible. He does resolve retrospectively that it is possible to give an account, but he refuses to grant it as a requirement for theology. It is helpful to recall from our discussion of Barth's theology of revelation that for Barth the principles of theological knowing are only known in reflection on the gift of the knowledge of God. Providing an account of how the knowledge of God becomes a human possibility cannot be a required first move, *prior* to reflecting on the actually given knowledge of God. In fact, Barth believed that it did not necessarily undermine the scientific character of theology if it had no prolegomena whatsoever.[47] It could be sufficient to note that beginning with reflection on the fact of the *esse* (being) of the knowledge of God renders its *posse* (possibility) a foregone conclusion requiring no account.[48] So the possibility of theological knowing was a valid assumption, not on the basis of a foregoing confidence in human noetic capacity but only as *nachdenken* (reflection, lit. thinking after) on an already given reality.

Similarly, Barth only acknowledges retrospectively an obligation to give an account of the way of theological knowing. The obligation is seen in the light of an already given knowledge; it therefore cannot be understood as a foregoing obligation to establish the grounds for theological knowing. Granting an obligation as an initial assumption would be to suggest that one is required, or duty bound, to produce an account in order to have a right to the belief.[49] In Barth's view, it is only in accepting its designation as a science that theology recognizes an obligation to "submit to itself, i.e., everyone who has a share in it, an account regarding this path of knowledge."[50] What is clear here is that the knowledge is already granted. Never is the knowledge itself contingent

[47]"It cannot be taken for granted that this question can be explicitly raised and answered, and therefore that there can be such a thing as dogmatic prolegomena. . . . The lack of prolegomena, or at least of extensive prolegomena, might well indicate, not a naive attitude, but one which is scientifically mature and well-considered. Nor need such an attitude rest on an illusion. It might well have a solid basis in the simplicity of truth, in supreme scientific soundness" (*CD* I/1, p. 25).

[48]"Das *Ab esse ad posse valet consequentia* könnte ihre Rechtfertigung sein" (*KD* I/1, p. 24; *CD* I/1, p. 25).

[49]Cf. Plantinga on "classical deontologism" in *WCB*, pp. 85-88.

[50]*CD* I/1, p. 275; also see *CD* I/1, p. 8.

on fulfilling the obligation. Barth provides an account of theological knowing without granting the assumed obligation.

The general starting-point assumption. The general starting-point and access-foundationalist assumptions draw Barth's sharpest attacks. To grant these assumptions would be to commit to a foolishly optimistic and hopelessly insecure theology from below. Unlike the first assumption, these two assumptions cannot be affirmed even after the fact.[51] Barth has been charged with naiveté for suggesting that theology finds its noetic grounds in the object of theology itself and not in a general epistemology with indubitable, accessible foundations.[52] This charge cannot be sustained, however, as Barth demonstrates time and again that he is fully aware of the problems, issues and various alternatives in play. Moreover, he launches the countercharge that the real naiveté is displayed by those who uncritically accept these packaged assumptions.[53]

Barth is emphatic and relentless in his rejection of the general starting-point assumption. We simply don't have and cannot create for ourselves an independent ground on which to stand. He observes that

> [t]he *in abstracto* and *a priori* question of the possibility of the knowledge of God obviously presupposes the existence of a place outside the knowledge of God itself from which this knowledge can be judged. It presupposes a place where, no doubt, the possibility of knowledge in general and then of the knowledge of God in particular can be judged and decided in one way or another. It presupposes the existence of a theory of knowledge as a hinterland where consideration of the truth, worth and competence of the Word of God, on which the knowledge of

[51]Barth does not believe it is possible, even retrospectively, to "deduce any independent, generally true insights that are different from God's Word and hence lead up to it" (*CD* I/1, p. 131).

[52]Bultmann accuses Barth of having "failed to enter into debate with modern philosophy and naively adopted the older ontology from patristic and scholastic dogmatics" (Bernd Jaspert and Geoffrey W. Bromiley, eds., *Karl Barth-Rudolf Bultmann Letters, 1922–1966* [Grand Rapids: Eerdmans, 1981], p. 38). Harnack sees in Barth's unscientific notion of revelation a teetering between "absolute religious scepticism and naive biblicism" (BHet, p. 53). Harnack's critique is aimed at Barth's failure to meet the second assumption. Barth's account of theological knowing is ailing because it is not subsumable "under one generic concept" and is therefore not scientific. The accusation that Barth heralds an uncritical neo-orthodoxy is in this same vein.

[53]"The confidence of the Enlightenment in the right and the power of rational thought was naïve, untested and therefore unsecured, stuck fast in half-truths and open to all kinds of counter-blows" (Karl Barth, *Protestant Theology in the Nineteenth Century: Its Background and History* [London: SCM Press, 1972], p. 394).

God is grounded, can for a time at least be suspended. But this is the very thing which, from the point of view of its possibility, must not happen.[54]

Barth was clearly not the first to reject the requirement that the way of knowing in theology must be grounded in a general epistemology. It can and has been argued that Barth was following in the footsteps of Albrecht Ritschl and Barth's Marburg professor Wilhelm Herrmann.[55] Both Ritschl and Herrmann sought independent epistemological footing for theology that would protect its scientific character while keeping it epistemically differentiated from philosophy. It will be helpful in clarifying the dissent that Barth was registering with the Enlightenment project to briefly examine to what extent he was or was not simply reiterating the positions of Ritschl and Herrmann. We will look at Ritschl in connection with the general starting-point assumption and at Herrmann in connection with the access-foundationalist assumption.

Like Barth, Ritschl rejects the possibility that the way of knowing in theology can be anchored in a general epistemology that serves as the basis for all philosophical knowing. While agreeing with Ritschl's conclusion, Barth does not agree with the reasons he employs in its support. Ritschl holds that cognition in theology and cognition in philosophy are of two fundamentally different kinds, namely, *Natur und Geist* (nature and spirit). The way of knowing followed in religion and pertaining to morals is sui generis. The search for a shared foundation between natural and spiritual knowing cannot be conducted without obscuring their fundamental differentiation.[56] This move serves to insulate theology from philosophy and vice versa. In a time when the scientific character and academic legitimacy of theology were often in question, this move to carve out an independent noetic position for theology was strategic. Reductionist tendencies in materialism and idealism that cast doubt on the

[54]*CD* II/1, p. 5.

[55]Simon Fisher argues that in Barth's early writings he "appears as an authentic, though sometimes critical, follower of Ritschl and Herrmann" (Fisher, *Revelatory Positivism? Barth's Earliest Theology and the Marburg School* [Oxford: Oxford University Press, 1988], p. 171).

[56]"Any investigation of the common foundations of all being must set aside the particular characteristics by which one represents the difference between nature and spirit. . . . Such an analysis is inadequate for grasping the form and peculiarity of the spirit, and in that sense is without value" (Albrecht Ritschl, *Three Essays* [Philadelphia: Fortress, 1972], pp. 154-55).

object and foundation of theology as a science were avoided by Ritschl's firm epistemological dualism. On his view, philosophical reasoning cannot be used to undermine Christian truth claims. By the same token, attempts to establish theology with general metaphysical arguments simply "fall short of their goal."[57]

Barth does agree with many of Ritschl's conclusions. Vis-à-vis the other sciences, dogmatics "does not have to justify itself before them, least of all by submitting to the demands of a concept of science which accidentally or not claims general validity."[58] He even agrees on a sui generis concept of knowledge for theology, which "cannot be definitively measured by the concept of the knowledge of other objects, by a general concept of knowledge."[59] For Barth, however, the uniqueness of the way of knowing in theology is entirely dependent on the uniqueness of its object and not a dualist epistemology[60] that merely nuances general knowing into two types, leaving them both anchored in general human noetic capacity. In Barth's view Ritschl did not prevail over the Enlightenment by overturning its false assumptions. Quite to the contrary, he sees Ritschl's thought as the "quintessence"[61] and the "fulfillment"[62] of the Enlightenment. Barth recognizes in Ritschl little more than a return to the Kantian division between theoretical and practical reason.[63] It is

---

[57]He has in mind here particularly the traditional proofs for the existence of God (Ritschl, *Three Essays*, p. 154).

[58]*CD* I/1, p. 8.

[59]*CD* I/1, p. 190 (*KD* I/1, p. 198, "Der Begriff seiner Erkenntnis durchaus nicht ultimativ an dem Begriff der Erkenntnis anderer Gegenstände, an einem allgemeinen Erkenntnisbegriff gemessen warden darf"). The English translation unnecessarily inserts in this sentence an *or*, which I have removed to more accurately render the original.

[60]Barth explicitly rejects the notion that human cognition in theological knowing is of a different kind from other instances of human cognition: "We are speaking of the human knowledge of God on the basis of this revelation and therefore of an event which formally and technically cannot be distinguished from what we call knowledge in other connexions, from human cognition" (*CD* II/1, p. 181).

[61]"It was a tired age that thought it could see a gleam of hope in the theology of A. Ritschl, which in the event merely reached back over Idealism and Romanticism to the quintessence of the Enlightenment" (*CD* I/1, p. 276).

[62]Regarding Ritschl, Barth writes "We can ask whether the entire theological movement of the century resulted not at all in an overcoming of the Enlightenment, of its decisive interest of man in himself, but in its fulfillment" (*Protestant Theology in the Nineteenth Century*, pp. 655-56).

[63]"He [Ritschl] energetically seized upon the theoretical and practical philosophy of the Enlightenment in its perfected form. That is, he want back to Kant, but Kant quite definitely interpreted as an antimetaphysical moralist" (Barth, *Protestant Theology in the Nineteenth Century*, p. 655).

not the freedom of God to determine for us the way to know God; rather, it is a general principle of practical reason that provides and anchors theological knowing.

Another important difference with Ritschl is Barth's seeming nonchalance about the scientific character of theology, which was, for Ritschl, an essential demand. On Ritschl's scheme the rational credentials of theology depended on its scientific character flowing from the principles of *geistiges Leben* (spiritual life). Barth's concern is that no systematic constraints be put in place that would interfere with or limit the freedom of God in revelation, or presume a foregoing human access to God. He even allows that "it would make not the slightest difference to its real business if it had to rank as something other than science."[64] For Barth, the way in which theology goes about its task can be considered "scientific,"[65] but whether theology is viewed from the outside as a science according to criteria external to theology is unimportant. Ritschl's concern to preserve theology as a science, in contrast, stems from his conviction that prevailing scientific standards really did have a proper claim on theology if theology was to be considered a rational enterprise. The distinction between Barth and Ritschl is crucial though somewhat counterintuitive, and therefore often missed. Ritschl's division of knowledge is in fact positivistic[66] but derives from an underlying commitment to an Enlightenment movement of knowledge flowing from general and generally accessible principles of reason. On the other hand, Barth, often accused of positivism,[67] is actually much more concerned with the direction rather than the division of knowledge. He is not pitting revelation against reason, or "giving up the integrity of reason,"

[64]*CD* I/1, p. 8.

[65]Barth gives practical reasons for considering theology a science, but never would he allow the direction of interpretation to begin from a general notion of science; on the contrary, simply by pursuing its task theology "shows what it means by true science" (*CD* I/1, pp. 10-11).

[66]*Positivism* is an elusive term, often casting more shadow than light. I am using the term in the sense defined by Paul Janz: "Positivism in theology is any position that seeks to uphold the integrity of transcendence (or revelation) by giving up the integrity of reason or of natural enquiry" (Janz, *God, the Mind's Desire: Reference, Reason and Christian Thinking* [Cambridge: Cambridge University Press, 2004], p. 5).

[67]We have already considered this charge in Pannenberg. Perhaps Dietrich Bonhoeffer is the first to level the critique of positivism, though without much development in *Letters and Papers from Prison,* enlarged ed. (London: SCM Press, 1971), pp. 280, 286, 328-39.

as is often suspected.[68] He is merely rejecting the assumed priorities of an Enlightenment view of reason concerning what it means for theology to be reasonable or scientific. Unlike Ritschl, Barth is willing to grant that theology does not "know an object of enquiry necessarily concealed from other sciences."[69] The distinction that Barth makes, once again, is that theology is not held to the same way of knowing that may govern contemporary science because the way of the knowledge of God does not begin from below with a general theory of knowledge.

The access-foundationalist assumption. This brings us to the access-foundationalist assumption, the final of the three mentioned assumptions traditionally smuggled in with the question of the way of knowing in theology. The assumption here is that theological knowledge, like every other set of beliefs that aspires to the rank of knowledge, must spring from trustworthy grounds that are readily accessible to the theologian. This assumption is at the heart of the modernist commitment to classical foundationalism so roundly criticized in the latter half of the twentieth century.[70] It is important to note that there are two parts to this assumption, just as there are two aspects to the traditional foundationalist claim.[71] On the one hand, there is a thesis about the *structure* of human knowing; on the other hand, there is a requirement that the human knower have self-reflective *access* to the basis of that structure. The first claim is that theological knowledge must spring from solid and dependable grounds. This means that there exist bedrock experiences or ideas that yield foundational beliefs that can be trusted to be true and that all knowledge must either be an instance of such a belief or in a linear inferential relationship to it. The second claim is that these grounds are readily accessible. This means that the human knower must be in a

---

[68]Janz, *God, the Mind's Desire,* p. 5.

[69]*CD* I/1, p. 5.

[70]Bruce Marshall surmises that "few theologians any longer will admit to being foundationalists" (Marshall, *Trinity and Truth,* Cambridge Studies in Christian Doctrine [Cambridge: Cambridge University Press, 2000], p. 80). A widely discussed critique of foundationalism from analytic philosophy is found in Laurence BonJour, "Can Empirical Knowledge Have a Foundation?" *American Philosophical Quarterly* 15, no. 1 (1978): 1-14.

[71]In the next chapter we will look at Plantinga's challenge to foundationalism, where he helpfully distinguishes various stripes of foundationalist doctrine. What we are here calling evidentialist foundationalism is what Plantinga distinguishes as classical or strong foundationalism.

position to provide a reason for accepting a belief by demonstrating how that belief is inferentially connected to a foundational belief or itself could not fail to be true.[72] I'll refer to the first claim as the *foundation requirement* and the second claim as the *accessibility requirement.*[73] The distinction between these two claims will be crucial for a proper understanding of Barth and for the prospect of bringing him into fruitful dialogue with Plantinga. I will argue here that it is clear only that Barth rejects the second of the two claims. Once again, Barth's position can be clarified by distinguishing it from one of his theological predecessors—this time his most esteemed Marburg mentor, Wilhelm Herrmann.[74]

The most obvious attempts to meet the requirements of the access-foundationalist assumption have been through philosophical proofs for the existence of God or of the truth of Christianity, beginning with Descartes's *Meditations* and proceeding with more or less subtlety right up to the present day.[75] Herrmann thoroughly rejected the use of ra-

[72]This is the accessibility requirement often associated with epistemological internalism, which BonJour defines as follows: "a theory of justification is *internalist* if and only if it requires that all of the factors needed for a belief to be epistemically justified for a given person be *cognitively accessible* to that person, *internal* to his cognitive perspective" (Laurence BonJour, "Externalism/Internalism," in *A Companion to Epistemology*, ed. Jonathan Dancy and Ernest Sosa [Cambridge, MA: Blackwell, 1992], p. 132, emphasis original). In William P. Alston's explanation of internalism he distinguishes between *perspective* and *access* (Alston, *Epistemic Justification: Essays in the Theory of Knowledge* [Ithaca, NY: Cornell University Press, 1989], pp. 185-226). The idea here is consistent with Michael Bergmann's explanation of internalism in terms of an "awareness requirement" (Bergman, *Justification Without Awareness: A Defense of Epistemic Externalism* [Oxford: Oxford University Press, 2006], p. 9).

[73]Bruce Marshall divides foundationalism into three claims, which map to our discussion as follows: his (F1) and (F2) taken together are the accessibility requirement, while his (F3) is the foundational requirement (Marshall, *Trinity and Truth*, p. 54).

[74]Barth came to Marburg to study under Herrmann in 1908. "Finally in the summer of 1908, various circumstances brought it about that I was able to visit Marburg, which I had earnestly wanted to do because of Herrmann. I was now able to hear whom I wanted. . . . These three semesters in Marburg easily form my happiest memory as a student. I absorbed Herrmann through every pore" (Barth, *Karl Barth-Rudolf Bultmann Letters*, p. 153). Kenneth Oakes observes, "The story of Barth on theology and philosophy is the story of a recovering Herrmannian" (Oakes, *Karl Barth on Theology and Philosophy*, p. 245).

[75]See especially the Third Meditation in René Descartes's *Meditations on First Philosophy*, trans. John Cottingham, rev. ed. (Cambridge: Cambridge University Press, 1996), pp. 24-36. At present, Richard Swinburne is probably best known for his pursuit of evidentialist arguments and natural theology, e.g., Swinburne, *The Resurrection of God Incarnate* (Oxford: Oxford University Press, 2003), pp. 204-16. Approaches since the Enlightenment are arguably different in character from medieval natural theology. For a defense of this point with respect to Aquinas's *Five Ways*, see Fergus Kerr, *After Aquinas: Versions of Thomism* (Malden, MA: Blackwell, 2002), pp. 52-72.

tional proofs in theology, whether as prolegomena or apologetics. Barth's summary of Herrmann's position is close to a stating of his own: "The thought underlying such proofs—God is Lord of all—has validity only as an idea of religion itself; not as a road to religion."[76] On the freedom of God in revelation tied to the impossibility of a scientific demonstration, it appears Barth was a dutiful disciple of Herrmann: "The God of faith is neither 'demonstrable' reality nor is he merely a possibility. . . . He is known only where he reveals his life; and where and to whom he will reveal it is his concern alone."[77] There is no hint in these quotations of an epistemological dualism (à la Ritschl) employed to secure theology's independence. It would seem that the independence of theology is itself secured by God's freedom in revelation and not the sui generis quality of a general ethical/religious knowing. Does this agreement between Herrmann and Barth, however, extend to the rejection of the access-foundationalist assumption?

Barth acknowledges his indebtedness to Herrmann for imparting to him "one essential truth." He writes, "This truth, followed out to its consequences, later forced me to say almost everything else quite differently and finally led me even to an interpretation of the fundamental truth itself which was entirely different from his."[78] Barth is undoubtedly speaking here of what Herrmann sometimes referred to as the *autopistia* of Christian truth, "the conviction of Christian truth as based on itself."[79] In Barth's view, however, this insight did not receive the stress and clarity it required.[80] It was shrouded instead by Herrmann's emphasis on the role of individual human experience in getting theology off the ground. Barth seizes on this statement of Herrmann to illustrate his point: "Knowledge of God is the expression of religious experience wholly

[76]Barth, however, would never use the term *religion* generically when referring to the revelation of God in Christ. Herrmann's "has validity only as an idea of religion itself" could be understood here to be suggesting that the validity of the claim only holds within a particular sphere of human knowing (i.e., religion). Herrmann's point is rather about *from where* the validity is secured, not about the scope of that validity (DHet, p. 243).

[77]Ibid.

[78]Ibid., p. 239.

[79]Ibid., p. 258.

[80]Ibid., pp. 268-70.

without weapons."[81] Barth hails the "without weapons" precisely because of his rejection of the accessibility requirement, which requires the human knower to come armed with an argument to defend the knowledge claim. For Barth a human defense is not possible.[82] "He [God] Himself will uphold and defend it without human help or strength."[83] "Only the Logos of God Himself can provide the proof."[84] It is because of the principle of *autopistia* that such knowledge "has no basis or possibility outside itself."[85] This also explains why Barth cannot countenance Herrmann's double-mindedness,[86] which while insisting that Christian truth is self-grounded, persistently undermines this claim with an appeal to the "inherent power of our (that is the believing Christian's) experiencing intuition."[87] Conscience (*Gewissen*) becomes the human point of contact with God.[88] It is important to see that the difference between Barth and Herrmann on this point is not a minor nuance or trivial detail; in Barth's view, the separation is "only by a blade's breadth and yet by a chasm's depth."[89] It finally makes the difference between an outright dismissal of the requirement for human access to the grounds of knowledge and merely a slight modification of that requirement, which remains essentially unchanged. At this point Herrmann is more akin to Ritschl; the kind of human access granted to the basis of the religious knowledge claim does not take the form of syllogistic reasoning or scientific proof. Nevertheless, the basis remains ac-

---

[81]Ibid., pp. 248, 259.

[82]This impossibility of human demonstration leads William Abraham to conclude that Barth's "central epistemological claims about divine revelation have been a disaster, leaving its adherents stripped of help in confronting competing claims" (Abraham, *Crossing the Threshold of Divine Revelation* [Grand Rapids: Eerdmans, 2006], p. 3).

[83]*CD* I/1, p. 31, quoting Luther (*Fastenpostille*, 1525, *Werke, Weimarer Ausgabe*, 17.2, p. 108, l. 26).

[84]*CD* I/1, p. 163.

[85]*CD* I/1, p. 120.

[86]Barth often anguishes over the tension in Herrmann between two contradicting points of view and the lamentable conclusion that the emphasis in Herrmann was on the wrong view. "If we ask first on which of the contradictory positions which he presented Herrmann himself, his heart, his professional character, is to be sought, there can be no doubt of the answer" (DHet, pp. 266-67). See also *CD* I/1, p. 86.

[87]DHet, p. 265.

[88]"Auf jedes noch einigermaßen rege Gewissen wirkt die Verbindung jener beiden Thatsachen in seiner Person als eine befreiende Offenbarung" (Wilhelm Herrmann, *Die Gewissheit des Glaubens und die Freiheit der Theologie*, 2nd rev. ed. [Freiburg im B.: Mohr, 1889], p. 30).

[89]*CD* I/1, p. 213.

cessible in the intuition of human experience,[90] what Herrmann often calls, "das innere Leben des Glaubens."[91] One might argue that Herrmann does not claim that accessibility is required, only that it exists. But this is all we need to differentiate his position from Barth's.

Distinguished from Herrmann, it should be clear that Barth makes a clean break with the accessibility requirement of the access-foundationalist assumption. Theological knowing does not require human access or defense in order to be considered legitimate knowing, primarily because it is self-grounded by its object—God. Barth denies not only cognitive accessibility to epistemic grounds as a requirement but also he denies the very possibility that we could ourselves provide a complete and independent justification or demonstration of the basis of our theological knowing.

Having addressed the accessibility requirement, we now turn to the foundational requirement. It is possible to be a foundationalist without accepting the accessibility requirement—without accepting the requirement to have an independent means of demonstrating the legitimacy of foundational beliefs.[92] Barth rejects the accessibility requirement because it violates the above-to-below way of theological knowing encountered in revelation. His is a theological epistemology that eschews all *human* foundations. We should resist, nevertheless, referring to Barth's position as "non-foundational," as if it lacked grounding altogether.[93] Barth is a foundationalist—not a classical foundationalist, but a theo-foundationalist.

In its most unassuming form, the foundational requirement stipulates that the structure of knowledge includes and is anchored in trustworthy

---

[90]Religion is unlike "Wissenschaft und Kunst" (Wilhelm Herrmann, *Warum bedarf unser Glaube geschichtlicher Thatsachen? Vortrag zur Feier des 22. März 1884 in Marburg gehalten,* 2nd ed. [Halle: Niemeyer, 1891], p. 22).

[91]Alternatively, Herrmann employs the phrase "persönliche Leben" (*Der Verkehr des Christen mit Gott: Im Anschluss an Luther dargestellt,* 2nd completely rev. ed. [Stuttgart: Cotta, 1892], pp. 8-12, 75-101).

[92]It is possible to be a foundationalist without being an *evidentialist* foundationalist.

[93]Nowhere does Barth commend an insulated coherentism. Barth would have warmed to aspects of Ronald Thiemann's "non-foundational" theology, while firmly repudiating the suggestion that "theology seeks its criteria of judgment within the first-order language of church practice" (Thiemann, *Revelation and Theology: The Gospel as Narrated Promise* [Notre Dame, IN: University of Notre Dame Press, 1985], p. 75). Although Thiemann, like Barth, emphasizes God's prevenience, the criterion for Barth is God in his revelation—the act of divine self-disclosure. The criterion is not something handed over to the church by means of this revelation (e.g., the "narrated promise").

foundational beliefs. In Barth's view, our knowledge of God is anchored in a trustworthy foundation. Barth's theological epistemology, based on the reality of revelation breaking through from above to below, certainly rules out non-foundationalism or *pure* coherentism.[94] What serves as the trustworthy foundation in Barth's theological epistemology is unambiguously God himself who is his speaking to us. The speech of God is his Word, Jesus Christ, self-revealed as we are brought into communion with God by the Spirit. This being-revealed-to is the trustworthy foundation and wellspring of all human knowing of God. Is there such a thing then as a foundational *belief?* The answer to this question, and therefore the answer to the question about Barth's attitude toward the foundational requirement, turns on what counts as a foundational belief. It is clear that human knowledge of God for Barth involves believing. Knowing God is the gift of faith, in which knowing, believing and obeying the Truth are inseparable. We are given the gift of trustworthy foundational believing, but we are not given the gift of the knowledge of God packaged in individual, foundational truth statements.[95] As discussed earlier, individual propositional expressions in human language do not have the power to contain the Truth.[96] That is not to say that there are not objectively better and worse ways of striving to express in human terms the trustworthy human knowledge of God. But these expressions are always second-order reflections, derivative of and dependent on the actual knowing relation.

What we have then is an affirmation of the absolute certainty of the foundation but a rejection of any confidence in human attempts to build to it. We should acknowledge that this is to undo completely what the foundational requirement was intended to do. The foundational requirement assumes that truth can be adequately conveyed in belief state-

[94]On a coherentist model the mutual support of beliefs is an intuition that characterizes the entire structure of knowledge. Coherentism, in its purest form, considers coherence with the belief structure to be the only criteria for belief justification. See *WCB,* pp. 78-80.

[95]"The concept of truths of revelation [*Offenbarungswahrheiten*] in the sense of Latin propositions [*lateinischen Sätzen*] given and sealed once for all with divine authority in both wording and meaning is theologically impossible. . . . The freely acting God Himself and alone is the truth of revelation [*Offenbarungswahrheit*]" (*CD* I/1, p. 15).

[96]See again *CD* I/1, p. 165. The distinctions between true propositions about God, their expression in human words and grasp in human conception are taken up in greater detail in chapter 8.

ments and furthermore that truth value can be transferred to belief statements in a direct inferential relationship to previously established belief statements. At one level, we should recognize that this is indeed rightly how we strive to build our knowledge. It is an implicit assumption in all human reasoning.[97] For Barth, however, this striving, which is indeed part of the task of theology, is ever only a striving after the given foundation in an inevitably imperfect effort to aim at the truth of revelation, in which we only succeed by the grace of the Holy Spirit.[98] This means that the foundation of our theological knowing is also its apex.[99] We cannot independently build self-secured structures on this knowledge but only revel in, reflect on and point to it, again and again subjecting our speech to the criterion of Christ the one and only True Revelation of God.[100] Truth in this sense is not transferred to our belief statements but rather sits in judgment over them. Another way to put this is that Barth is not first an epistemological foundationalist but first an ontological foundationalist.[101] The ontological foundation of theological knowing is taken to provide the epistemological foundation and basis for judging all theological reflection.

This brings us to the close of our brief excursus on Barth's rejection of

---

[97]F. LeRon Shults correctly observes that "inferential patterns in thinking" and the "intuition that being rational includes having good reasons as a basis for our beliefs" are even for nonfoundationalists "evident in their argumentative performance" (Shults, *The Postfoundationalist Task of Theology: Wolfhart Pannenberg and the New Theological Rationality* [Grand Rapids: Eerdmans, 1999], p. 30).

[98]Barth states that the real task of dogmatics is to question the church's talk about God in light of God's self-revelation. He distinguishes dogma from dogmas and dogmatic propositions. The formulation of dogmas and dogmatic propositions is always only a striving to aim at the truth of revelation without any possibility of succeeding outside of the grace of God. The truth of revelation cannot be isolated and contained in a mere human proposition, "in abstraction from the person of Him who reveals it and from the revelatory act of this person in which it is given to other persons to perceive" (*CD* I/1, pp. 267-70).

[99]It is worth noting that there is an ambiguity in our use of the term *foundation.* With respect to foundationalism, *foundation* refers to that set of our beliefs which is accepted without an inferential ground in other beliefs. The way I am using the term here, however, is in the sense of the foundation undergirding our foundational beliefs, which is for Barth an undemonstrable free act of God. Theo-foundationalism, therefore, calls into question the stability of foundational belief by highlighting our epistemic dependence on a foundation for our believing.

[100]"The criterion of past, future and therefore present Christian utterance is thus the being of the Church, namely, Jesus Christ, God in His gracious revealing and reconciling address to man" (*CD* I/1, p. 4).

[101]Regarding the Bible and church proclamation, "both renounce any foundation apart from that which God has given once and for all by speaking" (*CD* I/1, p. 120).

the epistemological assumptions of the Enlightenment. I have argued that it is on the basis of the way of knowing established by the ontological priority of God's self-revelation that Barth refuses to accept these assumptions, with their attending contrary ontological presuppositions. On the basis of this discussion we can conclude that, for Barth, theology is not required to accept the obligations, direction or rules of any philosophy that would impinge on its way of knowing. In short, Barth's theo-foundationalism shares the conviction that knowledge has a ground, while granting nothing to Enlightenment foundationalist assumptions about the nature of that ground. What conclusions can be drawn from this about the relationship between theology and philosophy, and therefore the prospects of finding in Barth's theo-foundationalism a constructive engagement with analytic epistemology?

THE BOUNDARY OF PHILOSOPHY

We have discussed Barth's recognition that engagement with the realm of philosophy is inevitable for theology[102] and that "familiarity with the thinking of the philosopher"[103] is a requirement for the theologian. We have also seen that Barth's theology of revelation dethrones philosophy as the founder and judge of theological knowledge. From these two assertions, one affirming and the other cautioning, we can conclude that in Barth's view there is a proper though constrained role for philosophy in theology. The boundaries of philosophy are established by revelation in its movement from above to below. The implications of these boundaries for Barth were evident in our discussion of his rejection of Enlightenment foundationalism. But what is to guide the theologian in the proper use of philosophy?

An excellent source for locating Barth's material concerns for the interaction with philosophy is his 1929 essay "Schicksal und Idee in der Theologie." Here he highlights the benefits and dangers for theology of realism and idealism, which he sees as opposite poles in philosophy. Barth begins with realism because he finds a measure of realism to be

[102]"[Theology] involves a fundamental reflection upon reality by means of that very same thought which is also the tool of the philosophers" (SITet, p. 32).

[103]*CD* I/1, p. 283.

an unavoidable (we might even say incorrigible) starting point. "If we are going to talk about God as the object of theology, then we will already be advancing a typically realist proposition."[104] God is objectively real, and by claiming that God is real we include God in the reality in which we experience ourselves and the world.[105] But philosophical realism must be kept in check. The danger, if taken uncritically, is that the realist will suppose that knowledge of God can be read directly from the data of given experience, whether subjectively or empirically. But the confidence with which the theologian knows God is a "confidence in God's self-giving," which is "rather different from realism's confidence in God's givenness."[106] A confidence in God's givenness entails an unwarranted anthropological assumption that we have a properly functioning human capacity to know God by means of the use of our own endowments applied to the data of given experience. This assumption is not entailed in the presupposition of revelation; in fact, the order of knowing in revelation and the powerlessness of the creaturely form independently to deliver the knowledge of God suggest quite the opposite. The knowledge of God requires the accompanying action of God breaking through to us in revelation, in which he himself is the very content.[107] God lifts our reason to give us a knowledge of himself through the medium of creaturely experience. "Reason's normal activity is not interrupted; but it is directed, guided and ordered by something superior to itself, something that has no part in its antithesis."[108] While encountering us through the data of given experience, however, the knowledge of God can never be reduced to that experience or derived from it independently from the determining act of God.[109] This is where the chastening of idealism is helpful.

---

[104]SITet, p. 35.

[105]Ibid., p. 36.

[106]Ibid., p. 40.

[107]"'The Word became flesh and dwelt among us'—what does that mean if not that the Word, and hence the God with whom we have to do, entered into our own particular mode of being, that of nature and history? Jesus Christ as the Word of God to us and therefore himself as God is the content of revelation. And also the Holy Spirit, who illumines the Word for us and us for the Word, is himself God, is the content of revelation" (ibid., p. 35).

[108]Ibid., p. 50.

[109]Ibid., p. 49.

In its pursuit of truth, idealism is critically reflective about the limits of human knowing.[110] Idealism recognizes the problem of our inability to secure a neutral ground of knowing outside of ourselves, a *view from nowhere*. We have no unobscured access to the knowledge of God through the data of experience. If we are to know God, God must make himself known to us. "If theology is to remain grounded in God's revelation, then the idealist is going to have to dampen his ardor for a generally accessible truth, and to join forces with the realist."[111] But the chastening of a critical idealism should never be seen to repudiate what Barth has affirmed in a proper critical realism—namely, that God truly reveals himself to us in otherwise inadequate creaturely thoughts, experience and words, without becoming identical to them.[112] The fact that knowing God is, from below, a human impossibility does not change the fact that God, from above, has made it possible for humans to know him. While much is made of the influence of Kantianism or neo-Kantianism on Barth,[113] it is clear that in Barth's view Kantian idealism could not

---

[110]Ibid., pp. 42-43.

[111]Ibid., p. 47.

[112]Those who would claim Barth for postmodernism are in danger of hearing the second word of chastening idealism as a repudiation of the first word of critical realism, which stakes its confidence in the Word that became flesh. See especially Graham Ward, *Barth, Derrida and the Language of Theology* (Cambridge: Cambridge University Press, 1995), pp. 27-33. Ward suggests that Barth presents two antithetical views without providing a way to move between them. He presents these as two competing models of language that reflect, respectively, a naive realism and a strong idealism. "Barth needs to provide a . . . coherent account of the interplay between two antithetical models for the nature of language. One offers a direct correspondence between signifier and signified, word and Word, but constitutes a natural theology and dissolves the distinction between the creaturely and the divine, the human and God as Wholly Other. The other denies the possibility of moving beyond mediation and, therefore, the possibility of any true knowledge of God as Wholly Other" (ibid., p. 33). Word become flesh is not enough for Ward. See critical reviews in Bruce L. McCormack, "Graham Ward's Barth, Derrida and the Language of Theology," *Scottish Journal of Theology* 49, no. 1 (1996): 97-109; and David Guretzki, "Barth, Derrida and *Différance:* Is There a Difference?" *Didaskalia* 13, no. 2 (2002): 51-71.

[113]There is, of course, Bonhoeffer's famous praise of Barth's second Romans edition, "in spite of all the neo-Kantian egg-shells" (Bonhoeffer, *Letters and Papers from Prison*, ed. Eberhard Bethage, enlarged ed. [London: SCM Press, 1971], p. 328). Simon Fisher stresses the early influence of neo-Kantianism on Barth but rightly points to Bonhoeffer's caution that Barth merely "makes use of the philosophical language of neo-Kantianism" and that it would be "rash to call him a neo-Kantian" (quoted in Fisher, *Revelatory Positivism?* p. 185). In the same way, Bruce McCormack stresses that while Marburg neo-Kantianism was an important influence on Barth, even in his early theology Barth made use of it only "where to do so strengthened the case he wanted to make theologically—or at least, did not infringe upon that theology" (McCormack, *Karl Barth's Critically Realistic Dialectical Theology*, p. 42).

get past its antithesis with realism,[114] and theology admits no more of a proof from practical reason than it did from pure reason.[115] Kantianism may be helpful in its critique of realism, but it has no privileged philosophical status with Barth.[116]

What we can see from this example of Barth's interaction with philosophy is that the guiding principle he employs for determining the boundaries of philosophy is the very same criterion that guided his rejection of Enlightenment foundationalism. Philosophy is of use to theology so long as it allows theology to remain grounded in God's self-revelation. Revelation breaks through to us in a creaturely form, bringing us face to face with the very Word of God in that creaturely form. Philosophy may not trespass the dynamics of revelation by separating or collapsing the form and content—by equating the creaturely form with the divine or by suggesting that we can have direct access to the divine content without the creaturely form. "The one would be realistic theology, the other idealistic theology, and both bad theology."[117] The criterion regulating the use of philosophy is therefore the same criterion that regulates theology itself, Jesus Christ the Word of God, the Revelation of God, self-revealed to human beings in a creaturely form.

---

[114]"Kant still moves within this antithesis of the singular and the general, the empirical and the rational" (*CD* I/1, p. 146). Barth saw evidence of this in Kant's rejection of the incarnation: "If, according to Kant, something corresponding to what is called the 'Word' in the prologue to St John's Gospel exists, there is certainly, according to him, no suggestion that this Word might by any chance have become flesh" (Barth, *Protestant Theology in the Nineteenth Century,* p. 288).

[115]Neil MacDonald is right to protest that "Barth's theology itself, is not dependent on Kant's anthropocentric turn implicit in his critique of the bounds of reason" (MacDonald, *Karl Barth and the Strange New World Within the Bible: Barth, Wittgenstein, and the Metadilemmas of the Enlightenment* [Carlisle, UK: Paternoster, 2000], p. 11).

[116]It has recently been suggested in John Hart's very useful translation and commentary on the Barth-Brunner correspondence that Barth proclaims Kantianism to be "the most desirable and helpful position" (Hart, "The Barth-Brunner Correspondence," in *For the Sake of the World: Karl Barth and the Future of Ecclesial Theology,* ed. George Hunsinger [Grand Rapids: Eerdmans, 2004], p. 29). Daniel Migliore picks up on this supposed concession as an example of Barth's position not being isolationist with respect to other faiths (Migliore, "Response to the Barth-Brunner Correspondence," in *For the Sake of the World: Karl Barth and the Future of Ecclesial Theology,* ed. George Hunsinger [Grand Rapids: Eerdmans, 2004], p. 50). The translation, however, is flawed. "Was ich höchstens als wünschenswert und hilfreich bezeichnen könnte" should be translated "what I could *at most* denote as desirable and helpful." This is far from an emphatic endorsement of the superiority of Kant.

[117]*CD* I/1, p. 175.

CONCLUSION

Barth saw Feuerbach's critique of religion as a clarion call to Christian theology. Feuerbach exposed the fact that Christian theology, when justifying itself by an analogy from the human being to the divine being, grounded God in man. This is precisely why there can be no philosophical compromise on the priority of the particularity of God's self-revelation in theological knowing. Barth's no to philosophy is aimed at precluding the possibility that the object of theology might become a human invention. Our objective in this chapter has been to understand better Barth's restrictions on philosophy for theological knowing. We began with what Barth believes to be the only basis for the knowledge of God, God himself in his self-revelation. Barth's theology of revelation, which is itself intended to be a thinking after revelation, motivates Barth's theological epistemology. The way of knowing in theology is initiated by and in God from above to below. Human knowers are given clear and unambiguous knowledge of God when they are brought by the power of the Spirit into communion with Christ and given a sharing in his knowledge. This knowing is transformative and personal but also cognitive. God comes to us in a verbal creaturely form and, without giving himself over as the form, is really given to the knower *in* the form by the miracle and mystery of grace. Revelation is not itself propositional statements, but it may be delivered by means of them. It is this theological epistemology derived in reflection on from-above revelation that is driving all of Barth's pronouncements *against* philosophy.[118]

I have endeavored to show that these pronouncements are not directed at the language, questions and tools of the realm of philosophy—all of which are available to theology and with which theologians must work. On the contrary, Barth's denunciation is leveled against philosophy's presumed competency, based on an ungrounded ontological

[118]As Thomas F. Torrance maintains, Barth does not endorse "the rejection of philosophical thinking" but offers instead "the development of a rigorous rational epistemology governed by the nature of the object, namely, God in his self-communication to us within the structures of our human and worldly existence" (Torrance, *Karl Barth, Biblical and Evangelical Theologian* [Edinburgh: T & T Clark, 1990], p. 122).

assumption,[119] to regulate and establish *from below* truth about God independent of revelation. It was this presumed competency that inveigled the theology of the nineteenth and twentieth centuries to accept the demands of Enlightenment foundationalism without notice of the cost. And yet, Barth still holds out the possibility for a Christian philosophy or philosopher who also works in the light of and strives for obedience to the revelation of God. Philosophy can and must be employed in a way that observes the dependence of human theological knowing on the grace of the miracle and mystery of God's self-revelation.

With a clarified understanding of Barth's theological epistemology and its qualified openness to a constructive dialogue with philosophy, we will now turn to the Christian analytic epistemology of Alvin Plantinga. Unlike Barth, Plantinga endeavors to challenge philosophical arguments against Christian belief using general philosophical argumentation. He frames his account of revelation within a general epistemology—just the thing that Barth declares unnecessary (at least as an a priori obligation for theology). As was explained earlier, Barth and Plantinga appear to be unlikely associates. I will argue, on the contrary, that there is great potential for combining their views to yield a complementing theologically rigorous and philosophically robust response to the epistemological issues confronting theology.

[119]The ontological assumption that Barth opposes is "that the Word of God is one of the realities that are universally present and ascertainable and therefore created" (*CD* I/1, p. 159).

4

PLANTINGA'S CHRISTIAN PHILOSOPHIZING AND WARRANT

◆

Nearly twenty-five years since James Tomberlin and Peter van Inwagen declared that Alvin Plantinga "is widely recognized as the most important philosopher of religion now writing,"[1] it may still be true. In the analytic tradition, his rival is not to be found. A sampling of Plantinga's contributions includes penetrating treatments of questions in modal logic, modal metaphysics, agency and causation, philosophy of mind, and philosophy of religion. What we are most concerned with presently are his celebrated studies in epistemology[2] and the theological epistemology defended in them.[3] His renowned defense of a particular Christian approach to epistemology has had a deep and reverberating impact. Referring to Plantinga, the late Dallas Willard declared, "No one today has clearer insight into knowledge and belief than he does."[4] The intent of the next two chapters is to elucidate Plantinga's theological epistemology as I have Karl Barth's, looking closely at any positive theological construction alongside his assumptions about the right range and

---

[1]James Tomberlin and Peter van Inwagen, eds., *Alvin Plantinga* (Dordrecht: D. Reidel, 1985), p. ix.

[2]Plantinga's work has come to be known as *reformed epistemology,* though Plantinga himself at one time referred to it as "Calvinist Epistemology" (Plantinga, "Self-Profile," in Tomberlin and Inwagen, *Alvin Plantinga,* p. 55). Particular attention will be given to *Warranted Christian Belief (WCB),* the culmination of Plantinga's warrant trilogy.

[3]We will continue to use the term *theological epistemology* to designate views about the way and nature of human knowledge of God.

[4]Willard, *Knowing Christ Today: How We Can Trust Spiritual Knowledge* (New York: HarperCollins, 2009), p. 21.

role of philosophy in responding to questions of theological knowing. We will then be positioned to address the main question of this work—the pursuit of a thoroughly Christian epistemology of revelation that speaks to the dilemma generated on the one hand from Christian theology's high view of the knowledge of revelation and on the other hand from its low view of the unaided capacities of the human recipients of revelation.

It is important to note that Plantinga and Barth differ greatly in their goals and methods. They are approaching a common subject—the knowledge of God—from two different angles of inquiry. We are therefore guaranteed a certain degree of descriptive parallax, which might be mistaken for real variance. What we are most interested in determining is to what degree their thought is centrolineal—moving along separate lines from and toward a common midpoint. What core assumptions are held in common, and are these shared assumptions enough to keep their projects from colliding so that the combined light cast on the center is mutually illuminating?

In this chapter, we will focus on Plantinga's understanding of Christian scholarship and the role of Christian philosophy in relation to theology. I will argue that the fundamental lineaments of Plantinga's conceptions of truth and knowledge are clear and very much in line with Barth's critique of the philosophical approach to theological knowing, while also flagging for later exploration tensions over subsidiary issues (e.g., natural theology and apologetics). In the next chapter we will take up Plantinga's epistemology of Christian belief, tracing first his positive, conditional model for how Christian belief might have warrant and then diving into his defense of Christian belief against overreaching atheological arguments. I will argue that Plantinga's project shares the heart of Barth's concern: that we recognize that the knowledge of God is only secured by God's self-revelation—that it "derives and is to be considered only from outside all human possibilities, i.e., from the acting of God Himself."[5]

---

[5]*CD* I/1, p. 38.

THE CONCERN OF THE CHRISTIAN PHILOSOPHER

Plantinga concludes his well-known "Advice to Christian Philosophers" with the following charge: "We who are Christians and propose to be philosophers must not rest content with being philosophers who happen, incidentally, to be Christians; we must strive to be Christian philosophers."[6] Taking a look at Plantinga's notion of what it means to be a Christian philosopher is a helpful entry point into his more fundamental epistemological convictions. These convictions shape not only his ideas about Christian philosophy but all of Christian scholarship.

On Christian scholarship. Arguably, Plantinga's greatest contribution to the Christian academic community has been his defense and championing of the right and responsibility of every Christian scholar to approach unapologetically his or her discipline from a Christian perspective. We might label this Plantinga's call for *constructive Christian scholarship.*

> Take a given area of scholarship: philosophy, let's say, or history, or psychology, or anthropology, or economics, or sociology; in working at these areas, shouldn't we take for granted the Christian answer to the large questions about God and creation, and then go on from that perspective to address the narrower questions of that discipline? Or is that somehow illicit or ill-advised?[7]

---

[6]Plantinga, "Advice to Christian Philosophers," *Faith and Philosophy* 1, no. 3 (1984): 271. Writing his "self-profile" in 1983, right before his move to the University of Notre Dame, Plantinga details his goals for the future and makes the following comment: "Finally I hope to continue to think about the question of how Christianity bears on philosophy. Although I have devoted considerable thought to these issues, I have much less to show for it than I'd like. What difference does being a Christian make to being a philosopher?" (Plantinga, "Self-Profile," p. 94). He fulfilled this objective on November 4 of the same year in his inaugural address as John A. O'Brien Professor of Philosophy at the University of Notre Dame, "Advice to Christian Philosophers." The position he adopts here he maintains consistently and further elaborates in the following: Plantinga, "On Christian Scholarship," in *The Challenge and Promise of a Catholic University*, ed. Theodore Hesburgh (Notre Dame, IN: University of Notre Dame Press, 1994), pp. 267-95; Plantinga, "The Twin Pillars of Christian Scholarship: 1989 Stob Lectures," in *Seeking Understanding: The Stob Lectures, 1986–1998* (Grand Rapids: Eerdmans, 2001), pp. 117-61; Plantinga, "Augustinian Christian Philosophy," *Monist* 75, no. 3 (1992): 291-320; and Plantinga, "Christian Philosophy at the End of the Twentieth Century," in *Christian Philosophy at the Close of the Twentieth Century: Assessment and Perspective*, ed. Sander Griffioen and Bert M. Balk (Kampen, Netherlands: Uitgeverij Kok, 1995), pp. 29-53.

[7]Plantinga, "On Christian Scholarship," p. 290.

For Plantinga, the reasoning is clear: when seeking the right answer to any problem, it is best to avail oneself of all potentially relevant information.[8] Being a Christian involves assent to some theological presuppositions that, if true, bear significantly on the questions scholars wrestle with. Suppressing important information leaves unexplored avenues to greater clarity, synthesis and depth. This is particularly the case for the sciences and humanities when the data in question have broad implications for a general understanding of the world and human beings. On Plantinga's view, Christian belief includes a legitimate claim to knowledge that has these broad implications. Christian scholarship will therefore not ignore but will begin with those pivotal Christian truth claims.[9] In order for Christian scholars to forge ahead without abandoning their Christian assumptions, however, requires that they allow themselves greater independence from the arbitrary prohibitions of the academic establishment against what is permitted to serve as grounds for scholarly judgments.[10] The greatest threat to constructive Christian scholarship is an acceptance of dominant cultural assumptions that are fundamentally at odds with Christian belief. For this reason, in addition to the constructive task there is an important critical work to be done; this we could call *critical Christian scholarship.*[11] If the focus of the constructive task is to clarify, deepen and systematize Christian thought, the aim of the critical task is to analyze and engage with alternative projects "so that their relationship to Christian ways of thought is made evident."[12]

[8]"What we need here is scholarship that takes account of all that we know, and thus takes account of what we know as Christians" (ibid., p. 291). "The best way to do these sciences, says the Augustinian, is to use all that we know, including what we know by faith or revelation" (Plantinga, "Twin Pillars of Christian Scholarship," p. 159).

[9]"The Christian philosopher has a perfect right to the point of view and prephilosophical assumptions he brings to philosophic work; the fact that these are not widely shared outside the Christian or theistic community is interesting but fundamentally irrelevant" (Plantinga, "Advice to Christian Philosophers," p. 258).

[10]Addressing Christian philosophy in particular, Plantinga writes, "my plea is for the Christian philosopher, the Christian philosophical community, to display, first, more independence and autonomy: we needn't take as our research projects just those projects that currently enjoy widespread popularity; we have our own questions to think about" (ibid., p. 269).

[11]Plantinga refers to the constructive task as "positive Christian science" or simply "Christian scholarship," while calling the critical task "Christian cultural criticism." See Plantinga, "On Christian Scholarship," p. 291, and Plantinga, "Twin Pillars of Christian Scholarship," p. 160.

[12]Plantinga, "Christian Philosophy at the End of the Twentieth Century," p. 45.

The constructive task seeks to build inwardly, while the critical focus is to engage externally. Plantinga encourages Christian scholars to see that the dominant cultural perspectives are not neutral alternatives to the Christian position but actively opposed to Christian belief. He identifies "perennial naturalism" and "creative anti-realism" as two currently dominant strands of thought antithetic to Christian belief and demanding critical attention.[13] So, Christian scholarship of every type ought to attend to both its constructive and critical tasks; in this regard Christian philosophy is not different from other disciplines.

Theology and Christian scholarship. It is worth asking whether Plantinga considers Christian theology itself to be a scholarly discipline with this same twofold task. Barth, it would appear, is loath to accept a definition of theology's task as a particular instantiation of a more general academic principle. But there is little reason to doubt that both Barth and Plantinga would regard theology, along with the rest of Christian scholarship, as having both constructive and critical responsibilities. Barth frames the very definition of Christian theology in terms of its critical dogmatic task—that of the church criticizing its own talk about God.[14] And as for the unique constructive task of Christian theology, Barth affirms Anselm's *fides quaerens intellectum*.[15] Theology's positive scientific work is one of reflecting on God's address to us in faith. The crucial point for Barth is that theology remain autonomously theo-

---

[13]Plantinga consistently identifies naturalism and creative anti-realism as the primary contemporary rivals to Christian thought, though sometimes giving more emphasis to the offspring of creative anti-realism: "relativism and anti-commitment" (Plantinga, "On Christian Scholarship," p. 291). In his charge to Calvin College graduates he simply mentions naturalism and relativism. "There are at present three main spiritual responses to the world, three main pictures of the world or perspectives on it, three main ways of thinking about the world and what the world is really like and what we ourselves are really like, and what we must do to live the good life. One of these, of course, is Christianity, and I needn't say much about that to this audience. In addition to the Christian perspective, however, there are fundamentally two others. The first is what I'll call naturalism. . . . There is another rival to Christian ways of thinking, another perspective, and I'll call it relativism" (Plantinga, *"Our Vision": Calvin College Commencement Address, May 20, 2000* [Grand Rapids: Calvin College, 2000], DVD). In his March 2, 2011, address at Taylor University, Plantinga issued a similar challenge, highlighting the contrast with naturalism and relativism.

[14]"Theology as a science, in distinction from the 'theology' of the simple testimony of faith and life and the 'theology' of the service of God, is a measure taken by the Church in relation to the vulnerability and responsibility of its utterance" (*CD* I/1, p. 4).

[15]Barth, *Anselm, Fides Quaerens Intellectum: Anselm's Proof of the Existence of God in the Context of His Theological Scheme* (London: SCM Press, 1960), pp. 16-18.

foundational. This means that theology is done in obedience to the object of theology—God made known by God's own self-revelation. The starting point does not require the impossibility of an external prolegomenous validation. The concern for autonomy and the defense of the presumption of Christian faith are shared by Plantinga. The rightful autonomy not just of theology but of all Christian scholarship is a main plank of Plantinga's platform.

It should be clear, therefore, that Barth and Plantinga agree that theology and all of Christian scholarship are free to start, and must start, with a given. A crucial question, however, remains: do Barth and Plantinga agree about just what this given is and whether it is the same for theology and the rest of Christian scholarship? This is a question about epistemological foundations, however, and must therefore be deferred until we have taken a closer look at Plantinga's epistemology of Christian belief. For now, a few provisional comments on Plantinga's understanding of the relationship between faith and reason will help to sharpen the question.

For Plantinga, Christian scholarship is done by appeal both to the deliverances of faith and to the deliverances of reason. The deliverances of reason are employed in the service of "explicating the bearing of the faith on some part of the discipline in question."[16] The given for Christian scholarship appears therefore to be the content of the deliverances of faith. What then is delivered by the deliverances of faith? One suggestion is that the deliverances of faith deliver particular expressed propositions that are fundamental to Christian belief. "It is crucial to Christian belief to suppose that such propositions as *God created the world* and *Christ's suffering and death are an atonement for human sin* are true."[17] But does this view come too close to the conclusion that the gift of faith involves the clean transfer of truth about God into propositional statements in human language? This is an idea that Barth, as we have seen, strongly rejects. Plantinga and Barth agree that the gift of faith is a gift of knowledge. Barth, moreover, is very clear that this knowledge is the self-revelation of the person of God in Christ by the Spirit, and

---

[16]Plantinga, "Twin Pillars of Christian Scholarship," p. 159.

[17]*WCB*, p. 425, emphasis original.

not a collection of standalone propositions. Revelation is cognitive and verbal, but the form of human language is never adequate to the content of the knowledge of God outside of the gracious work of the Spirit, who gives us a participation in the "triune circle of God's self-knowing."[18] Plantinga moves much more quickly to propositions. He appeals to Calvin's definition of faith, which "involves an explicitly cognitive element; it is, says Calvin, knowledge—knowledge of the availability of redemption and salvation through the person and work of Jesus Christ—and it is revealed to our minds."[19] There certainly seems to be a tension here between Barth and Plantinga at a foundational level regarding the nature of the knowledge of God, with Barth emphasizing the personal and Plantinga the propositional.

There are good reasons to suspect that the tension is not as severe as it may seem; however, due to the importance and complexity of the issue, we will leave off here and return to it again in greater detail in chapter eight, where we explore more deeply the nature of faith and its relation to reason. Before leaving it altogether, however, let me make one observation that moves in the direction of concord.

I mentioned above that while Barth might agree with Plantinga that theology, like the rest of Christian scholarship, has a critical and constructive task, the particularities of that task for theology are quite unique. That task has to do with measuring the church's talk about God by the church's very being, Jesus Christ, the personal revelation of God. The pronouncements of theology are therefore second-order reflections, faith seeking understanding, derivative and dependent on the actual knowing relation.[20] Plantinga concurs with Barth in two important ways. First, for Plantinga, theology has a role unique from and pivotal to the rest of Christian scholarship (including Christian philosophy). Theology helps us to understand the deliverances of faith. The rest of

---

[18]This is Trevor Hart's apt phrase picking up on Barth's "this event presents a self-enclosed circle" (*CD* I/2, p. 280; *KD* I/2, p. 304); see Hart, "Karl Barth, the Trinity, and Pluralism," in *The Trinity in a Pluralistic Age: Theological Essays on Culture and Religion,* ed. Kevin J. Vanhoozer (Grand Rapids: Eerdmans, 1997), p. 135.

[19]*WCB,* p. 244.

[20]Barth affirms what he takes to be Anselm's view that, for theology, *intellectus* is always *intellectus fidei,* "das im *Credo* vorgesagte nachdenken" (*Fides Quaerens Intellectum,* p. 37).

Christian scholarship works from a theological foundation, employing reason to determine the implications of this foundation for each discipline.[21] Plantinga, like Barth, reserves a special and primary place for the theological task;[22] moreover, he seems to affirm theology as a second-order reflection on faith.[23] If the knowledge of faith comes fully and lucidly prepackaged in propositional statements such that the deliverances of faith are transparently self-evident to all Christian scholars, then the theological task would involve no interpretive reflection, only a reiterating of these statements and an unpacking of their logical entailments. In an illuminating comment, however, Plantinga affirms that "theology is both important and necessary" and that it helps us "to know what we know by faith."[24] If there is work to be done in order to know what we know by faith, then there must be a distinction between first-order knowing of faith itself and the second-order reflection of theology. While propositions are quite definitely among the deliverances of faith, it is safe to say that there is more going on than a simplified, direct, propositional transfer of knowledge in Plantinga's view of faith and revelation. This of course leaves still a number of pressing questions, some of which will be given greater consideration in chapter eight.

Christian philosophy. I have outlined Plantinga's views on the constructive and critical task of all Christian scholarship, a task that begins unapologetically with central theological convictions, seeking the implications of those convictions for each discipline, by the light of reason. Now it is time to return to the main question of this section: what is the task of the Christian philosopher? For our purposes we also want to pay particular attention to how Plantinga conceives of the difference between philosophy and theology.

---

[21]We can acknowledge that Plantinga may speak with more confidence and less provisionality about the propositional knowledge generated by the theological task; however, this may be more a matter of emphasis than material disagreement.

[22]For Barth, it is not necessary that the theological task be performed as an independent discipline, but that detracts in no way from the uniqueness and importance of the theological task (*CD* I/1, p. 5).

[23]Paul Helm includes Plantinga's project in his treatment of the faith-seeking-understanding tradition (Helm, *Faith and Understanding,* Reason and Religion [Edinburgh: Edinburgh University Press, 1997], pp. 182-203).

[24]Plantinga, "Twin Pillars of Christian Scholarship," p. 157.

To begin with, we have already established that Christian philosophy shares with other disciplines in the twofold task of Christian scholarship. We have also touched on Plantinga's distinction between theology and all the other disciplines, including philosophy. What then is Christian philosophy's special function? Plantinga's main answer to this question is simply that Christian philosophy is to address itself to the particular questions of its discipline from a Christian perspective. His "Advice to Christian Philosophers" is devoted to challenging Christian philosophers to have the courage, independence and integrity to allow Christian theological convictions to set the agenda for their work.[25] This has direct implications for the relationship between philosophy and theology. Philosophy is not the beginning of the road—faith is. "The Christian philosophical community, quite properly starts, in philosophy, from what it believes."[26] Plantinga seems to accord with Barth that theological knowledge does not require the grounding of a philosophical argument. This does not mean, however, that there is no role in Plantinga's thought for philosophy marshaled in the defense and clarification of Christian belief. In fact, much of what Plantinga does as a Christian philosopher is employ philosophical reasoning to just these ends. Consistent with this, Plantinga highlights two roles for philosophy, roles that are in addition to its twofold task; these are the important functions of apologetics and philosophical theology.[27] Here we face another potential contrast with Karl Barth.

Barth maintains that if Christian theological convictions are really properly held independent of philosophical grounding, there is no need for a philosophical defense of them (i.e., apologetics). For Barth, we need not even enter into debate about the basis of our theological knowing or questions about God's existence.[28] He is not averse to using rather extreme language about such attempts: "all planned apologetics and po-

[25]Plantinga, "Advice to Christian Philosophers," p. 269.

[26]Ibid.

[27]Plantinga, "Christian Philosophy at the End of the Twentieth Century," p. 37.

[28]*CD* I/1, p. 30. We should not understand Barth here to forbid consideration, reflection on or speaking about the ground of theological knowing. It is rather that the ground of the knowledge of God is not up for discussion, uncertain and in need of defense. The knowledge of God is self-grounded in God's self-revealing act.

lemics have obviously been irresponsible, irrelevant and therefore ineffective."[29] It is difficult indeed to reconcile Barth's views here with Plantinga's. Although Plantinga has been charged with dismissing Christian apologetics altogether, he clearly maintains that apologetics, both in its negative and its positive forms, is a notably valuable and important endeavor.[30] Even though philosophical arguments do not provide justification or warrant for Christian belief, they still have an important role to play.[31] He appeals to Calvin, and suggests that philosophical arguments can be helpful in the process of coming to belief and in the believer's struggle with doubt.[32] Sorting out just where Plantinga and Barth agree and disagree on the questions of natural theology and apologetics is complicated by two factors. The first difficulty is that it is not at all clear that even the most basic terms are being used in the same way by Barth and Plantinga. And, second, their approach vectors to these issues are so different that the parallax mentioned earlier is nearly unavoidable. I will argue that there is a defensible way of interpreting Barth and Plantinga such that they are in fundamental continuity with each other and with the Reformed tradition to which they belong.[33] Nevertheless, due to the complexity involved and given the acuteness and importance of the disagreement, a separate chapter, chapter seven, will be devoted to this subject.

Along with apologetics, Plantinga mentions philosophical theology as an important division of Christian philosophy. The very mention of philosophical theology raises important questions for the relationship between philosophy and theology. Plantinga defines philosophical the-

---

[29]Ibid.

[30]In Plantinga's reply to the critique of R. Douglas Geivett and Greg Jesson, he clarifies that while apologetical arguments "are not necessary for rational faith . . . of course it doesn't follow for a moment that such apologetical work is inconsequential. It can be of use in many different and important ways: for example, in moving someone closer to the great things of the gospel. Such arguments can also provide confirmations, what John Calvin calls 'helps'" (Plantinga, "Internalism, Externalism, Defeaters and Arguments for Christian Belief," *Philosophia Christi* 3, no. 2 [2001]: 384-85). For similar affirmations see Plantinga, "Christian Philosophy at the End of the Twentieth Century," p. 217; and Plantinga, "Rationality and Public Evidence: A Reply to Richard Swinburne," *Religious Studies* 37 (2001): 215-22.

[31]Plantinga, "Christian Philosophy at the End of the Twentieth Century," p. 39.

[32]Ibid., p. 40.

[33]See RBG, p. 72, where Plantinga points out the fundamental agreement among Barth, Calvin, Kuyper and Bavinck.

ology as "a matter of thinking about the central doctrines of the Christian faith from a philosophical perspective; it is a matter of employing the resources of philosophy to deepen our grasp and understanding of them."[34] We have noted that for Barth theology cannot but engage with the tools, resources and language of philosophy, for theology is done "within the framework of philosophy."[35] This raises several questions: What theology is not philosophical theology? Is the Christian philosopher practicing philosophical theology really doing theology? If so, is theology properly understood as a branch of Christian philosophy?

A few observations will help to clarify where Plantinga and Barth stand with respect to these questions. Beginning with Plantinga, it is significant that he sees philosophical theology as important work for both Christian philosophers and theologians, adding that it would benefit from the coordinated involvement of both.[36] It also seems reasonable to conclude that, for Plantinga, as the name suggests, philosophical theology is theology. Plantinga, again, sees theology as the working out of what we know from the deliverances of faith, while Christian philosophy, in its constructive task, is working on the implications of what we know from the deliverances of faith for the questions in philosophy. Philosophical theology seen as theology, therefore, would be employing the resources of philosophy in the task of working out what we know from the deliverances of faith. Plantinga, however, describes philosophical theology as helping to clarify the central doctrines of the Christian faith. It is possible, therefore, that he understands philosophical theology to be one step removed from theology, clarifying what theology means in its clarifications of what we know from the deliverances of faith.[37] Philosophical theology viewed in this way would

---

[34]Plantinga, "Christian Philosophy at the End of the Twentieth Century," p. 41.

[35]SITet, p. 27.

[36]Regarding philosophical theology undertaken by Christian philosophers, Plantinga states, "No doubt some of this work could profit from closer contact with what theologians know" (Plantinga, "Christian Philosophy at the End of the Twentieth Century," p. 42). The study we are conducting here could be characterized as an effort in philosophical theology endeavoring to bring closer contact between Christian philosophy and theology.

[37]Just how this "clarifying" proceeds is of critical importance. Does philosophy actively shape content and meaning on the basis of its own independent criteria, or simply explore the implications and inner coherence of theology?

be a third-order reflection on a second-order reflection (theology) on the first-order knowledge of God given in faith. In either case, it seems clear that Plantinga does not think that all theology must be philosophical theology. Plantinga might agree with Barth that using the language and concepts of philosophy is unavoidable for the theologian, but he seems to have in mind here a particularly self-conscious, explicit and formal engagement with philosophical thought.

Turning back to Barth for a moment, it is helpful to remember that his primary objection to philosophy is an objection to any attempt to replace theology's particular, intractable, God-given ground and starting point with a general pseudoground established on human reason. Here, Barth and Plantinga are in complete agreement. Barth also agrees with Plantinga that theology and Christian philosophy may overlap and mutually inform.[38] He leaves the door open to the possibility of a philosophy that respects its boundaries and does not "subordinate theology to its own nexus of problems."[39] Nevertheless, it must be granted that the emphasis of Barth's thinking with respect to philosophical theology, like apologetics, is overwhelmingly negative. History teaches that going down this path nearly always results in a much too optimistic view of the capacity of human language, concepts and reason to grasp and independently convey divine truth. He worries that any positive assessment of the contribution of philosophy to theology may cause one to forget that "the intractability of faith and its object guarantees that divine certainty cannot become human security."[40] Plantinga would no doubt disagree about just how negative history's lessons are regarding the relationship between philosophy and theology. At no point, however, is Plantinga in disagreement with Barth about the proper ordering or the potential trespasses of philosophy in the service of theology. In fact,

[38]Recall here Barth's observation of the "common difficult tasks" of philosophy and theology and his suggestion that "the existence of the philosopher may be helpful to him [the theologian]" (PTet, pp. 80, 93).

[39]*CD* I/1, p. 39.

[40]*CD* I/1, p. 13. This is precisely the concern that motivates him to reject "a philosophical theology or theological philosophy in which the attempt would be made to reason 'theonomously.'" "All that men may here and now undertake is *human* theology . . . *theologia ektypa viatorum*, theology typical not of God but of man" (Karl Barth, *Evangelical Theology: An Introduction*, trans. Grover Foley [London: Weidenfeld & Nicolson, 1963], pp. 113-14). See also *CD* I/1, p. 269.

Plantinga's work on the nature of Christian scholarship (as we have seen) and the epistemology of Christian belief (as we shall see) is aimed at undercutting the Cartesian/Lockean quest for a general, anthropological and theologically neutral epistemic basis.[41]

The nature of truth and the nature of knowledge. What has been given so far is a rather condensed account of Plantinga's views on Christian scholarship, but this should be sufficient to support a few key observations about Plantinga's thought. Plantinga's position on Christian scholarship is motivated by at least two commitments that are of fundamental importance to understanding his epistemology of Christian belief, one about the nature of truth and the other about the nature of knowledge. Regarding truth, Plantinga asserts that the Christian perspective entails a commitment to the unitary, universal and objective nature of truth. We can distinguish this view from two confused, though popular, rivals. The first rival is a version of the Ritschlian dualism that Barth rejected. Plantinga would find no reason to accept a *Natur/Geist* disjunction of the realms of faith and reason. It is difficult to see whether the Ritschlian split is really a rival view of truth or simply the more popular notion that Christianity makes only ethical, and not metaphysical, claims.[42] In either case Plantinga does not countenance this division: Christian truth claims have implications for the natural sciences as well as ethical theory. The second rival view of truth is subjective relativism, where truth is multiple, individual and subjectively determined. Plantinga excoriates relativism in his critiques of creative anti-realism. Creative anti-realism suggests that there is no reality per se independent of the thinking human subject. Human thought is what creates and determines reality.[43]

---

[41]D. Z. Phillips attacks Plantinga's position on just this point, noting that Plantinga has abandoned the modern ideal of "disinterested enquiry" (Phillips, "Advice to Philosophers Who Are Christians," *New Blackfriars* 69, no. 820 [1988]: 426-30).

[42]One way to understand the Ritschlian split is as a kind of factual dualism where spiritual truths and natural truths both apply simultaneously. It is spiritually or ethically true that God created the world while it is naturally true that the world is uncreated. Under this view, truth is not necessarily subjective, but it is nevertheless a form of relativism if we suppose that there can be a real contradiction of meaning in two true propositions. The more popular interpretation is just to reduce Christian truth claims to merely ethical propositions, but this then shifts us to a question about the nature of Christian truth claims and not about the nature of truth and reality itself.

[43]Plantinga does allow, however, for a *divine* creative anti-realism. See his "How to Be an Anti-Realist," *Proceedings and Addresses of the American Philosophical Association* 56, no. 1 (1982): 68-70.

Like Barth, Plantinga rejects any thoroughgoing idealism[44] of this kind as "incompatible with Christianity."[45] If the existence of all things is dependent on our noetic activity, then "in a stunning reversal of roles, [God] would owe his existence to us."[46] Plantinga also considers this view to suffer from "deep problems with self-referential incoherence."[47] However, it is significant that his critique aimed at its logical inadequacy appears to be secondary to his concern that creative anti-realism is not a neutral option but rather wholly inimical to the Christian view.[48] In a statement that resonates with Barth's affirmation of an essential realism, Plantinga reasons:

> Clearly one of the deepest impulses in Christian thought is the idea that there really is such a person as God, who has established the world a certain way: there really is a correct or right way of looking at things; this is the way God looks at things.[49]

There is, therefore, no room on Plantinga's view for the possibility that propositions about God and the world might be personally true for the Christian but not publicly true for the scholar. Often popular postmodern thought embraces this kind of personal relativism.[50] But postmodern intuitions are not all wrong in Plantinga's judgment. After all, central to postmodernism is a critique of Enlightenment modernism's commitment to classical foundationalism with all of the requirements discussed in

---

[44]Plantinga traces creative anti-realism back to the ancients but credits its popularity and influence with a particular understanding of Kantian idealism. Whether this is the correct interpretation of Kant is beside the point. Plantinga gladly concedes that "Kant himself did not take creative anti-realism globally and neat. . . . No doubt there are restrictions of Kantian creative anti-realism that are compatible with Christianity, and ought to be explored as among the possibilities as to how things are" (Plantinga, "Christian Philosophy at the End of the Twentieth Century," p. 33). Plantinga also explores alternative interpretations of Kant in the first chapter of *WCB*.

[45]Plantinga, "Christian Philosophy at the End of the Twentieth Century," p. 32.

[46]Ibid., p. 33.

[47]Plantinga, "Twin Pillars of Christian Scholarship," p. 131.

[48]Ibid., p. 132.

[49]Plantinga, "Christian Philosophy at the End of the Twentieth Century," p. 35.

[50]It is worth noting that the kind of postmodernism embraced by the likes of Walter Lowe, Graham Ward and William Stacy Johnson is skeptical not about the notion that there really is a way that things are and an objective truth about it, but rather about the possibility of human access to that truth. Stanley Grenz and John R. Franke remind us that "the wholesale identification of the term postmodern with radical relativism . . . is simply too narrow to do justice to the actual breadth of the phenomenon" (Grenz and Franke, *Beyond Foundationalism: Shaping Theology in a Postmodern Context* [Louisville, KY: Westminster John Knox, 2001], p. 19).

chapter three, including the accessibility requirement. In other words, postmodernism helpfully challenges the possibility of autonomous, neutral human objectivity. This is the critical aspect of Barth's critical realism, namely, the chastening of idealism, which highlights the limits of independent human knowing from below. Plantinga, with his powerful critique of classical foundationalism, seems wholeheartedly to agree.[51]

By encouraging Christian academics to approach their disciplines with the assumption of the truth of Christian belief, Plantinga is allied with Barth and shares the intolerant chastisements that Barth receives from Harnack and Pannenberg. Presuming the Christian point of view, it is alleged, is a baleful transgression of the foundational principle of academic neutrality upon which the progress of universal human knowledge depends. Such a retreat to Christian ghettos amounts to a blind fideism, a hopeless subjectivism and, worst of all, as Peter van Ness worries, "raise[s] specters of Christian triumphalism."[52] Plantinga's response to this is similar to Barth's, just as it is aligned with Plantinga's Dutch ascendants Bavinck and Kuyper.[53] Human knowers occupy a stance of epistemic dependence. There simply is no privileged, neutral point of view, as this critique with all its resonating hopefulness invariably assumes. However, it quite obviously does not follow from the fact that humans have no independent objective access to the truth that truth must therefore be a subjective human construction.[54] Nor does it

[51]Plantinga points out that a critical recognition of the Enlightenment's mistaken optimism in human objectivity is hardly news to his own theological tradition. This critique "would of course have received the enthusiastic support of Kuyper and Dooyeweerd" (Plantinga, "Christian Philosophy at the End of the Twentieth Century," p. 35). Nicholas Wolterstorff makes the observation that long before Barth, Kuyper arrived at postmodern views regarding autonomous human objectivity (Wolterstorff, "What New Haven and Grand Rapids Have to Say to Each Other: 1992 Stob Lectures," in *Seeking Understanding: The Stob Lectures, 1986–1998* [Grand Rapids: Eerdmans, 2001], p. 278).

[52]Peter H. van Ness, "Philosophers Who Believe: The Spiritual Journeys of 11 Leading Thinkers," review of *Philosophers Who Believe,* ed. Kelly James Clark, *Journal of the American Academy of Religion* 64, no. 4 (1996): 889.

[53]This is especially true for our knowledge of God, where, as Abraham Kuyper advises, "man no longer stands *above,* but *beneath* the object of his investigation, and over against this object he finds himself in a position of entire *dependence*" (Kuyper, *Encyclopedia of Sacred Theology: Its Principles* [London: Hodder & Stoughton, 1899], p. 248, emphasis original).

[54]Plantinga quips, "As you have no doubt noticed, this is a whopping *non sequitur;* that hasn't curbed its popularity in the least" (Plantinga, "Christian Philosophy at the End of the Twentieth Century," p. 34).

follow that a lack of guaranteed and demonstrable certainty about the truth we believe we know undermines the validity of our natural conviction that we do indeed have at least approximate knowledge of the objective truth.

This last observation provides a nice bridge into the second motivating conviction for Plantinga's charge to Christian scholars, one having to do with the nature of knowing. But before plunging headfirst into his epistemology of Christian belief, let us take brief stock of what has been observed so far. Already in Plantinga's views on Christian scholarship there is a strong indication that he agrees with Barth's rejection of the three interconnected facets of Enlightenment modernism discussed in chapter three. Like Barth, Plantinga's view is properly understood as a kind of critical realism.[55] He begins his defense of this view arguing first from the implications of what is known by Christian faith. He in no way accepts the *obligation assumption,* which would require the scholar to demonstrate the legitimacy of Christian knowledge claims, nor does he grant the *general starting-point assumption,* with its stipulation that one may only proceed from knowledge claims that are generally accepted within the broader academy.[56] He critiques classical foundationalism's *accessibility requirement,* which sought truth-validation of belief from an independent human epistemic footing. He therefore recognizes the validity of critical idealism's critique of objective human certainty,[57] but does

[55]Which affirms both the underlying reality of the object of knowing and recognizes the active and constitutive role of noetic processes in the shaping of knowledge.

[56]Worthy of particular note for our interests is Plantinga's conclusion that Christian biblical scholars should not be limited by only what can be known through "ordinary scientific investigation" (Plantinga, "Sheehan's Shenanigans: How Theology Becomes Tomfoolery," *Reformed Journal* 37 [1987]: 25). See also his arguments against the stipulations of Troeltschian historical biblical criticism, in *WCB,* pp. 412-21.

[57]*Certainty* is a notion with two senses that can be quite unhelpfully ambiguous if not properly distinguished. In the sense of confidence or credence, *certainty* indicates maximal credence in or commitment to a particular belief. In the sense of clarity or infallibility, *certainty* indicates that one could not be mistaken. It is this ambiguity and the inadequacy of infallibility as an epistemic ideal that leads Esther L. Meek to commend confidence over certainty (Meek, *Longing to Know* [Grand Rapids: Brazos Press, 2003], pp. 137-40). It is important to see that it is possible to have an undoubting confidence in one's belief without pretending to see how it is impossible that one's belief could fail to be true. In other words, it is possible to rightly believe without doubt that a belief is true without being able to demonstrate how it could not be false. The possibility that all knowledge is infected with error (uncertain) does not necessarily invalidate the propriety of being maximally convinced (certain) that something we believe we know is true. Christian belief is

so without abandoning realism's commitment to a unitary, universal and objective reality—a reality that is only known with objective certainty by God. What Plantinga also does, that Barth does not do, is point out the logical inconsistency in the creative anti-realist and relativist positions.

Plantinga takes a fundamentally realist stance, affirming that there is a truth to be known about the world and about God. This truth is objective in that it is "the way God looks at things." The impossibility of *independent* human objectivity does not count against the possibility of a genuine human knowledge of that truth. While Plantinga never says as much, the implication of his position is that genuine human knowledge of God is in some way a participation in the way God looks at himself—which is precisely Barth's view. The task before us as we move into a consideration of Plantinga's epistemology is to discern just how compatible it is with Barth's from-above theo-foundationalism, in which the security of the gift of faith rests in the Giver and not in the earthen vessel such that our theological knowing remains *theologia ektypa viatorum* (provisional human theology, not perfected, but in process).[58]

PLANTINGA'S EPISTEMOLOGY AND WARRANT

It might be considered foolhardy to attempt a condensed summary of Plantinga's work in epistemology, not only because of its breadth and depth but also because, in general, epistemology is so conceptually challenging.[59] My aim here will need to be the more modest undertaking of

---

consistent with doubt about all human knowing while affirming the power of God to affirm to us the truth of our belief, despite our noetic fallibility. As we will soon see from Plantinga, the key question with respect to propriety is what warrants our belief. I will argue that, for both Barth and Plantinga, maximal conviction in our theological beliefs is always only warranted by the top-down action of divine revelation. For more on believing and knowing what we know is true, see Plantinga, "Internalism, Externalism, Defeaters and Arguments for Christian Belief," pp. 386-87.

[58]See Barth, *Evangelical Theology*, pp. 113-14.

[59]As Plantinga notes: "Epistemology is extremely difficult, in many ways more difficult than, say, the metaphysics of modality. The latter requires a fair amount of logical acumen; but it is reasonably easy to see what the basic concepts are and how they are related. Not so for epistemology. *Warrant, justification, evidence, epistemic normativity, probability, rationality*—these are all extremely difficult notions. Indeed, each of those terms is really associated with a whole class of difficult and analogically related notions, where a big part of the difficulty is discerning how the members of each class are related to each other and to the members of the other classes. Coming to clarity on them and their relatives and discerning the relations among them is strenuous and demanding; yet it is the only way to progress in epistemology" (*WCD*, p. vi).

clarifying for our particular question the central pivot points and the cumulative import of a hundred deft and nimble moves. We are helped considerably in this thanks to the painstaking clarity of Plantinga's writing. But the warning remains that these are deeply troubled waters, and despite Plantinga's best efforts, many—even of his admirers—have found it easy to misunderstand him at points. We will begin with an exploration of Plantinga's general account of how our beliefs might have *warrant.* Here I will highlight Plantinga's recognition that the possibility of human knowledge requires the purposive arrangement of elements both external and internal to our own noetic equipment. For Plantinga, knowledge, which is more than mere true belief, cannot originate from below.

Why warrant. Possibly the most significant distinction that Plantinga draws in his epistemological work is among the notions of warrant, justification and rationality. Failure to appreciate the importance of the differences in Plantinga's employment of these notions for understanding his contributions to epistemology is one of the most common mistakes made by Plantinga critics.[60] Some internalist and evidentialist critics, for instance, are inclined to reduce the question of *warrant* to the question of *justification,* conceived of in terms of fulfilling one's duty vis-à-vis accessible public or private evidence. A chief aim of Plantinga's *Warrant* trilogy, however, is to challenge the assumption that *justification* so conceived is either sufficient or even necessary for one's beliefs to have *warrant.*[61] He argues, in addition, that Christian belief cannot be challenged as irrational or unjustified.[62] Everything hinges on whether

[60]See Evan Fales, review of *Warranted Christian Belief,* by Alvin Plantinga, *Noûs* 37, no. 2 (2003): 353-70; Richard Feldman, "Proper Functionalism," *Noûs* 27, no. 1 (1993): 34-50; R. Douglas Geivett and Greg Jesson, "Plantinga's Externalism and the Terminus of Warrant-Based Epistemology," *Philosophia Christi* 3, no. 2 (2001): 329-40; Timothy McGrew and Lydia McGrew, "On the Historical Argument: A Rejoinder to Plantinga," *Philosophia Christi* 8, no. 1 (2006): 23-38; Philip Quinn, "In Search of the Foundations of Theism," *Faith and Philosophy* 2, no. 4 (1985): 469-86; and Richard G. Swinburne, "Plantinga on Warrant," review of *Warranted Christian Belief,* by Alvin Plantinga, *Religious Studies* 37 (2001): 203-14. What is often missing in these critiques is real engagement with Plantinga's argument against accepting internalist justification as necessary and sufficient for warrant.

[61]This is dealt with most comprehensively in *WCD.* See especially chapter 2, "Classical Chisholmian Internalism."

[62]*Rationality* for Plantinga has to do with the proper functioning of our reason in the apprehension of experience, the formation of belief, etc. (*WCB,* pp. 110-12), while *justification* is taken to refer

Christian belief has warrant, which ultimately hinges on whether Christian belief is true.[63] Consequently, a successful argument against the adequacy of Christian belief in general would have to target the truth of the belief itself.

What then is *warrant* in Plantingian parlance? The oft-repeated definition in fullest form is "warrant is a normative, possibly complex quantity that comes in degrees, enough of which is what distinguishes knowledge from mere true belief."[64] He develops this notion of warrant in response to Edmund Gettier,[65] who notably upset the near consensus in epistemology, though largely implicit until Gettier, that in order for a belief to count as genuine knowledge it must fulfill three essential requirements. It must of course be believed, it must in fact be true, and the belief must be formed in a way that entitles one to the belief—you can't say you know something if it's just a random belief that by blind luck happens to be true. This third requirement, which entitles one to a belief, is commonly expressed as *justification.* Putting all three requirements together, we arrive at the justified-true-belief theory of knowledge. Plantinga, however, after a long, hard look at the range of what epistemologists tend to mean by justification, argues that justification does not adequately address the concern for the connectedness of belief formation and truth. In other words, justification in its common construals does

---

to the epistemic duties we must fulfill to be within our epistemic rights to hold a belief (ibid., pp. 99-102).

[63]Ibid., pp. 187-89.

[64]*WCD,* p. 4. Plantinga traces the distinction between the notions of warrant and justification back to Locke. This emerges in his "Justification in the 20th Century," *Philosophy and Phenomenological Research* 50, supplement (1990): 52.

[65]In three pages, Edmund Gettier's "Is Justified True Belief Knowledge?" *Analysis* 23, no. 6 (1963): 121-23, both made explicit the justified-true-belief theory of knowledge and cast serious doubt on it. "It is almost as if a distinguished critic created a tradition in the very act of destroying it" (*WCD,* p. 6). Gettier was one of Plantinga's most influential colleagues in the Wayne State philosophy department, given special mention in the original preface to Plantinga's *God and Other Minds* (p. xvii). Plantinga has often commented on the uniqueness of Gettier's three-page piece in the ratio of its pages to the number of pages it has provoked. See especially Plantinga, "Self-Profile," pp. 28-29. Although Plantinga has pressed Gettier's work into the service of philosophical arguments that defend the possibility that Christian belief has warrant, Gettier himself strongly rejected Christian belief. Plantinga notes that, while at Wayne State, Gettier attacked his Christianity "with great verve and power" (Plantinga, "A Christian Life Partly Lived," in *Philosophers Who Believe: The Spiritual Journeys of 11 Leading Thinkers,* ed. Kelly James Clark [Downers Grove, IL: InterVarsity Press, 1993], p. 64).

not adequately distinguish knowledge from mere true belief.[66] An alternative to *justification* is needed, and Plantinga calls it *warrant*.[67] In order to appreciate the need for a new term and an alternative to traditional notions of justification in knowledge, we would do well to peel back another layer and look a bit closer at Plantinga's critique.

Where Plantinga and the vast majority of epistemologists throughout history are in agreement is that knowledge requires something more than belief and a belief's happening to be true. If the truth of belief candidates were absolutely transparent, obvious and somehow guaranteed, then a third requirement might not be necessary. To know something implies that there is some nonaccidental connection between belief formation and truth—something in the process that generates belief so that it is the truth of what is being believed and not something else that is motivating the believing.[68] This, therefore, is what we are after in our search for a proper third requirement for knowledge, a dependable, nonaccidental connection between belief formation and truth. Where Plantinga takes exception with the diverse tradition is in his contention that most notions of justification do not provide either what is sufficient or what is necessary for a dependable, nonaccidental connection between belief formation and truth—i.e., *warrant*.[69] Plantinga takes a penetrating look at the notions of justification on offer and consistently comes back to two key problems.

The failure of epistemic justification. *Warrant: The Current Debate* is the

---

[66]We shall see below that Plantinga uses *justification* primarily to refer to the rights and duties of belief, i.e., deontology.

[67]Plantinga originally opted for Roderick Chisholm's expression, calling it "positive epistemic status," but later explains that that was just too cumbersome a term. He also mentions Earnest Sosa's "epistemic aptness" as a synonym for *warrant* that has less deontological baggage (*WCD*, pp. 4-5).

[68]Plantinga helpfully points out that often the aim of belief in a case of knowledge is better understood as *verisimilitude* rather than *truth*. The aim may not be the production of a veridical proposition but rather the generation of conceptions that are accurate depictions of reality (*WPF*, p. 43).

[69]Plantinga's analysis of warrant is approached inductively by taking largely agreed instances of knowledge and critically by highlighting the weaknesses in alternative accounts. In Plantinga's view, it is simply a matter of the way things are that a concise definition of necessary and sufficient conditions for warrant is not possible. "This is a way in which philosophy differs from mathematics. . . . Our concept of warrant is too complex to yield to analysis by way of a couple of austerely elegant clauses" (*WPF*, p. ix). The inductive approach is also his tack in the analysis of proper basicality. See Plantinga, "Is Belief in God Properly Basic?" *Noûs* 15 (1981): 50.

place to find Plantinga's most sustained treatment of the various proposals made to address the elusive third requirement in knowledge. He takes a systematic look at various notions of the importance of and relationship among justification, rationality, evidence, epistemic duty, coherence and the like. Informed by attention to its origins in Descartes and Locke, Plantinga undertakes a percipient examination of epistemic internalism. Internalism affirms what I have called the *accessibility requirement.*[70] "The basic thrust of internalism in epistemology . . . is that the properties that confer warrant upon a belief are properties to which the believer has some sort of special epistemic access."[71] Plantinga's *ad fontes* argument is that internalism is motivated by an underlying commitment to a deontological conception of justification—where justification consists in doing one's epistemic duty, variously construed. In terms of our discussion with Karl Barth, it is appropriate to note that justification so construed is a decidedly from-below approach to knowing. As Plantinga suggests, "here our destiny is entirely in our own hands."[72] As an account of warrant, it is a veritable epistemic-works righteousness, where what principally matters is the conscientious discharge of duty. In the case of evidentialism, this is the duty to proportion belief to the evidence. Plantinga characterizes the attitude this way: "I may be wholly and hopelessly deceived. Even so, I can still do my epistemic duty; I can still do my best; I can still be above reproach."[73] The duty of the internalist, however, is to do everything possible not to be deceived. A thoroughgoing internalist, therefore, might only count as knowledge a belief that is based on evidence, the grounding truth of which is directly, internally

---

[70]Paul K. Moser expresses this internalist requirement as being "capable of calling to attention evidence which justifies the proposition" being believed. He, therefore, determines that "externalism falls short of capturing the primary sense of 'justified belief'" (Moser, *Empirical Justification* [Dordrecht: D. Reidel, 1985], pp. 246, 248). It is the appropriateness of this sense of justification as a criterion for knowledge that Plantinga critiques.

[71]*WCD,* p. 6. Paul Helm mistakenly argues that Plantinga's externalism is "logically parasitic on some form of internalism." This conclusion only follows because Helm places internalist constraints on what could serve to warrant externalism when this is exactly what the debate itself hinges on (Helm, review of *Warrant: The Current Debate* and *Warrant and Proper Function,* by Alvin Plantinga, *Religious Studies* 31 [1995]: 133).

[72]*WCD,* p. 15.

[73]Ibid.

apprehended or apprehensible.[74] Plantinga maintains that it is the notion of duty undergirding internalism that is its chief motivator—without which internalism of any variety loses its drive.[75] From this root, he goes on to trace the development of various alternative construals of justification, some internalist and others externalist.[76] In each case he explains that the proposal fails to serve as an adequate account of how our beliefs could have warrant. He employs a number of criticisms and counterexamples to cast doubt on each of the warrant candidates. In almost every case, however, he returns to one or more of the following three problems. First, there are counterexamples that point out that the proposal in question does not give us enough to distinguish knowledge from mere true belief. Then, there are counterexamples in which the proposed requirement would not even be necessary for warrant. And finally, Plantinga notes that many of the proposals misconstrue the relationship between warrant and belief and cannot account for the important fact that warrant comes in degrees. We will examine each of these briefly, giving us an opportunity to illuminate Plantinga's alternative in the light of his critiques.

The failure of epistemic justification: degrees of warrant. Starting with the last first, some versions of justification fail to grasp that what is conferred is a "quantity that comes in degrees."[77] Warrant is not an all-or-nothing Boolean value; it can be acquired at varying strengths.[78] There is a threshold, though not quantitatively defined, at which warrant becomes strong enough to serve, with belief and truth, as the third criteria for knowledge. The notion that warrant comes in degrees is, for Plantinga, an obvious fact, one related to the observation that our beliefs come in

[74]The representatives of evidentialist internalism highlighted by Plantinga are Earl Conee and Richard Feldman. See especially Earl Conee, "The Basic Nature of Epistemic Justification," *Monist* 71, no. 3 (1988): 389-404; and Earl Conee and Richard Feldman, "Evidentialism," *Philosophical Studies* 48, no. 1 (1985): 15-34.

[75]"Internalism flows from deontology and is unmotivated without it" (*WCD*, p. 29).

[76]A nice summary of the various combinations and permutations of the warrant candidates Plantinga has considered is found in the opening to *WPF*, p. 3.

[77]*WCD*, p. 4.

[78]The inability to deal adequately with this phenomenon of warrant is part of Plantinga's critiques of Laurence BonJour's coherentism, John Pollock's epistemic norms and Alvin Goldman's reliabilism (ibid., pp. 109-11, 169, 198-99, 209).

degrees of strength.[79] Part of the significance of Plantinga's observation about gradations of warrant is the relationship between warrant and belief. While Plantinga offers no precise account of this relationship, he does affirm that when things are working properly, "in the typical case, the degree to which I believe a given proposition will be proportional to the degree it has of warrant."[80] So close is the link that Plantinga can assert: "the degree of warrant [a belief] enjoys depends on the strength of the belief."[81] Such an assertion, however, could easily be misinterpreted. Is Plantinga really suggesting that we control the warrant for our beliefs by regulating the strength of our convictions? And, if not, then is warrant something that we independently perceive, to which we accordingly adjust the firmness of our beliefs? Either interpretation is ruled out by Plantinga's views on the nature of belief formation, seen particularly in his notion of the operation of internal rationality and his rejection of strict doxastic voluntarism.[82]

Internal rationality is concerned with forming the right beliefs on the basis of experience. In many cases, however, the function of internal rationality does not involve deliberation—reflecting on the nature of the experience and deciding on that basis what to believe and how firmly. Oftentimes, as when reflecting on our memories, we simply find ourselves in possession of a belief. The belief "seems *right, acceptable, natural;* it forces itself upon you; it seems somehow inevitable."[83] Theories of justification must be able to account for the phenomenology of belief—for the fact that our beliefs and their relative strengths are not (at least not entirely) in our control. Plantinga recognizes this and, therefore, rejects the notion that our beliefs are determined by deliberative choice. This rejection of strict doxastic voluntarism has led some to conclude that Plantinga's epistemology is "nonvoluntarist" to the extreme.[84] On

[79]Ibid., p. 109; *WPF,* p. 9; *WCB,* p. 114.

[80]*WPF,* p. 9.

[81]*WCB,* p. 156.

[82]Doxastic voluntarism is the view that beliefs are under the believer's voluntary control.

[83]*WCB,* pp. 110-12, emphasis original.

[84]See Laura L. Garcia, "Natural Theology and the Reformed Objection," in *Christian Perspectives on Religious Knowledge,* ed. C. Stephen Evans and Merold Westphal (Grand Rapids: Eerdmans, 1993), pp. 121-22; Linda Zagzebski, "Religious Knowledge and the Virtues of the Mind," in *Rational Faith: Catholic Responses to Reformed Epistemology,* ed. Linda Zagzebski (Notre Dame,

this view, one's beliefs are entirely determined by external factors, such that warrant becomes a matter of luck. These critiques miss their mark quite simply because Plantinga does maintain a place for deliberative choice in belief formation. The role of deliberative choice, however, is not primary for warrant. It is perfectly consistent with Plantinga's model that a person willfully resist the formation of right belief and thereby sabotage the proper functioning of their own cognitive processes.[85] However, while willful resistance may undermine warrant, choosing to believe does not convey warrant.

Pressing Plantinga on the nature of belief formation with respect to warrant raises interesting questions. Where does warrant ultimately come from, and what explains its gradation? In many of Plantinga's examples we are clearly in a position of epistemic dependence with regard to warrant. Warrant appears to be somehow given. He maintains that these examples are an indication that we neither do nor could provide the grounds or conditions for the warrant for our own beliefs. Instead he proposes that there must be an ultimate external grounding that provides a purposive connection between belief formation and truth—"a design plan successfully aimed at truth." What warrants our beliefs is that they are formed properly according to this designed connection to truth.[86] We are dependent on both an environment and cognitive faculties oriented toward and functioning in accordance with this plan. This means that there are a number of different factors that could influence the degree of warrant enjoyed by a belief. On the one hand, degree of warrant can be affected by malfunction. In the case of malfunction, of course, the actual degree of warrant could only be reduced, not increased. It might be the case that, due to some defect in my internal rationality, I fail to believe with the appropriate strength.[87] This

IN: University of Notre Dame Press, 1993), p. 202; and Keith A. Mascord, *Alvin Plantinga and Christian Apologetics* (Milton Keynes, UK: Paternoster, 2006), pp. 181-82, 198.

[85]Plantinga notes that proper function may be "impeded and overridden by lust, ambition, greed, selfishness" (*WCB*, p. 151).

[86]The specification of a design plan aimed at truth meets John L. Pollock's concern for "reason-guiding" epistemic norms and thereby refutes Pollock's argument against externalism (Pollock, *Contemporary Theories of Knowledge*, Rowman & Littlefield Texts in Philosophy [Totowa, NJ: Rowman & Littlefield, 1986], pp. 124-26).

[87]Plantinga distinguishes different "propositional attitudes," which amount to varying degrees of

would, in effect, diminish the warrant for the belief. If, however, I believed with more strength than was in fact proportionate to the warrant for the belief, I would not thereby increase the warrant of the belief.

So there is an important link between the strength of belief and the degree of warrant. To clarify further, the regulation of the strength of our belief is not a response to the warrant for a belief but part (maybe the last part) of a belief's becoming warranted. Consider the possibility that maximal warrant for a belief could be obtained and, nevertheless, we find ourselves with a low degree of confidence in this belief. This is technically not possible in Plantinga's conceptuality of warrant and belief formation because warrant applies not to the knower but to beliefs. Part of warrant is allocating the appropriate strength of belief. The basis for that strength may have to do with the clarity and/or proper functioning of our apprehension of experience,[88] but the destination of warrant is the belief itself. Depending on the suitability of environment and cognitive function oriented toward and functioning according to the designed connection between belief formation and truth—if everything is properly oriented and functioning—the full degree of warrant will, without attenuation or intensification, be reflected in and finally established by the proper proportionate strength of belief.[89] If that degree of warrant is high enough, then the belief qualifies as knowledge.[90] As far as other theories of justification go, they are deficient to the extent that they cannot accommodate the fact that *warrant is a quantity that comes in degrees.*

---

confidence that a proposition is true. If confidence is strong enough, we call it belief (*WPF*, p. 166). See also his discussion on Chisholm's "terms of epistemic appraisal" (*WCD*, p. 31).

[88]This is what Plantinga calls *external rationality*, referring to our part in the formation of experience, both sensuous experience, on which perceptual beliefs are based, and doxastic experience, on which beliefs from the likes of memory and a priori reason are based.

[89]In a parallel discussion on the objective conditional probability of a proposition, Plantinga maintains that a successful design plan would aim to match our propositional attitude with objective probability (*WPF*, p. 166).

[90]It is worth noting here that one of the particularities of Plantinga's warrant alternative to traditional notions of justification is that warrant as a third criteria actually subsumes the other two, belief and truth. It is impossible for a belief to have a high degree of warrant and not be believed, and indeed believed strongly. Also, given the necessity for warrant of environmentally suited and properly functioning processes operating according to a design plan successfully aimed at truth, it would be difficult for a belief to have a high degree of warrant and be false. Therefore, in Plantinga's scheme, a high degree of warrant is the sufficient condition for knowledge. For a dissenting view, see Richard Greene and N. A. Balmert, "Two Notions of Warrant and Plantinga's Solution to the Gettier Problem," *Analysis* 57, no. 2 (1997): 132-39.

The failure of epistemic justification: insufficient criteria. We now turn to the two most significant reasons Plantinga gives for rethinking what might give our beliefs positive epistemic status, beginning with the problem of the insufficiency of the criteria for justification. The insufficiency of most construals of justification for warrant is highlighted in situations where, despite fulfilling (by most accounts) one's epistemic duties, there occurs some kind of deception, mistake or malfunction in the process. A favorite subgroup of such counterexamples is Gettier problems.[91] In every Gettier-like example[92] there is an instance of belief that happens to be true for which there appears to be justification, and yet the belief clearly fails to be an instance of knowledge.[93] The justified true belief is enabled by a justified false belief.[94] The belief happens to be true even though the work done by the justification has failed, and the fact that the belief is true is actually against all odds.[95] One popular Gettier-like situation, found prior to Gettier, is Bertrand Russell's clock: "If you look at a clock which you believe to be going, but which in fact has stopped, and you happen to look at it at a moment when it is right, you will acquire a true belief as to the time of day, but you cannot be correctly said to have knowledge."[96] Russell was not pressing the point of justification, but his example has been used to show that a true belief, justified by the available evidence, is not sufficient for knowledge. The supposed justification has failed, and the fact that the belief is nevertheless true is a *felix culpa.* Gettier, by way of counterexample, shows that what we have called the accessibility requirement is not sufficient for knowledge. As Plantinga puts it, "the essence of the

[91]"What Gettier points out, of course, is that belief, truth and justification are not sufficient for knowledge" (*WPF,* p. 32).

[92]The credit here goes largely to Gettier, though Plantinga appeals to several Gettier-like examples that come from others. Plantinga specifically mentions examples taken from Keith Lehrer, Carl Ginet and Bertrand Russell.

[93]In Linda Zagzebski's analysis of Gettier examples, "what generates the problem for JTB, then, is that an accident of bad luck is cancelled out by an accident of good luck" (Zagzebski, "The Inescapability of Gettier Problems," *Philosophical Quarterly* 44, no. 174 [1994]: 66).

[94]*WPF,* p. 32.

[95]As Plantinga puts it, "these beliefs could *much better* have been false" (*WPF,* p. 33, emphasis original).

[96]Bertrand Russell, *Human Knowledge, Its Scope and Limits* (London: Allen & Unwin, 1948), p. 113; cf. pp. 170-71.

Gettier problem is that it shows internalist epistemologies to be wanting."[97] Gettier problems are for Plantinga a decisive blow to typical accounts of knowledge and justification, but they point to an even larger looming problem for such accounts. Gettier examples turn on a minor mistake, so minor that the common internalist proposal might comfortably allow a bit of Gettier slippage or, with a Gettier exception clause, rest content that the internalist approach is *nearly* correct. But, instead of a minor mistake, what about the possibility of large-scale epistemic deception or malfunction?

Internalism, in its various forms, makes justification dependent on the likes of doing one's duty,[98] maintaining a coherent set of beliefs,[99] satisfying the constraints of Bayesianism[100] and having the right epistemic norms.[101] But these criteria are quite plainly inadequate in cognitive environments that are massively misleading, or in situations where one's own cognitive equipment is not functioning properly. Either we might be subject to some kind of imperceptible external deception, as in the case of the Cartesian demon or any variant of the brain-in-a-vat scenario,[102] or we might have an undetectable defect in our cognitive faculties, as in the case of the Cartesian madman or Plantinga's Epis-

---

[97] *WPF,* p. 36.

[98] *WCD,* pp. 15-25. Descartes and Locke are given as the progenitors.

[99] Ibid., pp. 87-113. See especially Laurence BonJour, *The Structure of Empirical Knowledge* (Cambridge, MA: Harvard University Press, 1985). Jonathan L. Kvanvig argues against the view that in coherentism all beliefs are basic but fails to challenge the problems Plantinga raises with respect to proper function and truth (Kvanvig, "In Defense of Coherentism," *Journal of Philosophical Research* 22 [1997]: 299-306). Tomoji Shogenji considers the problem of the possibility of malfunction or a misleading cognitive environment where coherent beliefs are less likely to be true. He concludes that coherence may play a significant role in warranting a belief (what he calls "channeling of justification"); however, he agrees with Plantinga that coherence among beliefs does not provide warrant (Shogenji, "The Role of Coherence in Epistemic Justification," *Australasian Journal of Philosophy* 79, no. 1 [2001]: 90-106).

[100] *WCD,* pp. 114-31. Plantinga finds the term *probabilistic coherentism* to be the best description of Bayesianism. Plantinga entertains Bayesian coherentism, but Bayesian probability theory is also the staple of some foundationalist evidentialists. E.g., Timothy and Lydia McGrew, "Strong Foundationalism and Bayesianism," paper presented at the Formal Epistemology Workshop, UC-Berkeley, May 25-28, 2006; and Richard Swinburne, *Epistemic Justification* (Oxford: Oxford University Press, 2001), pp. 102-10.

[101] *WCD,* pp. 162-81. Pollock is particularly in mind.

[102] A favorite BIV scenario for Plantinga is of Alpha Centaurian cognitive superscientists who have the power to manipulate our cognitive faculties so that our beliefs are aimed not at truth but at some other end. See *WCD,* pp. 111-12, 129-31; *WPF,* pp. 24, 28, 52, 58; *WCB,* p. 237.

temically Inflexible Climber.[103] In all these cases either there is an impact to the formation of the experience that presents itself to us or there is an impact to the production of belief on the basis of that experience.[104] Unlike in Gettier problems, what challenges justification in these situations is not the possibility of an unlucky mistake but the possibility of wholesale epistemic unreliability that is entirely beyond our ability to detect or manage. While the examples Plantinga gives are imaginative, colorful and humorous, the epistemic blind spots they expose are to be taken quite seriously. They reveal not merely a potential for deception or malfunction but a situation of radical epistemic dependence, where the justification criteria for knowledge—which connect the way in which a belief arises and the truth of what is being believed—are finally outside of our control. The affinity with Barth on epistemic dependence should be clear: our theory of warrant cannot proceed unilaterally from below. In *Warrant: The Current Debate* Plantinga finds that the positive contemporary proposals for what warrants belief fail to recognize the prominent role of proper function,[105] an essential element of warrant that is outside of our control. His *Warrant and Proper Function* is devoted primarily to developing this notion.

The failure of epistemic justification: unnecessary criteria. So, one of the major problems with contemporary views of justification is that, by ignoring our epistemic dependence on the aptness of our cognitive environments and function, they do not provide sufficient conditions for warrant. But, in addition to being insufficiently prescriptive, they can also be seen to be unnecessarily proscriptive. There are after all several everyday cases of belief that we would all agree are instances of knowing for which most notions of justification are entirely irrelevant. In the development of Plantinga's thought, this takes us back to his first book devoted to a defense of Christian belief: *God and Other Minds.* He begins with an appraisal of the classical arguments of natural theology and natural atheology. He con-

[103] *WCD,* p. 82.

[104] Plantinga distinguishes between "external rationality," which has to do with the formation of the right kind of experience, and "internal rationality," which has to do with the production of the right beliefs on the basis of that experience (*WCB,* pp. 110-12, 255-56).

[105] *WCD,* p. 212.

ıes that there are no noncircular arguments or evidence to support belief either for or against God. Under the common conception of justification, however, in the absence of a reason to support belief, belief must be withheld. At this stage Plantinga had not yet revived the lost distinction between warrant and justification. Nevertheless, the move he makes strikes at the reigning evidentialist, classical foundationalist criteria for justification. Plantinga suggests that our common and mostly uncontested belief in other minds is "in the same epistemological boat"[106] as belief in God. There is no noncircular argument or evidence to which we can appeal in support of our belief that there are other thinking beings. Therefore, if belief in other minds is rational, belief in God may be also.[107] In the 1960s Plantinga had not yet formulated his penetrating objections to classical foundationalism,[108] evidentialism and internalism's accessibility requirement, but he was already raising all of the questions.[109] The conclusion remains the same: fulfilling contemporary criteria for justification is in some cases unnecessary for a belief to count as knowledge. This led to his famous defenses of the proper basicality of belief in God,[110] to his dismantling of the evidentialist objection[111] and finally to his analysis of and constructive work on warrant. The list of counterexamples excluded under the criteria of deontological

---

[106]*GOM,* p. xvi.

[107]Ibid., p. 271. This has been referred to as a "permissive parity argument" (Terence Penelhum, *God and Skepticism: A Study in Skepticism and Fideism,* Philosophical Studies Series in Philosophy 28 [Dordrecht: D. Reidel, 1983], p. 150). It is important to see that Plantinga is not arguing that belief in God is true because it is like belief in other minds, only that there is no reason to disqualify its being accepted in the basic way if we allow that it is rational to accept belief in other minds in the basic way.

[108]As I point out in chapter 2, there is a dangerous ambiguity in our use of the term *foundation.* With respect to foundationalism, *foundation* refers to that set of our beliefs that is properly basic. When I use the term in the sense of theo-foundationalism, however, I mean to refer to the foundation underneath our foundational beliefs, to the indemonstrable anchor that secures the truth of our beliefs—that is, what ultimately serves to warrant our beliefs.

[109]Ironically, after raising these questions, Plantinga interjects, "These are obviously some of the most difficult and persistent problems of epistemology. A direct assault on them would be bold indeed, not to say foolhardy" (*GOM,* p. 188). Of course a direct assault is exactly what Plantinga went on to mount in "Is Belief in God Rational?" in *Rationality and Religious Belief,* ed. C. F. Delaney (Notre Dame, IN: University of Notre Dame Press, 1979), pp. 7-27.

[110]Plantinga, "Is Belief in God Properly Basic?" *Noûs* 15 (1981): 41-51.

[111]RBG (1983).

justification grew from belief in other minds to also include memory beliefs, perceptual judgments, a priori intuitions and beliefs based on introspection, sympathy, moral sense and the like. Plantinga prefers to think of these beliefs as being generated by rational powers or faculties.[112] They are properly basic with respect to the foundations of our knowledge structures in that they are not based on inferences from other beliefs. Plantinga does not reject foundationalism per se.[113] He rejects classical varieties of foundationalism with their overly restrictive legitimizing criteria for basicality and failure to account for what warrants those beliefs.[114] In his constructive model for how Christian belief might have warrant, the means by which we *receive* the knowledge of God are treated as analogous processes that deliver properly basic warranted belief independent of argument or evidence. The counterexamples of memory, introspection and others indicate that knowledge formed in this way is not necessarily deficient.[115] In many cases, for belief to have warrant, it is simply not required that—prior to assent—one fulfill epistemic obligations stipulated by a criterion of justification. What does, however, emerge on Plantinga's account is that the proper functioning of these faculties or processes is *necessary* (though not in and of itself sufficient) for warranting the beliefs they produce. This brings us back once again to the priority of our epistemic *dependence* on the aptness of environments and processes beyond our scope of management or direct perception. What we are specifically dependent on is the purposeful alignment of the contingent elements of our epistemic environments and processes

---

[112]See *WPF,* chaps. 3–9; *WCB,* pp. 145-48.

[113]Plantinga is often classed as a "modest" foundationalist (e.g., David K. Clark, "Faith and Foundationalism," in *The Rationality of Theism*, ed. Paul K. Moser and Paul Copan [London: Routledge, 2003], p. 41). Though Plantinga demolishes strong foundationalism, Kevin Vanhoozer and Bruce Marshall are incorrect to assume that Plantinga is not still rightly considered a foundationalist in his view of the structure of knowledge with respect to basic beliefs. See Bruce Marshall, *Trinity and Truth,* Cambridge Studies in Christian Doctrine (Cambridge: Cambridge University Press, 2000), p. 87; and Kevin J. Vanhoozer, *Is There a Meaning in This Text? The Bible, the Reader, and the Morality of Literary Knowledge* (Grand Rapids: Zondervan, 1998), p. 288.

[114]RBG, pp. 55-63.

[115]When it comes to the knowledge of God, Plantinga argues that belief formed in the properly basic way is stronger than belief that depends on inference (*WCB,* pp. 304-6).

such that they are, in Plantinga's words, "successfully aimed at truth."[116] Foremost, we are dependent on a design plan.

The design plan. I have characterized the place of the design plan in Plantinga's notion of warrant as the ultimate external grounding that provides a purposive connection between belief formation and truth. Warrant is dependent first on this plan and next on cognitive environments and function aligned to it. *Design* may appear to be a theologically loaded term, one that directly implies God or at least a designer agent. Plantinga advises, however, that while design typically connotes "*conscious* design or purpose," it need not initially rule out the possibility that a design plan governing the proper operation of our cognitive faculties was generated by evolution without an origin in active, conscious agency.[117] In other words, the fundamental account of warrant that Plantinga presents is not a particularly Christian account of warrant, nor does it even require theism. This fact alone should raise suspicion about the compatibility of Plantinga's approach with that of Karl Barth. For Barth, we will recall, there is no movement that builds from a general epistemology to a Christian epistemology;[118] there is no clarity gained by standing outside of belief.[119] Earlier in this chapter, however, we concluded that Plantinga also rejects the general starting-point assumption. An oft-made mistake in Plantinga interpretation is to assume that he is building a traditional-style deductive argument to the ultimate conclusion that Christian belief has warrant.[120] What Plantinga is doing is

---

[116]E.g., one of Plantinga's earliest formulations of his warrant proposal, when he was still using Chisholm's term, "positive epistemic status": "what confers positive epistemic status is one's cognitive faculties working properly or working as designed to work *insofar as that segment of design is aimed at producing true beliefs*" (Plantinga, "Justification and Theism," *Faith and Philosophy* 4, no. 4 [1987]: 414, emphasis original). In a more mature form: "a belief has warrant for a person *S* only if that belief is produced in *S* by cognitive faculties functioning properly (subject to no dysfunction) in a cognitive environment that is appropriate for *S*'s kind of cognitive faculties, according to a design plan that is successfully aimed at truth" (*WCB,* p. 156).

[117]*WPF,* pp. 20-21, emphasis original; *WCB,* p. 146. For a detailed analysis of design plan see *WPF,* pp. 11-64.

[118]*CD* I/1, p. 190. See the discussion in chapter 3 on Barth's rejection of the general starting-point assumption.

[119]*CD* I/1, p. 30.

[120]This is a misinterpretation of Plantinga that befalls Richard Swinburne. He believes that the question Plantinga should be tackling is whether Christian belief does in fact have warrant, and he is convinced that the most sensible approach to this question is to argue from the evidence. So when Plantinga speaks of proper function and design, Swinburne seems inclined to under-

nearly the reverse. He is arguing, often inductively, that it is fallacious to require that Christian belief be built on deductive arguments from generally accessible grounds in order for it to have warrant. This does of course make a contribution to philosophy in general as it is an attack against a general philosophical presumption against Christian belief taken in the basic way. It should be clear, however, that Plantinga is not arguing that Christian belief has warrant on the basis of his theory of warrant. It is quite the opposite. As we will encounter in the next chapter, Plantinga goes on to offer a specific Christian model for how Christian belief might have warrant on the account of warrant we have already discussed. Plantinga argues that *if* Christian belief is true, then something like his Christian model of how Christian belief might have warrant is correct.[121] The source of warrant is not an argument given by Plantinga; that would clearly be a circular argument.[122] So too, the fact that Plantinga does not build his Christian model until he has cleared the justification deck and established a new outlook on warrant does not mean that he is arguing from a general principle to a theological one. His Christian model is not deduced from his general model any more than Plantinga's belief that Christian belief has warrant (i.e., is true) is deduced from his Christian model of warrant. The argument flows the other direction. Another way to put this is that Plantinga believes that if he is warranted in believing that he is correct about his general account of warrant itself, it will be because in arriving at that belief the relevant cognitive capacities were operating in a propitious environment according to a design plan—of the God made known in Jesus Christ—which is successfully aimed at truth. While Plantinga is obliged to point out that his general model does not mandate theistic design, it is clear that, *on his view,* the original warrant-generating impetus for all our knowledge is a design of the triune God.[123]

---

stand Plantinga to be treating them as evidence supporting his claims. It is no wonder that Swinburne is unimpressed with the results and misses much of what Plantinga has to offer. See especially Swinburne, "Plantinga on Warrant," p. 2; and Plantinga, "Rationality and Public Evidence: A Reply to Richard Swinburne."

[121]*WCB,* p. 351.

[122]"If the source of the warrant of my Christian belief were this argument, then indeed the project would suffer from vicious circularity. But it isn't, and it doesn't" (ibid., p. 352).

[123]As a bonus, Plantinga gives an argument against the major alternative to his Christian model,

CONCLUSION

In this chapter we have discussed Plantinga's views on the nature of Christian philosophy, his critically realist stance and his general account of warranted belief. We established the key features of Plantinga's solution to the problem of the elusive third criteria for knowledge, resolving the severally necessary and jointly sufficient criteria for beliefs to have warrant. We saw that Plantinga's constructive case is an alternative to the particular inadequacies of traditional views of justification. I argued that, both in Plantinga's views on Christian scholarship and in his general account of warranted belief, Plantinga is aligned with Barth in rejecting specific assumptions of Enlightenment modernism and in confirming the radical epistemic dependence of the human knower.[124]

Plantinga has, furthermore, achieved something that Barth's approach cannot do and might prefer to avoid.[125] As an undertaking in negative apologetics, Plantinga has undercut a host of potential defeaters for Christian belief, those that argue that acceptable Christian belief must meet some traditional version of justification with respect to public evidence or duty.[126]

In *Warranted Christian Belief*, Plantinga stakes out two projects. The first he calls "an exercise in apologetics and the philosophy of religion." My presentation thus far has been confined mostly to this first project.[127]

---

namely, naturalistic evolution. The argument here is that if evolution were somehow responsible for our design plan, there would be no reason to have any confidence that the design plan is aimed at truth rather than evolution's chief motivation, the promotion of survival, adaptive behavior or reproductive fitness (ibid., pp. 227-39).

[124]David Brown also briefly connects Barth and Plantinga in their "rejection of Enlightenment assumptions" (Brown, *Tradition and Imagination: Revelation and Change* [Oxford: Oxford University Press, 1999], p. 10).

[125]The question of the compatibility between Barth and Plantinga on the nature and acceptability of apologetics will be taken up in chapter 7.

[126]"Might I not be perfectly responsible even if I did not always require a reason for belief?" (*WCD*, p. 98). For Plantinga's own assessment of this contribution, see "Internalism, Externalism, Defeaters and Arguments for Christian Belief," p. 399, and "Rationality and Public Evidence: A Reply to Richard Swinburne," p. 222.

[127]The broader apologetical argument that runs throughout *WCB* is that there is no viable objection to the acceptability of Christian belief that does not depend on a refutation of the *truth* of Christian belief. Plantinga challenges the notion that one may remain agnostic about the truth of Christian belief while seeing that there is no acceptable way to arrive at that belief—the idea that, true or not, Christian belief is irrational, unjustified or lacks warrant. Plantinga undermines

In chapter five we will turn to Plantinga's second task, which he calls "an exercise in Christian philosophy," offering "a good way for Christians to think about the epistemology of Christian belief."[128] With respect to the knowledge of God, our chief concern, Barth has pronounced that it "derives and is to be considered only from outside all human possibilities, i.e., from the acting of God Himself."[129] So far we have seen that Plantinga's externalism suggests that the warrant for all human knowing ultimately derives "from outside." The linchpin of Plantinga's epistemology is the design plan, tailored to suitable environments, successfully aiming at truth. In Plantinga's view it is this divine design, from "outside all human possibilities," that enables the possibility of human knowing. It is now time to look at whether and in what way Plantinga sees the knowledge of God to be divinely initiated self-revelation—"from the acting of God Himself."

---

this position by showing that the only viable option for such an alethically neutral argument would be in the area of warrant. On the model Plantinga defends, however, the only way to show that Christian belief lacks warrant is to argue against the truth of the belief itself (*WCB*, pp. viii-xiii).

[128] Ibid., p. xiii.

[129] *CD* I/1, p. 38.

5

PLANTINGA'S EPISTEMOLOGY OF CHRISTIAN BELIEF

The Warrant of Revelation

◆

The discussion of Plantinga's constructive proposal with respect to acquiring theistic and specifically Christian belief will be limited to the scope of our chief concern—that of understanding its consonance with Barth's theology of revelation, with a view to a unified response to the epistemological issues facing theology. For this reason, I will present its primary components with minimal treatment of the numerous debates it has spawned.

We begin with two important cautions for approaching Plantinga's theological proposal. The first applies to the proposal itself; the second regards the wider philosophical argument within which the proposal is situated. Following these comments we will briefly consider what latitude Plantinga allows philosophy in challenging Christian belief, before finally moving into a discussion of his positive theological proposal.

PRELIMINARY CAUTIONS

Caution 1: an intentionally underspecified proposal. What Plantinga gives us in chapters six through nine of *Warranted Christian Belief* is a theological account of how theistic or Christian belief is formed in believers. Theologians in particular, however, should be warned that Plantinga is nowhere attempting to present a thoroughgoing, fully nuanced theological system. In order to understand Plantinga and conduct a judicious assessment of the compatibility of his work with Barth's theology of revelation, it is important to note just what Plantinga is and is not intending to do. Far from a detailed theology of revelation, all Plantinga needs for his purposes is a rough model of how things might go—just enough to show how a theistic or Christian belief could meet his general criteria for warrant. He does give us, in fact, quite a bit more than this. To begin with, he provides not just *a* model, but two models. The first is intended to show how generally theistic belief might have warrant. This model is then extended into a second model, giving an account of how explicitly Christian belief could have warrant.[1] Although some have complained about the minimalist character of Plantinga's models,[2] Plantinga could have held himself to a far more generic account, or no model at all.[3] It would have been sufficient for Plantinga's core argument simply to have suggested that if Christian belief is true then it is probable that there are special cognitive faculties and processes divinely designed to impart true beliefs about God and central Christian teachings. If this is so, then warrant for theistic and Christian belief may come about by the proper function of these special cognitive operations, in the basic way.

Plantinga, nevertheless, chooses to give a model, where these special, divinely designed, cognitive operations are named and described. He paints in broad brushstrokes the contours of an inclusive, though Reformed-leaning, theological proposal, noting particularly the contributions of Aquinas and Calvin. As an exercise in *Christian* philosophy, Plantinga is attempting to show that his account of how beliefs have warrant not only is philosophically defensible but also fits with the way in which the warranting operations for Christian belief proceed according to standard Christian teaching. Providing a model has the advantage of

---

[1]From the perspective of Christian theology these two models represent the classical though potentially distorting division between general and special revelation—the Book of Nature and the Book of Scripture.

[2]E.g., James K. Beilby, *Epistemology as Theology: An Evaluation of Alvin Plantinga's Religious Epistemology* (Aldershot, UK: Ashgate, 2005), pp. 135-36.

[3]Plantinga reminds those who criticize his model for not defining the relationship between divine action and human freedom that "the fewer such stands it takes the better; for the fewer such stands it takes the weaker the main premises of my argument are; and the weaker the premises are (provided they do in fact warrant the conclusion) the stronger the argument is" (Plantinga, "Internalism, Externalism, Defeaters and Arguments for Christian Belief," *Philosophia Christi* 3, no. 2 [2001]: 395).

giving not merely principles but also a tangible way to think Christianly about how Christian beliefs might legitimately be taken as knowledge, and, as one might expect, the model outlines Plantinga's own theological views on the matter. For this reason, it seems fair to include Plantinga's proposal in our theological discussion and assessment while recognizing that it is intentionally underspecified. We should certainly not expect that Plantinga's theological proposal would be as comprehensive as Barth's. Consequently, our line of questioning will focus on the conformity of Plantinga's affirmations with Barth's main concerns and an overall evaluation of the compatibility and contribution of Plantinga's approach. Plantinga's theological proposal is intentionally underspecified because of the role it plays in his wider philosophical argument. This may have the ring of theology being pressed into the service of philosophy. Whether this violates a Barthian anathema, however, will depend on whether the shape of the philosophical argument grants the appropriate freedom and priority to theology. We move now to our second caution.

Caution 2: what the argument is. In what immediately follows I will only be referring to Plantinga's argument with respect to his extended model for how specifically Christian belief may have warrant. What I say, however, also applies mutatis mutandis to Plantinga's model for merely theistic belief. In our discussion of the place of the design plan as fundamental to warrant, I noted that it is sometimes mistakenly assumed that Plantinga is building a deductive argument that would provide persuasive reasons to conclude that Christian belief is in fact warranted. It is worth repeating here that the flow and intent of the argument is quite unlike a traditional, evidentialist apologetic.[4] Plantinga's chief aim is not to present a case, or provide an argument, for why it is we should favor his specific theological proposal over other alternatives. As we have seen, Plantinga has done a good deal of precise philosophical work to develop a rigorous general account of warrant.

[4]Plantinga's approach could be construed as a kind of externalist evidentialism if the notion of evidence is allowed a wider sense than merely propositional evidence, such that memory, sense perception and faith might all be cognitive operations that make the truth of the matter *evident*, the deliverances of which could therefore be considered *evidence*. Evidence understood in this way refers generally to the *grounds* for one's belief. See Plantinga, "Is Belief in God Properly Basic?" *Noûs* 15 (1981): 44-45.

He is in a position now to consider whether specifically Christian belief could be warranted on this account, and warranted in the basic way. Again, the argument here is inductive in shape. Plantinga is not starting from outside belief in an attempt to show the skeptic that Christian belief does in fact have warrant. This would be to show how Christian belief can be accepted on the basis of an inference from some generally accepted starting point. Plantinga frankly admits that he knows of no such arguments the strength of which would warrant Christian belief.[5] "Of course this is nothing against either their truth or their warrant; very little of what we believe can be 'demonstrated' or 'shown.'"[6] The tactic Plantinga adopts, therefore, is to give a hypothetical account of how it could be that Christian belief might arise from cognitive processes operating in the right kind of environment according to a design plan successfully aimed at truth. The power of the hypothetical model Plantinga chooses is that, being itself a piece of Christian theology, it relies on the truth of Christian belief. What this secures for Plantinga is that if—independent of the argument—Christian belief is true, then it follows that Christian belief likely does have warrant either in the way described, or in some similar way.[7] As suggested earlier, this is not a circular argument because the argument itself is not trying to provide the warrant for Christian belief.[8] On the contrary, the argument is aiming to reveal how it could be that no argument is required for Christian belief to have warrant. Plantinga's argument is that if warrant for Christian belief were in fact obtained in the way suggested in standard Christian teaching, then the believer would be warranted to believe in the basic way and not as the conclusion of some chain of inference.

---

[5]*WCB*, pp. 170, 201, 499. "Any argument for its warrant, therefore, would also be an argument for its truth. But I don't know of good philosophical arguments for the claim that Christian belief is true (and I don't know of conclusive philosophical arguments for the claim that theism is true); hence I can't sensibly argue that Christian belief is in fact warranted. Of course my not knowing of any such arguments is wholly compatible with my knowing that both Christian and theistic belief are, in fact true, and in my better moments, I think, I do know that they are" (Plantinga, "Internalism, Externalism, Defeaters and Arguments for Christian Belief," p. 387).

[6]*WCB*, p. 170.

[7]Ibid., p. 285.

[8]Ibid., pp. 351-52.

The notion of holding Christian beliefs in the basic way strikes many Christian philosophers as a rather weak position to take. They presume that Christian belief, like any belief, would have a stronger footing if it were supported by reasons in the form of a good argument.[9] To these detractors, Plantinga's project appears to be a trivial diversion from the more important task of providing reasons to think that Christian belief is true. Swinburne complains that the real question is whether Christian beliefs actually do have warrant: "[Plantinga] has shown that they do, if they are true; so we might hope for discussion of whether they are true."[10] (It is worth noting that Swinburne makes a similar request of Barth.[11]) James Beilby is similarly troubled that while Plantinga argues that Christian belief is a viable epistemic option, "he does not address the reasons to think that the Christian worldview is not only permitted but true, persuasive, compelling."[12] Still others regret that Plantinga's approach leaves him unable to affirm the truth of Christian belief, or the possibility of knowing that one knows that it is true.[13] These are important objections, all of which fail adequately to appreciate the nature of Christian belief, whose warrant derives from God's revealing action. Briefly responding to these objections will help to underscore our point of caution with respect to Plantinga's argument and reinforce the compatibility here between Barth and Plantinga.

Plantinga nowhere claims that arguments or evidence cannot provide some support for Christian belief.[14] His chief objection is to the *requirement* that it *must* be supported by ulterior propositional inference in

---

[9]Deane-Peter Baker develops this criticism of Plantinga as the "Inadequacy Thesis" (Baker, "Plantinga's Reformed Epistemology: What's the Question?" *International Journal for Philosophy of Religion* 57 [2005]: 77-103).

[10]Richard Swinburne, "Plantinga on Warrant," review of *Warranted Christian Belief*, by Alvin Plantinga, *Religious Studies* 37 (2001): 206.

[11]See Richard Swinburne, *Revelation: From Metaphor to Analogy*, 2nd ed. (Oxford: Clarendon Press, 2007), pp. 360-61.

[12]Beilby, *Epistemology as Theology*, pp. 141-42.

[13]R. Douglas Geivett and Greg Jesson, "Plantinga's Externalism and the Terminus of Warrant-Based Epistemology," *Philosophia Christi* 3, no. 2 (2001): 331. In the same volume we find Richard Fumerton's dissatisfaction with Plantinga's approach in its failing to give some "assurance of truth" (Fumerton, "Plantinga, Warrant, and Christian Belief," *Philosophia Christi* 3, no. 2 [2001]: 351). See note 30 below on the "KK-thesis."

[14]"Of course they *could* be accepted on the basis of other propositions, and perhaps in some cases are" (*WCB*, p. 250, emphasis original).

order to have warrant sufficient for knowledge.[15] As we have already noted, Plantinga's pronouncements against natural theology are more modest than Barth's.[16] But Plantinga does clearly take exception to the presumption that Christian beliefs would have a stronger footing if they were accepted on the basis of inference from propositional evidence rather than in the basic way. Unless one were operating under coherentist assumptions,[17] it seems unlikely that ulterior inferential support could in every case enhance the strength of a belief. If this were so, then nonbasic beliefs would be stronger than the basic beliefs from which they derive their strength by inference. In fact, if there is a margin for error in the process of inference, nonbasic beliefs will be less secure than the beliefs supporting them.[18] Plantinga argues that if Christian beliefs can be properly basic, then the "most satisfactory way to hold them will not be as the conclusions of argument."[19] When warrant is obtained by a divinely designed and intended doxastic experience whereby the truth of Christian propositions becomes apparent without inference from other propositions, there is an analogy to direct perception.[20] The warrant for the belief is obtained by a process wherein the believer is enabled immediately to apprehend the truth of the belief. If that apprehension is sufficiently clear, then, because this kind of belief is more direct[21] than one that is *mediated* by inference, it is arguably a firmer and more satisfactory way to believe—in the same way that seeing for oneself is superior to depending on external testimony.[22] This echoes Barth's contention that

---

[15]Ibid., p. 93.

[16]I have reserved chapter 7 for an extensive discussion of this tension.

[17]The coherentist would not make this claim to begin with. On this view, coherence itself, and not inferential support, is crucial to the degree of warrant a belief enjoys. See *WCD,* pp. 79-80, where Plantinga also explains that coherentism is, in fact, a special case of foundationalism, "the variety according to which the only source of warrant is coherence."

[18]Plantinga takes this further in noting that arguments from historical evidence depend on a chain of "dwindling" probabilities (*WCB,* pp. 271-80).

[19]Ibid., p. 210. Plantinga seems to agree with Calvin's view that, as Plantinga puts it, "the Christian ought not to believe on the basis of argument; if he does, his faith is likely to be unstable and wavering" (Plantinga, "The Reformed Objection to Natural Theology," in *Philosophical Knowledge* [Washington, DC: American Catholic Philosophical Association, 1980], p. 53).

[20]Unlike perception in its phenomenal imagery, but analogically related to perception in being a direct apprehension (*WCB,* pp. 181, 286-89).

[21]Ibid., pp. 259, 262.

[22]This position is strengthened further by Plantinga's treatment of the affective aspect of the gift of faith, which we have not yet discussed. Here it is not merely the truth of the proposition that

a knowledge grounded in the free act of God's grace is more secure than one anchored in something we independently possess.

So for Plantinga, believing in the basic way is superior, though he does not deny that some basic beliefs could receive additional warrant by means of an argument from inference. Plantinga appeals to Calvin's notion that arguments might serve as secondary confirmations or aids.[23] Historical evidence for the resurrection, for instance, could boost the warrant one has for believing it.[24] But in Plantinga's view, while such arguments could play a supporting and secondary role, they would in no way be sufficient on their own to deliver the kind of warrant necessary for knowledge and paradigmatic Christian belief. An argument from public evidence might show that Christian belief is somewhat more probable than not, but this "is insufficient for its being warrantedly believed with *any* degree of firmness."[25] In summary, Plantinga's argument is that Christian belief can be properly held on grounds that are in fact firmer than the insufficient though not insignificant warrant delivered by propositional or historical evidence.

Returning now to Plantinga's detractors, Swinburne, Beilby, Geivett, Fumerton and others criticize Plantinga for giving insufficient attention to the question of the truth of Christian belief. For Plantinga along with Barth, however, the truth of the matter is paramount. As Plantinga affirms, "this is *the* really important question."[26] Plantinga's whole program is designed to move the question of the truth of Christianity back to center stage, by undercutting the objections to the knowability of that

---

is made evident but also its loveliness, beauty and desirability. This affective component is also more satisfactorily arrived at in the immediate, basic way rather than on the basis of argument. See ibid., pp. 304-6.

[23]Alvin Plantinga, "Christian Philosophy at the End of the Twentieth Century," in *Christian Philosophy at the Close of the Twentieth Century: Assessment and Perspective,* ed. Sander Griffioen and Bert M. Balk (Kampen, Netherlands: Uitgeverij Kok, 1995), pp. 39-40; Plantinga, "Internalism, Externalism, Defeaters and Arguments for Christian Belief," p. 385; and Plantinga, "Reply," *Philosophical Books* 43, no. 2 (2002): 127 n. 4.

[24]In his response to Stephen Wykstra, Plantinga writes, "So suppose I'm a beneficiary of the IIHS [internal instigation of the Holy Spirit], but the warrant enjoyed by my belief in the resurrection doesn't come up to the standard for knowledge: learning of the historical evidence could bring it up to that standard" (Plantinga, "Reply," p. 128).

[25]Alvin Plantinga, "Rationality and Public Evidence: A Reply to Richard Swinburne," *Religious Studies* 37 (2001): 220, emphasis original. See also *WCB,* pp. 271, 274, 280, 379.

[26]*WCB,* p. 499, emphasis mine.

truth. One of the leading objections to knowability is the imposed requirement that knowledge requires a supporting reason in the form of a good argument. Beneath the charge that Plantinga has skirted the question of truth is the underlying assumption that without a good argument the grounds for a belief are less than satisfactory. But this is just what Plantinga is arguing against.[27] And this brings us nicely back to the main point of caution. We cannot confuse believing without propositional evidence with believing without any grounds whatsoever. Here the notion of *a reason* can be employed misleadingly.

If we take an R1 reason to mean a propositional argument, then it is correct to say that Plantinga is arguing that we can know that Christian belief is true without an R1 reason. But taken in this sense, as Plantinga notes in his response to Fumerton, God's own beliefs are not based on R1 reasons.[28] Instead, God's knowledge is grounded in his very nature, which leads us to the other sense in which a reason may be taken, R2 reason: the grounding or warranting connection between our beliefs and the truth of the matter. Taken in this way, it is not at all the case that believers are without a reason for believing as they do. The R2 reason for belief, according to Plantinga's theological proposal, is grounded in cognitive operations designed by God to deliver true belief. When operating without impedance, this R2 reason is far better than the R1 reason any argument could supply.[29] The implication is, of course, that the demonstration of the truth of Christian belief is something we *receive* and not something we could supply ourselves. It is not that Plantinga does not

[27]This central point is somehow missed for those like Thomas McHugh Reed who fail to grasp one of Plantinga's most fundamental assertions—that there may be nonpropositional grounds for belief. See Thomas McHugh Reed, "Christianity and Agnosticism," *International Journal for Philosophy of Religion* 52 (2002): 81-95. See also, John Zeis, "A Critique of Plantinga's Theological Foundationalism," *Philosophy of Religion* 28 (1990): 173-89.

[28]Plantinga, "Internalism, Externalism, Defeaters and Arguments for Christian Belief," p. 390.

[29]In Paul Helm's discussion of Plantinga's deployment of Calvin's *sensus divinitatis,* he seems to miss the significance of this distinction between R1 and R2 reasons—which in his discussion features as the distinction between grounds and evidence. Neither Plantinga nor Calvin suggests that belief may be reasonless. Furthermore, Plantinga's appeal to Calvin is not to prove the factual existence of a divinely designed faculty, as Helm worries, but to indicate precedence in the Christian theological tradition for the possibility of noetic equipment designed to yield properly basic belief in God. The fact that Calvin does not theorize about rationality does not prevent Plantinga from drawing the epistemological implications out of an ontological claim. See Helm, *Faith and Understanding* (Edinburgh: Edinburgh University Press, 1997), pp. 188-89, 197-201.

that Christian belief is true, or even know that he knows.[30] ...hat Plantinga believes that the grounds for his knowledge ...n of Christian belief are, to use his phrase, “beyond the competence of philosophy.”[31] He claims that (at least in his “better moments”[32]) he knows the truth of Christian belief in the basic way, and he claims to show *how* his beliefs could have sufficient warrant for knowledge. What he does not claim to show is *that* his beliefs are true.[33] And so it is in fact in deference to the importance of the truth of the matter that Plantinga holds that a sufficient human demonstration of its truth is not possible. Using the resources of the historic Christian tradition to support his theological proposal, Plantinga's argument shows that the answer to the key question about the truth of Christian belief, vainly sought in the weak demonstrations of human argument, is properly received from God above—exactly as Barth would have it.

The extended cautions at the outset of this chapter amount to a reminder that the warrant for Plantinga's model and Plantinga's wider argument ultimately derives from the action of God himself. This rec-

---

[30]Plantinga need not accept the suggestion made by Geivett and Jesson (“Plantinga's Externalism and the Terminus of Warrant-Based Epistemology,” pp. 330-31) that his externalism limits him from being able to know that he knows that Christian belief is true. Notice how a typically evidentialist conception of knowing is smuggled into this charge. The question seems reasonable: “how do you know that you know that what you believe is true?” But what kind of answer do we think we need? Why should an R1 reason be required for knowledge about knowledge? Clearly if first-order knowledge can be warranted for the externalist in the basic way then so could all other reflection on the status of that knowledge. The externalist can know *that* without knowing *how* and without having an R1 reason. This applies equally as well to knowing that one knows in Hintikka's famous “KK-thesis.” See Jaakko Hintikka, *Knowledge and Belief: An Introduction to the Logic of the Two Notions,* Contemporary Philosophy (Ithaca, NY: Cornell University Press, 1962), p. 28; and Risto Hilpinen, “Knowing That One Knows and the Classical Definition of Knowledge,” *Synthese* 21, no. 2 (1970): 109-32. Plantinga does in fact provide a way in which one might have an R1 reason for thinking that a warrant-basic belief has warrant (*WCB,* pp. 347-48). The premise from which the inference flows is itself taken in the basic way and provides by inference the R1 reason for the belief that one knows that one knows. Furthermore, this is exactly how Plantinga himself is arguing. Nevertheless, since the premise of the argument—which is the theological model—is taken in the basic way, the whole argument rests on whether the premise is the divinely given truth of the matter. Truth, which only God can demonstrate, is back at center stage. Similarly Barth notes that dogmatics “realises that all its knowledge, even its knowledge of the correctness of its knowledge, can only be an event, and cannot therefore be guaranteed as correct knowledge from any place apart from or above this event” (*CD* I/1, p. 42).

[31]*WCB,* p. 499.

[32]Plantinga, “Internalism, Externalism, Defeaters and Arguments for Christian Belief,” p. 387.

[33]*WCB,* p. 169.

ognition yields another significant intersection between Barth and Plantinga. In the third chapter we noted that while Barth concedes a priority to the epistemic question, in seeking its answer he remains committed to the fundamental ontological priority of the object of theological knowing. Plantinga draws the same conclusion. As we have seen, his argument has value, whether or not one is prepared to accept the truth of the premises. The *possibility* that Christian belief could have warrant in the way described undercuts the de jure objection. The stronger conclusion, that Christian belief does indeed have warrant, depends on whether one is willing to accept the truth of the premises. Since warrant for the premise is obtained in the basic way and not by argument, it is the case, as Plantinga says, that "the dispute as to whether theistic belief is rational (warranted) can't be settled just by attending to epistemological considerations." And so he concludes that "it is at bottom not merely an epistemological dispute, but an ontological or theological dispute."[34] One's theological, metaphysical commitments will determine what one will accept to be legitimate warrant-conferring conditions (which is of course an independent question from whether they in fact do confer warrant). The priority of ontology is what motivates Plantinga's argument and supports the conclusion that any successful objection to Christian belief must be aimed at the truth of the belief and not the epistemic inadequacy of its formation.[35]

PLANTINGA'S A/C MODEL OF THEISTIC BELIEF

Plantinga's theological proposal comes, as I have said, in two parts. The first part is a model, the Aquinas/Calvin (A/C) model, intended to explain how belief in God, broadly conceived, might have warrant. The second part is said to be an extension of this first model, the extended A/C model, describing how explicitly Christian belief could be war-

[34]Ibid., p. 190. "So if we trace the epistemological question back we find (with apologies to John Austin) an ontological question grinning residually up at us from the bottom of the mug" (Plantinga, "The Prospects for Natural Theology," *Philosophical Perspectives* 5 [1991]: 309).

[35]Cf. *WCB,* p. 191. See also William Alston's discussion of the relationship between metaphysics and epistemology in Plantinga's model (Alston, "Epistemology and Metaphysics," in *Knowledge and Reality: Essays in Honor of Alvin Plantinga,* ed. Thomas Crisp, Matthew Davidson and David Vander Laan [Dordrecht: Kluwer Academic, 2006], pp. 81-87).

ranted. As the name implies, the extended A/C model bears a relation to the A/C model, though it is clearly a different model altogether. It is correct to view Plantinga's proposal not as one model with two parts but as two discrete models, the second having an impact on the first. We will treat the A/C model and the extended A/C model separately, bearing in mind that all Plantinga hopes to achieve is an account that grows out of Christian teaching itself, an account that would explain the possibility that a given basic belief is the result of truth-oriented, environmentally suited, belief-producing operations[36] working according to plan.

The A/C model: overview. The key feature of Plantinga's A/C model is what Thomas Aquinas refers to as a general though confused knowledge of God "implanted in us by nature"[37] and what John Calvin calls a "sense of divinity" (*sensus divinitatis*) that is "engraved upon men's minds."[38] Neither Aquinas nor Calvin gives a detailed epistemological account of how this implanted knowledge arises in the human knower. It is, as Calvin says, "naturally inborn in all." Plantinga seems a bit unsatisfied with this notion of immediate implantation.[39] Instead, he originally refers to the *sensus divinitatis* as a "strong tendency or inclination toward belief"[40] and, in his exposition of the A/C model, as a "kind of faculty or a cognitive mechanism . . . which in a wide variety of circumstances produces in us beliefs about God."[41] Rather than interpreting *sensus divinitatis* merely to be a generally "numinous awareness of God"[42] implanted as a "seed of religion,"[43] Plantinga conceives of a faculty that is similar to our senses, in that it operates under certain trig-

[36]The word *operations* is chosen here to be more general than Plantinga's terms *faculty* and *process*, which are associated each with the A/C model and extended A/C model, respectively.

[37]For Aquinas, by this implanted knowledge we know of God's existence without being clear on exactly who God is (Aquinas, *Summa Theologica*, trans. Fathers of the English Dominican Province [New York: Benziger Bros., 1947], 1.2.1).

[38]John Calvin, *Institutes of the Christian Religion*, ed. John T. McNeill, trans. Ford Lewis Battles, Library of Christian Classics (London: SCM Press, 1961), 1.3.3.

[39]Immediate knowledge does not mean an unmediated experience of God but may refer to an implanted knowing that is not dependent on triggering conditions. What Plantinga has in mind does involve triggering conditions.

[40]RBG, p. 66.

[41]*WCB*, p. 172.

[42]From the translator's note on "*divinitatis sensum*," Calvin, *Institutes*, 1.3.3 n. 189.

[43]Calvin, *Institutes*, 1.4.1.

gering conditions. These conditions might range widely from an encounter with the wonders of creation to an experience of guilt or spontaneous thanksgiving.[44] Unlike a faculty of empirical sensation, Plantinga's *sensus divinitatis* does not give us a perception of God.[45] The triggering experience is only the occasion for the formation of true beliefs about God, beliefs that of course entail God's existence.

Another way to put this is that, while "the operation of the *sensus divinitatis* will always involve the presence of experience of some kind,"[46] our external rationality with respect to the *sensus divinitatis* does not regard the proper formation of phenomenal experience but only the proper formation of doxastic experience occasioned by it. Other noetic faculties deliver phenomenal experience, but the phenomenal experience they deliver is inseparable from their exhortation to belief. The relative strength of the belief recommendation is proportionate to the strength or clarity of the experience. For this reason Plantinga uses the term *doxastic experience.*[47] What is delivered by the *sensus divinitatis,* triggered as it is by various experiences, is not a perception of God but a doxastic experience of some truth about God.

Plantinga claims that the *sensus divinitatis* in his A/C model does the work that he needs done. It details a cognitive faculty that is part of God's design for human beings that, when functioning properly under certain conditions, produces warranted belief in the existence of God.[48] Plantinga concedes, as do Calvin and Aquinas, that there is one major problem with the *sensus divinitatis,* namely, that the human fall into sin has rendered this way of knowing largely if not completely inoperative.[49] Hopes for restoring this cognitive faculty to proper function are dependent on work done in the extended A/C

---

[44] *WCB,* p. 174.
[45] Ibid., pp. 180-84
[46] Ibid., p. 183.
[47] *Doxastic* derives from the Greek δόξα, having to do with opinion or belief. I thank Luke Tallon for reminding me that in the Septuagint and New Testament, δόξα is also used to refer to the glory of God. Plantinga never exploits this double meaning, but one could argue that the doxastic experience of the *sensus divinitatis* or the instigation of the Holy Spirit involves an encounter with the glory of God motivating true belief.
[48] *WCB,* pp. 179, 186.
[49] Ibid., pp. 184-86.

model by the Holy Spirit. Given the possibility that the noetic effects of sin may be sufficiently overcome to allow the adequate function of the *sensus divinitatis,* the A/C model is successful in explaining how it is that a general belief in God might be warranted. There remains, however, a number of important questions to ask about the A/C model. We will begin with a look at Plantinga's requirement for triggering conditions, then turn to reservations about the success of the A/C model, and finally note the tensions in the A/C model with Barth's theology of revelation.

The A/C model: acquired not implanted knowledge. Why is it that Plantinga seems to show an aversion to the notion of a merely implanted or inborn knowledge of God, preferring instead a faculty operating on the occasion of certain experiences? He appears to combine affirmations that in Aquinas and Calvin are kept separate.[50] Aquinas reasons that our being led to desire a happiness that can only be fulfilled in God implies an implanted form of the knowledge of God.[51] This implanted knowledge is different from the general knowledge of God that is acquired as a function of natural reason in consideration of the ways in which God is evidenced by his effects.[52] Likewise, for Calvin, there is a distinction between a knowledge of God that is a "deposit in our minds" and the manifestation of "his perfections in the whole structure of the universe."[53] Plantinga's move to combine these two elements into one

---

[50]Plantinga has been roundly criticized for misinterpreting Calvin on exactly this point; thus, James P. Moreland and William Lane Craig charge that Plantinga "seriously misrepresents Calvin on this score" (Moreland and Craig, *Philosophical Foundations for a Christian Worldview* [Downers Grove, IL: InterVarsity Press, 2003], p. 168). Michael L. Czapkay Sudduth criticizes Plantinga for failing to observe a distinction between the *implanted* knowledge Calvin speaks of in chapter 3 of book 1 of the *Institutes* and the *acquired* knowledge of God in chapter 5 (Sudduth, "Plantinga's Revision of the Reformed Tradition: Rethinking Our Natural Knowledge of God," *Philosophical Books* 42, no. 2 [2002]: 83-84).

[51]"To know that God exists in a general and confused way is implanted in us by nature, inasmuch as God is man's beatitude. For man naturally desires happiness, and what is naturally desired by man must be naturally known to him" (Aquinas, *Summa Theologica* 1.2.1). See also Aquinas, *Summa contra Gentiles* 1.5.1.

[52]"The existence of God, in so far as it is not self-evident to us, can be demonstrated from those of His effects which are known to us" (Aquinas, *Summa Theologica* 1.2.2). It is this nonimplanted knowledge that is in view in the passage Plantinga cites (*WCB,* p. 170 n. 3; 176-77), *Summa contra Gentiles* 3.38.

[53]Calvin, *Institutes,* 1.5.1.

capacity, while possibly obscuring Calvin's distinction,[54] helps to avoid a potential misinterpretation of Calvin on general revelation. Calvin nowhere suggests that unaided human reason by inference from the data of experience can demonstrate the truth of propositions about God. If the capacity of the *sensus divinitatis* is not operative in beholding the manifestations of God in creation, it would tend to promote the conclusion that the warrant for such beliefs as are triggered by experience comes by way of inference rather than the operation of a divine gift. Not only would this misrepresent Calvin (and Aquinas), but it would also be entirely unhelpful to Plantinga's contention that arguments for God's existence are not strong enough alone to support full-fledged Christian belief.[55] The price of placing Calvin's two notions under one heading appears to be the loss of a *sensus divinitatis* that might operate without triggering conditions. Michael Sudduth challenges Plantinga on just this point with the suggestion that Plantinga ignores Calvin's notion of "implanted knowledge," replacing it with an "innate capacity."[56] But is an implanted knowledge wholly without conditions really possible?

Consider how the notion of implanted knowledge might fit into Plantinga's own highly nuanced, general account of knowledge. In Plantinga's view, knowledge and belief are inextricably linked. It is impossible that one could know something without believing it. Aquinas and Calvin employ the term *knowledge* without honed epistemological constraints, such that an innate knowledge can be present without belief.[57] This is not a knowledge such as the demons may have, which involves assent but fails to have the appropriate affective response. It is a knowledge that coincides with an utter lack of cognitive assent, a lack of

[54]Plantinga's chief aim is not Calvin exegesis; "whatever Calvin thinks, however, it's our model" (*WCB*, p. 173). Nevertheless, Plantinga defends his interpretation against Sudduth's critique: "I'm no Calvin scholar, but I doubt that he intended a distinction between the knowledge of God as proposed in Chapter 3 and that affirmed in Chapter 5" (Plantinga, "Reply," p. 134).

[55]Plantinga is willing to countenance variations on his model that might involve a "quick inference" or a further boost in warrant from argument; but, in each case, inference alone is not sufficient (*WCB*, p. 176; Plantinga, "Reply," p. 128).

[56]Sudduth, "Plantinga's Revision of the Reformed Tradition," pp. 83-84.

[57]"In the present day not a few are found who deny the being of a God, yet, whether they will or not, they occasionally feel the truth which they are desirous not to know" (Calvin, *Institutes*, 1.3.2).

assent that is described as a denial or suppression of what is known.[58] Implanted knowledge of this kind is not implanted belief. What Calvin seems to have in mind at points would not be called knowledge in Plantinga's system but is rather something more like access to, or an intuitive grasp of, the truthfulness of some propositions about God—in other words, a given capacity. As Calvin describes it, even those in unbelief, "occasionally feel the truth which they are desirous not to know."[59] Furthermore, as Plantinga points out, it is "a bit far-fetched" to suggest that this capacity is producing belief from the moment of birth.[60] If what we are really talking about is an implanted capacity to grasp the truthfulness of some propositions about God, then environmental conditions do apply after all. Beliefs would not issue at some arbitrary stage but arise as one begins to grasp the meaning of the propositions whose truthfulness the *sensus divinitatis* enables one to "feel." In order to grasp the meaning of propositions about God, it could be argued, requires having experiences, maybe even the kinds of experiences that in Plantinga's model operate as triggers for belief.[61] So while Plantinga's A/C model may somewhat obscure a distinction in Calvin, there is no impact to the thrust of Calvin on general revelation, affirming an indispensable, though merely indirect, role for experience in the operation of a divinely de-

[58]On either view, it is agreed that the failure of the deliverances of the *sensus divinitatis* to result in belief is due to a disruption in proper function caused by sin, impairing the formation of the right doxastic experience and disrupting the correct formation of belief on the basis of it. Plantinga discusses these two impairments as the damage done to the *sensus divinitatis* on the one hand and a resistance to its deliverances on the other (*WCB,* p. 205).

[59]Calvin, *Institutes*, 1.3.2.

[60]Plantinga, "Reply," p. 134. Also see *WCB,* p. 173.

[61]If this is correct, then the beliefs formed by Calvin's *sensus divinitatis* would be more like the deliverances of reason, a priori beliefs that are formed "independently of experience" (*WPF,* p. 103). In an early exchange with Peter Losin, Plantinga withholds from the suggestion that belief in God's existence might be on the basis of seeing the truth of the proposition as with a priori beliefs. Instead he offers the knowledge we have by way of memory as a more favorable analogue (Plantinga, "Reformed Epistemology Again," *Reformed Journal* 32 [1982]: 8). In *WCB,* p. 173, however, Plantinga makes the analogy to our capacity for arithmetical knowledge. In the reply to Sudduth, Plantinga calls attention to the resemblance the question bears to the debate between Locke and Leibniz over innate ideas and registers a preference for an interpretation of Leibniz where knowledge emerges in response to experience (Plantinga, "Reply," pp. 122-35). What appears to be least appealing to Plantinga about implantation is the lack of explanation for the emergence of beliefs from it. This, I believe, is addressed if we understand Calvin's chapter 3 *sensus divinitatis* to refer to a capacity to grasp the truth of some propositions about God, a capacity that requires cognitive development to the point of understanding the meaning of those propositions.

signed, innate capacity.[62] This leaves open, of course, the question of the extent of the damage done by sin, which we will touch on next.

The A/C model: is it successful? We now turn to the question of whether the A/C model is sufficient for the purposes of Plantinga's wider argument. The most apparent weakness of the A/C model is one that is only exposed by the *extended* A/C model, for specifically Christian belief, where the noetic effects of sin are detailed. Sin has "damaged and deformed" the *sensus divinitatis* and twisted us to resist its deliverances.[63] Some Calvin scholars suggest that Calvin saw no role for the *sensus divinitatis* in a postlapsarian knowledge of God.[64] Plantinga does not see it this way. For Plantinga, it is merely that, because of sin and its noetic effects, the A/C model is "incomplete."[65] For the *sensus divinitatis* to yield some true belief about God first requires healing from this damage, which is a work of the Holy Spirit. Because of sin, the A/C model cannot stand alone but is dependent on components of the extended A/C model to function.[66] This is, however, not the most common objection to the success of the A/C model. The most common objection is that the A/C model fails to yield precisely what it must yield to serve Plantinga's argument: properly basic belief.

This objection comes in many varieties, all of which suggest that on the A/C model beliefs about God may still involve some kind of evidential support and are therefore, by definition, not basic. This objection, in most cases, is meant to apply to the extended A/C model as well. The most common formulations are as follows. First, some worry that unlike those beliefs arising directly from the proposed analogues—memory, sense perception and a priori intuition—beliefs arising from the *sensus divinitatis* are indirect, being grounded in some kind of perceptual or

---

[62]At least on this point, Sudduth's charge that Plantinga has revised the Reformed position on the natural knowledge of God fails to convince. We will encounter the Reformed position again vis-à-vis natural theology in chapter 7.

[63]*WCB*, p. 205.

[64]These scholars suggest that the impact of the noetic effects of sin on the *sensus divinitatis* is total (John Beversluis, "Reforming the 'Reformed' Objection to Natural Theology," *Faith and Philosophy* 12, no. 2 [1995]: 193-94; and Derek S. Jeffreys, "How Reformed Is Reformed Epistemology? Alvin Plantinga and Calvin's 'Sensus Divinitatis,'" *Religious Studies* 33 [1997]: 428-30).

[65]*WCB*, p. 186.

[66]John Beversluis argues that, for Calvin, salvation does not involve a repairing of the *sensus divinitatis*. Knowledge of God is by faith alone ("Reforming the 'Reformed' Objection," pp. 195-96).

doxastic experience.[67] This objection does not suggest that an inference is involved but points to a dependence that is allegedly unfitting for a basic belief.[68] Plantinga, however, has made it clear that he is not arguing for a notion of basicality that requires properly basic beliefs to be without ground.[69] It is rather that they are not grounded by arguments or inference from other beliefs. This objection, therefore, is no threat to the notion of basicality that Plantinga wishes to defend.

Second, it is noted that Plantinga is open to a variant of the A/C model that involves a "quick inference," where what is actually basic is assent to a premise in an argument the conclusion of which is a theistic belief.[70] On this variation, phenomenal experience would not be the occasion for theistic belief but rather the occasion for seeing the truth of a crucial premise in a quick argument to a theistic belief.[71] This openness is not a threat to the success of the model because, on the one hand, it is not required and is resisted by Plantinga,[72] and, on the other hand, even if it is granted that the theistic belief is itself technically inferred, it remains the case that the real work of the argument is done not

---

[67]Versions of this can be found in: Robert Audi, "Direct Justification, Evidential Dependence, and Theistic Belief," in *Rationality, Religious Belief, and Moral Commitment,* ed. Robert Audi and William J. Wainwright (Ithaca, NY: Cornell University Press, 1986), pp. 139-66; Paul Helm, review of *Warranted Christian Belief,* by Alvin Plantinga, *Mind* 110, no. 440 (2001): 1113; and Philip Quinn, "The Foundations of Theism Again: A Rejoinder to Plantinga," in *Rational Faith: Catholic Responses to Reformed Epistemology,* ed. Linda Zagzebski (Notre Dame, IN: University of Notre Dame Press, 1993), pp. 28-29.

[68]Richard Grigg advances a related objection also targeting analogies to more mundane basic beliefs but suggests that these beliefs actually rest on evidentially supported beliefs in the credibility of the faculties delivering them. Grigg does not seem to see that beliefs generated by these faculties are not derived by inference from a belief in the credibility of the faculty. The belief in the credibility of the faculty enables the unobstructed flow of warrant in the same way a defeater-defeater might operate (see the last paragraph of this section). See Richard Grigg, "The Crucial Disanalogies Between Properly Basic Belief and Belief in God," *Religious Studies* 26 (1990): 389-401.

[69]RBG, pp. 78-82; Plantinga, "Is Belief in God Properly Basic?" pp. 44-48.

[70]The example Plantinga gives is the premise "*the heavens can be gloriously beautiful only if God has created them*" (*WCB,* p. 176, emphasis original; see also p. 304).

[71]See Laura L. Garcia, "Natural Theology and the Reformed Objection," in *Christian Perspectives on Religious Knowledge,* ed. C. Stephen Evans and Merold Westphal (Grand Rapids: Eerdmans, 1993), pp. 118-20; and Keith A. Mascord, *Alvin Plantinga and Christian Apologetics* (Milton Keynes, UK: Paternoster, 2006), pp. 130-35.

[72]"On that model, it is not that one notes the experiences, whatever exactly they are, connected with the operation of the *sensus divinitatis,* and then makes a quick inference to the existence of God" (*WCB,* p. 330).

by human reason but by the gift of the deliverances of the A/C model.

Third, some hold that Plantinga gives space for natural theology to play an essential role in supporting some theistic belief. Although the arguments of natural theology would never be sufficient on their own, it is imagined that, in cases where revelation by means of the *sensus divinitatis* is somewhat muted, these arguments might provide the additional warrant needed to boost warrant to the level required for knowledge.[73] I have reserved the next chapter to look at tensions between Barth and Plantinga on natural theology. It is sufficient here to say that, while Plantinga does indeed seem open to this possibility, the objection fails as natural theology is categorically excluded from the A/C model.

Fourth, it has been argued that Plantinga's "no-defeater condition"[74] leaves belief in need of support from arguments thereby undermining its basicality. We will look at defeaters in more detail at the end of this chapter. Let's provisionally define a defeater as a belief that is rationally in tension with another belief that it either fully or partially defeats, thus requiring the suspension or attenuation of the defeated belief. A defeater-defeater would be yet another belief that defeats the defeating belief, which may allow the reinstating of the originally defeated belief. For the purpose of understanding the objection, it is enough to see that Plantinga grants that warrant can be disrupted if one finds oneself convinced by an argument that refutes or entails the refutation of the belief in question. In these situations warrant can only again flow unobstructed if the defeating argument is itself defeated to the satisfaction of the knower by a defeater-defeater. Since it is the case that most sophisticated adults do have defeaters, some argue that the A/C model depends on the support of defeater-defeaters to warrant theistic belief.[75] As Beilby

[73]Quinn, "Foundations of Theism Again," pp. 35-45; Sudduth, "Plantinga's Revision of the Reformed Tradition," p. 89; and Stephen J. Wykstra, "'Not Done in a Corner': How to Be a Sensible Evidentialist About Jesus," *Philosophical Books* 42, no. 2 (2002): 106. Plantinga's response grants this possibility (Plantinga, "Reply," pp. 127-28).

[74]Michael Bergmann coined this term in "Internalism, Externalism and the No-Defeater Condition," *Synthese* 110 (1997): 399-417.

[75]"Religious belief that systematically requires the neutralization of defeaters largely or even completely loses its basicality" (Christoph Jäger, "Warrant, Defeaters, and the Epistemic Basis of Religious Belief," in *Scientific Explanation and Religious Belief*, ed. Michael Parker and Thomas Schmidt [Tübingen: Mohr Siebeck, 2005], p. 97). "The defeater-defeater requirement suggests that the rationality of theistic belief, even construed in an externalist manner, sometimes demands

puts it, "the presence of defeaters for Christian belief often causes Christians to seek to *support* their religious beliefs by developing defeater-defeaters."[76] If belief requires the support of arguments, it is no longer strictly basic. Dewey J. Hoitenga asks, "If the proper basicality of theistic belief makes the arguments of natural theology unnecessary and inappropriate to its justification, why does that proper basicality not make apologetic defenses of that belief equally unnecessary and inappropriate to its justification?"[77] The problem with this objection is that even in cases where a defeater-defeater is operative, the defeater-defeater is not *supporting* or supplying warrant for belief in God.[78] The defeater-defeater is rebutting or undercutting another belief that is obstructing the flow of warrant. Far from being a challenge to the proper basicality of belief, the defeater-defeater allows belief to form in the properly basic way. Plantinga clearly allows that in some cases a defeater-defeater is needed to safeguard epistemically responsible belief. But in these instances the belief in no way derives by inference from the defeater-defeater—it is not in some way *based on* an argument.[79]

The A/C model: tensions with Barth's theology of revelation. While the A/C model raises some serious questions for compatibility with Barth, there is nothing new here that we have not flagged earlier. We have again encountered the apparent disagreement over natural theology, which

a degree of internalist reflective rationality whereby we acquire reasons for supposing that theistic belief has some epistemic excellence" (Michael L. Czapkay Sudduth, "The Internalist Character and Evidentialist Implications of Plantingian Defeaters," *International Journal for Philosophy of Religion* 45 [1999]: 182-83).

[76]Beilby, *Epistemology as Theology*, p. 197, emphasis mine.

[77]Dewey J. Hoitenga, *Faith and Reason from Plato to Plantinga: An Introduction to Reformed Epistemology* (Albany: State University of New York Press, 1991), p. 209.

[78]Though disagreeing, Beilby recognizes that for Plantinga "theistic belief is not based (epistemically) on the defeater-defeater. Rather, the belief continues to be grounded by the experience which occasioned the belief" (Beilby, *Epistemology as Theology*, p. 58).

[79]Plantinga has always been clear that negative apologetics does not provide a *basis* for belief. For instance, when employing the free will defense to defeat Democritus's objection to belief in God, Plantinga remarks, "Of course if this happens, my original belief may still be basic; I do not now accept it *on the basis of* my belief that Democritus' argument is unsuccessful" (RBG, p. 84, emphasis original). Plantinga later distinguishes proper basicality with respect to justification from proper basicality with respect to warrant. In the case where a defeater-defeater is required for epistemically responsible belief, it is still *proper* with respect to one's epistemic responsibilities (justification) that the belief be held without its being *based on* another belief. Likewise, and more clearly with warrant, the need for a defeater-defeater in no way affects the fact that belief may be properly (warrantedly) taken in the basic way. See *WCB*, pp. 177-78.

will occupy our attention in the next chapter. Other questions arise primarily around Barth's emphatic insistence that knowledge of God is a human possibility only by the self-revelation of God in Jesus Christ. In contrast, it may seem that there is nothing particularly Christian about Plantinga's A/C model—that it is proposing a knowledge of God outside of the work of the Spirit ministering Christ. On Barth's account there is no avenue to the knowledge of God that begins with generic theism or originates from an innate human capacity. We will return to this point in the chapter on natural theology. Suffice it to say that—except with extreme qualifications—we would not see Barth affirming a *sensus divinitatis* or developing models for mere theistic belief as Plantinga does. As we will see, however, in our treatment of the extended A/C model, due to the noetic effects of sin,[80] it is only by the gracious redemptive work of the Spirit that there is any hope for the gradual repair of the *sensus divinitatis.* Moreover, in Plantinga's view, because of the damage done by sin, "these beliefs do not come to the Christian just by way of . . . the *sensus divinitatis,* or any other of the cognitive faculties with which we human beings were originally created; they come *instead* by way of the work of the Holy Spirit."[81] Plantinga agrees that *post lapsus* Christian belief does not and could not originate from an innate human capacity. Furthermore, there is no room in Plantinga's model at any point for a knowledge of God that arises from innate ideas remembered.[82]

[80]Derek Jeffreys charges that Plantinga "obscures Calvin's insightful analysis of the noetic effect of sin" and therefore "ignores Calvin's harsh negative assessment of the *sensus divinitatis.*" (Jeffreys, "How Reformed Is Reformed Epistemology?" pp. 430, 425). In *WCB* Plantinga has clarified his position helpfully so that it is clear that the only adequate knowledge of God delivered by the postlapsarian *sensus divinitatis* is due to its regeneration by the Spirit as part of the gift of faith. "Our original knowledge of God and his glory is muffled and impaired; it has been replaced by stupidity, dullness, blindness, inability to perceive God or to perceive him in his handiwork" (*WCB,* pp. 214-15).

[81]*WCB,* p. 245, emphasis mine.

[82]It is assumed by some in dialogue with RBG that "Plantinga's epistemology is innatist in the tradition of Augustinian Platonism" (J. Wesley Robbins, "Belief in God, Proper Basicality, and Rationality," *Journal of the American Academy of Religion* 61, no. 2 [1993]: 339-40) and that Plantinga embraces a Platonic doctrine of innate ideas rather than a Thomistic or Aristotelian notion of an innate capacity (Thomas A. Russman, "'Reformed' Epistemology," in *Thomistic Papers,* ed. Leonard A. Kennedy [Houston: Center for Thomistic Studies, 1988], 4:195-200). Plantinga's *sensus divinitatis,* however, is not a maieutic faculty. The knowledge of God is not something that by nature resides unborn in human beings. See also Hoitenga, *Faith and Reason from Plato to Plantinga,* pp. xii, 238-40.

As for the concern about building from a generic theism, we have already discussed Plantinga's rejection of the general starting-point assumption and cautioned about misunderstanding the flow of his argument. The A/C model is not a premise in an argument for theistic belief. And since, due to sin, the A/C model is dependent on and largely replaced by the extended A/C model, it is in fact the case that defending any role for the *sensus divinitatis* is unnecessary to Plantinga's wider argument. If Plantinga is right, there cannot be a warranted theistic belief that is not the work of the Spirit's giving birth to faith in Jesus Christ.[83] It is to this extended A/C model that we now turn.

PLANTINGA'S EXTENDED A/C MODEL OF CHRISTIAN BELIEF

The extended A/C model: overview. The focus of Plantinga's model for warranted *Christian* belief is a "three-tiered cognitive process."[84] The three elements in the process are Christian scripture, the Holy Spirit and faith. Christian scripture is a humanly authored collection of writings that God has specially inspired to use as a means for his own communication. This action of God unifies the human texts into a grand narrative with a central theme, "the gospel, the stunning good news of the way of salvation God has graciously offered."[85] The second and driving element of the process is the "internal instigation of the Holy Spirit (IIHS)."[86] Whereas the A/C model treated a human cognitive faculty that is part of our "natural epistemic equipment,"[87] the *extended* A/C model involves a supernatural work of the Spirit. According to the model, the context of the IIHS is the reading or hearing of the message of scripture. The IIHS enables a kind of perception whereby a person comes to grasp the truth of that primary gospel narrative. In other words, the experience of the work of the IIHS is a *doxastic experience* recom-

[83]This is not to say that other theistic religions could not leverage some of Plantinga's work in the creation of their own models for how their beliefs might have warrant (*WCB*, p. 350). But it does mean that according to Plantinga the model for human knowledge of God is irreducibly Christian.

[84]*WCB*, pp. 243-44

[85]Ibid., p. 243.

[86]Ibid., p. 324.

[87]Ibid., p. 256.

mending to us belief in the truth of the "main lines of the Christian gospel."[88] The IIHS makes the truth evident, not on the basis of propositional evidence but with the immediacy that characterizes self-evident truths or the deliverances of our memory.[89] The evidentiality of the truth made known does not have the kind of phenomenology attending sense experience but is nevertheless rightly considered a real perceiving. The belief to which the IIHS gives birth is the third element of the process, faith. I have already mentioned that Plantinga appeals to Calvin's definition of faith, recognizing its essential cognitive content. The gift of faith is a gift of knowledge—that is, a gift of warranted true belief. Plantinga also treats faith's vital affective component as well, and even notes the affective parallels to warrant.[90] And, because faith is the end product of this special Spirit-driven, three-tiered cognitive process, Plantinga typically refers to the whole process as the "cognitive process of faith."

As a cognitive process, in most respects, the cognitive process of faith is like our other natural cognitive faculties; it is a cognitive endowment designed by God to yield true belief, subject to similar functional and environmental conditions. If one is functioning properly with respect to external rationality, then the doxastic experience delivered by the IIHS will be a strong and clearly perceiving endorsement of the truth of the gospel. If one is fully internally rational and operating in an appropriate environment, then the full degree of warrant for a belief arising from the testimony of the Holy Spirit will be reflected in the strength of the belief produced—and overall coherence with one's wider set of beliefs will be pursued.[91] The cognitive process of faith is unique in that the beliefs it produces are the direct result of a *donum supernaturalis,* but this is no

---

[88]Ibid., p. 248.

[89]Ibid., pp. 262, 265.

[90]See ibid., pp. 309-11. This renders curious the denouncement of Harriet A. Harris that "Plantinga confines his attention to faith as a cognitive activity and does not expand his notion of cognitive activity in a way that recognizes the constitutive roles of affections or the intelligence of emotions" (Harris, "Does Analytical Philosophy Clip Our Wings? Reformed Theology as a Test Case," in *Faith and Philosophical Analysis: The Impact of Analytical Philosophy on the Philosophy of Religion* [Aldershot, UK: Ashgate, 2005], p. 115).

[91]Plantinga details how the cognitive process of faith meets the four essential criteria in his warrant formula, in other words, the four essential criteria for knowledge. See *WCB,* pp. 246, 256-57.

slight difference. For while the supernatural character of the input to this process does not change the humanness of the knowing produced or alter the essential criteria for warranted belief, the fact that the cognitive process of faith involves a direct encounter with God the Spirit means that this cognitive process entails the very remedies needed to ensure warranted believing. The part of Plantinga's Christian model that we have already treated in some detail is its recognition of the devastating noetic effects of sin. Wrapped up with the gift of faith is a transformational work of the Spirit whereby "the ravages of sin (including the cognitive damage) are repaired, gradually or suddenly, to a greater or lesser extent."[92] Here the question of proper function cuts both ways. The cognitive impact of sin has a distorting and attenuating effect on the doxastic experiences of faith, while at the same time the very presence of the Spirit drawing us to Christ begins to rehabilitate and restore proper function.[93] Consequently, until a human knower is completely renewed, there will be varying interference in the deliverances of faith that will reduce warrant and weaken belief.[94] In keeping with Plantinga's general account of warrant, we find that the deliverances of faith are also open to the possibility of defeat. And good doxastic practice will require, for some, investigating arguments against belief as part of remaining internally rational.

Many of the same questions raised for Plantinga's A/C model may also be raised for his extended model. Is it successful as an account of Christian belief taken in the basic way that fulfills Plantinga's general account of warrant? What issues does the extended model raise for the

---

[92]Ibid., 244.

[93]Why the restoring work of the Spirit is evidenced in some and resisted in others is not a question Plantinga seeks to resolve with his model.

[94]Surprisingly, Plantinga has been criticized for giving an "ideal" account of faith and, in so doing, failing to "describe the actual epistemic situation of typical believers" (Beilby, *Epistemology as Theology*, p. 139). But Plantinga is fully aware that typical cases of faith remain troubled by doubt to some degree (*WCB*, pp. 260 n. 35, 264 n. 43). Does this undermine the model as an account of how typical Christian belief can have warrant? The fact is that for many Christians faith fluctuates and with it so does the degree of warrant for Christian belief, exactly as Plantinga's model describes. We will meet this objection again in our discussion of whether defeater-defeaters or natural theology might preserve or boost warrant. For similar complaints see Mascord, *Alvin Plantinga and Christian Apologetics*, p. 199; and Andrew Chignell, "Epistemology for Saints," *Books & Culture* 8, no. 2 (2002): 20-21.

question of Plantinga's congruity with Barth? In some cases of parallel concern, nothing new need be said than has already been said, but in other cases new issues surface that require clarification. We will confine ourselves to what seem to be the three issues of greatest concern and treat them in conversation with Barth.

The extended A/C model: authentic human Christian belief. At one point in Plantinga's explanation of the cognitive process of faith, he describes the Holy Spirit as one "who gets us to accept, causes us to believe, the great truths of the gospel."[95] Facilitating acceptance and causing belief, however, seem to be two rather different notions, and possibly Plantinga is offering them as just this, two alternative conceptions, both of which are compatible with the model. However, some have raised the concern that Plantinga's model may be endangered by this tension. Paul Helm suggests that if there is a role for human acceptance or rejection of the gift of faith, such a "metaphysically independent act of the will" would "threaten the proper basicality of faith."[96] James P. Moreland and William Lane Craig worry that if beliefs are formed in the believer by someone other than the believer, this may not be a case of authentic human believing.[97] If we combine Helm's concern with Moreland and Craig's, the question becomes, Is Plantinga's model an account of authentic human Christian belief, and, if so, does this compromise its warrant basicality? A brief consideration of Barth's perspective on authentic human knowing will be helpful here, both to advance our primary objective and to focus the issue with respect to Plantinga.

Barth is more emphatic than Plantinga that the agent who is entirely responsible for the possibility of human knowledge of God is God alone. "The Word of God becomes knowable by making itself known."[98] Both

---

[95]*WCB,* p. 245.

[96]Helm, review of *Warranted Christian Belief,* p. 1112.

[97]"Certainly, the belief is formed in me, but I am not the one who formed it, and, therefore, I have not truly believed" (Moreland and Craig, *Philosophical Foundations for a Christian Worldview,* p. 169). Pierre Le Morvan and Dana Radcliffe express a similar concern that distinct human personhood is violated if "the Holy Spirit performs this activity as *part* of the person's cognitive system and so as a part of the person herself" (Le Morvan and Radcliffe, "Notes on Warranted Christian Belief," *Heythrop Journal* 44, no. 3 [2003]: 348, emphasis original).

[98]*CD* I/1, p. 246.

Plantinga and Barth see that revelation and redemption are inextricably linked, part of a unified movement of grace by the Spirit ministering Christ in the miracle of faith. Neither redemption nor revelation, therefore, is a human work, though it enlivens and enables human response.[99] Should we then conclude that Moreland and Craig have a legitimate complaint? If God is the active agent in the generation of knowledge and belief, is this an obstruction to real human knowing and believing? Barth does not think so. He denies that God's activity implies any human passivity. "If God is seriously involved in experience of the Word of God, then man is just as seriously involved too. The very man who stands in real knowledge of the Word of God also knows himself as existing in the act of his life, as existing in his self-determination."[100] The concern at the bottom of this debate seems to be that of human freedom in Christian belief. While Barth utterly denies the efficacy of human work in revelation, he clearly does not deny human activity, life and freedom. Human freedom, however, is improperly conceived when understood as human autonomy or choice made independently from God. In Barth's view, we are designed for dependence on God, so that the fullest and freest expression of being human is a living and choosing in fellowship with the will and act of God. He writes:

> Where God is truly served . . . the willing and doing of God is not just present as a first or second co-operating factor; it is present as the first and decisive thing as befits God the Creator and Lord. Without depriving the human element of its freedom, its earthly substance, its humanity, without obliterating the human subject, or making its activity a purely mechanical event, God is the subject from whom human action must receive its new and true name.[101]

Barth acknowledges that there will and must be a human response but that the power and enabling for this response are also the Spirit's gift. Plantinga's extended A/C model corresponds in most ways to Barth's theology of revelation. Clearly, the power to overcome the stifling

---

[99]Appealing to Calvin, Plantinga notes the importance in coming to faith of the "renewal and redirection of affections," for which the Holy Spirit is responsible (*WCB*, p. 292).

[100]*CD* I/1, p. 200.

[101]*CD* I/1, p. 94.

noetic effects of sin is the work of God in Christ. The knowledge of God is enabled by a Spirit-driven process whereby we are given faith. But Plantinga does seem to remain open, in a way that Barth is not, to the possibility of an independent human response serving as a kind of necessary human contribution to the process.[102] There is agreement, nevertheless, that the primary agency and enabling of the Spirit do not conflict with full, active and free human engagement.[103]

A related concern could and has been raised with respect to the freedom of the Spirit in the cognitive process of faith.[104] Plantinga is happy to describe the work of the Spirit as an "extraordinary cognitive process or belief-producing mechanism."[105] This manner of speaking might give the impression that the Spirit himself is conceived to operate impersonally, mechanistically and with predictable necessity. Nothing could of course be further from Barth's conception, where the hallmark of revelation is the freedom of God in his self-revelation.[106] Knowing is left open to the freedom of the object of knowing.[107] Plantinga fully agrees. "Faith doesn't go just by natural laws or regularities, working instead by way of the free cooperation of a person—God himself—whose speaking in Scripture is, of course, free."[108] The IIHS, like the great things of the gospel, is understood by Plantinga to be "a result of God's free and gracious action."[109] The choice of the language of *process* or *mechanism* is strictly with a view to the way in which a freely Spirit-

---

[102]See *WCB*, p. 212, where Plantinga agonizes over the problem of evil and the fall, attempting to come to grips with the fact of sin's origination. See also ibid., p. 257, where Plantinga is clear that his model "need take no stand" on the questions of sovereignty and human freedom, though he is expressly open to the possibility that "there is a contribution to this process that I myself must make, a contribution that I can withhold."

[103]The implication of this conclusion is that Laura Garcia, Linda Zagzebski and Keith Mascord are incorrect in charging Plantinga with extreme nonvoluntarism regarding belief formation (Garcia, "Natural Theology and the Reformed Objection," pp. 121-22; Zagzebski, "Religious Knowledge and the Virtues of the Mind," p. 202; and Mascord, *Alvin Plantinga and Christian Apologetics*, pp. 181-82, 198). Mascord concludes that, for Plantinga, unbelievers "are not the beneficiaries of the internal instigation of the Holy Spirit" (*Alvin Plantinga and Christian Apologetics*, p. 182)—a claim that Plantinga never makes.

[104]Le Morvan and Radcliffe, "Notes on Warranted Christian Belief," pp. 347-48.

[105]*WCB*, p. 256.

[106]*CD* I/1, p. 206. Barth declares, "Revelation is simply the freedom of God's grace" (*CD* I/1, p. 117).

[107]*CD* I/1, p. 190.

[108]*WCB*, p. 258.

[109]Ibid., p. 261.

driven enabling of belief might address the conditions for warrant. The parallel Plantinga wishes to highlight between the cognitive process of faith and our other cognitive faculties is with the mechanics of warrant, not a mechanism of origin. With respect to origin, Plantinga is clear that the work of the Spirit is "extraordinary."

For both Plantinga and Barth, therefore, Christian belief is free and authentic human knowing made possible by the free decision of God. What then of Helm's concern, that the integration of the cognitive process of faith with human noetic equipment, occasioned as it is by a reading or hearing of the human testimony of scripture, serves to threaten the suggestion that Christian belief is being held in the basic way? For Helm, it seems that a thoroughgoing monergism of the Spirit that ruled out human participation might safeguard proper basicality. But this objection possesses the same defect encountered in the objections to proper basicality in Plantinga's A/C model. It is sufficient for basicality that what grounds one's belief is not inference from other beliefs. It is sufficient for the *properness* of basicality if the beliefs so held have sufficient warrant. It is not required for basicality that a belief originate ex nihilo and without any connection to the rest of human thinking, willing and believing. As for warrant, it seems to me that Plantinga's model clearly conforms to the conditions for warrant he earlier develops.

The extended A/C model: individualism and the community of believers. Another common objection to Plantinga's extended A/C model is that it is "radically individualist"[110] and fails to appreciate the nurturing role of believing communities.[111] If the driving component of Plantinga's model is the *internal* instigation of the Holy Spirit, acting on the individual, is it fair to suggest that the role of the church in shaping Christian belief has been neglected? For Barth, a strictly individualist

---

[110]Terrence W. Tilley, review of *Warranted Christian Belief*, by Alvin Plantinga, *Theological Studies* 62 (2001): 389.

[111]Harris, "Does Analytical Philosophy Clip Our Wings?" pp. 100-118. These critiques are indicative of a wider trend that largely dismisses the value of the analytic approach as "(white western) masculinist: individualist, cut off from the body, from emotion, from humour, . . . from collaboration, and from creative imagination" (Grace M. Jantzen, *Becoming Divine: Towards a Feminist Philosophy of Religion* [Manchester: Manchester University Press, 1998], p. 69).

knowledge of God would be inconceivable.[112] The subject of the knowledge of God is never people in general or the isolated individual but always the "man *in the Church.*"[113] But it is important to note that this being in the church does not, for Barth, become a ground or basis for our knowledge of God, any more than association with the Christian community provides warrant in Plantinga's scheme. Barth maintains that the church is not an independent entity any more than the individual is. The church to whom the knowledge of God is given is always the church of Jesus Christ.[114] Revelation in Christ given to the church by the Spirit is the only possible basis for knowledge of God.

Where does this leave Plantinga's model? Do the charges of individualism and ecclesial neglect stick? The short answer is no, but to see why, we need to disentangle two assertions easily confused in the critique. The first assertion is about proper function for fundamentally relational beings, where the nurturing *koinōnia* of the community of faith is seen to be decisive for Christian belief formation. The second assertion is drawn from reflection on the social construction of belief and asseverates that the community of faith itself provides at least part of the warrant for Christian belief. I contend that Barth and Plantinga each affirm the first and deny the second.

Starting with the second assertion, we should recognize that, despite his detractors, Plantinga does acknowledge the importance of Christian community as the context within which properly basic belief develops.[115] "It is the church or community that proclaims the gospel, guides the neophyte into it, and supports, instructs, encourages, and edifies believers of all sorts and conditions."[116] But this does not mean that the community somehow anchors the warrant for the members' own belief.

---

[112] The revelation of God is given to the church, such that "there is no possibility of dogmatics at all outside the Church" (*CD* I/1, p. 17).

[113] *CD* I/1, p. 189, emphasis mine.

[114] *CD* I/1, p. 257.

[115] RBG, pp. 33-34; *WCB*, p. 202. Beilby seems to overstate Plantinga's silence on the role of the Christian community though he draws the right conclusion that Plantinga's model does not undercut such a role (*Epistemology as Theology*, p. 184-85; Beilby, "Plantinga's Model of Warranted Christian Belief," in *Alvin Plantinga*, ed. Deane-Peter Baker [Cambridge: Cambridge University Press, 2007], pp. 140-41).

[116] *WCB*, p. 244 n. 8.

If it did, there might be some truth to the unexpected conclusion of Harriet Harris that "Plantinga tends toward the view, though he does not state it, that the degree to which a belief is warranted depends on how many people hold it."[117] We can also easily rule out the suggestion that Plantinga's defense of the privileged epistemic status of the beliefs of the Christian community is in the neighborhood of "epistemological behaviorism."[118] What warrants these beliefs is not their being believed but the truth of what they confess regarding the redemptive and revelatory purposes of God. Denying that the church is the primary source of warrant for Christian belief does not imply a denial of a vital role for the church in the formation of Christian belief.

Another way of approaching this question is to ask whether openness to a role for the church in shaping Christian belief threatens the propriety of accepting Christian belief in the basic way. Some critics who want to see from Plantinga more acknowledgment of the social constructedness of knowledge assume that this would inevitably undermine basicality. Terrence Tilley declares that if an account of belief formation were to include the "social practices which trigger those beliefs . . . then our basic beliefs will be shown to be based on others' beliefs and the practices we share with them."[119] This is, however, either a non sequitur or a fundamental confusion about the nature of basicality with respect to belief. A belief that is based on the received testimony of another person may not be based on some other belief in one's belief structure. For this reason Plantinga counts credulity as one of our distinct rational powers "whereby we learn from others."[120] It is not as though belief in testimony must pass through an intermediating inference from the belief that the witness is trustworthy. One may in fact hold a belief in the

[117]Harris, "Does Analytical Philosophy Clip Our Wings?" p. 112.

[118]J. Wesley Robbins, "Is Belief in God Properly Basic," *International Journal for Philosophy of Religion* 14, no. 4 (1983): 246.

[119]Terrence W. Tilley, "Reformed Epistemology and Religious Fundamentalism: How Basic Are Our Basic Beliefs?" *Modern Theology* 6, no. 3 (1990): 254. Similarly, Frank Schubert argues that to the extent that belief depends on ancestral testimony it is "belief which is not properly basic" (Schubert, "Is Ancestral Testimony Foundational Evidence for God's Existence?" *Religious Studies* 27 [1991]: 499-500).

[120]*WCB*, p. 147. Because of Swinburne's acceptance of a "Principle of Credulity," Plantinga does not consider him an evidentialist (ibid., p. 91 n. 43).

general trustworthiness of a witness without that belief serving as a basis for accepting the truth of the testimony conveyed. It is perhaps better to think of beliefs generated by the acceptance of testimony as conditional on the lack of a defeater for the truthfulness of the testimony. *Credulity* implies a default position of trust that requires no further inferential propping up.[121] Therefore, even if it were true that on Plantinga's model warrant for Christian belief is obtained from human testimony, this would not threaten the basicality of that belief. The fact is, however, that Plantinga's model does not posit human testimony as the source of warrant for Christian belief. Instead, human testimony becomes an essential occasioning condition in the process whereby we are given a view of the truth[122] by the power of the Holy Spirit.[123] Scripture and the church are not diminished in importance, but they do not function as the ultimate warranting basis for Christian belief.

The significance of the community of believers to the formation of Christian belief is, of course, not exhausted by its service in the process of relaying the message of the gospel. It also serves as the arena of personal relationship within which believers encounter and live out the transforming truth of that gospel. If this is true, then the church is used by God in the restoration of proper function and in the creation of suitable environments for growth in faith. Admittedly, Plantinga does not spend a great deal of time on the role of the community of faith in the facilitation and restoration of proper function. But, with reference to our earlier caution, it is important to understand what Plantinga is and is not intending to achieve in his volumes on Christian epistemology.

---

[121]What further confuses the notion of basicality when considering beliefs based on testimony is that while the beliefs may be properly accepted in the basic way, there is an additional dependency with respect to warrant such that "belief on the part of the testifiee has warrant only if that belief has warrant for the testifier" (*WPF,* p. 86).

[122]Plantinga frequently refers to the work of the IIHS as enabling the human knower to have some kind of direct apprehension of the truth (e.g., *WCB,* pp. 83, 256, 281, 302, 340). It is a great distortion, however, to thereby conclude as Christopher J. Insole does that this being afforded a view for oneself implies a "rational self-sufficiency" (Insole, "Political Liberalism, Analytical Philosophy of Religion and the Forgetting of History," in *Faith and Philosophical Analysis: The Impact of Analytical Philosophy on the Philosophy of Religion,* ed. Harriet A. Harris and Christopher J. Insole [Aldershot, UK: Ashgate, 2005], p. 160).

[123]In Plantinga's model, Christian belief is based on an extraordinary kind of testimony, the testimony of the Holy Spirit, which uniquely includes our being enabled to grasp the truth of the testimony. See *WCB,* p. 252.

He is not attempting a comprehensive account of all aspects involved in a thick description of Christian belief formation. He is sketching an intentionally minimalist structure to give account of the principal way in which Christian belief receives warrant. In this account Plantinga mentions the importance of the gradual repairing of proper function and the criticality of suitable environment without becoming entrenched in the details. In agreement with Barth, Plantinga affirms that the principal means of restoration and revelation is the work of the Spirit applying the redemption of Christ. This does not nullify the fact that one chief way in which the Spirit works is in and through communities of faith, as Plantinga himself notes: "Presented in this brief and undeveloped way, this model can seem unduly individualistic. But of course it doesn't at all preclude the importance of the Christian community and the church to the belief of the individual Christian."[124]

Leaving this aspect of Christian belief formation undeveloped does not mean that there is something deficient in Plantinga's account of warrant. There is no deficiency because, on Plantinga's model, warrant does not originate from the Christian community wherein it arises. This also answers Beilby's concern that "if most of the interesting and efficacious work is being done by the *sensus divinitatis* and the internal testimony of the Holy Spirit, what of importance is left for the Christian community to do?"[125] Although the Christian community does not itself ground the connection between belief formation and the truth of what is being believed, it may still be critical to suitable cognitive environment and proper function. Perhaps, rather than lament Plantinga's lack of detail here, we should appreciate the openness of his theologically oriented structure for developing—as this book attempts to do—fuller accounts of the formation of warranted Christian belief. Constructively, these critiques are helpful in pointing out the connectedness of cognitive environment and proper function. Part of the restoration of proper function, facilitating warranted belief formation, driven by the self-revelation of God, is the Spirit's work to engender conducive *ecclesial* cognitive environments.

---

[124]Ibid., p. 244 n. 8.

[125]Beilby, *Epistemology as Theology*, p. 185.

The extended A/C model: can human arguments defeat Christian belief? Theological knowledge of the kind most central to Christian belief is not established by philosophical argument on Plantinga's account. But this leaves open the possibility of a negative role for philosophical arguments. Does Plantinga grant to philosophy the power to undercut or diminish the warrant for Christian belief? Does a human argument have the power to torpedo the work of the IIHS in the cognitive process of faith? In our earlier discussion of *defeaters,* we clarified that an argument that refutes an argument against belief (a *defeater-defeater*) does not supply warrant for a belief but removes obstructions to warrant. For this reason defeater-defeaters, while sometimes crucial to warrant, do not alter the proper basicality of a belief. The question we are raising now is not about the role of defeater-defeaters but about the nature of the possibility of defeaters in the extended A/C model. Though human arguments are not needed for belief to have warrant according to the model, is it possible that human arguments could inhibit specifically the warrant for Christian belief instigated by the Holy Spirit? And, if so, how does this *not* clearly constitute what Barth would deem a gross violation on the part of philosophy?

The issues surrounding this question are easily confused, as we saw in our earlier discussion of defeater-defeaters; therefore, it will serve us well to briefly highlight the salient features of Plantinga's understanding of the nature of defeaters. I gave this provisional definition of a defeater earlier in the chapter: A *defeater* is a belief that is rationally in tension with another belief, which it either fully or partially defeats, thus requiring the suspension or attenuation of the defeated belief.[126] But this definition really only applies to the most commonly discussed kind of defeater, what Plantinga calls a "rationality defeater." Rationality defea-

[126]Plantinga follows the penetrative work of John Pollock on defeaters, including his original distinction between Type I (rebutting) and Type II (undercutting) defeaters. See John L. Pollock, "The Structure of Epistemic Justification," *American Philosophical Quarterly* monograph series 4 (1970): 62-78; and John L. Pollock and Joseph Cruz, *Contemporary Theories of Knowledge,* 2nd ed., Studies in Epistemology and Cognitive Theory (Lanham, MD: Rowman & Littlefield, 1999), pp. 195-202. Plantinga calls defeasibility a "crucial but puzzling notion" (*WCD,* p. 216). His most involved treatments can be found in *WCD,* pp. 216-21; *WCB,* pp. 357-67; and "Naturalism Defeated" (unpublished, 1994; available at www.calvin.edu/academic/philosophy/virtual_library/articles/plantinga_alvin/naturalism_defeated.pdf).

sibility, understood to result from beliefs in conflict, is a concern of the proper function of "internal rationality." Earlier, we saw that internal rationality has to do with forming the right beliefs on the basis of experience. But, for Plantinga, this also requires conducting some epistemic due diligence, such as ensuring the sufficient coherence of one's beliefs, looking for defeaters and considering objections.[127] We may recall, however, that in Plantinga's system internal rationality is only one aspect of the delivery of warrant. It is possible to have what Plantinga calls a "warrant defeater," which is not a belief in conflict with another belief but is instead a failure of some kind in the noetic processes on which we depend.[128] Given the facets of warrant elucidated by Plantinga, this could be a failure in the truth orientation of our design plan, in the appropriateness of our environment with respect to that plan or in cognitive function—perhaps in the area of external rationality.

With respect to the defeasibility of Christian belief, therefore, we can see at least two closely related concerns. The first is whether Christian belief might be undermined by antagonistic philosophical arguments; the second is whether warrant might be impeded by a wider range of epistemic problems. Our primary concern here is with the first of these—rationality defeaters from philosophical arguments. Warrant defeaters due to epistemic problems caused by the noetic effects of sin are fully expected by both Barth and Plantinga. The work of the Spirit, repairing the damage of sin, may be done "gradually or suddenly, to a greater or lesser extent."[129] Plantinga speaks of "paradigmatic" instances of faith,[130] but full and complete repair of our cognitive faculties and environments is an eschatological reality. This suggests a provisional answer to the question of the defeasibility of Christian belief in general: the extent to which warrant defeat of the deliverances of faith is possible is directly related to the extent that the noetic effects of sin distort proper function and render our environments misleading. But does this adequately address the specific question of rationality defeat? Maybe so, if all instances

[127] *WCB*, pp. 112, 255.
[128] Ibid., pp. 359-60.
[129] Ibid., p. 244.
[130] Ibid., pp. 256, 260, 264.

of the rationality defeat of Christian belief arise from an error stemming from cognitive malfunction or a misleading cognitive environment.[131]

There is good reason to think that in Plantinga's view this provisional answer does extend to all instances of the defeat of Christian belief, including the possibility of the defeat of Christian belief by philosophical argument. If this is true, then the possibility of the defeat of Christian belief by philosophical argument is not explained by the inherent power of human argument but arises only as a consequence of the impact of human sin. The power of reason to undermine faith is a reality created by an underlying epistemic distortion that disrupts the service of reason in the formation of true beliefs. This understanding of the nature of the rationality defeasibility of Christian belief is the inevitable consequence of Plantinga's other commitments. The nature of defeasibility in general obviously depends on a commitment to the principle of noncontradiction. If Christian belief is true, then any belief that either contradicts or entails a contradiction with it must be false, and no false belief can have warrant sufficient for knowledge. On Plantinga's general scheme, false beliefs can be traced back to problems in the truth orientation of the design plan, unsuitable environments, improper cognitive function upstream or downstream from experience or some combination of these. But if Christian belief is true, there is no problem with the truth orientation of the design plan with respect to Christian belief.[132] We can conclude, therefore, that all instances of the rationality defeat of Christian belief arise from an error stemming from cognitive malfunction or a misleading cognitive environment. In other words, any philosophical argument that contradicts Christian belief arises from some underlying epistemic problem, is therefore unwarranted and consequently cannot count as knowledge.

Should we conclude, therefore, that according to Plantinga any belief that contradicts Christian belief is irrational and unjustified? Not at all.

[131]In this argument I am assuming that anything in our environments that would mislead us with respect to the proper deliverances of faith can be understood to be an environmental consequence of sin.

[132]It may be that aspects of the design plan are aimed at things other than true belief or things *in addition to* true belief, but clearly for Plantinga the part of the design plan that governs the formation of Christian belief is aimed at true belief. See *WPF,* p. 195, as well as *WCB,* p. 257.

Plantinga's position is fully consistent with the reasonability of philosophical arguments against Christian belief and with the justification of accepting their conclusions. This is in fact one of the great strengths of the sophistication and nuance of Plantinga's epistemology. Warrant involves a number of considerations wholly external to the human faculty of reason and to the fulfillment of epistemic duties. Arguments against Christian belief may be reasonable, and one may be justified in believing their conclusions—even though the resulting beliefs fail to have warrant. Arguments against Christian belief may be valid while relying on dodgy premises. Assessment of probability may be accurate, but background knowledge skewed. Plantinga's system does not suggest that the work of the Spirit makes Christian believers smarter than unbelievers in terms of their felicity with logic, their ability to avoid incoherence within their network of beliefs or their capacity to deduce entailment. The principal cognitive work of the Spirit, on Plantinga's model, is to give a perception of the truth of Christian belief. This involves an initiation of the repair of the noetic effects of sin but does not necessarily transform believers into brilliant philosophers. Just as unbelieving philosophers with high-functioning faculties of reason can be justified in believing Christianity false without knowing that their beliefs lack warrant, so also the warranted beliefs of simple-minded Christian believers are rational and justified without any complex reasoning process required to support them.[133]

But can the simple-minded Christian really be justified in his or her belief without defeater-defeaters for known objections to Christian belief? Is it rational to accept Christian belief in the face of known objections for which one has no refutation whatsoever? The answer to this depends on what might count as refutation. Plantinga advises that we not narrow our notion of refutation to merely that which takes the form of a philosophical counterargument. Resolution of belief conflict may be conducted purely on the basis of the relative strength of warrant of the beliefs themselves. In Plantinga's parlance, a belief that is in a stronger

[133]By "reasoning process" I mean just that work done by the faculty of reason to determine the "deductive and probabilistic relations among propositions" (*WCB*, p. 78). The wider *cognitive* process supporting belief is the robust cognitive process of faith by the IIHS.

position with respect to warrant may serve as an *intrinsic* defeater-deflector for a conflicting belief.[134] One may find oneself unconvinced by an argument or evidence not on the basis of any deficiency seen in it but simply because the conclusion conflicts with a belief that has a firmer footing.[135] Plantinga's contention here is similar to G. E. Moore's response to David Hume on skepticism about the existence of material objects.[136] The move Moore makes has become known as Moore's "shift." Rather than taking on the validity of the argument or the truth of the premises, one may simply have a more firmly held belief that the conclusion is not true. In this case then, the refutation of the objection is just to restate the objection as a reductio ad absurdum:[137] if it is true that if the argument is valid and the premises are true, then the conclusion must follow, then if we are in a stronger position to see that the conclusion is not true, we are safe to conclude that the argument has a problem, without needing to identify that problem precisely. For Moore on perception, it is perfectly rational to maintain that the direct perceptual experience of a material object provides the best refutation of Hume's potential defeater. For Plantinga, the deliverances of faith, if strong enough, may provide the best refutation for any particular objection to belief.[138]

---

[134]Alvin Plantinga, "The Foundations of Theism: A Reply," *Faith and Philosophy* 3, no. 3 (1986): 311-12. Philip Quinn, to whom Plantinga is replying, accepts the possibility of intrinsic defeater-defeaters but doubts that typical believers have enough warrant for their theistic beliefs to operate as intrinsic defeater-defeaters for all the potential defeaters typically encountered. See Quinn, "Foundations of Theism Again," p. 39. Similarly, see Sudduth, "Internalist Character and Evidentialist Implications of Plantingian Defeaters," pp. 181-82. For cases where a defeater is never actually acquired, only repelled, Plantinga has introduced the term *defeater-deflector* as a more felicitous descriptor (Plantinga, "Reply to Beilby's Cohorts," in *Naturalism Defeated? Essays on Plantinga's Evolutionary Argument Against Naturalism,* ed. James Beilby [Ithaca, NY: Cornell University Press, 2002], p. 224).

[135]Plantinga's classic example pits a person's memory beliefs against circumstantial evidence. See Plantinga, "Foundations of Theism: A Reply," p. 310, or *WCB,* p. 371. Following Chisholm, Plantinga calls this approach "particularism" (RBG, pp. 77-78). See Roderick M. Chisholm, *The Problem of the Criterion* (Milwaukee: Marquette University Press, 1973), p. 15.

[136]From a lecture delivered in 1911 at Morley College in London (G. E. Moore, "Hume's Theory Examined," in *Some Main Problems of Philosophy* [New York: Humanities Press, 1953], pp. 108-26).

[137]Or as Plantinga suggests, if your belief in God is firmer than your belief in the premises of an argument against that belief, "you would go *modus tollens* and take it that you had an argument against the premises" (from an unpublished letter to Kelly J. Clark, printed in Clark, "Plantinga vs. Oliphint: And the Winner Is . . ." *Calvin Theological Journal* 33 [1998]: 164 n.).

[138]This includes the objection that Plantinga must provide an *independent* reason for believing that

According to the extended A/C model, there is no inherent tension between faith and reason. Where tensions do arise, this may suggest no deficiency of reasoning but rather a lingering hindrance in environment or proper function. By distinguishing warrant from rationality and justification, Plantinga is able to show that one may be both rational and justified in accepting the deliverances of faith over the conclusions of philosophical argument. Philosophical arguments may swamp weak or fluctuating faith not because reason is conceived to be a rival or independent source of knowledge but because its exercise in the pursuit of truth is dependent on broader epistemic conditions darkened by sin. It should be clear, therefore, that for Plantinga Christian belief does not require the tools of reason for it to be rational and it need not enter the fray of philosophical exchange for it to be justified.

CONCLUSION

I have attempted to show that there is a striking compatibility between Plantinga's approach to Christian epistemology and Barth's theology of revelation. In chapter four we looked at Plantinga's understanding of Christian philosophy and its relationship to theology, along with his general account of epistemic warrant. There we found that Plantinga not only affirms Barth's rejection of various potential philosophical encroachments on theological knowing but also offers further philosophical argument against them. The same set of assumed obligations and human epistemic responsibilities that Barth decried as noetic works righteousness Plantinga also rebuffs as neither necessary nor sufficient for knowledge. What is critical for knowledge, that is, warranted true belief, is functioning according to the right kind of truth-oriented design in a suitable environment. This, along with Plantinga's externalism and inductive procedure, yields an epistemology of

there is such a thing as the IIHS. The deliverances of the cognitive process of faith themselves provide the grounds for concluding that Plantinga's model or something like it is correct. Evan Fales fails to grasp this when he suggests that "the morally checkered history of Christendom, and the conflicting moral testimony of Scripture" count as prima facie defeaters for Plantinga's model in the absence of some kind of independent validation of the IIHS (Fales, review of *Warranted Christian Belief*, by Alvin Plantinga, *Noûs* 37, no. 2 [2003]: 363-64). For Plantinga, the work of the Spirit is sufficient to produce an intrinsic defeater-defeater.

Christian belief that derives ultimately "from outside all human possibilities."[139]

In this chapter we examined Plantinga's models for theistic and specifically Christian belief, taking special note of key objections and potential tensions with Barth's theology of revelation. It should be evident that Plantinga agrees with Barth that what is beyond human possibilities is possible with God. Plantinga sees the knowledge of God to be divinely initiated—"from the acting of God Himself." The gift of faith in its paradigmatic forms is the gift of knowing that we know by the special instigation of the Holy Spirit. Demonstration of the truth of what is known is not required for knowledge, nor is it even within the competency of philosophy to offer.[140] Despite all the philosophical weaponry Plantinga mobilizes, Herrmann's expression of a knowledge of God "wholly without weapons" still applies in the sense that Barth so enthusiastically endorsed. What anchors the warrant for and therefore strength of our belief is not the strength of arguments in its favor but the very content of the truth that is believed. Moreover, the priority in origination and formation of Christian belief resides with the free action of God, without at any point undermining or overriding its thoroughgoing humanness. These are strong alignments between Barth and Plantinga on the knowledge of God.

With sufficient clarity, I hope, we have now on the table the relevant positive elements of Barth's and Plantinga's epistemologies of revelation. In the next chapter I will attempt briefly to summarize and harmonize Barth's and Plantinga's proposals into a unified account. This will offer the reader an opportunity to regroup or even jump into the discussion midstream. Then, in the second half of this book, I will

---

[139]Quoted earlier, Barth maintains that the knowledge of God "derives and is to be considered only from outside all human possibilities, i.e., from the acting of God Himself" (*CD* I/1, p. 38).

[140]The from-above approach means that we are in a position of dependence where our only option is to trust. Plantinga points out that this is true of all kinds of human knowing. In his response to Steup's distinction between the use and function of cognitive faculties, Plantinga notes: "at a certain basic level I must simply trust my cognitive faculties; I have no alternative. At that basic level, the issue of using them well or ill doesn't arise: how they function and whether they function reliably (a) isn't up to me, and (b) is such that I can't determine it without assuming it" (Plantinga, "Reliabilism, Analyses and Defeaters," *Philosophy and Phenomenological Research* 55, no. 2 [1995]: 444).

test, elucidate and deepen the combined Barth/Plantinga epistemological proposal by examining its fruitfulness for contributing to four areas of theological debate and considering the objections that emerge from them.

6

SUMMARIZING INTERLUDE

The Unified Barth/Plantinga Approach to Christian Theological Epistemology

◆

It's time to look back over the ground covered and attempt to bring together the insights of Barth and Plantinga into an emerging unified proposal. I say "emerging" because I intend to press for further development of our grasp of their thought, both in concord and in contrast, as we engage with specific epistemological difficulties in the latter half of this book. This will also give me an opportunity to emphasize general points that may have been lost in the sometimes more technical theological and philosophical discussions. I do not plan to affirm anything in this chapter that has not already been affirmed in detail in the previous chapters. My hope is merely to clarify the features I take to be most salient in the theological epistemologies of Plantinga and Barth for the epistemological dilemma facing Christian theology discussed in chapter one.

In chapter one we used an engagement with skepticism as a heuristic to sharpen our focus on the fundamental epistemological issue confronting Christian theology. In that discussion I resolved that Christian theology, at least as traditionally conceived, is committed to the reality of a God who can be known. The skeptical challenge to knowledge requires a noncircular demonstration of grounds. Modernist apologetics attempts to meet the skeptic's burden of proof through the arguments of natural theology.[1] Unfortunately, there seem to be no noncircular ways to demonstrate and secure for ourselves theological knowledge. Christian theology (and every other discipline for that matter) should readily and without anxiety concede that the skeptic's burden of proof cannot be met. In so doing, we simply acknowledge the kinds of human epistemic limitations observed by Christian anthropology and perhaps any sensible view of the human knower.

The typical ways of accommodating for human epistemic limitations generally include, on the one hand, reducing or removing the commitment to knowledge altogether (some form of skepticism) and, on the other hand, adjusting what is meant by the truth of such knowledge (typically forms of "non-realism"[2]). Neither of these is an option for Christian theology as traditionally conceived. This brings us to the dilemma. Defending theological knowledge by providing a noncircular demonstration of its grounds is not a human possibility. Nevertheless, Christian theology confesses that the knowledge of God—as God really is—is a human possibility. It seems obvious that escaping this dilemma will require us to reject one or more of the skeptic's assumptions about knowledge that come embedded with what we have called modernity's Enlightenment project.

As we have seen, both Barth and Plantinga recognize the inherited epistemological dilemma. Barth characterized it as the choice between "Fate and Idea," which can be distinguished as naive realism and anti-realism.[3] Plantinga and Barth each adopt a critically realist position, acknowledging that there is no objective neutrality for the human

---

[1]Hilary Putnam's account of the possible responses to skepticism begins with this one, which he calls the "traditional approach, and the one that is still that of the Roman Catholic Church." The other two responses he discusses are forms of fideism. He concludes in favor of William James and the view that neither reason nor experience can ground or guide belief (Putnam, "The Depths and Shadows of Experience," in *Science, Religion, and the Human Experience,* ed. James D. Proctor [Oxford: Oxford University Press, 2005], pp. 79-82).

[2]This is not always called "non-realism" or "anti-realism." Karin Johannesson proposes a "non-metaphysical realism." See Johannesson, *God Pro Nobis: On Non-Metaphysical Realism and the Philosophy of Religion* (Leuven: Peeters, 2007).

[3]It is important to note that the *realism/anti-realism* distinction can be confusing in theological writing because of the very different ways it is deployed. Here I use *realism* to signal the ontological commitment discussed in chapter 1—affirming a coherent, external, independent reality with which our beliefs, in order to be true, must in some sense correspond.

knower while maintaining a realist position and strongly affirming the possibility of theological knowledge. Both chart an escape through the horns of this dilemma by rejecting certain core epistemological assumptions of modernity. Plantinga identifies its origins in the unreasonable deontology associated with classical foundationalism. Barth heralds the pre-engaged givenness and self-grounding of divine self-revelation.

Together, they provide a well-reasoned epistemology of revelation that is both deeply theological—arising from the resources of Christian theology itself—and philosophically astute, aware of and able to engage with the critical issues and concerns arising internally and externally to Christian theology. The theological depth comes largely from Barth and the philosophical strength largely from Plantinga, but the overlap is considerable, and where there is overlap there is strong agreement. In what follows I will recap what I take to be the central points in an emerging unified Barth/Plantinga proposal.

PRIMARY COMPONENTS OF THE EMERGING UNIFIED PROPOSAL

The proposal I am attempting to piece together from the works of Barth and Plantinga is aimed at clarifying how Christian theologians ought to think about theological knowledge given the dilemma that Christian theology traditionally conceived confesses real human knowledge of God by epistemically inadequate and fallible human beings. The ten components listed below summarize the points defended by Barth, Plantinga or both that we have discussed in the preceding chapters, providing a touchstone as we move on to test and further elucidate their ideas in the chapters ahead.

What is the character of theological knowledge?

1. *Real gift:* Knowledge of God is the free gift of God's self-revealing. It cannot be grasped from below but only received from above. By its very nature it cannot be deduced or demonstrated by unaided human reason. It is the inbreaking of the independent reality of God himself, emerging within but not from human conceptuality, so as to commandeer and judge strictly human ideas.

2. *Theo-foundational:* God, in his act of self-revelation, creates and enables our capacity to receive the knowledge of him. God is not just the object of theological knowledge but is also the means and even cosubject of that knowledge. God the Spirit enables and receives in us the revelation of the Father through the Son. The triune revelation of the triune God is knowledge by participation in God's being, in God's own self-knowledge. The knowledge of God is theo-foundational, given by God, grounded in God himself. The knowledge of God is not properly referred to as non-foundational, as if it lacked foundation or grounding altogether.
3. *Freely transformational:* The revelation of God is transformational, enabling personal receptivity through communion with God. In order to enable participation in divine self-knowledge, the free gift of God's self-revealing transforms earthen vessels, rehabilitating and restoring proper function to faculties injured by the noetic effects of sin.
4. *Corporately known:* Knowledge of God is not an isolated individual experience but the self-revelation of God by the Spirit shared in and through the body of Christ. Revelation and transformation are corporate realities experienced personally but not merely privately. While the church is not the ground or basis for our knowledge of God, God gives himself to be known for the restoration of communal knowing. The Spirit's work to engender conducive ecclesial cognitive environments is part of the restoration of cognitive function, facilitating the formation of warranted belief, driven by the self-revelation of God.
5. *Knowledge of God by grace alone:* All knowledge of God depends in some way on the grace of God. A human knowledge of God—that surpasses mere abstract and impersonal information about God—is given only by the enabling of the self-revealing action of God. It is not grasped independently of the knowing relation created and sustained by the fellowship of the Spirit within the body of Christ. The legitimate starting point of theology is one that grasps the knower but is not grasped *by* the knower independent of the given knowing relation.

6. *Personal and cognitive:* The knowledge of God is objective, personal and cognitive. It is knowledge of God as God really is. It is knowledge of God, given by God, without at any point undermining or overriding its thoroughgoing humanness. It is genuine human knowledge of God, with cognitive (i.e., propositional) content.
7. *Mediated—but not reduced to the medium:* The knowledge of God is communicated when one is confronted by the creaturely forms of God's speech, but in such a way that the divine content does not become the creaturely form. Neither God, nor the knowledge of God, is reduced or transferred into propositions, experiences, nature or human faculties. While the knowledge of God has propositional content, it is neither reducible nor transferrable to others or to ourselves strictly and independently by means of human thought, concepts and language. Scripture and the church are not diminished in importance, but they do not function as the *ultimate* warranting basis for Christian belief.
8. *The only secure ground:* Freely given communion with God provides the only truly secure grounding for the knowledge of God. God's own self-attestation, far from being arbitrarily fideistic, is the only escape possible from the ghettos of human reason. It is, as such, more secure than beliefs that depend merely on human reasoning. What anchors the warrant for and therefore strength of our belief is not the strength of arguments in its favor but the free act of God restoring proper function and conducive environments according to his personally tailored, truth-aimed design plan for knowing him.
9. *Theological epistemology not prolegomena:* Christian theological epistemology is faith seeking understanding. It does not provide a theoretical basis for a reality but instead thinks in light of a reality about its basis. Theological epistemology begins with the givenness of the reality of the revelation of God. It begins as having been revealed and works back from this given. It begins with ontological commitment and then turns to the epistemological account. Already on the way, it seeks to give an account of a divinely established way of knowing. Philosophy can and must be employed in a way that observes the

dependence of human theological knowing on the grace of the pre-engaged miracle and mystery of God's self-revelation.

10. *Coherent and warranted:* While the warrant for theological knowledge is certainly not provided by a general theory of knowledge, it is defensible and may be coherent with a general theory of knowledge. The one advanced here is an externalist theory of knowledge that hinges on divine design and in which it is seen that several important aspects of warrant are beyond human control or demonstration. Warrant for theological knowledge is, in this sense, not different from warrant for any other human knowledge. Theological warrant is not accounted for in an ad hoc way that might suggest special pleading, and it does not face any extraordinary difficulties that do not also attend other instances of genuine human knowing. Warrant for theological knowledge is occasioned by a mediated testifying encounter within a thoroughly human context engaging the broad spectrum of human experience. The warrant itself for such knowledge is conveyed by means of a self-confirming, Spirit-enabled, belief-producing process that transforms cognitive capacities and environments in alignment with a design plan successfully aimed at truth.

On these ten points we find a great deal of alignment between Barth and Plantinga. That is not to say that they would each affirm every point in the language given above. I only argue that these affirmations either stem directly from their expressed views or are mutually consistent with them. What we have seen thus far is that two giants, one in Christian theology and the other in Christian philosophy—sharing crucial core commitments but taking sometimes seemingly antagonistic approach vectors—enjoy an enormous amount of agreement about the nature and means of the knowledge of God.

In the previous chapters, I also flagged some potentially critical areas of tension between Barth and Plantinga. In the remaining chapters we will turn to these troubled areas and others as a way not just to deepen our understanding of the compatibility and complementarity of the contributions of Barth and Plantinga but also to see how their theological epistemologies may provide commendable navigations of those difficulties. We will spend one chapter each on the following tensions: theology and reason, faith and revelation, scripture and theology, and fallibility and assurance. Beginning with theology and reason, in chapter seven we look at Barth's notorious and unrelenting ban on both apologetics and natural theology alongside Plantinga's openness to a role for apologetics and his endorsement of a *natural* knowledge of God by means of a divinely given human cognitive capacity.

PART TWO

A Unified Barth/Plantinga Response to Theology's Contemporary Epistemological Issues

7

THEOLOGY AND REASON

Natural Theology and the Reformed Objection

◆

If English-speaking philosophers of religion know one thing about Karl Barth, it is that he emphatically denounces natural theology.[1] In theological circles as well, Barth's position on natural theology is considered to be entrenched and uncompromising, or "simply preposterous."[2] Anthony Thiselton expresses the widely held view that Barth is "the most outspoken opponent of natural theology in modern times."[3] On this basis, it is reasonable to suspect that we would find sharp differences between Plantinga and Barth. The critical task is to specify where precisely the differences lie and to assess their significance. Since natural theology is one strategy for bridging philosophy and theology,[4] signif-

---

[1]E.g., Brian Davies, *An Introduction to the Philosophy of Religion,* 2nd ed. (Oxford: Oxford University Press, 1993), p. 9; Nancey Murphy, "Theology and Scientific Methodology," in *Philosophy of Religion: Selected Readings,* ed. Michael Peterson, William Hasker, Bruce Reichenbach and David Basinger (Oxford: Oxford University Press, 2001), p. 514; and Richard Swinburne, "The Value and Christian Roots of Analytical Philosophy of Religion," in *Faith and Philosophical Analysis: The Impact of Analytical Philosophy on the Philosophy of Religion,* ed. Harriet A. Harris and Christopher J. Insole (Aldershot, UK: Ashgate, 2005), p. 41.

[2]James Barr, *Biblical Faith and Natural Theology: The Gifford Lectures for 1991, Delivered in the University of Edinburgh* (Oxford: Oxford University Press, 1993), p. 9. Wolfhart Pannenberg suggests that Barth takes Ritschl's negative view of natural theology to an "extreme" (Pannenberg, *Offenbarung als Geschichte,* ed. Wolfhart Pannenberg, 3rd ed. [Göttingen: Vandenhoeck & Ruprecht, 1965], p. 7).

[3]Anthony Thiselton, *A Concise Encyclopedia of the Philosophy of Religion* (Oxford: Oneworld, 2002), p. 196.

[4]E.g., Brian Hebblethwaite, who considers Barth's objection to natural theology to be extreme and, therefore, unhelpful to Hebblethwaite's hopes for a "rapprochement between the philosophers and the theologians" (Hebblethwaite, *Philosophical Theology and Christian Doctrine* [Oxford: Blackwell, 2005], p. 5).

icant disagreement here could threaten broader conclusions about compatibility and complementarity between Barth's theology of revelation and Plantinga's epistemology of Christian belief.

Initial impressions are not all bad in this case. Barth and Plantinga share some measure of agreement about natural theology: both raise vocal objections to it,[5] though Barth's objection certainly appears to be more categorical than is Plantinga's. Plantinga, we will see, remains open to a limited role for natural theology, which Barth resists. The task of penetrating the differences between Barth and Plantinga is made somewhat easier by Plantinga's own consideration of Barth's position.[6] Barth's ban on natural theology is in fact the only aspect of Barth's theology that Plantinga gives detailed comments on in his published writings. Plantinga agrees with what he understands to be Barth's primary motivation but withdraws from Barth's "*in toto*" rejection.[7] No doubt this blanket rejection is in mind when Plantinga later cites Barth as an "extreme example" of a theological objection to natural theology.[8] Plantinga's treatment of Barth, however, does not engage with the full scope of Barth's concern and, while highly valuable, is for this reason only of limited use. One of our aims, therefore, will be to identify those aspects of Barth's position that Plantinga does not examine and evaluate their impact on the question.

The remainder of this chapter will be devoted to pinpointing where Plantinga and Barth agree and disagree on the question of natural theology. We will begin with an exploration of the driving concerns that motivate Barth's "extreme" position and clarify just what was the *natürliche Theologie* he so spurned. We will then take a look at Plantinga's engagement with Barth and Plantinga's explanation of his own position.

---

[5]Barth's most famous and forceful objection is, of course, his *Nein! Antwort an Emil Brunner* (Munich: Kaiser, 1934). Plantinga sees his own views as aligned with a traditional Reformed objection to natural theology. See RBG, pp. 63-73; Plantinga, "The Reformed Objection to Natural Theology," in *Philosophical Knowledge* (Washington, DC: American Catholic Philosophical Association, 1980), pp. 49-62; Plantinga, "The Reformed Objection Revisited," *Christian Scholar's Review* 12 (1983): 17-61; and Plantinga, "The Prospects for Natural Theology," *Philosophical Perspectives* 5 (1991): 287-315.

[6]RBG, pp. 68-72.

[7]Plantinga, "The Reformed Objection Revisited," p. 58.

[8]Plantinga, "Natural Theology," in *A Companion to Metaphysics,* ed. Jaegwon Kim and Ernest Sosa (Oxford: Blackwell, 1995), p. 347.

In conclusion, I will assess the significance of our findings and determine if and how we might need to revise our emerging unified proposal and what has been, up to this point, a positive assessment of the compatibility, complementarity and centrolineality of their thought.

PART 1: BARTH'S DRIVING CONCERNS AND THE NATURAL THEOLOGY HE REJECTS

Most of what we need in order to understand Barth's rejection of natural theology has already been unearthed in the first two chapters. What we will attempt here is an unpacking of the implications that Barth himself saw for the question of natural theology.

Rejecting the move from below. Barth's primary motivation for rejecting natural theology is no different from his primary concern about the relationship between philosophy and theology. Thomas F. Torrance captures it well when he writes: "what Barth objects to in natural theology is not its rational structure as such but its *independent* character, i.e. the autonomous rational structure which it develops on the ground of 'nature alone' in abstraction from the active self-disclosure of the living God."[9] If it were reason, per se, that Barth was objecting to, then we might be able to understand him as a thoroughgoing Ritschlian—positing a chasm between nature and grace. Instead, for Barth, the fundamental problem with natural theology is its presumption of an independently accessible knowledge of God on the basis of an innate human capacity. We saw in chapter two that, when it comes to theological knowing, Barth rejects the general starting-point assumption and the accessibility requirement of Enlightenment modernism. In both cases we saw that Barth's underlying conviction is that the knowledge of God can be established not from below on the basis of human thought or capacity but only from above on the basis of divine self-revelation. So just as Barth, in rejecting philosophy's pretension to have access to an independent source of the knowledge of God, does not reject philosophy per se—the very realm in which theology must inevitably do its business—so also with human reason, he does not dismiss or reduce its

[9] Thomas F. Torrance, "The Problem of Natural Theology in the Thought of Karl Barth," *Religious Studies* 6 (1970): 128.

importance and centrality. He is quite clear that the knowledge of God by faith in the grace of divine self-revelation is a communication of divine reason with human reason. "The encounter of God and man takes place primarily, pre-eminently and characteristically in this sphere of *ratio.*"[10] The problem with natural theology is not the importance assigned to human reason but its latent presumption that human reason could provide neutral and independent access to the knowledge of God apart from encounter with and transformation by God.

A similarly qualified, positive claim can be made for creation, history, culture and humanity. While these all lack an inherent capacity to effect revelation, Barth is still able to affirm their role in the activity of divine self-revealing. In a 1926 lecture that has proven confusing for some interpreters,[11] Barth is content to affirm that there is a "buried and forgotten truth of creation" and that "culture can be a witness." He even hints that there might be an acceptable way of conceiving of natural theology![12] These statements, however, can prove rather misleading without the crucial qualification that creation and culture are only instruments of revelation by the grace of Jesus Christ in the activity of divine self-revealing. Nevertheless, as instruments, the media God freely chooses to use are not insignificant, arbitrary or inconsequential.[13] Bruce McCormack helpfully recommends distinguishing between the

---

[10]*CD* I/1, p. 135.

[11]Karl Barth, "Church and Culture," trans. Louise Pettibone Smith, in *Theology and Church: Shorter Writings, 1920–1928* (London: SCM Press, 1926), pp. 334-54; originally published as "Die Kirche und die Kultur," in *Vorträge und Kleinere Arbeiten, 1925–1930,* ed. Hermann Schmidt (Zurich: Theologisher Verlag, 1926). Hans Urs von Balthasar believes that Barth's rift with Brunner arose because Barth did not stick to his 1926 position (Balthasar, *Karl Barth: Darstellung und Deutung seiner Theologie* [Cologne: J. Hegner, 1951], p. 96). I will argue that there is no discontinuity between Barth's objection to Brunner's natural theology and his statements in the 1926 lecture.

[12]Barth, "Church and Culture," pp. 342-43 ("Die Kirche und die Kultur," pp. 22-24). See also *CD* I/1, pp. 130-31.

[13]Barth's notorious comment about the freedom of God to speak through any creaturely medium could easily be taken to indicate the arbitrariness of the medium. "God may speak to us through Russian Communism, a flute concerto, a blossoming shrub, or a dead dog" (*CD* I/1, p. 55). To conclude this would be to ignore Barth's warning that immediately follows, that unless we consider ourselves to be prophets of a new church, our proclamation is to be based on "an exposition of some portion of the biblical witness to revelation." Ignoring the secular form of the word would be the hallmark of "idealistic theology," which is for Barth "bad theology" (*CD* I/1, p. 175). See also Trevor Hart's helpful discussion in *Regarding Karl Barth: Essays Toward a Reading of His Theology* (Carlisle, UK: Paternoster Press, 1999), pp. 19-26.

locus of revelation and the "source (the power) by means of which revelation (in the Bible or in nature and history) [is] actualized."[14] It is accurate to say that on Barth's view, Emil Brunner did not adequately grasp this distinction.

The legendary exchange between Barth and Brunner in 1934 is Barth's most resolute statement against natural theology and is particularly helpful in distinguishing Barth's view from other objections to natural theology. Brunner seems to have heard Barth's positive statements but failed to comprehend their strict qualifications, thereby overestimating Barth's agreement with his own position.[15] Barth perceives that by beginning with a human "capacity for revelation" (*Offenbarungsmächtigkeit*) Brunner fails to maintain the absoluteness of human dependence on God for the knowledge of God.[16] He believes that this move inevitably leads to a suppression and distortion of revelation with potentially disastrous consequences, like those unfolding in Germany at the very time of his writing. Barth's acerbic reply to Brunner should be viewed in light of the capitulation of German Christians to Nazi national theology and the alarming events beginning in 1933, which involved an appeal to German culture as a source of natural revelation.[17]

Despite Brunner's protests, Barth contends that by allowing a revelation that issues from below, Brunner violates the Reformers' *sola gratia.*[18] Brunner's surprise and confusion over Barth's rebuke leads to one of the most illuminating aspects of the debate. Brunner assumes

---

[14]Bruce McCormack, *Karl Barth's Critically Realistic Dialectical Theology: Its Genesis and Development, 1909–1936* [Oxford: Oxford University Press, 1995], p. 306 n. 51.

[15]Emil Brunner, *Natur und Gnade: Zum Gespräch mit Karl Barth* (Tübingen: Mohr, 1934), p. 6; translated by Peter Fraenkel as "Nature and Grace," in *Natural Theology,* ed. John Baillie (London: Centenary Press, 1934), pp. 18-19.

[16]Karl Barth, "No! Answer to Emil Brunner," trans. Peter Fraenkel, in *Natural Theology,* ed. John Baillie (London: Centenary Press, 1934), p. 78. It might be that the word *capacity* is too neutral and passive to convey the connotation of *mächtigkeit.* A more literal translation—"power for revelation"—might also better account for Barth's strong reaction.

[17]Particularly in mind here are the establishment of the German Evangelical Church, its assimilation with the state and the appointment of the *Reichsbischof.* In 1933, Barth decries the zeal to find a church leader "in the concrete form of Adolf Hitler and leaders under him." He expresses his dismay that the pursuit of a national bishop "has made the Evangelical Church look ridiculous," and with chilling prescience he warns, "the consequences may turn out to be worse than all the actual and imagined evil of the past" (Barth, *Theological Existence To-Day! A Plea for Theological Freedom,* trans. R. Birch Hoyle [London: Hodder & Stoughton, 1933], pp. 34, 41).

[18]Barth, "No!," pp. 80, 85.

that he and Barth are in essential agreement, each rejecting a natural theology that begins from below, independent of the light of grace. He claims to stand with the Reformers in insisting that "the light of the revelation in Christ must shine into nature in order to light up this foundation."[19] He then distinguishes this view from what he understands to be the positions of Roman Catholicism and Enlightenment rationalism.[20] This is helpful in that it provides us with at least three alternative positions on natural theology that can be contrasted usefully to distinguish Barth's own position.

Brunner, Roman Catholicism and Enlightenment rationalism. Of the four positions Brunner identifies, Enlightenment rationalism clearly offers the most permissive or optimistic attitude toward natural theology. On this view, human reason apart from grace becomes the sole and independent organ for arriving at knowledge of God. Divine special revelation is subordinated in such a way as to become irrelevant or is denied altogether. Barth and Brunner agree that such a positive view of natural theology must be opposed, and their agreement seems to stem from a shared opinion about the limitations of human reason. The optimism of Enlightenment rationalism regarding the essential capacities and uncorrupted condition of human reason makes it untenable. The limitations of human reason, however, arise from two considerations that should be highlighted separately—limitations that obtain as a result of human sin and limitations that obtain merely as a consequence of being human. With respect to the noetic effects of sin, it would seem that Barth and Brunner generally agree. According to Barth, "the discernment of the creation of man which is also the revelation of God, has, however, been taken from us by the fall, at least according to Reformation ideas of the extent of sin, and it is restored to us in the Gospel, in *revelatio specialis*."[21] But for Brunner, once the blindness of sin is removed by the grace of Jesus Christ, there is restored a human capacity to grasp a rudimentary knowledge of God "imprinted" on creation.[22] So, for Brunner,

---

[19]Brunner, "Nature and Grace," p. 47.
[20]Ibid., pp. 45-48.
[21]*CD* I/1, p. 130.
[22]Brunner, "Nature and Grace," p. 25.

natural theology, rightly construed, is not a "self-sufficient rational system."[23] We must begin with the grace of special revelation from above, which then enables a proper general revelation from below. For this reason, Brunner can give qualifications that appear quite compatible with Barth's position. For instance, Brunner states, "Only the Christian, i.e. the man who stands within the revelation in Christ, has the true natural knowledge of God."[24] Moreover, Brunner agrees with Barth that philosophical arguments are inadequate to serve as the basis for Christian belief.[25] All these qualifications must be made for Brunner because of the limitations imposed by the pervasive effects of human sin.

We move now to a second alternative, Brunner's characterization of the Roman Catholic view. Brunner believes that his assessment of the impact of sin on the powers of human reason separates his Reformed position from the Catholic view.[26] According to Brunner, the Roman Catholic position divides the realms of faith and reason cleanly. Truths that can be known by the power of human reason are not made any less accessible by a noetic impact of sin. Natural theology is independent of revealed theology and may even provide the basis for grounding the claims or apparatus of faith. Here again Barth and Brunner agree. This view of natural theology must be opposed, though we will see that Barth believes Brunner has misunderstood the Catholic position. They both strongly deny that the knowledge of God might have a prior foundation in philosophical argument or any other independent human grounding.[27] In other words, Brunner agrees with Barth's objections to the general starting-point assumption and the accessibility requirement. With so much agreement, what then is the basis for Barth's scathing disapprobation? The difference between Barth and Brunner is not a difference over the noetic effects of sin but rather a disagreement about wider human limitations with respect to the knowledge of God. I will expand

---

[23]Ibid., p. 46.

[24]Ibid., p. 27.

[25]Ibid., p. 58.

[26]Ibid., p. 46.

[27]Brunner denies that his eristic theology has anything to do with providing an external foundation for theology and objects to what he takes to be the Roman Catholic enterprise of seeking philosophical proofs or foundations (ibid., p. 35 nn. 14, 46).

on this as we now turn to a third alternative, Brunner's own position.

Brunner maintained that a genuine and relatively independent natural theology was possible, but only in the light of grace, which restores a natural sight once robbed by sin. Creation itself is endowed with a natural capacity to reflect the attributes of its Creator, and human beings, as created in the image of God, have a natural capacity to apprehend the knowledge of God reflected in creation.[28] This human capacity for apprehension is obliterated by sin and restored by grace in Christ. But Brunner also stresses the importance of maintaining that, while capacities constituting the *material* image of God are destroyed, the *formal* image of God is not destroyed by sin. The untouched formal image of God must remain intact to provide the "point of contact" for divine grace.[29] Unless sin were to destroy the human completely, it cannot take away the passive receptivity to divine address that human beings possess in virtue of being created in the image of God. In all of this, there is no material capacity or human contribution, so the principle of *sola gratia* is never violated. Brunner believes that a formal possibility must be affirmed if human beings are to remain responsible.[30] Furthermore, this formal passive receptivity becomes the basis of a qualified negative apologetics Brunner calls "eristics."[31]

Barth's sharp disagreement with Brunner is at root an objection to Brunner's positive assessment of human capacity on the basis of the unbroken *formal* image of God. Barth does not dispute the claim that a formal image of God remains intact in sinful humans.[32] But he rejects the suggestion that this entails any form of natural human capacity, receptivity or predisposition for revelation. "Man has completely lost the capacity for God."[33] No matter how passive, any human predisposition that might function to explain the possibility of receiving grace is seen

[28]"In every creation the spirit of the creator is in some way recognisable. The artist is known by all his works" (ibid., p. 24; see also the German original, *Natur und Gnade,* p. 11: "jedes Werk lobt seinen Meister").

[29]Brunner, "Nature and Grace," p. 31 (*Natur und Gnade,* p. 18: "Anknüpfungspunkt").

[30]Emil Brunner, "Die andere Aufgabe der Theologie," *Zwischen den Zeiten* 7 (1929): 273.

[31]Brunner, "Nature and Grace," p. 59.

[32]"In this formal sense the original image of God in man is not destroyed. Indeed not, we may well say. Even as a sinner man is man and not a tortoise" (Barth, "No!," p. 79).

[33]*CD* I/1, p. 238.

by Barth as a human contribution and therefore a violation of *sola gratia*.[34] He contends that Brunner's position is, in fact, much closer to the Roman Catholic view.

Barth finds Brunner's caricature of the Catholic conception of natural theology to be "sadly distorted."[35] Brunner suggests that Roman Catholicism holds that the deliverances of human reason with respect to natural theology are unaffected by sin and are therefore not in need of a restoring grace. According to Brunner, what sets his position apart is its appeal to the prevenience of grace so that while natural theology is independent of revealed theology, it is nevertheless subordinated to it. But, as Barth argues, in Roman Catholic theology "a true knowledge of God derived from reason and nature is *de facto* never attained without prevenient and preparatory grace."[36] The real Catholic position is very close to Brunner's, and the outcome is similar as well—two sources of the knowledge of God: one delivered by human reason in contemplation of the imprint of the Creator on creation and the other delivered by faith, the supernatural self-revelation of God in Christ and through scripture. Brunner believed that he had sufficiently distinguished his view from the Roman Catholic approach by objecting to philosophical proofs and the pursuit of an externally grounded rational basis for theology.[37] But this seems to assume that Catholic theology accepts the presuppositions of Enlightenment rationalism, even prior to the Enlightenment.[38] The

---

[34]This would be, in Trevor Hart's terms, the "smuggling in of a material sense" (*Regarding Karl Barth*, p. 171). Hart offers a helpful distinction between active and passive capacities, noting that in Barth's view, Brunner's formal/passive capacity has traces of the material/active sense (ibid., pp. 167-71).

[35]Barth, "No!," p. 95.

[36]Ibid., p. 96.

[37]Brunner, "Nature and Grace," p. 58.

[38]What Brunner gives us here is a common caricature of the Catholic attitude toward *fundamental* theology that has been helpfully questioned not least by Barth himself in his interpretation of Anselm's *Proslogion 2–4* (*Fides quaerens Intellectum: Anselms Beweis der Existenz Gottes im Zusammenhang seines theologischen Programms*, Forschungen zur Geschichte und Lehre des Protestantismus 4 [Munich: Kaiser, 1931], 3:76-199). For a clarification of the Catholic view, see also Walter Kasper, *Der Gott Jesu Christi* (Mainz: Matthias-Grünewald-Verlag, 1982); translated by Matthew J. O'Connell as *The God of Jesus Christ* (New York: Crossroad, 1984); Eugene F. Rogers, *Thomas Aquinas and Karl Barth: Sacred Doctrine and the Natural Knowledge of God* (Notre Dame, IN: University of Notre Dame Press, 1995); and Nicholas Wolterstorff, "The Migration of Theistic Arguments: From Natural Theology to Evidentialist Apologetics," in *Rationality, Religious Belief, and Moral Commitment: New Essays in the Philosophy of Religion*, ed. Robert Audi and William J. Wainwright (Ithaca, NY: Cornell University Press, 1986), pp. 38-81.

Roman Catholic view agrees to the distinction between natural and revealed theology but also agrees to the priority of revealed theology and the dependence on grace for each. As Walter Kasper clarifies, in Catholic thought the possibility of natural theology is presupposed on the basis of revelation, and there is no natural capacity independent of grace.[39]

Barth's insistence on the direct action of God in all revelation. No matter how cautious or humble, any suggestion of a source of the knowledge of God outside of God's own activity of self-revelation cannot be countenanced on Barth's view. In Barth's view, this is what really separates him from Brunner and the Roman Catholic position. The impact of sin was not to disrupt an otherwise neutral and relatively independent created capacity either in nature to reflect the knowledge of God or in human beings to apprehend this reflection. The impact of sin was not to disrupt a *natural* order instituted as an impersonal witness within the order of grace. The impact of sin was to disrupt fellowship with God, within which God's self-disclosure, enabling creatures to hear and creation to speak, was always given *supernaturally.* "Only retrospectively is it possible to reflect on the way in which he 'makes contact' with man, and this retrospect will ever be a retrospect upon a *miracle.*"[40] It is not enough to stipulate that a natural knowledge of God is enabled by God indirectly—that a capacity for independent discovery is "infused by God."[41] All revelation, no matter what its medium, to the extent that it is an enabling of a real knowledge of God, is a miraculous, supernatural gift. For this reason Barth rejects any strong division between two books or two types of revelation.[42] Geoffrey Bromiley has suggested that Barth's critique of natural theology should be differentiated from an objection to "natural revelation."[43] There is, however, every reason to think that Barth strongly resists the notion of natural revelation, where creation is endowed with the capacity successfully to reveal God. While Barth may allow that it is proper to creation to serve as a witness in the supernatural miracle of

---

[39]Kasper, *Gott Jesu Christi*, pp. 70-77.

[40]Barth, "No!," p. 121, emphasis original.

[41]*CD* I/1, p. 216.

[42]*CD* III/1, p. 414.

[43]Geoffrey W. Bromiley, "Karl Barth," in *Creative Minds in Contemporary Theology*, ed. Philip Edgcumbe Hughes (Grand Rapids: Eerdmans, 1966), p. 55.

divine self-revelation, it is not a property *of* creation so to serve. Consequently, the provision of a natural revelation, independent of the domain of supernatural revelation is rejected on the same grounds as Barth's rejection of natural theology. Critical to understanding Barth's objection is seeing that, in his view, revelation cannot be revelation unless it is an instance of direct divine self-disclosure.

But why is Barth so unflinching about the direct action of God in revelation? Why not think that God has endowed human beings with a faculty, we might call it the *sensus divinitatis,* that can operate in relative independence from the direct action of the Holy Spirit? Why not think that when this faculty is regenerated and functioning properly, it can lead us to a real knowledge of God purely from a consideration of creation, which God has similarly endowed with a capacity to witness to God in relative independence from the work of the Spirit? To get to the heart of what is motivating Barth's position we need only return to what we have already established in the first two chapters regarding Barth's theology of revelation, starting with Barth's rejection of the general starting-point assumption—his resistance to grounding a theology of revelation in any a priori claims about revelation.

Barth intends his dogmatics to be a reflection on the one a priori event of revelation itself. Barth's theo-foundationalism eschews any anthropological bases or foundational philosophical assumptions. The only foundation is the one God himself establishes in his divine self-disclosure. This is an approach that is quite like Plantinga's own particularism, working inductively from what has already been made known.[44] In fact, *particularism* is the term George Hunsinger adopts to indicate Barth's strictly inductive approach. Hunsinger maintains that Barth's particularism is a key motivator for Barth's rejection of natural theology.[45] This is not to suggest that particularism itself is for Barth an

[44]See the discussion in chapter 4. Plantinga begins not with a general criteria for proper basicality but with instances of knowledge already known and held in the basic way.

[45]Hunsinger also quite rightly finds that natural theology is in conflict with what he has identified as the Barthian motifs of *actualism* and *objectivism.* In Barth's eyes, all these motifs unfold from the foundation that God himself establishes in his self-revelation (Hunsinger, *How to Read Karl Barth: The Shape of His Theology* [New York: Oxford University Press, 1991], pp. 96-99).

a priori methodological assumption.[46] Hunsinger is quite clear that the Barthian motifs he identifies are not a priori philosophical principles or foundational commitments; rather, they are to be taken as forms of thought arising out of or "implicit in" the event of revelation itself.[47] In other words, Barth is not guilty of adopting particularism as a *general* principle. Instead, his particularism describes the realization, in the light of divine self-revelation, that the Creator who is making himself known is truly sui generis, utterly transcending the created media of revelation. His particularism is motivated by an encounter with the uniqueness of the one doing the self-revealing. He writes: "A result of the uniqueness of this object of knowledge might well be that the concept of its knowledge cannot be definitively measured by the concept of the knowledge of other objects or by a general concept of knowledge but that it can be defined at all only in terms of its own object."[48] The uniqueness of God creates a problem for any revelation that moves from creation to Creator. In fact, the uniqueness of God is problematic for revelation in general.[49]

This problem is often discussed as a problem of theological reference[50] or the problem of the inadequacy of human language and concepts for the knowledge of God.[51] For Brunner, the solution seems to be found in the *imago Dei* as the point of contact for human beings.[52] Barth believed that the Roman Catholic solution was based on an *analogia entis.*[53]

---

[46]Thomas F. Torrance notes the interesting parallels between what we have called Barth's particularism and what he calls "*a posteriori* science." We should be careful, however, not to think that an analogy to science provides Barth a basis for or a validation of the way in which he proceeds theologically. It is potentially misleading, therefore, to conclude that "Barth's exclusion of natural theology is seen to rest on the two-fold ground of theological content and scientific method." The only ground for the knowledge of God, as Torrance thoroughly affirms, is "its objective ground in God himself" (Torrance, "Problem of Natural Theology in the Thought of Karl Barth," p. 128).

[47]Hunsinger, *How to Read Karl Barth,* pp. 29-30.

[48]*CD* I/1, p. 190.

[49]This amplifies the problem Kierkegaard engages at the beginning of the *Fragments.* If, in ignorance of the truth, we lack also the condition for recognizing the truth, how can truth be learned? (Kierkegaard, *Philosophical Fragments*, trans. Howard V. Hong and Edna H. Hong [Princeton, NJ: Princeton University Press, 1985], pp. 9-22).

[50]See Aquinas's famous treatment of the names of God (*Summa Theologica* 1.13).

[51]Plantinga addresses a version of this problem in the first chapter of *WCB.*

[52]Brunner, "Nature and Grace," p. 31.

[53]*CD* I/1, p. xiii. In Keith Johnson's lucid study on Barth's opposition to the *analogia entis,* he rightly notes that Barth softens his rhetoric in *CD* II/1 after his exchange with Söhngen, allowing that

In the development of Barth's own thought he wrestles with the fact that the God who makes himself known is known to be so independent and transcendent as to cast doubt on a genuine human possibility of knowing him.[54] In order to preserve the revealed truth of God's freedom and uniqueness, Barth concludes that not just the knowledge of God but all conditions for the possibility of the knowledge of God must come from outside creation, from God alone. God himself provides, indeed is, the possibility of his own knowability. "Man must be set aside and God himself presented as the original subject, as the primary power, as the creator of the possibility of knowledge of God's Word."[55] More specifically, as we saw in chapter two, Barth's solution takes shape within his doctrines of the Trinity and incarnation. The problem of the possibility of human reception of divine revelation—the subjective appropriation of revelation—is overcome in that God is his own revealedness. God is both the object and, as the Spirit, the subject of his revealing. The Revealer and revealing act are one with the success of that act. This does not spiritualize revelation in such a way that it ceases to be creaturely knowledge or such that creaturely mediation becomes irrelevant. Barth is, instead, insisting that the possibility of genuine human knowing is the gift of our participation in the incarnate Christ by the ministry of the Spirit.[56] Creaturely mediation remains without a betrayal of God's

---

the Catholic position may have changed (Johnson, *Karl Barth and the* Analogia Entis [London: T & T Clark, 2012], p. 180). We will take a closer look at the problem of analogical predication in the next chapter.

[54]Helpful treatments of Barth's development from *Der Römerbrief* on the issue of the possibility of revelation include Balthasar, *Karl Barth;* McCormack, *Karl Barth's Critically Realistic Dialectical Theology,* pp. 241-374; and Wolfhart Pannenberg, "Die Subjectivität Gottes und die Trinitätslehre: Ein Beitrag zur Beziehen zwischen Karl Barth und der Philosophie Hegels," in *Grundfragen systematischer Theologie: Gesammelte Aufsatze* (Göttingen: Vandenhoeck & Ruprecht, 1980), pp. 96-98.

[55]*CD* I/1, p. 247.

[56]Here once again we should emphasize that while the doctrine of the Trinity is at the heart of Barth's solution to the freedom of God in his revelation, this does not mean that the *doctrine* of the Trinity is the fundamental presupposition upon which Barth deduces his theology of revelation. God is the ground for our knowledge of God. It is not that a doctrine or presupposition about God is the ground for Barth's conception of revelation. It is in this light that we should understand Pannenberg's conclusion that "die immanente Trinität ist somit der Grundstein für Barths Konzeption der Selbständigkeit Gottes in seiner Offenbarung" ("Die Subjectivität Gottes und die Trinitätslehre," p. 98).

radical uniqueness.[57] Though the power to mediate divine revelation is not a capacity inherent in or transferred to creaturely media, nevertheless, through the gift of faith,[58] creaturely media serve as the vehicles of divine communication. As Barth says, "the power of this reference does not lie in itself; it lies in that to which it refers."[59]

We can conclude that Barth's unflagging insistence on the direct action of God in revelation and his resistance to any creaturely capacities for the knowledge of God fundamentally stem from two reflections on the event of God's self-revelation. The first is that God is really, genuinely, humanly and cognitively known in his revelation. The second reflection is that the God we meet in God's self-revelation is so utterly unique that no creaturely phenomenon could explain the possibility of his being humanly known. The only solution that can maintain both affirmations is one where the possibility for real human knowing of God is in no way given over to or implanted in creation. This explains Barth's disagreement with Brunner and his rejection of any form of natural theology that might compromise God's freedom and transcendence by implying that the source and power of the revelation of God could be anything other than God himself. This also begins to explain the bluntness and urgency of Barth's response.[60] Barth saw that the consequences of a compromise of God's freedom and transcendence in his revelation could be disastrous. The inevitable outcome of a conceiving of God from human ideas rather than from the givenness of revelation was a loss of the knowledge of God altogether and a fulfillment of the suspicions of Feuerbach. Such a move would be "the end of all, yes, *all* certainty."[61] Granted, the particular historical situation out of which

---

[57]See Bruce McCormack's enlightening exposition of Barth's discovery of this affirmation with respect to the incarnation accomplished in the "anhypostatic-enhypostatic" christological dogma (McCormack, *Karl Barth's Critically Realistic Dialectical Theology*, pp. 325-463).

[58]Instead of an *analogia entis*, Barth suggests an *analogia fidei*, in which our knowledge of God is in our being known by God. "It is the divine act of knowledge which takes place on man rather than through man that distinguishes those whose knowledge is grounded in love of God and therefore in true fellowship with Him, in the presence of God" (*CD* I/1, p. 244).

[59]*CD* I/1, p. 197.

[60]John Webster describes Barth's response to Brunner as "rude" and "rather savage" (Webster, "Introducing Barth," in *The Cambridge Companion to Karl Barth*, ed. John B. Webster [Cambridge: Cambridge University Press, 2000], p. 6).

[61]*CD* I/1, p. 216, emphasis original.

Barth was writing highlighted these dire consequences,[62] but it is quite unlikely that Barth imagined a situation in which opposing this error was anything less than imperative for a theologian of the church.[63]

Finally, God's direct action is always essential to revelation because "revelation in fact does not differ from the person of Jesus Christ nor from the reconciliation accomplished in Him."[64] God is who he is, and is known to be who he is, in his action of drawing us into relationship with him by the person and work of Jesus Christ through the ministry of the Spirit.[65] There cannot be a full-fledged human knowledge of God that is not incorporated into this activity of transforming grace. This is what we find at the heart of Barth's objection to natural theology. It seems that in Barth's view all natural theology, including Brunner's qualified endorsement, is guilty of conceiving of a positive knowledge of God derived by human beings independent of direct active encounter with the sovereign, triune God who by his own revelation overcomes all barriers to revelation. Barth will grant that such knowledge is possible, but only as a mere abstraction, which—on its own—does us no good.[66]

Assessment of Barth on natural theology. It is safe to conclude that the fundamental difference between Barth and Brunner is not over their estimation of the noetic effects of sin, or the perseverance of a formal *imago Dei,* or the possibility that creation and culture might be used in

---

[62]Thomas F. Torrance maintains that Barth's contemporary situation "explains why Barth was so angry with Emil Brunner's mediating pamphlet 'Nature and Grace,' for to those fighting the battle of resistance in Germany it appeared to fortify the basis on which the so-called 'German Christians' were advocating conciliation with the Nazi régime" (Torrance, "Problem of Natural Theology in the Thought of Karl Barth," p. 125).

[63]We should not take as a retraction Barth's 1966 message to Brunner stating that he no longer felt he needed to say no. Nor should we see this as an indication that the historical situation no longer necessitated a strong opposition to the notion of an independent, though restored-by-grace, natural capacity for revelation. Brunner was on his death bed, and Barth simply wanted to emphasize God's gracious yes to humanity as the source of life: "sagen Sie ihn *doch ja,* die Zeit da ich meinte, ihm ein 'Nein!' entgegenrufen zu müssen, sei längst vorüber, wo wir doch alle nur davon leben, daß ein großer un barmherziger Gott zu uns allen sein gnädiges Ja sagt" (Barth, *Karl Barth—Emil Brunner Briefwechsel 1916–1966,* ed. Eberhard Busch, complete works 5 [Zurich: Theologischer Verlag, 2000], p. 391).

[64]*CD* I/1, p. 119.

[65]This seems to be what Hunsinger has in mind in his identification of Barth's "actualism" as an important motif in shaping Barth's attitude toward natural theology (Hunsinger, *How to Read Karl Barth,* pp. 96-99).

[66]*CD* IV/1, p. 765.

the service of divine self-revelation. We do have a human capacity to be made recipients of revelation, but it is a divinely given and divinely actualized capacity. What Barth rejects is the possibility of building our knowledge of God on the foundation of a general revelation unrelated to God's encountering us in Jesus Christ by the Spirit. This does not entail that creation and culture cannot serve as media of divine revelation whereby encounter with Jesus is actualized by God. For Barth it *is* possible to know God by his effects but not *merely* by his effects. Even knowing God by his effects requires God's immediate act. What this does entail is either eradication or a heavy blurring of the distinction between general or natural revelation and special or supernatural revelation. Barth emphatically denounces the separation of nature and grace into two books of revelation.[67] All revelation, whether through reflection on the cosmos or by means of the testimony of prophets and apostles, is an activity of divine grace and, more specifically, a gracious encounter with Jesus Christ by the transformative work of the Spirit.

Barth's position can be clarified further by distinguishing it from other options with respect to two considerations frequently operative in stronger demarcations between special and general revelation—namely, the availability of revelation and the kind of grace active in revelation. Starting with the question of the availability of revelation, we saw in chapter five that Plantinga follows Aquinas and Calvin in affirming some kind of innate capacity for a rudimentary knowledge of God activated in the presence of triggering conditions that might include an inward or outward experience of created existence. This is a *natural* knowledge in that the human cognitive equipment involved is part of the original design plan. We might continue to follow Calvin and suggest that this is a universal knowledge, in that the original design plan expresses an intention for every human being.[68] Barth is willing to go along up to a point. In his exposition of Romans 1:18-21, Barth grants that "it is unquestionable that knowledge of God is here ascribed to man in the cosmos, and knowability is ascribed to God."[69] For Barth, however,

---

[67]Barth rejects what he calls the "dual system of book-keeping" (*CD* III/1, p. 414).

[68]John Calvin, *Institutes*, I.ii-v.

[69]*CD* II/1, p. 119.

the very rubric of "universally available" knowledge is perilously misleading. The knowledge of God is never like a cache of information deposited either in human nature or in the created order, as if it were a substance at our disposal that could be mined and acquired. Knowledge of God, no matter how rudimentary—in order to qualify as knowledge of the true God—is personal, freely given, trinitarian self-disclosure. So Barth quickly adds, "There can be no doubt that Paul meant by this the revelation of the grace of God in Jesus Christ."[70] Edward Adams argues convincingly that for Calvin even the universal, natural knowledge of God is *revealed* knowledge. Though Calvin speaks of an implanted knowledge of God, "it does not come to human beings, nor do human beings come to it, apart from God's action but as a direct consequence of divine initiative."[71] This is patently the case for Barth, who (also like Calvin) would for this reason never speak of a knowledge of God arising from a natural "capacity." The fact that it is part of the original, designed intention for human beings to come to know God in no way changes Barth's conviction that a human knowledge of God—that surpasses mere abstract and impersonal information about God—involves the essential enabling action of the Spirit. This takes us to the second consideration, regarding kinds of grace.

It should be obvious that for Barth if there is no positive knowledge of God outside of active divine self-revelation, there is no natural knowledge of God independent of grace. Merely recognizing the necessity of grace for knowledge of God does not, however, distinguish Barth's view. Without further definition, an insistence on grace might only amount to what Henri de Lubac calls the rejection of the hypothesis of "pure nature,"[72] a relatively modest claim regarding the dependence of nature on divine sustaining. In this regard, Aquinas grants that "for the knowledge of any truth whatsoever man needs divine help, that the

[70]Ibid.

[71]Edward Adams, "Calvin's View of Natural Knowledge of God," *International Journal of Systematic Theology* 3, no. 3 (2001): 281-82. See also T. H. L. Parker, *The Doctrine of the Knowledge of God: A Study in the Theology of John Calvin* (Edinburgh: Oliver & Boyd, 1952); and the dissenting view of Edward A. Dowey, *The Knowledge of God in Calvin's Theology* (New York: Columbia University Press, 1952).

[72]Henri de Lubac, *The Mystery of the Supernatural*, trans. Rosemary Sheed (London: Chapman, 1967), pp. 53-74.

intellect may be moved by God to its act."[73] Aquinas grants this pervasive divine activity, which upholds and moves our natures, but distinguishes it from the activity of *sanctifying grace,* which adds something to our nature, thereby enabling a knowledge that surpasses what can be known by natural light. Some later Reformed thought observes a similar distinction, articulated as the difference between common grace and special or saving grace. Common grace, which accounts for general revelation, is a divine work that exerts a rational or moral influence but "leaves the heart unchanged."[74] For Barth, none of this will do. Genuine knowledge of God involves personal encounter with God, which cannot leave us unchanged. Revelation is both personal and transformative in a way that defies a clean separation of mind, heart and life. In other words, revelation requires the gift of faith to be received. Barth's dictum that "it is faith that hears, understands and obeys God's speech"[75] applies equally to all of God's speech, whether the medium is scripture or the starry heavens. For this reason, with respect to the gift of revelation, there can be no division of God's grace into kinds.

In conclusion, Barth's rejection of natural theology is required by his understanding of revelation and should be understood only as a rejection of the possibility of an intimate and genuine knowledge of God outside of active, triune self-disclosure through gracious, personal and transformative encounter with Jesus Christ by the ministry of the Spirit. If there is room for a properly construed and constrained *theologia naturalis,* as Barth himself suggests, it will be "included and brought into clear light"[76] in the theology of revelation.

Barth's position is not, in fact, as extreme as it is sometimes thought to be. There is no denial in his view of the significance of human cognition and reasoning in the reception of revelation, nor of the possibility that the created order or our general experience as creatures might indeed serve as a witness to the Creator. Barth is merely denying that created human capacities, even once renewed from the deleterious ef-

[73]Thomas Aquinas, *Summa Theologiae,* 1–2.109.1.

[74]By contrast, special grace is "spiritual and re-creative" (Louis Berkhof, *Systematic Theology,* 4th rev. ed. [Grand Rapids: Eerdmans, 1969], p. 437).

[75]*CD* I/1, p. 135.

[76]Barth, "Church and Culture," p. 342.

fects of sin, are ever in and of themselves sufficient. Vigilance here is required, not only for German Christians in 1934 but wherever the church is tempted toward the inevitable idolatry that results from seeking a way to the knowledge of God that is other than God's way to us. To choose to begin elsewhere constitutes disobedience and a de facto rejection of God's self-disclosure. General revelation and natural theology are not dismissed, only their illusory status as independent of "special" divine action.[77] If there is a *sensus divinitatis,* it operates within the realm of the action of the Holy Spirit.

Having seen ourselves clear of several misconceptions of Barth's position and having ventured a clarification of his core concerns, we are now ready to look at Plantinga's thoughts about natural theology in order to determine the extent and seriousness of his disagreement with Barth. But before we do, it is worth acknowledging two areas for further investigation that bear on the discussion of natural theology, but which we have mostly left unanalyzed. The first has to do with what qualifies as "knowledge of God." In principle, Barth thinks of the knowledge of God in a holistic sense, including propositional knowledge, personal acquaintance and even obedience. Barth hesitates to call simply knowing an isolated fact about God "knowledge of God," though for the analytic epistemologist, knowing an isolated fact about God does typically qualify as knowledge of God. Barth is interested in the kind of knowledge that comes with restored relationship with God. This is the only kind of knowledge on which theology can be rightly grounded. The second area for further investigation is intimately related to the first. It has to do with the nature of faith, which I have noted plays an essential noetic role in Barth's theology of revelation. Faith and the knowledge of God will occupy our attention in the next chapter. Both of these questions are raised by an obvious difficulty for Barth's position—namely, that it certainly seems that some who do not have Christian faith still possess at minimum a rudimentary knowledge of God. The discussion of natural theology tees up these questions nicely,

[77]As we have already pointed out, mere divine sustaining of the natural capacities is not enough. For Barth, the grace of revelation can never be taken to be an unspiritual, semiautomated process in which God remains personally distant and we remain unchanged.

and until they are addressed in the next chapter, the conclusions of this chapter remain incomplete.

PART 2: PLANTINGA ON NATURAL THEOLOGY

One of Alvin Plantinga's central contributions to the epistemology of religious belief has been to defend the possibility that accepting belief in God without an argument may be a perfectly rational and sensible thing to do. In the early days of his development of what would later be known as Reformed epistemology, one way in which Plantinga advanced his argument was by looking at what he termed "the Reformed objection to natural theology." In its first published form, Plantinga examined the positions taken by Herman Bavinck and John Calvin,[78] but when he incorporated it into his truly seminal essay, "Reason and Belief in God," it was expanded to include a treatment of "the Barthian dilemma."[79] For our purposes, we will first attempt to establish Plantinga's position with respect to natural theology and then turn to the connection with Barth.

The natural theology that Plantinga rejects. The *natural theology* Plantinga considers—under that name—is much more narrowly defined than the natural theology debated by Barth and Brunner. Plantinga uses the term to identify strictly "the attempt to prove or demonstrate the existence of God."[80] He does not, for instance, extend the definition to the possibility of arriving at a knowledge of God by the application of our natural faculties. Given this narrower definition, it is accurate to say that a central thrust of Plantinga's work has been to attack the notion of the necessity of natural theology for belief in God.[81] The nonnecessity of natural theology is a corollary of his rejection of Cliffordian eviden-

[78]Plantinga, "The Reformed Objection to Natural Theology," in *Philosophical Knowledge* (Washington, DC: American Catholic Philosophical Association, 1980), pp. 49-53.

[79]RBG, pp. 68-71. Unfortunately, this is the only point in Plantinga's corpus where he engages in any detail the thought of Karl Barth. Plantinga once conveyed to me that he has always been favorably disposed to Barth and might have engaged more with his writings except that Barth's particular nonanalytic style tends to interfere with one's gaining a clear understanding of his views.

[80]Ibid., p. 63; and Plantinga, "The Reformed Objection to Natural Theology," p. 49.

[81]In Philip Quinn's debate with Plantinga, he identifies the need for natural theology as the issue of deepest disagreement between them. "A great deal hangs on the fate of natural theology" (Quinn, "The Foundations of Theism Again: A Rejoinder to Plantinga," in *Rational Faith: Catholic Responses to Reformed Epistemology*, ed. Linda Zagzebski [Notre Dame, IN: University of Notre Dame Press, 1993], p. 162).

tialism and his defense of the proper basicality of theistic belief. Plantinga clearly sees himself in line with a tradition of Reformed thought on this point. He does not stop here, however; nor does the tradition with which he finds himself aligned. Not only is natural theology unnecessary for belief in God; but there is also something fundamentally improper about it.[82]

As we noted in chapter five, according to Plantinga, "if Christian beliefs are true, then the standard and most satisfactory way to hold them will not be as the conclusions of argument."[83] The impropriety of natural theology is its suggestion that rational inference from more certain, antecedently held beliefs provides the best foundation, not only for Christian belief but even for brute theism. Plantinga argues for the definitive superiority of a "testimonial model."[84] It is not rational inference but the testimony of God the Spirit that is the truly adequate and stable source of warrant for belief. He cites a conclusion Calvin reaches in Calvin's discussion of the proper basis for accepting the authority of scripture: "we ought to seek our conviction in a higher place than human reasons, judgments or conjectures, that is, in the secret testimony of the Spirit."[85] While Calvin is directly addressing the authority of scripture, Plantinga contends that the same holds true for belief in God's existence.[86] But what is it about the arguments of natural theology that make them unfitting grounds for belief in God?

Plantinga seems to have two responses to this question, both of which suggest that stable belief requires a degree of warrant that is not delivered by human arguments. At some points, Plantinga simply says that he has never come across an argument for Christian or generally theistic belief that confers a degree of warrant sufficient for knowledge

---

[82]Plantinga would disagree sharply with Norman Kretzmann's assertion that "natural theology still offers the best route by which philosophers can, as philosophers, approach theological propositions" (Kretzmann, *The Metaphysics of Theism: Aquinas's Natural Theology in Summa Contra Gentiles I* [Oxford: Clarendon Press, 1997], p. 22).

[83]*WCB*, p. 201.

[84]Ibid., pp. 255-68.

[85]Plantinga, "Reformed Objection to Natural Theology," p. 53; RBG, p. 67; and *WCB*, p. 267; quoting John Calvin, *Institutes of the Christian Religion*, ed. John T. McNeill, trans. Ford Lewis Battles (Philadelphia: Westminster Press, 1960) 1.7.4, p. 79.

[86]I am deliberately postponing for now the question of the role of the Spirit in belief formation involving the *sensus divinitatis.*

and strong conviction.[87] But at other points he seems willing to suggest that such arguments are inherently inadequate.[88] In chapter five we saw that, on Plantinga's model, properly basic beliefs hold a stronger position than the nonbasic beliefs inferred from them. He argues that a probabilistic argument from public evidence and historical investigation could never, by itself, produce warranted belief in either the existence of God or the "great things of the gospel." For Plantinga, the only adequate source of warrant for these beliefs exceeds the capacities of the arguments of natural theology and involves directly the design and action of God.

> If it's to be the case that at least some people actually know some of the claims of Christianity, or even are rational in actually believing them, there will have to be a separate source of warrant for such belief, something like, following Calvin and Aquinas, the internal testimony (Calvin) or instigation (Aquinas) of the Holy Spirit.[89]

So, for Plantinga, the rejection of natural theology is a recognition that human arguments are neither necessary nor sufficient for theistic or Christian belief. As I mentioned in chapters four and five, however, the arguments of natural theology retain, in Plantinga's view, considerable value.

Plantinga's role for arguments and inference. Plantinga emphatically denies the charge that he considers efforts to develop arguments for Christian belief to be "wrongheaded and inconsequential."[90] On the contrary, he maintains that such arguments "can be of use in many dif-

---

[87]E.g., "I don't know of good philosophical arguments for the claim that Christian belief is true (and I don't know of conclusive philosophical arguments for the claim that theism is true)" (Plantinga, "Internalism, Externalism, Defeaters and Arguments for Christian Belief," *Philosophia Christi* 3, no. 2 [2001]: 387). Or, "I don't know of an argument for Christian belief that seems very likely to convince one who doesn't already accept its conclusion" (*WCB*, p. 201). In *God and Other Minds*, Plantinga concludes that there are no noncircular arguments or evidence to support belief either for or against God.

[88]Arguments cannot deliver the kind of firm conviction that comes when belief is warranted in the basic way. "They have (or can have) much more firmness and stability than they could sensibly have if accepted on the basis of rational argument" (*WCB*, p. 264).

[89]Plantinga, "Rationality and Public Evidence: A Reply to Richard Swinburne," *Religious Studies* 37 (2001): 221.

[90]R. Douglas Geivett and Greg Jesson, "Plantinga's Externalism and the Terminus of Warrant-Based Epistemology," *Philosophia Christi* 3, no. 2 (2001): 338.

ferent and important ways."[91] In order to see the value of the arguments of natural theology for Plantinga, we will need to relax his above-cited definition of *natural theology*. The proper function of the arguments of natural theology is not to prove or demonstrate God's existence; nevertheless, such arguments can assist belief. For Plantinga, this assistance may be apologetical, assisting unbelievers in attaining belief, or pastoral, assisting believers in sustaining belief. In either case, arguments may be used by God to boost the positive epistemic status of belief or to neutralize arguments against belief and dispel doubt. In my treatment of Plantinga's position, I will look first at the pastoral role of natural theological arguments and then turn to their apologetical function.

Plantinga believes that rational arguments, which draw conclusions by inference from other beliefs, may be useful for those who have already arrived at theistic or Christian belief. That the arguments of natural theology might serve a pastoral role in the life of the believer is a possibility created by the reality that faith has not yet been made perfect. Like Barth, Plantinga recognizes that our faith finds itself in tension to some degree with our unbelief.[92] For Barth, our proper attitude is that of the father in Mark 9, who cries out to Jesus, "I believe; help my unbelief" (Mk 9:24).[93] In Plantinga's view, help from the Lord may come in the form of an argument that "can help dispel the doubt."[94] The idea here seems to be that at points when faith is waning an argument for the reasonableness of faith in light of other beliefs may help to prop up faith. Clearly, for Plantinga, Christian or theistic belief should not require the support of argument. Arguments only serve this purpose under less than optimal conditions, namely, when faith is in a weakened state.

Plantinga's thought diverges from Aquinas in an important way at

---

[91]Plantinga, "Internalism, Externalism, Defeaters and Arguments for Christian Belief," pp. 384-85.

[92]Plantinga defers to Calvin: "in the believing mind certainty is mixed with doubt" (Plantinga, "Christian Philosophy at the End of the Twentieth Century," in *Christian Philosophy at the Close of the Twentieth Century: Assessment and Perspective,* ed. Sander Griffioen and Bert M. Balk [Kampen, Netherlands: Uitgeverij Kok, 1995], p. 40, quoting John Calvin, *Institutes of the Christian Religion,* ed. John T. McNeill, trans. Ford Lewis Battles [Philadelphia: Westminster, 1960] 3.2.18, p. 564). See also *WCB,* pp. 260 n. 35, 264 n. 43.

[93]*CD* I/1, p. 24. He also writes, "Even and precisely in the depths of unbelief faith hears the new summons to faith" (*CD* I/1, p. 255).

[94]Plantinga, "Christian Philosophy at the End of the Twentieth Century," p. 40.

this point. Plantinga repeatedly distinguishes his understanding of the relationship between faith and reason, or philosophy and theology, as Augustinian rather than Thomist.[95] At the heart of this distinction is the assertion that, for the Thomist, taking something by faith is epistemically inferior to knowing it by reason.[96] The knowledge of faith is indirect, requiring an act of the will trusting in testimony, rather than the direct apprehension (*scientia*) provided by the light of reason. "Hence the knowledge of faith is more like hearing than seeing."[97] Plantinga rejects this Thomist characterization of faith and knowledge, and recommends instead an Augustinian view. On this view, knowing something by way of testimony is not necessarily inferior to knowing something by way of deductive argument. Thinking back to Plantinga's general model for how beliefs may have warrant, key conditions like design plan, truth orientation, environmental aptness and proper function are consistent across a number of different faculties. There is nothing on Plantinga's model to support the Thomist class distinction between testimony and demonstration. In fact, as Plantinga argues, there are many objects of knowing that are better known by testimony than by any other means (e.g., the speed of light or one's own name). Knowledge of God is a prime example. Genuine knowledge of God cannot be arrived at by reasoning alone but requires God's self-revealing design and action. In the case of God, therefore, hearing is better than seeing—or we might even say that hearing is a better seeing than that afforded by otherwise unassisted human intellectual vision.

Plantinga unflinchingly maintains that the arguments of natural theology are neither necessary nor sufficient for Christian or theistic belief. How is it then that on Plantinga's account of warrant, in times of

---

[95]See Plantinga, "Augustinian Christian Philosophy," *Monist* 75, no. 3 (1992): 316-20; Plantinga, "On Christian Scholarship," in *The Challenge and Promise of a Catholic University*, ed. Theodore Hesburgh (Notre Dame, IN: University of Notre Dame Press, 1994), pp. 157-59; and Plantinga, "Faith & Reason: A Response to Pope John Paul II's Encyclical Letter, Fides et Ratio," *Books & Culture* 5, no. 4 (1999): 29-31.

[96]The *locus classicus* for this in Aquinas is *Summa Theologiae*, 1.12. Here we find that faith's advantages over reason have to do with the limitations of reason. Knowledge by faith, however, is without intellectual vision and therefore lacks real understanding. Knowledge of God's essence is not available in this mortal life but awaits the beatific vision that surpasses faith because it is a direct seeing.

[97]Aquinas, *Summa Contra Gentiles*, 3.40.3.

weakened faith, such arguments may serve to assist belief and dispel doubt? Nowhere are we given a detailed answer;[98] however, Plantinga does suggest that the warrant for a single belief could come from multiple sources that together boost warrant to a level required for knowledge.[99] This affords an opportunity for the arguments of natural theology to play a positive role. In chapter five we saw that the impact of sin on cognitive environments and proper function may distort and attenuate doxastic experience and belief formation motivated by the operation of the *sensus divinitatis* or the internal instigation of the Holy Spirit (IIHS). The impact may diminish warrant to such a degree that it is no longer sufficient for knowledge. In this situation the warrant boost of a probabilistic or evidential natural theological argument may be such that, together with the deliverances of faith, "the combination of the two sources *is* sufficient for knowledge."[100]

We entered this discussion focused on the pastoral role of arguments, but the dynamics of the relationship between the deliverances of reason and the deliverances of faith are similar for the apologetical role. For the believer in the throes of doubt, struggling to maintain conviction in what once seemed more certain, arguments may be useful in either neutralizing or overwhelming doubt. Doubt may come because of specific defeating doubts, or it may indicate the weakening of the deliverances of faith, or both.[101] The arguments of natural theology may serve to defeat doubt directly or strengthen belief formation, or both. The same is the case for the unbeliever whose warrant for belief is disrupted by defeaters or weakened by the noetic impact of sin.[102] The apolo-

[98]Graham Oppy laments that Plantinga leaves the faith-bolstering role of arguments "seriously underdeveloped" (Oppy, "Natural Theology," in *Alvin Plantinga,* ed. Deane-Peter Baker [Cambridge: Cambridge University Press, 2007], p. 43).

[99]See Plantinga, "The Prospects for Natural Theology," *Philosophical Perspectives* 5 (1991): 311-12.

[100]Plantinga, "Reply," *Philosophical Books* 43, no. 2 (2002): 127-28, emphasis original. Plantinga is even willing to suggest that these two sources together may provide an "excess of warrant." Perhaps this is how we are to understand Plantinga's frequent suggestion that the arguments of natural theology may serve as *confirmations.* In the light of faith, such arguments are not only more convincing but actually confer an excess of warrant.

[101]I am suggesting not a weakening in what is offered by the Spirit but a weakening in its appropriation in the human knower.

[102]The noetic impact of sin, it should be remembered, is not confined to noetic degradation due to the personal rebellion of the knower in question but also includes a much broader form of noetic degradation due to brokenness in human relationships, thought forms and communication.

getical role of the arguments of natural theology will take either a negative role in the defeating of defeaters or a positive role in overwhelming defeaters (intrinsic defeater-deflectors) or in boosting warrant for belief in combination with the *sensus divinitatis* or IIHS.[103] Understood in this way, Plantinga is open to the usefulness of both negative and positive apologetics.[104]

Nonetheless, many of Plantinga's interlocutors have wanted to see a greater stress in Plantinga's work on the value of and need for the arguments of natural theology.[105] Plantinga's primary objective has been to show that theistic and Christian belief may be properly basic with no assistance from inferential reasoning. Some of Plantinga's more sympathetic objectors, however, while not disagreeing with Plantinga's main point, have been strongly critical of how understated the value of argument seems to be in Plantinga's models. Philip Quinn and James Beilby seem to agree that for many people living in the world today, theistic or Christian belief does require the assistance of argument to defeat defeaters or boost warrant.[106] In chapter five, I addressed the objection that Plantinga's "no-defeater condition" leaves belief in need of support from arguments, thereby undermining its basicality. There I argued that the employment of defeater-defeaters/deflectors, which is the enterprise of negative apologetics, does not undermine basicality because the arguments do not lend anything themselves positively to warrant. Instead, negative apologetical arguments work to remove ob-

---

[103]For Plantinga's thoughts on negative and positive apologetics, see Plantinga, "Augustinian Christian Philosophy," pp. 292-96; and Plantinga, "Christian Philosophy at the End of the Twentieth Century," pp. 37-40.

[104]Michael Sudduth is right to conclude that "Plantinga's criticisms of theistic arguments should not be construed as undermining positive apologetics, but rather as shaping it in a constructively critical manner" (Sudduth, "Reformed Epistemology and Christian Apologetics," *Religious Studies* 39 [2003]: 316).

[105]E.g., "I can't help but agree with David Basinger and the many critics of Reformed epistemology who echo his position, that the Christian has a duty to at least *attempt* to offer a positive apologetic for her beliefs" (Deane-Peter Baker, "Plantinga's Reformed Epistemology: What's the Question?" *International Journal for Philosophy of Religion* 57 [2005]: 100, emphasis original.)

[106]Quinn says this is the case for "intellectually sophisticated adults in our culture" (Quinn, "In Search of the Foundations of Theism," *Faith and Philosophy* 2, no. 4 [1985]: 481-84). Beilby argues that "typical believers" do not take theistic or Christian belief in the purely basic way (Beilby, *Epistemology as Theology*, pp. 135-37, 139; Beilby, "Plantinga's Model of Warranted Christian Belief," in *Alvin Plantinga*, ed. Deane-Peter Baker [Cambridge: Cambridge University Press, 2007], pp. 147-48).

structions to the flow of warrant. Surely, though, the same cannot be said for positive apologetics or the kind of arguments that might serve cooperatively to boost warrant when human appropriation of the deliverances of faith are attenuated by the personal and environmental, cognitive impact of sin. In these cases, theistic or Christian belief is no longer purely basic. We will return to this in a moment in discussion with Barth where I will make an irenic proposal for how best to understand Plantinga's notion of positive apologetics.

Plantinga and the Barthian dilemma. The only aspect of the theology of Karl Barth that Plantinga ever entertains at any depth is Barth's objection to natural theology, and even then it is only one aspect of Barth's objection to natural theology. Plantinga hones in on an argument Barth makes against an apologetical motivation for natural theology. This argument is lifted from a larger exposition on how it is that God may be known. Barth's broader theme in this section, simply put, is that the only explanation for the knowability of God is that in freedom God "gives Himself to us to be known, thus establishing our knowledge."[107] Revelation is "of the Father in Jesus Christ by the Holy Spirit."[108] Since the knowledge of God is only received as freely given from above, natural theology, which claims an independent knowledge of God in hand from below, is impossible. Barth then undertakes to examine why it is that natural theology is so popular. One motivation he considers is the apologetical impulse, seizing on the mistaken assumption that natural theology could provide "a common basis of communication between the Church and the world."[109] Barth strongly affirms the apologetical impulse:

> How can the Church be the Church if it is not actively engaged in this work; in the work of inviting and guiding from one point to the other, from the ignorance to the knowledge of God, and therefore from ungodliness to salvation; in the work of pointing the way that leads from the one to the other, and to that extent certainly also in the work of striving for a common basis of communication?[110]

---

[107] *CD* II/1, p. 69.
[108] *CD* II/1, p. 68.
[109] *CD* II/1, p. 91.
[110] *CD* II/1, p. 92.

The problem with attempting to deploy natural theology in the service of this "work of love" is that it pretends to take a different starting point than the only possible starting point, which is faith. Instead, faith *masks* itself as unbelief. This creates a dilemma.

Plantinga's reading of the dilemma is, I think, slightly different from what Barth actually proposes to be the dilemma. On Plantinga's read, the problem is that the believer must either genuinely abandon the standpoint of faith or be dishonest toward the unbeliever. The resolution to this dilemma, according to Plantinga, is simply for the believer not to wear the mask of unbelief at all. In Plantinga's view, the believer may deploy the resources of natural theology in the service of apologetics while being quite upfront about the fact that "her belief in God is not based on its relation to the deliverances of reason"[111] and, furthermore, that optimally belief in God is not based on arguments. For Barth, however, the whole enterprise of natural theology, as we have seen, rests on the assumption that there is a knowledge of God that can be accessed wholly from below, without God's deliberative, personal, self-revealing action. It might be the case that the existence of a being bearing a few of the abstract metaphysical attributes of the classical definition of *God* does follow or is highly likely given other propositions affirmed by the unbeliever. Moreover, attempting to point this out to the unbeliever may be a charitable Christian act. The grave danger of this endeavor is that it appears to suggest that a genuine knowledge of God is humanly accessible without the Spirit's immediate, deliberative, personal, self-revealing activity in the gift of faith.

Barth's dilemma is slightly different from the one Plantinga finds. For Barth, the apologetical deployment of natural theology entails a masking of faith. The first horn of the dilemma is not that faith would actually abandon itself to remain genuine but that masquerading faith would achieve a "successful" result. The second horn is that masquerading faith would fail to convince. Either result will not be the genuine knowledge of God that can only come with the gift of faith but rather a hardening toward faith. In the case of "success" (the first horn) it might be that the

---

[111]RBG, p. 71.

unbeliever agrees that something like theism could be affirmed on the basis of inference from propositions already held. The problem with this is that it is not faith, it is not a genuine knowledge of God, and it has not served to move the unbeliever out of self-sufficient reliance on the deliverances of reason to receive a genuine knowledge of God by the Spirit's gift of faith. What is more likely to happen, in Barth's estimation, is that this weak "success" will inoculate the converted against Christian belief. By the introduction of a weak belief under the human steam of "reason alone," "unbelief will . . . fortify itself all the more against faith."[112] In the case of failure (the second horn), "unbelief will be of the opinion that it has successfully defended itself against faith,"[113] serving to bolster all the more the self-assurance of unbelief. The unbeliever will think that the claims of faith have been considered and found wanting. In reality, the unbeliever has been allowed to resist a real encounter with the claims of faith, which are not met like a set of proposals to be considered from an academic distance according to their knowability in light of existing beliefs. The claims of faith not only make assertions about what is true and false about God and the world but are also accompanied by the authority of God's own testimony known in a personal encounter with God by the Spirit where the criterion for evaluation of the asserted propositions is included itself with the gift. The deployment of natural theology in the service of apologetics fails because instead of challenging human rational self-sufficiency, it panders to it.

Plantinga's conclusions from his brief excursus on Barth are right on target, even if they provide an incomplete picture of Barth's position. Plantinga is certainly correct that Barth rejects classical foundationalism and the notion that belief itself should be based on what we can infer from what we already believe. Though Plantinga is happy to countenance a role for arguments in bolstering weak faith, Barth and Plantinga seem to agree that "the correct and proper way to believe in God . . . [is] not on the basis of arguments from natural theology or anywhere else."[114] There is, however, more to Barth's concern. For Barth, convincing

[112]*CD* II/1, p. 93.
[113]*CD* II/1, pp. 93-94.
[114]RBG, p. 72.

someone with an argument to affirm the existence of a being who possesses a number of the metaphysical attributes traditionally affirmed in classical theism is not a worthwhile accomplishment. Belief on the basis of argument could never be belief in the Christian God because an argument could never warrant genuine knowledge of the true God. By playing up to reason's assumed self-sufficiency, the approach of natural theology discourages faith.

It is intriguing to think about just what Barth might have made of Plantinga's proposal for escaping the dilemma. Plantinga's suggestion is that apologetics that makes recourse to the positive arguments of natural theology need not be conducted in such a way as to imply that its arguments ought to be taken as the *basis* for belief. If Plantinga is right, and I think he is, this suggestion appears to neutralize Barth's main concern. We could extend the proposal even further to address Barth's concerns by adding that the Christian apologist would underscore the difference between an affirmation of the conclusion of a natural theological argument and genuine knowledge of God. It seems to me that such provisos would mitigate Barth's concerns. The unbeliever who rejects the arguments of natural theology would not be encouraged to think that what has been rejected is the basis for Christian belief as taken from the perspective of belief. The unbeliever who accepts the conclusions of an argument from natural theology would see that the warrant for belief in the God who exists derives from God and not the argument.

PART 3: THE RELATIONSHIP BETWEEN BARTH AND PLANTINGA ON NATURAL THEOLOGY

The agreement between Barth and Plantinga on natural theology is substantial though not total. Both reject the common assumptions that have grown up around natural theology since the Enlightenment. They agree not only that human arguments are unnecessary for attaining a knowledge of God but also that the deliverances of human reason do not provide adequate warrant for Christian belief. It should not be a surprise that the ways they arrive at this shared conclusion are different. We saw that Barth reasons directly from his theology of revelation. God in his revelation is genuinely humanly known but also known to be utterly free and unique—a knowledge beyond all independent human capacity. Revelation must be from above; it must be the personal self-revelation of the Father. And it must address the inadequacies of human fallenness and finitude; it must transform the human knower by communion with Jesus Christ. Moreover, it must create its own capacity for human reception; the Spirit of God must provide for the human knower, in the gift of faith, the subjective reception of revelation. The *only* revelation of God to human beings provided by God is in this, his trinitarian act of self-revelation. This self-revealing describes, therefore, the only possible warrant for Christian belief.

Plantinga does not argue from a developed theology of revelation. His main point is to defend the possibility of the proper basicality of Christian belief from flawed philosophical objections. He is, in this sense, giving a negative apologetic—exposing the inadequacy of potential defeaters to divinely initiated revelation. His appeals to Christian theology are not an attempt to demonstrate the truth of the matter. Instead, he takes a model from Christian theology and argues that if it is true, then all philosophical objections to it fail. It is significant that for both Barth and Plantinga, the theology of revelation is the pivot point of their arguments. Barth, as a Christian theologian, assumes the basis of faith and argues from it. Plantinga, as a Christian philosopher, considers how a theological account of warrant would influence questions and assumptions in religious epistemology.

This is not to say that Barth and Plantinga fundamentally agree on all important aspects of the question of natural theology. There remain several areas of tension that need to be considered, which we will examine under the following three questions: (1) Do Barth and Plantinga agree on a negative role for natural theology? (2) Do they agree on a positive role for natural theology? (3) Do they agree about the nature of the *sensus divinitatis*?

Do Barth and Plantinga agree on a negative role for natural theology? To answer this question it is important to be clear about what is meant by a *negative* role. We are not concerned here with *via negativa* natural theology, which attempts to arrive at a knowledge of God through a consideration of what God is not. We are, instead, interested in the possibility of natural theology providing a negative service through a challenging of unbelief. There is a suggestion in Barth's writing that natural theology should not be allowed even a negative function. This arises particularly in connection with Brunner's eristics, which Barth understands to be a kind of negative apologetics that serves as a propaedeutic to faith by confronting the resistance of human rational self-sufficiency.[115] There are significant parallels to Plantinga's negative apologetical enterprise. Plantinga seeks to undermine the reigning rationally self-sufficient paradigms of justification and warrant in order to defend the possibility of warrant by faith. Why might Barth object to this? What Barth objects to is the idea that theology might depend in some way on the prolegomena of even a negative natural theology. What he opposes is the idea that a negative natural theology might contribute in any substantive way to the actualization of a genuine human knowledge of God. What we find, in fact, is that what Barth really rejects is the idea that negative natural theology might play a *positive* role in coming to faith.[116]

For Plantinga, negative apologetics responds to objections to Christian belief; it is aimed at defeating defeaters. In the language of warrant, we could class negative natural theology as an attempt to remove barriers to warrant for Christian belief, without contributing to that warrant. What moves a person to faith is not the human argument. It might seem unlikely, however, that Barth would be content even with these qualifications. Answering objections by appealing to reason might mean entering the realm of the "godless reason of man which is inimical to belief."[117] Faith has its own resources for defense. Revelation can defend itself. Should we understand Barth as opposed to the work of Christian philosophers defending the faith against objections? From the material already covered, it should be clear that this is not at all the point of Barth's comments on the rebellion of human reason and the self-vindicating nature of revelation. We can grant that Barth maintains that the struggle between reason and revelation should "not [be] ori-

---

[115]*CD* I/1, pp. 26-31.

[116]As it is first encountered in the *Church Dogmatics,* apologetics and eristics are considered and rejected as *necessary* prolegomena to dogmatics (*CD* I/1, pp. 25-31).

[117]*CD* I/1, p. 28.

ented to the contradiction of reason but to the declaration of revelation."[118] This view, however, is not necessarily at odds with Plantinga's approach. Optimally, faith will be so strong that it operates as an intrinsic defeater-deflector. Ideally, on the deliverances of faith alone, belief will be so compelling that any objection to it will be unbelievable and, therefore, not require refutation. But the fact that the refutation of objections is not required in ideal cases of belief does not mean that refuting an objection is somehow unhelpful or that it might not be useful in defusing doubt.

Extreme care is needed here to comprehend Barth's position. We ought to ensure that we not reinstate the caricatures that were challenged in chapter three. There we saw that it is not philosophy or human reason per se that Barth opposes; it is the orientation of human reason to unbelief and the false independence with which philosophy approaches the knowability of God. Plantinga's approach, however, is nothing like what Barth is opposing. He certainly understands that the Christian philosopher need not work independently from the light of faith. The Christian apologist need not adopt an orientation of unbelief or assume the autonomy of human reason. In addition, Barth never claims that human reason cannot give us some provisional knowledge of what is true about the world or the capacity to see in some instances what is logically impossible, even with respect to God. It is only the genuine knowledge of God that Barth insists must come by the transformative grace of God in Christ by the Spirit's gift of faith. Nothing Plantinga affirms about a negative role for natural theology seems to violate these worries. Moreover, Plantinga's position is entirely consistent with Barth's nuanced trinitarian theology of revelation. He acknowledges the helpfulness of removing objections in the service of belief, not because of inadequacies in the gift of faith but because of human resistance. If we consider what Barth means by "natural theology," we must conclude that Plantinga's negative natural theology is categorically not a subspecies thereof. In fact, it is exceedingly unlikely that Barth would place Plantinga's negative natural theology under the rubric of *theology*

[118] *CD* I/1, p. 29.

whatsoever. It is, perhaps, more accurate to classify Plantinga's negative apologetics as a concern of Christian philosophy, while in no way demoting its importance or value for the church. In conclusion, therefore, while Barth does not explicitly endorse any role for negative apologetics,[119] all things considered, Plantinga shows that it is possible to remain consistent with Barth's theology of revelation and the all-sufficiency of the deliverances of faith while maintaining a vital role for and Christian approach to negative apologetics. But can the same thing be said for a *positive* role for natural theology?

Do Barth and Plantinga agree on a positive role for natural theology? If negative natural theology removes barriers to warranted Christian belief without contributing to that warrant, positive natural theology attempts to bolster Christian belief by providing arguments that contribute directly to the warrant for belief. We saw that Plantinga is happy to endorse the benefits of such an enterprise. Arguments in support of Christian belief may be helpful when the warrant humanly received from the deliverances of faith is insufficient for knowledge and, therefore, belief. The value of natural theology is, again, the service it provides in the less than ideal situations of weakened faith. And Plantinga is clear that arguments of natural theology do not on their own provide sufficient warrant for belief. He seems to accept, nevertheless, the possibility that human arguments might in some small way contribute to the warrant for Christian belief. As we have seen, this just will not fly for Barth. The suggestion that the deliverances of human reason might be able to contribute even weakly to a genuine knowledge of God undermines Barth's uncompromising theology of revelation from above. Even to crack the door slightly would be to open the floodgates from below,

---

[119]Barth does in fact address the question of negative apologetics but has in mind something much different from Plantinga's proposals. The negative apologetics in Barth's crosshairs is an approach like Brunner's eristics, in which a positive case was built on an analysis of the problem of human existence (see Brunner's "Die andere Aufgabe der Theologie," pp. 255-76). Tjarko Stadtland suggests that Barth proposed a kind of negative natural theology (Stadtland, *Eschatologie und Geschichte in der Theologie des jungen Karl Barth* [Neukirchen-Vluyn: Neukirchener Verlag, 1966], p. 116). Bruce McCormack objects to Stadtland's proposal (McCormack, *Karl Barth's Critically Realistic Dialectical Theology*, pp. 259-60). Barth also refuses a negative point of contact in his "Antwort an Erwin Reisner," *Evangelische Theologie* 2 (1935): 51-66, and he objects to a *via negativa* approach to the knowledge of God in *CD* III/1, p. 372-75.

fueling the Feuerbachian suspicion and eclipsing any confidence in a genuine human knowledge of God from God. For Barth, we cannot afford to be epistemological semi-Pelagians. *Sola gratia* in theological epistemology must be guarded vigilantly. What is more, any concession here would affirm the possibility of a supplementary revelation to the revelation of God in Christ. This might imply that there is more that can be known about the Father than is revealed in Jesus Christ, a notion that would no less than shatter the unity of the Trinity.[120] The question we face is whether there might be any way to understand Plantinga's openness to a warrant-contributing role for natural theology that does not violate Barth's concerns.

We might begin with the question of whether and how it is possible that warrant for a single belief could come from multiple, combined sources. It seems to me that there are two ways this might go.[121] To make the distinction between these two ways more evident, let me offer the following ordinary kind of belief scenario:

> *The Mail Carrier:* At around ten in the morning as my wife is deeply engrossed in the translation of some French manuscript, she is distracted by a sudden though indistinct sound. She walks to the front window where she catches a glimpse of a person in the shadows, just exiting through the gate. She does not know what to conclude from this until she realizes the time and remembers that at about this time each day, and with consistent regularity, the mail carrier delivers the post through the slot in our front door. She immediately forms the warranted conclusion that she has seen the mail carrier and heard the sound of the mail coming through the door.

There are at least two ways to understand the nature of the combination of warrant in this scenario. One possibility (for ease of reference—CW_1) is that warrant for the belief actually derives by an in-

---

[120]"If revelation is to be taken seriously as God's presence, if there is to be a valid belief in revelation, then in no sense can Christ and the Spirit be subordinate hypostases. In the predicate and object of the concept revelation we must again have, and to no less a degree, the subject itself. Revelation and revealing must be equal to the revealer" (*CD* I/1, p. 353).

[121]It should be clear that the following analysis is not a theological argument; instead, I am adopting a Plantinga-like inductive approach from instances of ordinary belief in support of a proposal for how we might conceive of the contribution of natural theology within a Barthian theology of revelation.

ference made on the basis of beliefs that issue from multiple independent faculties. Sense perception weakly captures a sound and a figure and issues the belief, along with the attending obscure phenomenology, that a sound was heard and a figure seen. A belief about the time of day is formed perhaps purely on the basis of circadian rhythm, and a belief about the regularity and punctuality of the mail carrier issues from memory. At this point, reason takes on a coordinating role, forming the belief on the basis of inference from other beliefs that the mail carrier was seen and heard. As with any case of inference, the warrant for the inference in CW_1 will only be as strong as the warrant for the beliefs it is inferred from. In CW_1 there is a real combination of sources. If any of the sources mentioned is removed, warrant for the conclusion would be diminished.

There is, however, a second possibility for how things might go—CW_2. CW_2 proceeds exactly as CW_1 except that something interesting happens with respect to the faculty of sense perception. The faculty of sense perception does not always complete its task immediately. As my wife is processing the other sources of warrant for her conclusion, the phenomenal experiences of the faculty of sense perception are still fresh in mind. In CW_2 the suggestion of the inference assists either external rationality in its formation of the phenomenal experience or internal rationality in its forming of the appropriate belief in response to that phenomenology. In other words, the inference serves as a catalyst for the proper functioning of the faculty of sense experience. My wife now more clearly perceives the sound that initially broke into her state of concentration and the figure she saw exiting our gate. The belief she holds about having heard and seen the mail carrier is no longer based on a deduction but, more securely, on a perception. The warrant for the belief now swings free from the other sources and the inference. It is even possible that she might discover she was incorrect about the time, or forgot that the post is wildly unpredictable in our town. But, if it were indeed the mail carrier she encountered, she may now be warranted in her belief, held in the basic way on the basis of sense perception alone,[122] even if

[122]Note that I take the faculty of sense perception to be more than the presentation of strictly empirical data. Sense perception also includes the learned apprehension of the forms of that data.

the same belief earlier held on the basis of the catalyzing inference was, in fact, unwarranted.[123]

Returning to the possibility of a positive role for natural theological arguments in the formation of Christian belief, we can now ask whether there is a construal of multiple sources of warrant along the lines of either CW_1 or CW_2 that would be free from Barth's proscriptions. It seems to me that this is exactly what we have if the relationship between inference and basic belief is as it is in CW_2. Consider another scenario, this time one of theistic belief:

> *Christian Belief* (IIHS + human testimony): Joe Bloggs does not believe the gospel, but he does notice that he has some inclinations to believe. Unbeknownst to Joe, the Holy Spirit is active in his life, offering him transforming faith. Unfortunately, because of internal and environmental resistance, the deliverances of faith are not yet strong enough in Joe to warrant belief. He does, however, have a few new friends who are strong believers and insist to Joe that Jesus is real and explain to him the gospel. On the basis of the testimony of his friends in combination with the otherwise insufficient deliverances of faith, Joe finds himself believing and warrantedly so.

The sources of warrant are different in this scenario from those in the previous scenario, though inference may still play a role. Belief on the basis of testimony may involve an inference from a basic belief in the credibility of Joe's friends and the earnestness of their conviction.[124] There is, in any case, a CW_2-like way to think about the relationship of the identified contributors to warrant. Warrant by way of human testimony could be seen to be acting as a catalyst for belief that will properly

[123]Perhaps a Gettier-type objection could be raised to the CW_2 construal, if it is possible, as I have suggested, that a mistaken assumption could motivate a fortuitous result. This would only be an effective objection, however, if the belief in question continued to depend on the mistaken assumption to deliver warrant sufficient for knowledge. On the CW_2 account above, however, warrant eventually swings free of the mistake and depends on the faculty of perception alone.

[124]If we follow Thomas Reid's thought on testimony and credulity, believing testimony involves no inference. Credibility is assumed, though it can be defeated by discrediting the witness. Credulity is an innate gift and a natural faculty—"a disposition to confide in the veracity of others and to believe what they tell us" (Reid, *Essays on the Active Powers of the Human Mind: An Inquiry into the Human Mind on the Principles of Common Sense,* ed. Dugald Stewart and G. N. Wright [London: T. Tegg, 1843], chap. 6, sec. 24, p. 567).

rest on divine testimony alone. If things go in the CW_2 way, Joe's belief will grow independent of the testimony and credibility of his friends. The testimony of friends serves the cognitive process of divine illumination whereby one is given a knowledge of God by God—in accordance with proper function. Human testimony cooperates with the testimony of the Holy Spirit, not as an independent source of warrant but as one condition under which faith by the Spirit is realized.

This scenario is particularly helpful for thinking about the general problem of the role of arguments in the formation of Christian belief. First, the scenario seems to capture the experience that many believers have when coming to belief. Many believers experience a transition from the partial support of the testimony of friends or parents to believing in the basic way. Second, the fact that this is so does not seem to violate any of Barth's concerns. This scenario of belief, even though it begins with a belief based partially on inference (or a natural capacity to believe testimony), fits well with Barth's theology of revelation. This is especially the case if we understand God to be directly involved with Joe's believing the testimony of his friends or perceiving their credibility. Third, we can quite easily alter the scenario by replacing the testimony of friends with a natural theological argument. If it is true that warrant from the IIHS and human testimony could combine in the CW_2 way and not violate Barth's concerns, then it should also be possible for warrant from the IIHS and an argument to combine in this way.

It seems that CW_2-type warrant collaboration is the best way to understand Plantinga's suggestion that other sources of warrant may combine with the deliverances of faith to bolster belief. Plantinga may tip his hat in this direction in the following comments on the warrant-boost of arguments:

> Theistic arguments can obviously be of value for those who don't already believe, they can move them closer to belief, and can bring it about that belief in God is at any rate among the live options for them. Only God bestows saving faith, of course, but his way of doing so can certainly involve cooperation with his children, as in preaching and even argumentation.[125]

[125]Plantinga, "Christian Philosophy at the End of the Twentieth Century," p. 40.

The view here seems to be of arguments functioning as warrant catalysts within the orchestration of the sovereign action of God. There is no sense of an independent rational capacity to bring oneself to belief or even to contribute to the warrant for faith. Plantinga, moreover, draws a parallel between the testimony of preaching and the function of arguments. Taken in the CW_2 way, what is compelling about a proclamation or what seems reasonable about an argument does not become a permanent fixture of the warrant for belief. Argumentation, like proclamation, serves (nonarbitrarily) as a catalyst by the power of God to clarify the deliverances of faith according to proper function. Read in the CW_2 way, Plantinga's notion of the positive role of natural theology does not conflict with Barth's theology of revelation.

There is a critical difficulty, however, with this proposal for harmonizing Plantinga with Barth. The problem is that, while Plantinga does seem to endorse the CW_2 construal of warrant-source collaboration, where mature belief will derive from the deliverances of faith alone, he certainly never repudiates CW_1, where knowledge is enabled partially on the basis of the supplementary warrant of natural theological argumentation. Is this one point, therefore, where Plantinga and Barth simply part ways? Has Plantinga compromised on epistemological *sola gratia*? Not necessarily. To see why, we need to remember that on Plantinga's system, the work of the Spirit and the deliverances of faith have a critical enabling impact on other sources of warrant. The IIHS is conceived of as part of a process that addresses the noetic effects of sin to restore proper function in other faculties. What is more, the deliverances of faith begin to transform one's interpretive grid in ways that may be enormously influential to internal rationality, which is the place where belief formation is completed for all belief-forming faculties or processes. Assessing the probabilities associated with historical evidence[126] or the strength of the premises of an argument depends to a significant degree

[126]While Plantinga is open to historical evidence supplementing warrant from the IIHS to boost the warrant for belief in the resurrection of Jesus, he is clear that properly judging the probabilities involved is not possible on the basis of the data alone. See *WCB*, pp. 271-80, and Plantinga, "Reply [Ad Wykstra]," pp. 124-28. Keith Mascord incorrectly suggests that Plantinga allows no role whatsoever for arguments from historical evidence in support of Christian belief (Mascord, *Alvin Plantinga and Christian Apologetics*, pp. 168-83, 207-9).

on the relative priorities of one's existing nexus of belief. It is, therefore, possible to maintain that even on the CW_1 construal of collaborative warrant, those sources of warrant that supplement the deliverances of faith, to the extent that they are contributing to the warrant for theistic or Christian belief, do so by the influence of the transformational work of the Holy Spirit. In this case, alternative sources of warrant are not understood strictly as catalysts for belief by the deliverances of faith but rather as extensions of the deliverances of faith. In this light, even arguments that support faith can be seen as operating not by mere human strength but by the deliberate action of God. God creates and sustains his own possibility of being known, making use of arguments from reason as the harmonic cognitive reverberations of faith, creating a crescendo of warrant sufficient for knowledge.

In summary, I have argued that there are good ways of thinking about the function of natural theological arguments that do not run afoul of Barth's anathemas. Barth's objections to natural theology are based on the impossibility of independent human sources of the knowledge of God outside of the deliberative action of God's self-revelation in Christ by the Spirit. If we understand the arguments of natural theology to function as catalysts to or extensions of the deliverances of faith, there is nothing independently natural about them. My proposal is not only that this gives us a way to understand Plantinga's notion of the positive role of natural theology in a way that does not conflict with Barth's theology of revelation or epistemological *sola gratia.* It also provides the best way to understand Plantinga's direct comments on the matter and their coherence with his wider corpus.

Do Barth and Plantinga agree about the nature of the* sensus divinitatis*? We return now to a question raised by Plantinga's A/C (Aquinas/Calvin) model in chapter five. In Barth's view, the dangers of natural theology have to do not only with human arguments but also with any natural human capacity for the knowledge of God that functions independently of the supernatural activity of divine self-revelation. Does this rule out the possibility of a *sensus divinitatis* as Plantinga conceives?[127]

[127]Barth comments in his *Table Talk* (ed. John Godsey [Edinburgh: Oliver & Boyd, 1963], p. 95) on the idea in Calvin of an *innata religio.* He concludes that Calvin was affirming something like

The distinction is drawn fairly clearly by Plantinga: "On my model, there is both natural knowledge of God by way of the *sensus divinitatis* ('SD') and non-natural or supernatural knowledge of God, knowledge that comes as a result of the IIHS."[128] The *sensus divinitatis* is "part of our original increated cognitive equipment."[129] The IIHS, by contrast, "consists in direct divine activity"[130] and was inaugurated as "a special divine response to sin."[131] Sin has a debilitating effect on the proper functioning of the *sensus divinitatis,* but "by virtue of the work of the Holy Spirit in the hearts of those to whom faith is given, the ravages of sin (including the cognitive damage) are repaired, gradually or suddenly, to a greater or lesser extent."[132] This means that on Plantinga's scheme a natural human capacity for knowledge of God can be restored to some degree as a result of the combined revealing and healing work of the Spirit, who ministers to us the benefits of Jesus Christ.

It would certainly appear that Barth dismissed Brunner for far less than this. Plantinga's *sensus divinitatis* seems to fit the description of exactly what Barth rejects—independent human access to a knowledge of God. But just what does the *sensus divinitatis* deliver? Plantinga's A/C model, which draws from Calvin's development of the *sensus divinitatis,*[133] is intended to explain how theistic belief might have warrant. The *sensus divinitatis* provides a rather minimalist "awareness of divinity," which, for Plantinga, does not amount to much more than an awareness that God exists and should be worshiped and obeyed.[134] Specifying the content of this knowledge is a slippery business. What is meant by any assertion depends in part on what is meant by the referring terms. If God is to be the referent of the affirmation of existence, and the affirmation is meant really to affirm something, then God must

---

a natural disposition and that even if it did not have "bad consequences" for Calvin, it was nevertheless a "bad example."

[128]Plantinga, "Reply [Ad Sudduth]," p. 132.

[129]*WCB,* p. 246 n. 10.

[130]Ibid.

[131]Ibid., p. 180.

[132]Ibid., pp. 243-44.

[133]"Here I want to propose a model based on Calvin's version of the suggestion, not because I think Calvin should be the cynosure of all eyes theological, but because he presents an interesting development of the particular thought in question" (ibid., p. 170).

[134]Ibid., p. 177. Plantinga is in this respect still following Calvin.

somehow be known by the referrer. It would seem that the *sensus divinitatis* cannot provide a knowledge of God's existence without an accompanying knowledge, however scant, of some of God's properties. What is the nature of this knowledge of the referent who is known to exist? This is a difficult but important question—one that will inform decisively our understanding of the relationship between theological knowledge and reason on our emerging unified proposal. The question turns on precisely what counts as knowledge of God, which we will be our focus in the next chapter.

CONCLUSION

The differences between Plantinga and Barth on the *sensus divinitatis* may be similar to the other differences on natural theology that we have considered. They do not expose a fundamental theological or philosophical incompatibility. The differences are better explained as the consequence of differences in the purpose and nature of their work. As a Christian theologian, Barth is attempting to reflect the inner priorities of Christian theology and emphasize those priorities over against critical areas of potential distortion. It would be antithetical to Barth's task if he were to highlight the virtues of our epistemological gifts without also emphasizing their utter inadequacy. They are powerless outside of God's giving of himself to be known and his decision to involve our faculties in his self-revealing. Plantinga's purposes are considerably different. He operates as a Christian philosopher with the particular goal of defending the possibility that belief could have warrant without reposing on an argument or demonstrable evidence. Plantinga's models are intentionally theologically minimalist. Though they are intended to be faithful to Christian theology, they make no pretenses of being comprehensive theological accounts.

In chapter six I brought together key insights from Barth and Plantinga to outline an emerging unified proposal for a Christian theological epistemology. My objective in this chapter has been to explore the implications of that proposal for the difficult question of the relationship between theology and reason. I did so by pressing on perceived tensions between Barth and Plantinga. I began with a clarification of the main concerns that drive Barth's objection to natural theology. I argued that the only construal of natural theology that would be compatible with Barth's theology of revelation is one that maintains that God can only be genuinely known in his personal, trinitarian act of self-revelation. Any aspect of the created order may serve as the locus of divine revealing, but not its source. I then turned to Plantinga's much more modest objection to natural theology, which consists of an argument for both the insufficiency and the nonnecessity of natural theological arguments for warranted theistic or Christian belief. Finally, I focused on the points where Plantinga's proposals threaten to encroach on Barth's concerns. I reasoned that natural theological arguments in Plantinga's thought are best understood as functioning within the realm of supernatural revelation and not independent from it. Such arguments are either strictly defensive, not contributing to the warrant for belief, or they function as catalysts to or extensions of the deliverances of faith. I left open for analysis in the next chapter the possibility that Plantinga's notion of the *sensus divinitatis* delivers the kind of natural knowledge of God that Barth rejects.

What does this mean for our understanding of the relationship between theology and reason on the unified Barth/Plantinga proposal? And what has this discussion contributed to clarifying and expanding that proposal? First, this discussion has offered a further rebuttal of the Ritschlian divide. A theo-foundational approach to theological knowledge in no way undermines or minimizes a significant and central role for human reason. We have already strongly affirmed the cognitive aspects of theological knowing and expressed this in conjunction with what I have called the thoroughgoing humanness of the knowledge of God. Now we can extend what that means particularly for rational arguments. While human reasoning is not the essential conduit for theological knowledge, rational thought processes and argumentation may participate in our growing in the knowledge of God. Our reason in the service of knowing God should not be seen to function as an ancillary process or an alternative means. Rather, to the extent that reasoning genuinely serves growth in knowing God, it is enfolded into the personal, trinitarian act of self-revelation.

We may also affirm the negative counterpart to this affirmation. Reason can participate in a helpful and cooperative way, but it may also compete against revelation, serving to obscure and distort. Human reasoning that is not submitted to the transformation of revelation itself may fail to function as designed and result in the obstruction of real hearing. In either instance, the significance of reason is maintained while its limitations and vital dependencies are acknowledged.

Second, this discussion of natural theology illustrates how the Barth/Plantinga approach can offer an adept response to typical criticisms without resorting to the extreme, if fashionable, *in toto* dismissal of apologetical arguments.[135] On the unified proposal, apologetics is dethroned but not discarded. I am thinking of three kinds of criticisms in particular that apologetical arguments face. The first criticism comes from a certain kind of evidentialism. It would hold apologetical arguments to the modernist requirements of the skeptical challenge and find those arguments wanting. Apologetical arguments have been, and perhaps continue to be, advanced in a way that accepts these requirements. It should be abundantly clear that the Barth/Plantinga approach does not accept these requirements or the inflated claims often attached to such arguments. Taking, however, a measured estimation of the place of rational arguments undermines the basis for this kind of modernist critique.

Another kind of criticism facing apologetical arguments comes from the recognition that human knowing is much fuller and more complex than merely reasoning in the form of drawing logical inferences from propositions. This criticism is itself a response to the myopia of classical evidentialism and takes many forms depending on what other aspects of human knowing are in view. It commonly comes from epistemologies that pay critical attention to the embodied, social, dialogical, historical and developmental nature of knowledge formation.[136] Another virtue of

---

[135] If it is fashionable to dismiss apologetics, it is hardly a new fashion. In 1947, for example, Princeton Seminary renamed its professorship in Apologetics and Christian Ethics to a professorship in Christian Philosophy. In that year, Emile Cailliet took the position, abandoning the original apologetic intentions of the Stuart Chair (Gordon Graham, "The Philosopher: A Christian Philosopher in a Theological Seminary," in *The Long Shadow of Emile Cailliet: Faith, Philosophy, and Theological Education,* ed. Abigail Rian Evans and Clemens Bartollas [Eugene, OR: Wipf & Stock, 2011], pp. 124-25).

[136] E.g., Alvin Goldman, *Knowledge in a Social World* (Oxford: Oxford University Press, 1999);

the Barth/Plantinga proposal is its readiness to incorporate the insights of these critiques. On the proposal, analytic philosophical reasoning is acknowledged as neither a necessary nor a sufficient component of the process of growing in knowing God. At no place in the proposal are any aspects of a holistic view of human knowing dismissed or displaced by the deliverances of faith—that is, the active self-revealing of God. By the power of the Spirit of God, they may be taken up, commandeered and brought into a process of transformation to function in correspondence with the purposes of revelation.

A third criticism often leveled against the enterprise of apologetics in general is the concern that apologetics is oriented toward persuasion and not truth. Barth himself, we saw, raised the concern that apologetics required the adoption of a disingenuous stance. The critique I have in mind, however, is very similar to Plato's classic critique of the Sophists. As Gordon Graham puts it, "Apologetics is primarily aimed at securing and protecting belief. Its purpose is to fend off attacks and restore the confidence of the person who already believes, not to inquire into what he or she ought to believe."[137] Two important responses can be given to this concern in light of our emerging Barth/Plantinga proposal and the discussion of this chapter. The first is that there need be no opposition between the desire to persuade and the desire to grow in a knowledge of the truth. One aim need not be pursued at the expense of the other. We saw that for Barth the work of love is to communicate truth. Apologetics is far from sophistry or mere rhetoric, at least if it is true to its use in scripture, where ἀπολογία is associated with giving "a reason for the hope that is in you" (1 Pet 3:15).

Perhaps the more significant response, however, to this third criticism of apologetical arguments is a rejection of one of its central presuppositions. Veiled in the criticism that apologetics is oriented to persuasion and not truth seems to be the assumption that the problem with apologetics is that it is not sufficiently neutral, whereas the proper ap-

---

Elizabeth Anderson, "Feminist Epistemology: An Interpretation and a Defense," *Hypatia* 10, no. 3 (1995): 50-84; and Michael Polanyi, *Personal Knowledge: Towards a Post-Critical Philosophy* (London: Routledge & Kegan Paul, 1958).

[137]Graham, "Philosopher," pp. 126-27.

proach to seeking the truth is to do so from a standpoint of neutrality. But this hypothetical neutrality is precisely what Barth found so disingenuous and Plantinga found dubious. It operates under the pretense that the knowledge of God is rationally discoverable from an ostensibly neutral human epistemic basis. So, to this third critique our emerging Barth/Plantinga proposal offers its own response and critique. It agrees that an orientation to truth must be maintained, but it disagrees with the supposition that the best vantage of that truth is from a stance of noncommitment.

These are significant gains in the attempt to refine and clarify our emerging unified Barth/Plantinga proposal for a Christian theological epistemology. We are still left with a number of important practical areas where the import of the proposal could be sharpened. One of those is a related issue that I explicitly deferred in the discussion on natural theology. This is the question of the relationship between faith and revelation—i.e., what constitutes a genuine knowledge of God. We covered this question in some detail in the first part of the book. It is an area where Barth's work is understandably more developed than Plantinga's. Consequently, we will spend more time engaged in conversation with Barth and his critics while appealing where helpful to Plantinga's work for clarification.

8

FAITH AND REVELATION

What Constitutes a Genuine Human Knowledge of God?

◆

In chapter seven we tackled the problem of the seeming incongruity between Barth and Plantinga on natural theology as a way to clarify how our emerging unified Barth/Plantinga proposal handles the role of human reason in theological knowledge. Taking advantage of the groundwork laid in chapters two and three, we established that Barth's principal concern is to maintain that a genuine knowledge of God is only possible by the free, self-revealing action of the Father through the Son by the Spirit. I argued that there are ways of thinking about revelation and rational arguments that preserve Barth's concern for the centrality of divine self-revealing action. I suggested plausible interpretations of Plantinga's thought in which free divine action retained an exclusive warrant-contributing role. In that discussion, however, we bracketed a crucial question. Do Barth and Plantinga have the same thing in mind when they speak about knowing God? A difference on this central point could be very significant indeed.

The purpose of this chapter is to clarify what constitutes a genuine human knowledge of God according to our emerging unified Barth/Plantinga proposal and to assess the impact of differences or disagreements. This chapter also deepens the discussion of the nature of Christian scripture, the writings of the Bible and its role in coming to a knowledge of God. We will find that because Barth provides greater theological resolution, he operates with a stricter notion of the nature of the knowledge of God. Plantinga avoids detailed commitments on some of the questions we raise but offers distinctions that are helpful to our discussion. I highlight important areas for clarification and analysis particularly regarding the relationships among transforming faith, personal revelation and rational propositions.

BARTH AND THREE ASPECTS OF THE KNOWLEDGE OF FAITH

In chapter two, we noted that, for Barth, revelation is the miraculous action of divine personal self-disclosure to human beings. Revelation is, in fact, personified in Jesus Christ, the incarnate Son[1]—"the Word which is nothing other than the Word of His revelation and reconciliation."[2] He is the real content of revelation. In the incarnation, scripture and preaching, God uses creaturely means to speak to creatures. Not even in the incarnation, however, does revelation become transferred to the creaturely veil. Christ's human nature remains human; it is not divinized. Christ's humanity does not in and of itself reveal the eternal Logos. Even in the face of the incarnate Christ, our inability to see God remains not only because of the noetic effects of sin but even more fundamentally because of the limits of creatures and creaturely media to *contain* divine revelation. Knowledge of God only becomes a human possibility by the free decision of God, who, through the work of the Spirit and by means of creaturely media, gives human beings a sharing in the knowledge of Christ. This process of coming to know God by means of the medium of revelation requires the gift of faith. Only in faith does the Spirit (the "revealedness" of God) become for us our subjective apprehension of the knowledge of God.[3]

For Barth, a human knowledge of God is genuine if and only if it is knowledge by faith. Our objective here, therefore, is to discern, so far as

[1]"For He is revelation, divine-human reality" (*CD* I/1, p. 18).

[2]*CD* II/1, p. 483.

[3]"If one asks about the reality of the knowledge of God, which is so inconceivable in its How, which can be revealed only by God, which can be proclaimed by man only in the service of God and in virtue of His presence; if one asks what this reality is in so far as the knowability of God is included within it, the only possible answer which is both accurate and exhaustive is that this reality is faith" (*CD* I/1, p. 228).

possible, what it means to know God by faith. We made significant progress in this direction in chapter two. There we saw, among other things, that for Barth the knowledge of God is personal, cognitive and transformative. It is worth unpacking these notions again briefly here.[4]

Perhaps the first thing to note is that *personal, cognitive* and *transformative* do not refer to three distinct kinds of knowing. It is better to think of these qualifiers as designating three aspects of an integrative, unitary knowing. We will seek to distinguish each qualifier, one from the other, for the sake of understanding the breadth of Barth's conception. It would be a serious mistake, however, to think that each of these three aspects of the knowledge of faith stands on its own or operates independently.

As we have already mentioned, the controlling feature of Barth's notion of revelation is the personal, free, trinitarian action of God. It is the personal nature of revelation that makes revelation both cognitive and transformative. The knowledge of God is said to be *personal* because it is fundamentally a being brought to Jesus Christ, the personal revelation of God. "Faith . . . is the gracious address of God to man, the free personal presence of Jesus Christ."[5] Knowledge by faith is not principally a transfer of information or abstract mental illumination. The knowledge of faith is personal on both the divine side and on the human side—it is God's personal encounter with human persons.[6]

One consequence of this personal encounter with God is human transformation, the inauguration of the healing of sinful humanity and the beginning of repentance. In Barth's view, revelation is reconciliation,[7] and the eschatological consummation of reconciliation is redemption.[8]

---

[4]Barth felt that the most appropriate word for describing the knowledge of faith was *Anerkennung* (acknowledgment); cf. *CD* II/1, p. 217. He identifies three characteristics of the Word of God as the speech of God. The Word of God is *spiritual, personal* and *purposive.* These correspond respectively to our *cognitive, personal* and *transformational.* See *CD* I/1, pp. 132-43, 205.

[5]*CD* I/1, p. 18 (*KD* I/1, p. 17: "der Glaube . . . ist . . . die gnädige Zuwendung Gottes zum Menschen, die freie persönliche Gegenwart Jesu Christi im Handeln des Menschen").

[6]Speaking of the Reformers, Barth writes, "they could understand the presence of the holy God among unholy men only as the grace of the strictly personal free Word of God which reaches its goal in the equally personal free hearing of men, the hearing of faith" (*CD* I/1, p. 68).

[7]"The work of the Son or Word is the presence and declaration of God which, in view of the fact that it takes place miraculously in and in spite of human darkness, we can only describe as revelation. The term reconciliation is another word for the same thing" (*CD* I/1, p. 409).

[8]"He is not just the Redeemer, so surely does redemption stand in indissoluble correlation with reconciliation, so surely does reconciliation reach its consummation in redemption" (*CD* I/1, p. 471).

Revelation does not instantly and absolutely eradicate the corruption of human conceptuality and language; nevertheless, it overcomes the noetic effects of sin to provide genuine human knowing, thereby initiating the proper human response. Consequently, the impact of personal divine address includes human acknowledgment of and submission to the One who is revelation. In Barth's assessment of πίστις in the New Testament, he concludes that, while the action and faithfulness of God is the foundational principle, the term also embraces faith's human impact and response.[9] The transformation of revelation is a feature of being drawn into participation by the Spirit in Christ's knowing of the Father.[10]

The other consequence of the personal nature of revelation is human cognitive content. As stressed in chapter two, Barth's affirmation of the personal character of faith should not be taken to mean that revelation is strictly noumenal, amorphously experiential or exclusively metacognitional.[11] He firmly underscores the cognitive, verbal and rational nature of divine address.[12] He writes:

> The fact that it has God not only for its object but also for its origin and that its primary and proper subject is the Father who knows the Son and the Son who knows the Father in the Holy Spirit, and that it is a sure and perfect and genuine cognition because God is known by God, does not mean either the abrogation, abolition or alteration of human cognition as such, and therefore of its formal and technical characteristics as human cognition.[13]

Despite Barth's forthright statements, his reserves about divine freedom and creaturely limitations leave some with the impression that

---

[9]"In the πίστις Ἰησοῦ Χριστοῦ we see the divine decision made about man. Only then and on this basis does the word slip down, as it were, into the sphere of human actions; now . . . πίστις is fairly frequently and clearly described as trust, as the attitude in men in which they honour and revere the worth of God" (*CD* I/1, p. 228).

[10]Knowledge of God is a "participation in the veracity of the revelation of God" (*CD* II/1, pp. 219, 220, 223). As Barth says, "the mutual indwelling and indeed the union of the divine and human *logos* in faith cannot be ignored or denied. This mutual indwelling or union is the knowability of the Word of God" (*CD* I/1, p. 242).

[11]It is noteworthy in this connection that Barth sharply dismisses Rudolf Otto's "das Heilige" as "irrational" and finally indistinguishable from "an absolutised natural force" (*CD* I/1, p. 135).

[12]See especially *CD* I/1, pp. 135-38.

[13]*CD* II/1, p. 181.

Barth is finally endorsing bald irrationalism.[14] It is my view that this confusion may have at its root a misunderstanding of Barth's fundamental attitude toward propositions with respect to revelation. Is propositional knowledge a facet of the genuine knowledge of God given by faith? Getting clear about Barth's views regarding propositions, furthermore, is important for our assessment of a tension raised in chapter four, where we noted that Barth tends to emphasize the personal character of revelation while Plantinga emphasizes the propositional. I will approach this question by considering briefly the assessments of C. Stephen Evans, Paul Helm and Nicholas Wolterstorff—each of which links Barth in some way to what might be called a nonpropositional view.

THE CRITIQUES OF EVANS, HELM AND WOLTERSTORFF

C. Stephen Evans associates Barth with "neo-orthodox theologians," who advocate a nonpropositional view of revelation.[15] Evans does not directly assert that Barth himself holds this view strictly, though it would be easy to mistake this as implied.[16] Evans presents the neo-orthodox, nonpropositional view as a reaction against liberal theology. Liberal theologians, adopting the "traditional understanding of revelation as propositional,"[17] subjected the propositions of the Bible to increasing suspicion, thereby compromising its authority. Evans concludes that the neo-orthodox response was to assert that revelation does not convey propositions. Revelation proceeds on the occasion of reading the Bible "as the Spirit of God illumines the *hearts* of those who read and listen with openness."[18] He helpfully points out, however, that one need not adopt a strictly nonpropositional view of revelation to appreciate the insight that "the *primary* object of revelation is God himself, not propositions about God, and the *primary* purpose of revelation is making possible a relationship with God."[19] We might term such a view the not-

[14]See discussion and references in chapter 2.

[15]C. Stephen Evans, "Faith and Reason," in *The Oxford Handbook of Philosophy of Religion,* ed. William J. Wainwright (New York: Oxford University Press, 2005), pp. 325-27.

[16]Evans, "Faith and Reason" has clarified that he does not mean to assert that Barth's view is best understood as the "strictly non-propositional" view.

[17]Evans, "Faith and Reason," p. 325.

[18]Ibid., p. 326, emphasis mine.

[19]Ibid., p. 327, emphasis original.

merely-propositional view over against the strictly nonpropositional view. It should be clear that the strictly nonpropositional view cannot apply to Barth. As we have already demonstrated, Barth is adamant that revelation engages the mind. It is rational and verbal. Unless this is absolute doublespeak, clearly he is affirming *some* propositional element to revelation. The not-merely-propositional view, I would suggest, is Barth's actual view—that revelation has both nonpropositional and propositional aspects. It is safe to say that Barth would agree with Evans's conclusion that revelation, in its paradigmatic verbal forms, cannot be strictly nonpropositional and that God's personal self-disclosure inevitably involves the revelation of "some truths about himself."[20]

Paul Helm draws a slightly different conclusion about Barth's notion of revelation. Helm determines that if revelation is propositional, it must be epistemically objective. Something is epistemically objective "if what is known by one person about that object can be remembered and communicated to others for them to know."[21] Helm says that Barth "denies the objectivity of revelation" because epistemic objectivity implies that revelation is static and subject to human control, which is a violation of God's sovereign freedom in revelation.[22] He concludes, therefore, that Barth rejects the possibility of revelation being propositional.[23] Helm's primary critique of Barth is that he is wrong to assume that epistemic objectivity gives an object over to the control of those who have epistemically objective knowledge of it.[24] Helm's analysis suffers from a misunderstanding of the logic of Barth's position. Barth is not worried that epistemic objectivity would subject God to human control. Barth is concerned to safeguard against the presumption that genuine human knowledge of God could be a human possession *outside* and *independent*

---

[20]Ibid. In fact, Barth's view comports quite well with Evans's later treatment of Kierkegaard and Plantinga (ibid., pp. 335-41).

[21]Paul Helm, *The Divine Revelation: The Basic Issues* (Westchester, IL: Crossway, 1982), p. 40. Plantinga's notion of "objectivity" as "being oriented toward . . . the *object* of knowledge" corresponds with Barth's view. "What is objective may be thought of as coming from the object rather than from myself as subject" (*WCB,* pp. 417-18, emphasis original).

[22]Helm, *Divine Revelation,* pp. 40-41.

[23]Ibid., p. 46.

[24]Ibid., pp. 45-46.

of divine self-disclosure in the gift of faith.[25] In fact, Barth has no problems with the epistemic objectivity of God, so long as it is not seen to be a function of an independently held human capacity rather than the epistemic objectivity of faith.[26] In Barth's view, the gift of faith—divinely enabled epistemic objectivity—is the basis for preaching, which is precisely an attempt to "remember and communicate" truth truly in the light of revelation.[27] Directed against conclusions like those of Helm, Barth gives the following plea: "We have made a positive assertion, pronouncing a definite Yes to the knowability of the Word of God. . . . Others ought not so stubbornly to hear only the No in what has been said."[28]

Nicholas Wolterstorff offers a more careful and penetrating analysis of Barth's theology of revelation. His conclusion, however, is similar to Helm's. Wolterstorff claims that despite all of Barth's talk about revelation as the speech of God, "there's less in Barth on God speaking than first appears."[29] Wrestling with many of Barth's intricate statements, Wolterstorff seems to grasp Barth's key distinction between revelation per se and the media of revelation.[30] He also grasps just how unflinching Barth is in maintaining that a medium of revelation can never be equated with revelation per se.[31] While apparently noticing Barth's insistence

---

[25]It is Barth's understanding of the nature of revelation as thoroughly divine gift, not subject to human demonstration or isolated possession, that also eludes Keith Ward. He makes the mystifying claim that Barth's view of revelation is motivated by pride and self-exaltation. "Of course one has an interest in thinking one's own religion is the only true one; it enables one to dismiss the others as of no account and so bask in the superiority of one's own possession of truth. . . . One can hardly get more proud, more self-righteous, and more short-sighted than that" (Ward, *Religion and Revelation: A Theology of Revelation in the World's Religions* [Oxford: Oxford University Press, 1994], p. 17).

[26]"We can grasp [God's Word] only in faith. We are set in the greatest clarity in relation to the one, in such clarity that we have very distinct and in themselves clear thoughts regarding what is said to us, and we can react thereto with the whole outer and inner attitude of our lives" (*CD* I/1, p. 174).

[27]"We must be very clear that the simplest proclamation of the Gospel can be proclamation of the truth in the most unlimited sense and can validly communicate the truth to the most unsophisticated hearer if God so will" (*CD* I/1, p. 83).

[28]*CD* I/1, p. 196.

[29]Nicholas Wolterstorff, *Divine Discourse: Philosophical Reflections on the Claim That God Speaks* (Cambridge: Cambridge University Press, 1995), pp. 58, 72.

[30]Ibid., p. 65. As we saw in chapter 1, Barth often refers to this as the distinction between content and form (*CD* I/1, p. 175).

[31]Wolterstorff, *Divine Discourse,* pp. 68-70.

that there is a real revealing, a real divine speaking through the media of revelation, the connection between God's speech and the medium of human speech is too tenuous for Wolterstorff. He draws the unfortunate conclusion that what Barth calls God's speech, when encountered through a medium, is not, in fact, appropriately referred to as speech.[32] Instead, what God does through the medium of human witness is to speak to the heart, not the head, of the hearer. This conclusion is simply untenable in light of Barth's consistent and emphatic declarations both that God speaks, particularly through scripture and preaching, and that this speech is verbal, cognitive and rational.[33] What has Wolterstorff missed? The chief failing in Wolterstorff's assessment is a failure to come to grips with Barth's view that a human medium could be appropriated for divine discourse without being equated with it. Scripture is not divine discourse, in and of itself. The qualifier "in and of itself" is absolutely crucial. This does not mean, for Barth, that God does not speak through scripture. It means that what drives and enables that speech is not a property or capacity of the medium. The human medium does not contain or convey the Word of God on its own, but it does serve as a genuine medium when accompanied by the work of the Spirit in the gift of faith.

There is, however, a deeper point to which Wolterstorff leads—one that is pivotal for understanding Barth's theological motivations. Wolterstorff says that to understand Barth one must "realize that he is the most relentlessly Chalcedonian of all Christian theologians."[34] It is clear from his discussion, however, that Wolterstorff is only thinking of one side of the Chalcedonian formula—that which stresses the unity of the natures in one person. From this he draws the mistaken conclusion that in the incarnation the humanity of Jesus unmediatedly communicates the divine. Barth has in mind both sides of Chalcedon, including the stipulation that in the unity of the person the natures are not to be con-

---

[32]Ibid., p. 72.

[33]It may be sufficient to observe that the first thing Barth says about the nature of the Word of God is that it is speech. And, according to Barth, part of what it means that the Word of God is the speech of God is that "the encounter of God and man takes place primarily, pre-eminently and characteristically in this sphere of *ratio*" (*CD* I/1, p. 135).

[34]Wolterstorff, *Divine Discourse,* p. 64.

fused.[35] Consequently, Barth does not hold, as Wolterstorff suggests, that veiling and unveiling do not apply to revelation by means of the human Jesus[36] or that the human speech of Jesus can be simply equated with divine discourse[37] without the provisos that attend other kinds of human media taken up in revelation.[38] For Barth, this mistake is at the heart of a cancer that plagues theology, which is precisely why the proper distinction between form and content in revelation is so important to grasp. Given the significance of this point, I'll include a longer excerpt from the *Church Dogmatics.*

> Can the incarnation of the Word according to the biblical witnesses mean that the existence of the man Jesus of Nazareth was as it were in itself, in its own power and continuity, the revealing Word of God? Is the *humanitas Christi* as such the revelation? Does the divine sonship of Jesus Christ mean that God's revealing has now been transmitted as it were to the existence of the man Jesus of Nazareth, that this has thus become identical with it? At this stage we can only reply that when this view has really been held, there has always been more or less clearly discernible the very thing which, as we have seen, the Old Testament tried to avoid with its concept of the holiness of the revealed God, namely, the possibility of having God disclose Himself through man, of allowing man to set himself on the same platform as God, to grasp Him there and thus to become His master.[39]

Barth's insistence on the independent inadequacy of the creaturely medium of revelation is held alongside his firm commitment to the divinely enabled possibility of a genuinely humanly received revelation of God. They are, as it were, united but not confused.

From these very brief exchanges with Evans, Helm and Wolterstorff,

---

[35]This is applied expressly to scripture as well: "It is neither divine only nor human only. Nor is it a mixture of the two nor a *tertium quid* between them" (*CD* I/2, p. 501).

[36]Wolterstorff, *Divine Discourse,* p. 65.

[37]Ibid., p. 73.

[38]As Trevor Hart explains, "The vehicle of revelation, even when it is hypostatically united with God, is not itself God. Information about Jesus' life, character, actions, death and resurrection is not knowledge of God in the sense that Barth intends it and in the event of revelation it is precisely *God himself* who is known" (Hart, "Revelation," in *The Cambridge Companion to Karl Barth,* ed. John B. Webster [Cambridge: Cambridge University Press, 2000], p. 52, emphasis original).

[39]*CD* I/1, p. 323.

we can affirm that Barth conceives of revelation as not merely propositional, as objective knowing in the gift of faith and as conveyed by, but not reducible to, a creaturely medium. The gift of faith is the total act of God's giving himself to be known, which enables the creaturely medium to serve God's purposes and optimally to result in a unified personal and propositional knowledge. This is a divine act in which we as receivers are called to participate with the totality of our being. The temptation is to divide the aspects or elements of the gift of faith. Focusing exclusively on the propositional aspect of revelation is a common way to give in to this dichotomizing temptation and in so doing to compromise the integrity of the gift of faith. In our discussion, I will not focus exclusively on the propositional, but I will give a more careful analysis of the nature of the propositional components of revelation in order better to understand how the Barth/Plantinga proposal comprehends the relationship between faith and knowledge. To that end, while I seek to keep the propositional connected to the personal, we first need to clarify what we mean by "propositional knowledge."

THE PROPOSITIONAL FORM AND CONTENT OF THE KNOWLEDGE OF FAITH

On propositional knowing. We have already suggested that the kind of knowledge Plantinga is primarily concerned with is propositional knowledge. Propositional knowledge is, simply, knowledge of propositions. In order to count as knowledge, of course, the proposition known must be true, it must be understood and it must be warrantedly believed. What constitutes a proposition? According to Plantinga, propositions "are the things that are true or false; they are also the things we believe, and the things expressed by our sentences."[40] Propositions are, therefore, distinct from the sentences used to express them. Plantinga explains further: "When one sincerely asserts a proposition *p*, then one believes *p* (and hence grasps or understands it) and asserts *p* by way of assertively uttering a sentence that expresses *p*."[41] I take it that when Plantinga

---

[40]Plantinga, "Replies to My Colleagues," in *Alvin Plantinga*, ed. James E. Tomberlin and Peter van Inwagen (Dordrecht: D. Reidel, 1985), p. 355.

[41]Ibid.

here says "a sentence expresses a proposition," this is shorthand for "a sentence is used by a person to express a proposition."[42] One way of judging the truth or falsehood of a sentence would be on the basis of the truth or falsehood of the proposition that is intended to be expressed by means of the sentence.[43] The suitability of a sentence as the vehicle of the expression of a proposition will depend on all of the many factors that affect communication. On its own, a sentence does not have the capacity perfectly to convey a proposition. Instead, as Plantinga affirms, the expression of a proposition by a sentence is successful when "my interlocutor, upon hearing the sentence I use, grasps or apprehends the very proposition in question—the very proposition I believe, intend to assert, and express by my sentence."[44] In Plantinga's view, our grasp or apprehension of a proposition is not an all-or-nothing venture; it is a matter of degree.[45] One more obvious point to make is that propositions are about things, things that are referred to in sentences under some description or designation. Sentences expressing propositions are typically composed of subjects, predicates and predicating terms; to grasp a proposition firmly, one must apprehend clearly what is meant by each of these components.[46]

---

[42]In other words, I believe the proposition Plantinga means to assert with "a sentence expresses a proposition" is better expressed by "a sentence is used by a person to express a proposition." That is not to say that there is not a distinction between what the sentence expresses and what a sentence may be used by a person to express.

[43]See Alvin Plantinga, "Divine Knowledge," in *Christian Perspectives on Religious Knowledge,* ed. C. Stephen Evans and Merold Westphal (Grand Rapids: Eerdmans, 1993), p. 43, where he also notes that not every sentence is intended to express a proposition.

[44]Plantinga, "Replies to My Colleagues," p. 355.

[45]Ibid., p. 356.

[46]It is important to note that the traditional "propositional" sentence is certainly not the only vehicle for expressing propositions. Propositions can be given expression by means of other linguistic genres (e.g., poetry, parable, etc.). Propositions can also be expressed through nonlinguistic means (e.g., gestures, sculpture, interpretive dance, etc.). These forms may serve to evoke or express more than propositions, though often not less. These forms may have the advantage of addressing noncognitive barriers to and personal dimensions of knowing. The advantage of the traditional sentence in "propositional form," adopted as the primary form in research literature, is the precision with which it is able to express an intended proposition. Some suggest, however, that the impotence of propositional form to address the fuller dimensions of knowing can so impede successful communication of meaning that other means of expressing propositions are, in fact, superior. Kevin Vanhoozer, for example, advocates "poetic analysis." He argues that "theologians must do more (but not less!) than 'narrow' analysis that simply distils clear propositions from texts in order to assess their cogency. This kind of analysis . . . yields only thin descriptions that overlook the cognitive significance of larger forms of discourse, such as literary genres" (Vanhoozer, "The

Propositional knowing may be distinguished from other kinds of knowing. Propositional knowing takes the form of knowing *that p* (where *p* is a proposition). There is also *practical* knowledge—knowing how to do *x* or being *capable* of doing *x*. There is *experiential* knowledge or the knowledge of acquaintance whereby one is familiar with *x*. The personal knowing we have discussed could be considered a special kind of experiential knowing. It is significant to note that practical knowledge, experiential knowledge and personal knowledge can and usually do have propositional content.[47] Practical, experiential or personal knowledge is accompanied by propositional knowledge about that which is known practically, experientially or personally. The relationship between propositional knowing and other kinds of knowing is complex.[48] Growing in propositional knowledge is often a means to growing in other kinds of knowledge. Growing in other kinds of knowledge often involves the discovery of new propositional knowledge.

Belief also has more than one sense. Belief as a component of propositional knowledge indicates assent to the truth of a proposition—*belief that p*. The kind of belief that indicates trust in or submission to something or someone takes the form of *belief in x*. Each of these distinctions regarding belief, knowledge, propositions and their means of expression will be important for avoiding ambiguity as we now pick up where we left off with Barth.

Barth and propositional knowing. We have already confirmed that, for Barth, revelation is principally personal divine self-disclosure. Revelation, therefore, cannot be reduced to propositions.[49] This leaves open the

---

Apostolic Discourse and Its Developments," in *Scripture's Doctrine and Theology's Bible: How the New Testament Shapes Christian Dogmatics,* ed. Markus Bockmuehl and Alan J. Torrance [Grand Rapids: Baker Academic, 2008], pp. 200-201).

[47]Vanhoozer makes this point: "Against the dichotomy between personal and propositional revelation, I am inclined to say that *all* our encounters with persons are 'propositional' in the sense of involving communicative action" (Vanhoozer, "God's Mighty Speech-Acts: The Doctrine of Scripture Today," in *A Pathway into the Holy Scripture,* ed. P. E. Satterthwaite and David F. Wright [Grand Rapids: Eerdmans, 1994], p. 179, emphasis original).

[48]This complexity is compounded by other noncognitive dimensions that directly affect knowledge structures. The interconnectedness of the affective and the cognitive is commonly acknowledged. See *WCB,* pp. 205-9, 301-10.

[49]On the question of whether revelation can be equated with doctrinal propositions, Barth's view is clear. "Will the truth of revelation submit to such materialisation and depersonalisation? Can one have it in abstraction from the person of Him who reveals it and from the revelatory act of

question of whether, in Barth's view, revelation has propositional content that is in some way available to human subjects. Does revelation as personal knowing eclipse the propositional? Does Barth believe that revelation is indifferent to propositional content, or merely that the propositional content of faith cannot be known outside of the gift of personal divine self-revealing? It may be helpful to look at some of Barth's sterner warnings regarding propositions.

> The concept of truths of revelation in the sense of Latin propositions given and sealed once for all with divine authority in both wording and meaning is theologically impossible if it is a fact that revelation is true in the free decision of God which was taken once for all in Jesus Christ.[50]

> We cannot view [revelation] in such a way that propositions may be taken from it which, isolated from the giving of God's Word in revelation, Scripture and proclamation, can be known as general truths by man, . . . so that they for their part can then be made—and this is the decisive point—the presupposition of an understanding of God's Word or the basis of theology.[51]

> It is for this reason and in this sense that we finally speak of the Word of God as the mystery of God . . . as one might put it, a theological warning against theology, a warning against the idea that its propositions or principles are certain in themselves like the supposed axioms of the mathematicians and physicists, and are not rather related to their theme and content, which alone are certain, which they cannot master, by which they must be mastered if they are not to be mere soap-bubbles.[52]

These are strong warnings, yet rather than supporting the conclusion that revelation has no propositional content, propositional content is assumed and given a strict qualification.[53] Barth's apparent anxiety about

---

this person in which it is given to other persons to perceive?" (*CD* I/1, p. 270).

[50]*CD* I/1, p. 15. Barth is not suggesting that the truth of what is revealed is relative to God's decision to reveal it rather than absolute, anchored in the reality of the object of revelation. It is rather that God's decision to reveal is part of who God is, as the object of revelation. God is also his revealing.

[51]*CD* I/1, p. 130.

[52]*CD* I/1, p. 165.

[53]It is clearly incorrect to conclude, as Laurence W. Wood does, that in Barth's understanding of revelation as inseparable from redemption and reconciliation, the result is a restriction such that "revelation is not a matter of propositions or objective events" (Wood, "Defining the Modern

propositions is directed at a view of revelation as the lossless transmission of divine data in self-contained human statements. In each instance, his intent is to highlight the utter incapacity of human words, conceptions and noetic equipment to contain the personal revelation of God. We must remember, however, that in the miracle of faith this incapacity is overcome. Having remembered this, we must not forget that even the propositional content of revelation remains ever dependent on the gracious action of divine self-disclosure—the gift of faith. It may be illuminating to consider how this might proceed for a particular proposition—one that would traditionally be considered a revealed truth.

Consider the proposition Plantinga often returns to: "God was in Christ, reconciling the world to himself."[54] How might grasping this proposition be related to Barth's notion of revelation such that, on the one hand, it constitutes a genuine human grasp of the proposition while, on the other hand, it remains fundamentally dependent on the personal knowing of faith? Throughout this analysis it will be important to keep in mind the difference between a proposition and its means of expression. The way in which the proposition in question is expressed may, of course, vary. The appropriateness of the expression will depend on a multitude of situational variables. Perhaps one hears a sermon that explicitly addresses the sentence "God was in Christ, reconciling the world to himself," or, what may be more likely, one encounters a presentation of the gospel narrative that expresses the proposition in question and many others. The question is: How might one be given a grasp of this proposition that is a genuine human grasp and also derivative of the faith-giving activity of the Spirit?[55]

Consider again what is involved in grasping a proposition. The strength of one's grasp of a proposition is dependent on how clearly one apprehends the subject, the predicate and the nature of the predication in-

Concept of Self-Revelation: Toward a Synthesis of Barth and Pannenberg," *Asbury Theological Journal* 41, no. 2 [1986]: 85).

[54]*WCB*, pp. 7, 36, 42, 56, 105, 244, 250, 260, 261, 267, 331, 376, 378-79, 448, 454; referencing 2 Cor 5:19.

[55]One impressive study that sets out to answer this question is Kevin Hector's *Theology Without Metaphysics: God, Language and the Spirit of Recognition* (New York: Cambridge University Press, 2011). See also the symposium on this book in the *Journal of Analytic Theology* 1, no. 1 (2013).

volved. There may be many ways in which one comes to acquire a new or strengthened apprehension of these things—through experience, inference, testimony and so on. There are also different ways of apprehending a proposition. It is possible to have no prior knowledge of a subject and still apprehend a proposition in a certain sense. Take for example the proposition expressed by a sentence that begins with an unknown proper name—such as "Newg is very friendly." One might have no other knowledge of who or what Newg is and still apprehend that someone or thing named Newg has the property of being very friendly. There is a difficulty with this, however. What is meant by the expression "being very friendly" depends, in part, on the nature of the thing about which it is expressed. Think of the difference it would make if Newg were an amoeba, a tropical storm, a personal computer or a newborn baby. We can see, therefore, that the stronger one's apprehension of the realities involved, the better one's grasp of a proposition about them.

Now let us consider what it takes to have a relatively strong grasp of the proposition that "God was in Christ, reconciling the world to himself." If we are correct in what we have said so far, it requires a relatively strong apprehension of what is being expressed by the proper names *God* and *Christ*, as well as what is meant by *reconciling* and other words in the sentence. Where might we turn to find greater clarity about these realities? Principally, Barth suggests, this clarification comes through God's own transforming work of self-revelation through the witness of the Bible and the proclamation of the church. In Christian scripture and preaching, however, we find yet more expressions in human words that are used together in an attempt to clarify what those expressions intend. The problem, which is for Barth patent, is that all those words are never adequate, by themselves, to give a sufficient grasp of the reality referred to by the proper names *God* and *Christ*.[56] Certainly one

[56]Like others, Hilary Putnam recognizes the epistemic difficulties surrounding the concept God and finds this to be the fundamental problem with attempts to prove God's existence (Putnam, "The Depths and Shadows of Experience," in *Science, Religion, and the Human Experience,* ed. James D. Proctor [Oxford: Oxford University Press, 2005], p. 80). Early in his career, Antony Flew further suggested that there is no coherent concept "God" (Flew, *The Presumption of Atheism and Other Philosophical Essays on God, Freedom, and Immortality* [New York: Barnes & Noble, 1976], pp. 131-32).

can become competent in using the words and still lack a basic understanding of and familiarity with the realities to which they refer.[57] Plantinga has a great deal to offer in navigating the subtleties involved with proper names, real referents and propositional utterances. One example that provides particular assistance on this issue is the connection Plantinga draws between essential properties and proper names.

Proper names and the essences they express. Early in Plantinga's career he began making contributions to debates in metaphysics in conversation with the likes of W. V. O. Quine and David Lewis. Central to some of these debates were theories of attribution and reference and the nature of proper names. Plantinga's own views on proper names provide us an illuminating conceptuality for thinking about the different kinds of propositional knowledge one might have of God.[58]

Proper names are used to refer to or pick out an individual being or object. On Plantinga's view, a proper name expresses properties that are essential to the thing named—but not just any properties that are essential to that thing, essential properties that are essentially unique to that thing. Following Boethius, Plantinga adopts the notion of an individual essence. An individual essence of something would be the essential properties of that thing that are essentially unique to that thing. So, what a proper name does is express the individual essence of a thing. On this view, the proper name for God, whichever one might be using, is used to express unique essential properties of God. If there were no more to Plantinga's view, it would leave open a number of concerns. How do we account for the fact that different people will have different ideas about God's essential properties in mind when they employ a proper name for God and that not all proper names for God seem to pick out the same essential properties? Questions also arise with respect to the

---

[57]As Plantinga notes, "a competent speaker could use his words to assert a proposition of which he has only an inchoate grasp or even no grasp at all" (Plantinga, "Replies to My Colleagues," p. 357).

[58]Some theologians will balk at references to essences and properties with a worry that contaminating metaphysical commitments attend them. This need not be the case. What we say here is intended to be clear of Barth's own similar concerns. For a discussion along these lines, see Kevin Hector's concerns about metaphysics and what he calls "essentialism" and his exchange with Oliver Crisp (Hector, *Theology Without Metaphysics*, pp. 14-15, 125-31; Crisp, "*Ad* Hector," *Journal of Analytic Theology* 1, no. 1 [2013]: 133-39; Hector, "Responses to *JAT*'s Symposium on *Theology Without Metaphysics*," *Journal of Analytic Theology* 1, no. 1 [2013]: 140-47).

uniqueness of God. To what extent are proper names for God different from other proper names? How does Plantinga's view of proper names fit with the biblical notion of God's name?[59]

As far as I know, Plantinga never explicitly discusses how proper names for God fit with his general view of proper names; however, it would be consistent with Barth to think that in most ways our use of language and the nature of reference would operate according to the same principles that apply to other things.[60] What is particularly helpful about Plantinga's view of proper names—we will see—is its ability to handle the concerns just mentioned about the variability of names, use and expression. This allows his view to accommodate Barth's view where hiddenness and real revealing coexist.

Plantinga saw that his idea that proper names express individual essences would not work if it meant that proper names express the comprehensive set of all essential properties that are essentially unique to the named thing. It could not be the case that proper names just pick out the complete and single individual essence of a thing.[61] Moreover, it need not be the case that different proper names for the same thing express the same essence of that thing. If that were the case, then what is expressed by a proper name or several proper names for the same thing could never vary epistemically. Two proper names for the same thing would have to have the same cognitive value or be in Plantinga's words, "epistemically equivalent." Plantinga considers Frege's Puzzle (which is the proper name for a puzzle about proper names). Frege notes that ancient Babylonians were not aware that the evening star, Hesperus, and the morning star, Phophorus, were one and the same planet, Venus. These proper names in fact refer to the same object, but they are clearly

[59]As Barth notes, the name God gives in Exodus 3:14, "I am that I am," suggests that God is beyond naming, and yet he reveals himself under this name. Barth further asserts that in the name of Jesus the manner of revelation is "incomparably more direct, unequivocal and palpable" (see *CD* I/1, pp. 316-19).

[60]Notice that I am not saying that God is known through, deduced by or confined to a general theory. What is special about the knowledge of God is God and the fact that, as Barth says, "by the grace of revelation our human views and concepts are invited and exalted to share in the truth of God" (*CD* II/1, p. 341).

[61]"In *The Nature of Necessity* I unwisely conceded that if proper names express essences, then it is plausible to suppose that different proper names of the same object express the same essence" (Plantinga, "The Boethian Compromise," *American Philosophical Quarterly* 15, no. 2 [1978]: 135).

epistemically inequivalent. Plantinga's understanding of the nature of proper names resolves this puzzle by allowing that an object may have many individual essences. Given this possibility, it is a further possibility that different proper names for the same thing can express different essences of that object. This is precisely what is happening in the case of Hesperus and Phophorus. Plantinga argues, however, that while the individual essences expressed may be epistemically inequivalent, they are logically equivalent.[62] They are logically equivalent because those properties expressed by the various individual essences of a thing are essential and essentially unique to that thing. So the thing in question could not be what it is and fail to have any of the properties expressed by its various proper names. Though the thing is singular, its names and the particular properties picked out by those names may vary.

Applying this back again to our broader discussion, Plantinga's Boethian view makes sense of the epistemic variability that accompanies human references to God. Variability not only comes from different names for a thing but potentially from "the same name on different occasions of use."[63] This is clearly the case for proper names for God. On one occasion of use, a proper name for God may express only the property of God's being the one who could create the world. On another occasion, it may express the property of God's being the one who is supremely powerful. On another occasion, it may express all of this and more. In other words, there can be broader and narrower expressions of God's essence by means of the same proper name for God.[64] In addition, of course, there can be occasions of using the words that are used to express a proper name for God and failing entirely to refer to God at all.

Barth does not have Plantinga's detailed conceptuality for parsing these distinctions. His interest is to point to a God-given knowledge of God that comes by means of communion with God. He intends so to de-

[62]"Different proper names of an object can express logically equivalent but epistemically inequivalent essences of that object" (Plantinga, "Boethian Compromise," p. 134).

[63]Plantinga adds this parenthetically (ibid., p. 138).

[64]Perhaps from God's point of view all of God's essential properties are in some sense indistinguishable, as certain construals of divine simplicity seem to suggest. From the human point of view, however, God's essential properties are epistemically distinct. I may know of some and not of others.

marcate the knowledge of God by faith that any knowledge or expression of God's uniquely essential properties that is epistemically inferior to it fails to be what I have called a *genuine* human knowledge of God. It fails to be genuine in its propositional content, at least in part, because those essential properties of God that remain unknown of God are crucial to a redeemed knowledge of God. We will return to this at the end of the chapter when we compare Barth and Plantinga on the *sensus divinitatis.*

Barth sees that the words themselves are insufficient to carry the freight. The words have no more power than the human speakers of the words to express all the essential and essentially unique properties of God that a redeemed propositional knowledge of God includes. That possibility comes by participation in God's self-knowledge, without which the words effectively hide more than they reveal. It is that potential for hiding or veiling God that we turn to next as the first of three difficult interconnected issues for coming to grips with Barth's theology of revelation. We will treat these in the following order: (1) the hiddenness of God, (2) the problem of analogical predication and (3) the significance of historical knowledge.

HIDDENNESS, ANALOGY AND HISTORY

The hiddenness of God revisited. As alluded to in chapter two, the hiddenness of God, for Barth, is neither an a priori assumption nor a demonstrable truth. What Barth means by God's hiddenness is that human language, conceptuality and noetic equipment are insufficient for arriving at a knowledge of God on their own. But knowing about God's hiddenness is only possible in the light of actual knowledge of God.[65]

> It is in faith, and therefore in the fulfillment of the knowledge of God, and therefore in the real viewing and real conceiving of God, that we can understand the fact that we know, view and conceive God, not as a work of our nature, not as a performance on the basis of our own capacity, but only as a miraculous work of the divine good-pleasure, so that, knowing God, we necessarily know His hiddenness.[66]

---

[65]We find a detailed treatment of this in *CD* II/1, pp. 179-204.

[66]*CD* II/1, p. 184. "Even knowledge of the impossibility of knowledge of the Word of God outside its reality is possible only on the presupposition of this real knowledge" (*CD* I/1, p. 197).

This is significant for our discussion in at least two ways. First, here we have another clear example of Barth affirming that the event of revelation has propositional content. The proposition that "human language, conceptuality and noetic equipment are insufficient for arriving at a knowledge of God" is a revealed truth. This very proposition is grasped on the basis of God's having overcome the insufficiency of human language, conceptuality and noetic equipment.

Second, the fact that Barth does not posit the hiddenness of God as a demonstrable presupposition keeps him from internal incoherence and direct conflict with Plantinga. One of the de jure objections to theistic belief that Plantinga dismantles is the argument that the existence of God is not something that could be known by human beings because human concepts cannot apply to God. At the heart of Plantinga's critique is the observation that to suggest that human concepts cannot apply to God is to apply at least one human concept to God.[67] It is also important to see that Barth never claims that human concepts *cannot* apply to God. What Barth claims is that human concepts are inadequate to deliver the fullness of what it is to know God.[68] What makes reference to God possible is not a capacity latent in human concepts.

> The Bible, the Church and theology undoubtedly speak this language on the presupposition that there might be something in it, namely, that in this language God's revelation might be referred to, witness might be given, God's Word might be proclaimed, dogma might be formulated and declared. The only question is whether this possibility is to be understood as that of the language and consequently of the world or man, or whether it is to be regarded as a venture which is, as it were, ascribed to the language, and consequently to the world or man, from without, so that it is not really the possibility of the language, the world, or man, but the possibility of revelation.[69]

---

[67]"One who makes the claim seems to set up a certain subject for predication—God—and then declare that our concepts do not apply to this being. But if this is so, then, presumably, at least one of our concepts—being such that our concepts don't apply to it—does apply to this being" (*WCB*, p. 6). See also ibid., p. 38.

[68]Barth asks in his lectures on ethics, "Does man really know God when he admittedly does not know him totally, in his nature, as the Lord in the pregnant and comprehensive biblical sense of the term?" *Eet*, p. 31.

[69]*CD* I/1, p. 339.

How does this help us with our question about the propositional content of revelation and the wider question of what constitutes a genuine knowledge of God for Barth? In addition to reaffirming once again that for Barth there is indeed propositional content to revelation, we also find a reaffirmation that the propositional content of revelation depends on a gracious divine enabling, and the creaturely form God enables to serve as the means of revelation may itself be an expression of propositions. We have also established that genuine knowledge of God for Barth must give us real reference to God. Minimally, this must entail that in the gift of faith what is meant by the proper name *God* is personally revealed.

We should be careful, however, what conclusions we draw from this. One is tempted to suggest that the knowledge of faith is the knowledge of religious experience,[70] such that how one knows God is principally by reference to an experience or memory of an experience of God. On this view, one's grasp of a proposition about God is dependent on understanding that the proper name *God* refers to "the one whom I religiously experience." One difficulty with this is the implication that the religious experience is strictly noumenal and utterly nonpropositional. This simply is not Barth's view.[71] God's personal revealing is inextricably connected to the propositions expressed in the medium of revelation. God's Word is speech; it is experienced as it is heard.[72]

The knowledge of God by faith (at least in the paradigmatic instances) puts us in contact with the real referent by means of human language, despite the inadequacies of human language and human cognition. In Barth's view, human cognition depends on human views[73] and human

[70]Barth was cautious in his use of the phrase "religious experience" (*CD* I/1, p. 193).

[71]Barth emphasizes that, while revelation is rightly construed as an experience (*Erfahrung*) of the Word of God, it is an experience that affects all "anthropological centres"—"intellect" as well as "feeling" and "conscience" (*CD* I/1, pp. 202-3).

[72]Some parallels can be found in William Alston's view of the relationship between beliefs about God's activity and an experiential awareness of that activity. See Alston, "Christian Experience and Christian Belief," in *Faith and Rationality,* ed. Alvin Plantinga and Nicholas Wolterstorff (Notre Dame, IN: University of Notre Dame Press, 1983), pp. 103-34; and Alston, *Perceiving God: The Epistemology of Religious Experience* (Ithaca, NY: Cornell University Press, 1991).

[73]"Views are the images in which we perceive objects as such" (*CD* II/1, p. 181).

concepts[74] and is expressed in words.[75] The grace of revelation gives us a participation in a view and conceptions of God expressed in words. We know this is possible again in retrospection on the knowledge of God given by faith. Barth reasons from the fact that God is known and can be successfully referred to in human words to the conclusion that it must be possible to "conceive (i.e., perceive and think) God."[76] This means that the knowledge of the real referent of the proper name *God* given in revelation is not independent of a clarified apprehension of the other elements of linguistic description, particularly predicates and predications.[77] This brings us to the second of three nodal issues—the problem of analogical predication.

The problem of analogical predication. Following the medievals, the way in which human language and concepts are said to refer to God is neither strictly univocally nor utterly equivocally but in some way analogically. When it comes to analogical predication, however, the devil is in the details.[78] One's grasp of what is predicated in a proposition typi-

---

[74]"Concepts are the counter-images with which we make these images of perception our own by thinking them, i.e., arranging them" (ibid.).

[75]As stressed in chapter 2, Barth is no Kantian with respect to pure reason. No doubt his thinking about cognition is shaped by Kant, but for Barth a cognitive human knowledge of the noumenal God is a real possibility thanks to God. Barth rejects Kant in explicitly Kantian terms when he says that the initiating divine action in faith generates a corresponding authentic and clear human knowing, from "intuitive apprehension to [linguistically] formulated comprehension" (*CD* I/1, p. 12). For Kant, the futility of a cognitive knowledge of God is a function of his being that which lies beyond our sensibility and understanding. See especially book 2, chapter 3 of the Transcendental Dialectic in Kant's *Critique of Pure Reason,* trans. Norman Kemp Smith (New York: Palgrave Macmillan, 2003), pp. 485-531.

[76]*CD* II/1, p. 181. Of course this is not a "possibility immanent in our viewing and conceiving (i.e., indwelling and proper to it as such" (*CD* II/1, p. 182).

[77]Trevor Hart draws the parallel to Christ's humanity. Though there is no "co-mingling of the divine and the creaturely which presents the divine to us immediately," there also can be no "docetic indifference to the humanity of the Lord," whose "life, death and resurrection constitute the primary objective locus or site of God's self-revealing" (Hart, *Regarding Karl Barth: Essays Toward a Reading of His Theology* [Carlisle, UK: Paternoster, 1999], p. 185; Hart, "Revelation," p. 52). So also, "God defines himself for us, assuming our words and conceptuality just as surely as he assumes our flesh in order to reveal himself, and yet doing so in such a way that it never lies within our grasp to cash out the metaphors in literal terms, any more than we can capture the eternal Son simply by analysing the humanness of the historical Jesus" (Hart, *Regarding Karl Barth,* p. 194).

[78]Barth's words are infamous: "I regard the *analogia entis* as the invention of Antichrist" (*CD* I/1, p. xiii). Over time Barth would soften his rhetoric, but as Keith Johnson argues, Barth did not change his fundamental view (Johnson, *Karl Barth and the* Analogia Entis [London: T &T Clark, 2012], p. 12).

cally relies, in part, on generalizing from previous knowledge based on direct or indirect experience. If I assert, for example, that my friend Dabgib "likes flowers," one's grasp of my assertion will involve picking out of the range of what it means to "like flowers" the sense or senses in which I mean to predicate "liking flowers" of Dabgib. As it stands, the assertion is rather ambiguous. It would be much less ambiguous were I to specify the sense of "liking flowers" I mean with the addition of "as is common to all herbaceous dinosaurs" or "just like any productive bumblebee." Grasping my assertion would then usually involve making an appropriate generalization from one's previous knowledge of what is typical of herbaceous beasts or bees. If this is a straightforward instance, my predication is univocal. I mean to assert that "liking flowers" applies to Dabgib in exactly the same way it applies to a general class of beings. Of course, I could be equivocating, prevaricating or simply being sarcastic. I might also employ a figure of speech, as in "Dabgib likes to stop and smell the roses." It is possible that Dabgib actually detests the smell of roses. In this case the predicate applies to Dabgib metaphorically.[79] There is a relation of some kind between what is literally predicated and what is actually predicated. In the way that some like to stop and smell roses, Dabgib likes to deviate from a regimented schedule to appreciate life's ad hoc gifts. What applies to Dabgib is a similarity shared with the predicate. Picking out the kind of relation intended is, like other communication skills, dependent on a complexity of environmentally conditioned rules and assumptions that structure human discourse within particular contexts. What is significant to notice is that even in cases of analogical predication, grasping what is predicated typically involves drawing the appropriate generalization. Whether univocally or analogically predicated, predication involves situating something with respect to generalizations drawn from existing beliefs or experience.

Barth sees that merely stipulating that reference to God is analogical is not sufficient to safeguard against the critique of Feuerbach. If our knowledge of God is finally derived from generalizations and extrapola-

---

[79]For our purposes, we need not be detained at this point with the distinction between analogy and metaphor. Cf. Swinburne, *Revelation: From Metaphor to Analogy,* 2nd ed. (Oxford: Clarendon Press, 2007), pp. 38-52.

tions of relations to human phenomena, then it seems we are destined to project a God in our own image. A knowledge of God originating from below cannot escape anthropomorphism. These concerns, which were at the forefront of Barth's rejection of natural theology, also drive his rejection of an *analogia entis* (analogy of being).[80] As Barth understood it, an *analogia entis* suggests that the being of God can be subsumed under a general category of being that applies to all beings, thus providing an analogical basis for a human knowledge of God.[81] On this view, the power of analogical predication to communicate truths about God resides in the suitability of the human knower's prior knowledge and experience to provide a noetic bridge according to a particular analogical relation.[82] For Barth, this is as good as having no hope whatsoever of knowing God.[83] Given the freedom and uniqueness of God, analogical predication of this sort requires two earth-shattering moves on the part of the human knower. The first is having a priori possession

[80]It has been well established that the notion of the *analogia entis* Barth so strongly criticized was not, in fact, held by Aquinas. While Aquinas affirms an *analogia entis* (*Summa Theologica* 1.4.3) and suggests that human language for God is analogical (*Summa Theologica* 1.13.10), it is far from clear that his notion of the *analogia entis* provides the basis for a "natural" knowledge of God. We find, furthermore, that for Aquinas the Holy Spirit bestows the natural light (*Summa Theologica* 1–2.109.1). An extremely illuminating discussion of Aquinas and Barth on the question of analogical predication is found in Alan Torrance, *Persons in Communion: An Essay on Trinitarian Description and Human Participation, with Special Reference to Volume One of Karl Barth's Church Dogmatics* (Edinburgh: T & T Clark, 1996), pp. 127-203. For other comparisons of Barth and Aquinas on analogy, see Henri Chavannes, *L'Analogie entre Dieu et le monde selon Saint Thomas d'Aquin et selon Karl Barth* (Paris: Éditions du Cerf, 1969); Battista Mondin, *The Principle of Analogy in Protestant and Catholic Theology* (The Hague: Nijhoff, 1963); and Albert Patfoort "Vers une réconciliation entre saint Thomas et Karl Barth," *Angelicum* 48 (1971): 226-32.

[81]The *analogia entis* is construed "as an analogy that can be surveyed and perceived, as an analogy that can be understood in a synthesis from an onlooker's standpoint." It posits "a being which the creature has in common with the Creator," resulting finally in "a deification of man" (*CD* I/1, p. 239).

[82]In *CD* II/1, where Barth will affirm the possibility of an analogy enacted by revelation, he remains steadfast in denouncing any view of analogy that moves from a "general analogy of the world to God." He calls this "the moderate doctrine of analogy in natural theology" (*CD* II/1, p. 232).

[83]"The question: What is God's Word? is utterly hopeless [*völlig hoffnungslos*] if it is the question as to the category in which God's Word is to be put or the syllogism by which it might be proved. Questions of category and syllogism obviously presuppose that the Word of God is one of the realities that are universally present and ascertainable and therefore created. All concepts tending in this direction, even that of a supreme being, an *ens perfectissimum* or an unconditioned, even that of the breaking through and knowledge of such a supreme being, are not as such—as general concepts—the concept of the Word of God. As general concepts, they suppress the essential point that the Word of God is a reality only in its own decision. The fact that the Word of God is decision means that there is no concept of the Word of God apart from the name of God, which we love and fear and worship because it is identical with the Bearer of the name" (*CD* I/1, pp. 158-59).

of knowledge and experience that may serve as a suitable analogue. The second is being able to discern the analogical relation—perceiving the boundaries of the sense in which the analogy holds.

Is Barth's rejection of an *analogia entis* equivalent to the rejection of any reference to God by means of analogical predication? Do all forms of analogy run aground on the shoals of anthropomorphism? Barth seems to concede that some form of analogy is the only option standing between the extremes of univocation and equivocation. The key qualification for Barth is that successful analogy is only made possible by means of divine self-revealing. Affirming what he sees as the right view of analogy, Barth writes:

> Between our views, concepts and words, and God as their object, there exists, on the basis of the revelation of God, the relationship of analogy, of similarity, of partial correspondence and agreement. On the basis of this similarity there is a true human knowledge of God and therefore the human knowledge of God reaches its goal.[84]

What Barth rejects is not analogy, but the presumption that a human potency enables its success. The problem arises when the power of analogical reference to God is "ascribed to the language, and consequently to the world or man, *from without*."[85]

The kind of analogy that is operative in revelation is not an *analogia entis* but the *analogia fidei*.[86] The critical difference is that, in the gift of faith, the power enabling the success of the analogical predication is the grace of God's own self-revealing. This means that, rather than relying on an a priori grasp of the analogue and a human perception of the precise range and sense of the analogical relation, God himself provides cognitively what human knowers cannot provide themselves. This involves a reversing of the epistemic relationship between subject and object that has tacitly informed all our illustrations up to this point. Rather than starting with the noetic capacities and preconditions of the

---

[84]*CD* II/1, p. 227.

[85]Quoted at length above, *CD* I/1, p. 339, emphasis mine.

[86]"Our reply to the Roman Catholic doctrine of the *analogia entis* is not, then, a denial of the concept of analogy. We say rather that the analogy in question is not an *analogia entis* but according to Rom. 12^6 the ἀναλογία τῆς πίστεως" (*CD* I/1, p. 243).

human knower, revelation proceeds—yes, *by means of* the analogy, but according to the self-interpreting priority of the object of knowing, the real referent God. Genuine human knowledge of God begins not with a human grasp but with God grasping the human by means of an encounter with the Word of God, which results in a corresponding human grasp.[87] Barth explains the *analogia fidei* in light of Galatians 4:8, where the priority of being known by God establishes a Christian knowledge of God.[88] This has a decisive impact on how we conceive of the propositional content of revelation.

Let us consider how this goes for specific analogues, for instance, our expression of God in Christ "reconciling" the world or the seemingly more straightforward ascriptions of God as "father," or even simply "person." No matter how much additional description we pile on to clarify the analogy from the disanalogy between God and our own prior knowledge and experience of mundane reconciling, fathers and persons, we can never lift ourselves out of the limitations inherent in human language, particularly in light of the sinfulness of the human condition and the uniqueness of God. Overcoming this problem, Barth believes, requires a reversal of the movement from mundane knowledge to divine knowledge. Barth's expression, encountered earlier, is again apposite here: "the power of this reference does not lie in itself; it lies in that to which it refers."[89] What anchors the analogical reference cannot be a conception of the mundane analogue but the active role taken by the object of knowing to illumine himself in the reference.[90] "By the grace of revelation our human views and concepts are invited and exalted to share in the truth of God and therefore in a marvelous way made instru-

[87]"Not therefore that man has grasped at the Bible but that the Bible has grasped at man" (*CD* I/1, p. 110).

[88]"This *analogia fidei* is also the point of the remarkable passages in Paul in which man's knowledge of God is inverted into man's being known by God. Paul calls Christians γνόντες θεόν only to amend it at once: μᾶλλον δὲ γνωσθέντες ὑπὸ θεοῦ. It is obviously this γνωσθῆναι that distinguishes their γιγνώσκειν as Christians from their previous non-knowing of God as pagans (Gal. 4:8f.)" (*CD* I/1, p. 244).

[89]*CD* I/1, p. 197.

[90]Jay Wesley Richards rightly identifies Barth's commitment to God's action in revelation as the motivation for his rejection of an *analogia entis* and an intrinsic *analogia attributionis* (Richards, *The Untamed God: A Philosophical Exploration of Divine Perfection, Immutability and Simplicity* [Downers Grove, IL: InterVarsity Press, 2003], p. 124).

ments of a real knowledge of God."[91] The analogue is commandeered and filled out by the referent. The object of knowing assumes epistemic priority over the human preconceptions and experience associated with the reference. The reconciliation, fatherhood and personhood of God are paradigmatic reconciliation, fatherhood and personhood. The mundane notions are derivative of the uniquely divine and thus paradigmatic instantiations. For Barth, this is the only solution to the problem of anthropomorphism. He therefore quips, "The doubtful thing is not whether God is person, but whether we are."[92]

We can now see with greater clarity why, for Barth, one cannot separate the question of the propositional or cognitive content of revelation from the personal and transformative character of revelation. Together they constitute a *genuine* human knowledge of God. In the *analogia fidei,* human noetic structures and linguistic forms are reconciled (though not yet fully redeemed) by the Spirit of God so that we may begin to grasp—or better, be grasped by—the propositions expressed in human language. In this action of revelation we receive a knowledge of the referent, God himself.

This also means that, for Barth, any successful reference to God or communication about God that counts as or results in a genuine human knowledge of God must always be *by faith*—that is, it must involve the free gift of active, personal, transformative divine self-disclosure. It is not possible, having been revealed to propositionally, to come as it were back down the mountain with those propositions in hand to conceive and speak of God outside of his presence and active self-revealing.[93] Of course this is not a reason to despair but merely a reminder of our faithful hope and confident dependence on God's grace.

As always, much more can be said about the nature of this transformative self-revealing. I may be guilty in this section of seeming to approach the question of propositional content as if such knowing were highly theoretical, abstract and individualistic. I have said very little here to recall discussions in chapter five of the importance of broader

[91]*CD* II/1, p. 341.

[92]*CD* I/1, p. 138.

[93]As Trevor Hart puts it, we cannot "climb up the vapour trails left by the divine descent, and find our way to heaven" (Hart, *Regarding Karl Barth,* p. 192).

environmental factors, particularly what I, using Plantinga's notion of a "cognitive environment," referred to as the Spirit's engendering of conducive ecclesial cognitive environments.[94] In Barth's view, our knowledge of God takes place within the true community of Jesus Christ, which "has its origin in [Christ's] revelation,"[95] established by the revealing and reconciling action of God giving us a participation in Christ by the Holy Spirit.

We have also, up to now, given relatively little explicit attention to the relevance of the historical dimension of the knowledge of God, which brings us to the third important element for understanding Barth's idea of the character of genuine human knowing and its relation to propositional content. In our discussion of the first two issues, the hiddenness of God and analogical predication, we established that Barth unambiguously affirms propositional content as a key element of revelation by faith in which God transforms human conceptions and language to give a knowledge of himself through propositional expression. Now we turn to the significance of the not merely abstract but *historical* nature of divine self-disclosure.

The significance of the historical character of divine self-revealing. Barth maintains that the Word of God is indivisible from God's concrete action in history.[96] Perhaps the most fundamental historical action may be taken to be God's eternal electing to be our reconciler and redeemer in the incarnation.[97] This is what Keith Johnson, following Eberhard Jüngel,

[94]For a fuller and far richer exploration of ecclesial, doxological and semantic participation and transformation in revelation, see Alan Torrance's *Persons in Communion.*

[95]*CD* IV/3.2, p. 792.

[96]For Wolfhart Pannenberg, grasping the historical character of revelation requires that one jettison Barth's notion of revelation as Word of God and as the self-revelation of God. Like Barth, Pannenberg wants to avoid the conclusion that revelation is handed over in complete, self-contained truths. The alternative for Pannenberg is to see that until the consummation of history, revelation remains provisional. For Barth, however, what enables the self-revelation of God as a truly successful, though irreducibly historical, speech-act is not a completeness of the medium but the gracious decision of God to draw human knowers, by the gift of faith, into a historical participation in Christ's knowledge of the Father through a verbal encounter with God's self-disclosure in history. Pannenberg draws the unfortunate conclusion that Barth's position is fundamentally Hegelian and unravels into a denial of the possibility of mediated revelation. See Pannenberg's "Einfuhrung" [Introduction] to *Offenbarung als Geschichte,* ed. Wolfhart Pannenberg, 3rd ed. (Göttingen: Vandenhoeck & Ruprecht, 1965), pp. 7-11.

[97]*CD* II/2, pp. 80-81, 94-145.

calls "Barth's decision to make the human Jesus of Nazareth the condition for the possibility of knowledge."[98] Real revelation of God is only possible as a participation in the incarnate Son's communion with the Father. Moreover, revelation is bound up with God's reconciling acts in history.[99] "In God's revelation . . . what is concerned is always the birth, death and resurrection of Jesus Christ, always His justification of faith, always His lordship in the Church, always His coming again, and therefore Himself as our hope."[100] On the inseparability of word and act in revelation, Barth writes:

> The distinction between word and act is that mere word is the mere self-expression of a person, while act is the resultant relative alteration in the world around. Mere word is passive, act is an active participation in history. But this kind of distinction does not apply to the Word of God. As mere Word it is act. As mere Word it is the divine person, the person of the Lord of history, whose self-expression is as such an alteration, and indeed an absolute alteration of the world, whose *passio* in history is as such *actio*. What God does when He speaks, in exactly the same way as what He says, cannot, of course, be generally defined either by way of anticipation or by that of reproduction. We can refer only to the *concretissima* of the acts which are attested in the Bible and which are also to be expected from God in the future.[101]

There are at least two inseparable though distinguishable senses in which, for Barth, the revealed knowledge of God is historical—two ways in which revelation is act. Revelation is historical in that it is simultaneously act that reveals and revelation that acts. It is historical in character with respect both to the acts of revelation proper and to the subsequent acts of witness to revelation. Barth, consequently, differentiates the historical concreteness of revelation into three "times." There is, first, the

[98]Johnson, *Karl Barth and the* Analogia Entis, p. 202, referencing Eberhard Jüngel, "Die Möglichkeit theologischer Anthropologie auf dem Grunde der Analogie," in *Barth-Studien* (Zurich: Gütersloh Verlagshaus Mohn, 1982), p. 212.

[99]Barth's emphasis on the historical content of revelation is thoroughgoing throughout the *Dogmatics* but particularly evident in his doctrine of reconciliation. "Revelation takes place as the revelation of reconciliation . . . as the self-declaration of this history, as the truth of this reality" (*CD* IV/3, p. 8).

[100]*CD* II/1, p. 262.

[101]*CD* I/1, p. 144.

time of Jesus Christ, who is revelation proper. This includes not only a period of the first century but also what Barth calls "the time of the direct, original speech of God Himself in His revelation, the time of Jesus Christ (which was also and already that of Abraham according to Jn. 8:56)."[102] The second time is the time of scripture, the written word and witness to revelation proper. Finally, the witness of the church in proclamation of the word is the third time. So, for Barth, revelation is always temporally located without being temporally constrained.[103]

Another way of getting at the inseparable though distinguishable twofold nature of the historical character of revelation is to think in terms of the distinction between the *content* of revelation and the *reception* of revelation. As we saw above, what it means for revelation to be concretely historical is that the speech of God, the act of God, involves "an absolute alteration of the world." The content of the knowledge of revelation, therefore, is knowledge of God in his absolute world-alteration, which is received by human knowers only by God's radical alteration of their world.[104] This is to say that there is an overlap between what it means that revelation is historical and all that we have already said about revelation being transformative. The work of the Spirit in human knowers to "open up man and make him capable and ready for Himself, and thus achieve His revelation in him"[105] is a concrete world-altering historical act. What human knowers are opened up to is God in his world-altering action. This distinction, therefore, is nothing more than the indivisible way in which God becomes both object and subject for us in his revelation.[106]

---

[102]*CD* I/1, p. 145.

[103]James A. Veitch makes the untenable assertion that, in Barth's view, revelation "never participates in world history." He nevertheless aptly describes Barth's view of the relationship between revelation and history as revelation's being located "in time" without being "relativised by the historical process" (Veitch, "Revelation and Religion in Karl Barth," *Scottish Journal of Theology* 24, no. 1 [1971]: 3-4).

[104]This radical alteration is the New Testament notion of μετάνοια (*metanoia*)—as Murray Rae describes: "variously translated in the English New Testament as 'repentance' or 'conversion,' the conjunction of *meta* and *nous* means literally, 'a change of mind,' but is employed by the New Testament writers to suggest a profound transformation of the whole person" (Rae, *Kierkegaard's Vision of the Incarnation: By Faith Transformed* [Oxford: Oxford University Press, 1997], p. 115; cf. *CD* I/1, p. 387).

[105]*CD* I/1, p. 450.

[106]With reference to Bonhoeffer, Paul Janz critiques the positivist tendencies in Barth's notion of

What are the implications of this twofold historical character of revelation for our discussion of revelation's propositional content and expression? We have already given some attention to the subjective or receptive nature of God's speech as action, but we have not considered what it means for the content of revelation, and therefore the propositions of revelation, to be fundamentally historical in character. Consider again the expression: "God was in Christ, reconciling the world to himself." In our discussion thus far of what it would mean to have a genuine human grasp of the proposition expressed by means of this expression, we have treated the notions of reference, analogy and belief in more or less abstract terms. For Barth, however, the knowledge of God is never a knowledge of God's essence in abstraction from his acts in human history.[107] Who God is is who God has made himself known to be in our atoning, resurrecting, ascending Lord.[108]

> But who is the Lord and therefore the God to whom the Bible is referring? As we have seen already, it is typical of the Bible in both the Old Testament and the New that its answer to this question does not point us primarily to a sphere beyond human history but rather to the very centre of this history.[109]

This means that all of our inquiries into the real reference of expressions used in the communication of revelation by faith finally come to rest on Jesus Christ—not an abstract *logos asarkos* but the incarnate Christ of human history. This confirms what we noted earlier, that a redeemed

---

revelation as act. He charges that the result of Barth's position is that God remains "non-objective," resulting in a "basic loss of rational integrity." This clash with reason comes when Barth tries to maintain that "in revelation God both 'posits' himself as a possible referent of rational discourse or thinking, and yet does so while contradictorily (and therefore 'miraculously') remaining entirely immune from the intrinsic obligations of the very rational discourse into which revelation posits itself" (Janz, *God, the Mind's Desire: Reference, Reason and Christian Thinking* [Cambridge: Cambridge University Press, 2004], pp. 118-20). Janz never demonstrates the contradiction in Barth, but more significantly, he fails to grasp that the whole purpose of God's action of bringing the human knowing subject into a participation in God's self-knowing is to enable not the contradiction of reason but the true miracle of an objective human knowledge of God.

[107]"This 'God with us' has happened. It has happened in human history and as a part of human history" (*CD* I/1, p. 116).

[108]Barth writes that the atonement is "the place and the only place from which as Christians we can think forwards and backwards, from which a Christian knowledge of both God and man is possible" (*CD* IV/1, p. 81).

[109]*CD* I/1, p. 384.

knowledge of God cannot merely consist of a subjective, backstage, noumenal encounter. To know what it means that God has the property of being the one who "reconciles the world to himself" involves thicker description of the concrete reconciling of the incarnation in his life, death, resurrection and ascension.[110] The way in which the Spirit transforms human concepts and language will be by means of exposure to this history and not in abstraction from it. Just as we have stressed all along that for Barth the knowledge of God is not reducible to mere propositions, so also here we see that an apprehension of the acts of God is not equivalent to having access to the right historical data. Nevertheless, Barth affirms that the propositional content of revelation has this irreducibly historical character in both reference and expression.

The obvious consequence of this is that genuine human knowledge of God in the full sense we have been considering from Barth involves knowledge of and therefore belief in historical details. Minimally, some grasp of and belief in the historical actuality of the incarnation seems to be required.[111] Plantinga explicitly references affirmations of the incarnation, suffering, death and resurrection of Christ as key components of Christian belief.[112] It is critical to see, however, that the way in which these beliefs have warrant is, for both Barth and Plantinga, not finally on the basis of inference from historical research and human testimony.[113] Witness to this history is the principal means by which the Spirit grasps us, and in this action we are given a participation in the knowledge of

---

[110]Though Barth is not expressly referenced, in a discussion of what it might mean for theological propositions to be true, Robert Jenson echoes Barth's thoughts on revelation and history when he asserts that "accounts of reality other than the biblical story are abstractions from the full account of what we actually inhabit, that is, they are abstractions from the story of God with his creatures." He laments that, for theology, "the fact of the Incarnation has made far too little difference; most of what we say could equally well be said if God's *Logos* were that immaterial mirror and Jesus simply a great prophet or rabbi—or beach-boy guru" (Jenson, "What If It Were True?" *CTI Reflections* 4 [2001]: 7, 15).

[111]Barth laments the "blind alley" of docetic Christology, which abstracts the "idea" of Jesus from history. "The fact that the manifestation of this idea was seen in Jesus of Nazareth was more or less accidental and indifferent, so indifferent that the concrete humanity of His earthly existence, or finally even its historical reality, could be queried" (*CD* I/1, p. 403).

[112]*WCB*, pp. vii, 117, 180, 205, 241, 243, 270, 285, 357, 374.

[113]Barth clarifies that "historical does not mean historically demonstrable or historically demonstrated" (*CD* I/1, p. 325). Plantinga, as we have discussed, does not regard historical evidence sufficient to warrant Christian belief. See *WCB*, pp. 268-80, 378-80.

revelation. It is the ministry of the Spirit in the gift of faith and not the historical propositions themselves that is their proof. Barth and Plantinga agree, furthermore, that this remains the case even for eyewitnesses.[114] Even at the interface between Barth's first two "times," when the prophets and apostles were confronted by the direct and original speech-act of God, hearing was by the gift of faith in the work of the Spirit.[115] So, the revelation of the hidden God given in the gift of faith fills and sharpens as the Spirit transforms our hearing by means of a confrontation with his historical witness.

What can we take away from this cursory sketch of the key facets of Barth's notion of the genuine human knowledge of God given by the Spirit in the gift of faith? We have established that the propositional content and character of revelation are fundamental to revelation, though derivative of the personal encounter with God wherein human knowers are given a participation in the risen Christ's knowledge of the Father by the Spirit. We have seen the impact of the transformational character of God's concrete speech-act, which enables real reference to God by liberating earthbound preconceptions, allowing the object of knowing to recondition human thought in language. All of this is included in what Barth calls "faith." Along the way we have made recourse to some of Plantinga's helpful distinctions and pointed out a few areas of explicit agreement.

We are ready now to draw some conclusions about the differences between Plantinga and Barth on the nature of faith and the knowledge of God. The fruit of this discussion helps further to clarify our emerging unified Barth/Plantinga proposal for a Christian theological epistemology.

---

[114]Barth writes: "What a neutral observer could apprehend or may have apprehended of these events was the form of revelation which he did not and could not understand as such. . . . The neutral observer who understood the events recorded in it as revelation would cease thereby to be a neutral observer" (*CD* I/1, p. 325). Plantinga discusses the limits of empirical perception: "It is certainly possible to perceive Jesus the Christ and perceive that he is saying that he is the Christ; still, can we perceive that Jesus actually is the Christ? That he actually is the second person of the trinity? I'm inclined to doubt it" (*WCB*, p. 288).

[115]Murray Rae, reflecting on Kierkegaard's *Fragments,* puts it this way: "Whoever sees the God-Man with the eyes of faith sees not only differently, but also more truthfully than the contemporary eyewitness" (Rae, *Kierkegaard's Vision of the Incarnation,* p. 129).

PLANTINGA AND BARTH ON FAITH AND KNOWING

For both Barth and Plantinga it is clear that knowledge of God has propositional content and that the means of its expression may be in propositional form. They each affirm the critical and indispensable role of the Spirit in coming to Christian faith. Moreover, they each affirm the importance of the transformative character of the Spirit's work in overcoming the noetic effects of sin. The important differences between them, it seems to me, lie in two areas that I will address in the following order: first, the manner and extent to which revelation is to be considered personal and, second, the scope that may be allowed for a knowledge of God that lies outside of faith.

In Barth's theology of revelation and Plantinga's epistemology of Christian belief, it is safe to say that knowledge merely consisting of assent to propositions falls short of the kind of knowing that is enabled by the self-revelation of God in the gift of faith. And yet, on Plantinga's model, the kind of knowledge that is delivered by the work of the Spirit in the cognitive process of faith is primarily propositional. For Plantinga, this follows from the fact that he is interested in an analysis of the possibility of warrant for Christian *belief,* and "what one *believes* are propositions."[116] For Barth, and ultimately for Plantinga also, propositional knowing—belief *that*—is built on something more foundational, a personal, transforming encounter with the self-revealing God. If you push the button on your Karl Barth action figure, it announces, "Revelation in fact does not differ from the *person* of Jesus Christ nor from the reconciliation accomplished in Him."[117] For this reason I have termed Barth a theo-foundationalist. The foundation for theology and the knowledge of God is not a basic proposition, but "the real encounter between God and man, which is faith."[118] Barth refers to this as the "personal quality"[119] of divine address. Propositional content does not therefore stand independent of the person, for God is "present in person in and with what is said by Him."[120] So it is the personal knowing of

[116] *WCB,* p. 248, emphasis mine.
[117] *CD* I/1, p. 119, emphasis mine.
[118] *CD* I/1, p. 18.
[119] *CD* I/1, p. 136.
[120] *CD* I/1, p. 137.

God in faith that provides the arena in which propositional knowledge is possible. Language and concepts are means through which God makes himself known, and thoughts or beliefs about God are assisted by God's personal self-revealing. The ground for all of this is God himself in the personal relationship he establishes with us. "For the point of God's speech is not to occasion specific thoughts or a specific attitude but through the clarity which God gives us, and which induces both these in us, to bind us to Himself."[121] While the final end is personal relationship, not mere propositional assent, propositional assent remains a natural outcome and important aspect of that relationship.

It might appear that this underlying personal nature of the knowledge of God is not a perspective shared by Plantinga,[122] and yet Plantinga clearly agrees with Barth that the final goal is a close fellowship with God, "some kind of *union* with God, a being united to, at one with him."[123] The difference with Barth is at least partially semantic. Plantinga acknowledges the personal character of Christian belief but distinguishes, for the sake of his project, propositional knowledge (belief *that*) from belief *in* God.[124] With appeals to Calvin, Aquinas and, of course, Jonathan Edwards, Plantinga differentiates between the noetic and affective impact of the work of the Spirit. He differentiates, but he does not disassociate them. The priority of the transformational encounter with the Spirit for propositional knowing is unambiguous. Plantinga calls it the "cognitive benefits of regeneration,"[125] and it involves not only restoring the *sensus divinitatis* but also the special revelation of new propositional knowledge. Plantinga writes:

---

[121]*CD* I/1, p. 175.

[122]Esther Meek believes this to be a lack in Plantinga that is helpfully addressed in the work of Michael Polanyi. It is certainly the case that Polanyi and others in the later twentieth century offer helpfully holistic views of human knowing that move beyond the traditional analytic impersonal and ahistorical tendencies. And it is unfortunate that in Plantinga's writings there is nothing to find of interaction with Michael Polanyi or Marjorie Grene. However, while Polanyi gives much more attention to the *development* of knowledge, there is nothing in Plantinga's epistemology that is incompatible with the central Polanyian insights. In my view, Meek misunderstands Plantinga on several key points and presents a thesis of conflict where there should in fact be a strong affirmation of complementarity (Meek, "Michael Polanyi and Alvin Plantinga," *Philosophia Christi* 14, no. 1 [2012]: 57-77).

[123]*WCB,* p. 317, emphasis original.

[124]See RBG, p. 18; *WCB,* pp. 291-94.

[125]*WCB,* p. 280.

> The work of the Holy Spirit goes further. It gives us a much clearer view of the beauty, splendor, loveliness, attractiveness, glory of God. It enables us to see something of the spectacular depth of love revealed in the incarnation and atonement.[126]

Barth in no way dismisses these cognitive benefits, but because of their radical dependence on the reconciling personal revelation of God in Christ by the Spirit, he does not emphasize a distinction between the noetic and the affective.

There may be, however, more than a mere semantic difference between Barth and Plantinga on the *nature* of the relationship between propositional knowledge and personal encounter with God. The priority of personal encounter is entailed in Plantinga's model, and propositional knowledge is dependent on it, but the nature of that dependency is mostly undefined.[127] Plantinga's presentation of the model might create the impression that the IIHS serves as a mechanistic trigger occasioning belief rather than a personal encounter of which propositional belief is one facet of a connected, organic and relational whole. The IIHS may be the trigger for its noetic and affective effects, but it is not clear that those effects remain connected to and derivative of personal fellowship with the Spirit, as they are for Barth. It is possible again on this point that we are merely coming up against the boundaries of the scope of Plantinga's project, focused as it is on warrant for propositional beliefs. Plantinga's description in many of these areas is intentionally minimalist. His intent is not to write a theology of revelation but instead to provide philosophical cover for the notion of Christian belief as a product of revelation enabled by the design and action of God.

The more pointed difference between Barth and Plantinga appears to be in the scope that Plantinga seems to allow for a knowledge of God

---

[126]Ibid., p. 281.

[127]Andrew Dole criticizes Plantinga for "giving faith not only the last, but the strategically crucial—but somewhat imprecise—word in what is otherwise a rigorous philosophical argument" (Dole, "Cognitive Faculties, Cognitive Processes, and the Holy Spirit in Plantinga's Warrant Series," review of *Warrant and Proper Function* and *Warranted Christian Belief,* by Alvin Plantinga, *Faith and Philosophy* 19 [2002]: 41). Dole believes the lack of definition leaves Plantinga open to the critique that the cognitive *process* of faith is not sufficiently similar to our other cognitive *faculties.* But why think that the work of the Spirit need have any other similarity with our other cognitive faculties than those set out in Plantinga's general requirements for warrant?

that lies outside of faith. This issue comes to a head in a question raised at the end of the last chapter regarding Plantinga's notion of the *sensus divinitatis.* It is fairly clear that what the *sensus divinitatis* delivers would not qualify as knowledge of God for Barth. A generic theism could only count as a positive knowledge of God for Barth if it were a knowledge given by God in his self-revealing. God can only be known in his act of revelation, which would have to be added to the *sensus divinitatis* to enable a genuine knowledge of God and therefore a knowledge of his existence. For this reason we have suggested that, for Barth, if there is a *sensus divinitatis,* it must operate within the realm of the action of the Holy Spirit. It is not enough to uphold a generic epistemological *sola gratia.* Plantinga would certainly affirm that the *sensus divinitatis* is a gift of grace; it is a gift of creation that involves God's gracious design and sustaining. For Barth, however, there is an additional stipulation: the grace of the knowledge of God can only be God's revelation in the action of self-revelation by the Spirit in Jesus Christ. "Only in the One who acts on us as the Reconciler through the cross and resurrection could we perceive the Creator."[128]

Does this mean that Plantinga and Barth simply disagree about the *sensus divinitatis?* It seems to me that they only disagree about what to call the knowledge delivered by it. Plantinga does seem to think of the *sensus divinitatis* as a natural faculty that was originally designed to function without the active, ongoing, personal, self-revealing action of the Spirit.[129] For Plantinga the IIHS is connected with the knowledge of the great things of the gospel occasioned by the fall. The *sensus divinitatis* is a created endowment existing prior to the fall. But, the fact is, Plantinga never claims that knowledge of God prior to the fall was achieved independently of personal engagement with God, and it is highly doubtful that he, Aquinas or Calvin[130] has this kind of independence in mind.

In my view, there is no glaring incompatibility here for Barth and

[128]*CD* I/1, pp. 412-13.

[129]*WCB,* p. 184.

[130]Recall the aforementioned argument of Edward Adams that, for Calvin, natural knowledge of God is *revealed* knowledge (Adams, "Calvin's View of Natural Knowledge of God," *International Journal of Systematic Theology* 3, no. 3 [2001]: 280-92).

Plantinga. Insofar as the *sensus divinitatis* operates independently of the personal, historical, transformative, reconciling action of God, it delivers only at best an affirmation of some true propositions *about* God. This, as we have seen, falls far short of Barth's notion of revelation. Not only does it lack the connection to fellowship with God, but, just in terms of cognitive content, it also falls short of the kind of knowledge of God human beings need. Recall Plantinga's understanding of the nature of proper names and the epistemic variability of the essential properties that may be expressed by them. The propositional knowledge delivered by a properly functioning *sensus divinitatis* is narrow and fails to disclose to us *who* God is. It may in some sense be similar to the knowledge that the demons have according to James 2:19: "Even the demons believe—and shudder!" For Barth, the demonic knowledge is mere abstract knowledge. "Taken alone, as an abstract knowledge of God and the world and even of Jesus Christ, it can only be described as unimportant."[131] Barth's main concern is relentlessly to challenge the tendency to think of our knowledge of God as building up from a foundation in this human capacity. The danger is not in acknowledging that there is a possibility—outside of reconciliation with God—of knowing something about God, including an awareness of his existence. The danger is in thinking of it as the originating basis for Christian theology and a full-fledged human knowledge of God. For Plantinga, what distinguishes demonic knowledge of God from Christian faith is twofold. It lacks both the affective transformation—believing in, trusting and loving God—and the cognitive benefits of regeneration. Barth is in complete agreement and considers those things utterly decisive for a genuine, redeemed human knowledge of God.[132] Plantinga concurs that "only God bestows saving faith."[133]

CONCLUSION

In this chapter, we have taken a closer look at Barth's understanding of

[131] *CD* IV/1, p. 765.

[132] "The demons, no doubt, are theists and also believe of God that he exists; the demons do not believe in God, because they do not trust and love God and do not make his purposes their own" (*WCB*, p. 294).

[133] Plantinga, "Christian Philosophy at the End of the Twentieth Century," p. 40.

what constitutes a genuine knowledge of God by faith. This is cognitive revelation with propositional content, which is expressible in propositional form by the enabling of the personal, historical, transformative work of the Spirit. In an effort to clarify Barth's views, we drew on Plantinga's work with respect to propositional expression and the character of assertion and belief. God makes himself known by giving us an apprehension of the real referent of statements about God—that is, the one true God made known in Jesus Christ. This knowledge, while mediated through historical witness, is not humanly accessible outside of the gift of faith. By means of the action of self-revelation in the gift of faith we are given a participation in genuine propositional knowledge of God through God-empowered, referent-anchored, analogical predication. The cognitive and transformative aspects of faith are indivisible acts of the personal self-revelation of God.

Plantinga agrees that Christian belief is a result of the work of the Spirit in the gift of faith. His notion of revelation is less developed—and quite understandably, given his objectives. Plantinga acknowledges the possibility for a warranted abstract knowledge of God independent of the work of the Spirit, which Barth also acknowledges but considers "unimportant" on its own. On our unified proposal, we conclude that knowledge of God, involving both its fuller cognitive and affective benefits, is only possible by means of the transforming gift of faith.

This chapter also addressed again the subject of the nature and role of Christian scripture in divine revelation. In the next chapter we will expand this discussion to consider more fully the implications of our emerging unified Barth/Plantinga proposal for thinking about scripture. We will bring together affirmations already made about what scripture is and consider how, on our proposed model, knowledge of the authority of scripture might have warrant.

9

SCRIPTURE AND THEOLOGY

Warrant and the Normativity of Scripture?

◆

Over the years, debates about the proper understanding of Christian scripture have come at great cost in lives and in pages penned in their pursuit. Who could estimate the blood and ink given in the struggle to grasp the nature, role and correct interpretation of the Bible? It has often been disagreements over the interpretation of scripture that pressurize debates about the more fundamental questions of its nature and authority. In this chapter, we will leave *specific* issues of interpretation aside, but of course we cannot avoid the question of hermeneutics altogether. After all, hermeneutics seems to be the foremost epistemological interest of contemporary theology vis-à-vis the Bible. If the proposal we have been developing is correct, however, when it comes to the Bible the foremost epistemological considerations hinge on its fundamental nature and function in divine self-revealing. Biblical scholarship often moves quickly past this more fundamental question, or assumes that the right way to approach the question is first to settle general issues of interpretation. Both in the seminary and in the broader academy there is a tendency to operate as if one begins with the mastery of basic principles of the *science* of hermeneutics and then applies them to the Bible to discern its meaning. We might even think that this is the right order of operations to allow scripture to answer for itself the question of what it is and how it functions in divine revelation. What is more, this sounds convincingly similar to the kind of epistemic humility that our proposal champions; nevertheless, the Barth/Plantinga approach urges a different starting point.

We begin as imperfect but already participating subjects of historically, ecclesially, *biblically* mediated divine revelation. We think retrospectively, not in ignorance of interpretive difficulties but wrestling with them in light of growing convictions about God *in* his revelation. It is therefore fitting—given that our goal in this chapter is to develop further and elucidate the implications of an emerging unified Barth/Plantinga proposal for thinking about Christian scripture—that our task would begin with a consideration of the fundamental nature of scripture and then turn to the question of its authority. As was the case in our discussion of the nature of faith, we will be leaning in different ways into Barth's theology of revelation and Plantinga's epistemology of Christian belief. In this connection readers are encouraged to look back to the expositions of Barth's theology of revelation, and particularly the function of creaturely mediation covered in chapters two, seven and eight. Though not always explicitly about scripture, much of what needs to be said here has already been said there. Then in the second half of this chapter we will turn to the questions of scripture's authority and interpretation, offering suggestions for how—given our proposal—belief in scripture's special divinely authorized normativity might have genuine epistemic warrant.

TOWARD AN ONTOLOGY OF SCRIPTURE

Christian Smith's 2011 publication *The Bible Made Impossible* provides an interesting entrance to the critical question of what scripture is. He argues there that the bankruptcy of a common evangelical view of the nature and role of scripture, namely "biblicism," can be seen in its inability to produce interpretive consensus (a problem he calls "pervasive interpretive pluralism").[1] Of course, degrees of interpretive dissonance have plagued the church throughout history, but Smith seems to think that this is particularly problematic for those who hold a biblicist view of the Bible. Moreover, he hopes that what he offers in place of biblicism will yield better or at least more self-consistent results.

[1]Christian Smith, *The Bible Made Impossible: Why Biblicism Is Not a Truly Evangelical Reading of Scripture* (Grand Rapids: Brazos Press, 2011), pp. 16-26.

His views are interesting and helpful for our purposes because he offers a proposal that features the contributions of Karl Barth, while differing in some important respects from our own reading. Barth's view of the Bible is notoriously controversial and not always easy to decipher.[2] Smith himself notes that worries about Barth's view of the Bible are widely regarded as the reason for Barth's relatively cool reception from American evangelicals.[3] Similarly, and not unexpectedly, Smith's critiques in *The Bible Made Impossible* have met with resistance.[4] Rather than become mired in detailed debate, our modest hope here is that through minimal engagement with Smith and others we will be able to clarify central convictions and concerns.

Christian Smith and the value of Barth's view of scripture. Smith identifies two principal "moves" that he finds helpful in Barth's view of scripture.[5] The first is Barth's placement of scripture in his well-known threefold form of the Word of God. The second, which can be read as a consequence of the first, is what Smith takes to be Barth's encouragement to read the Bible christocentrically. I've already introduced Barth's view of the Bible in chapter two and expanded on this again in chapter eight. It is correct to emphasize that, for Barth, revelation proper is Jesus Christ, the Word. Scripture is the written word and *witness* to Christ. As we covered earlier, Barth differentiates the historical concreteness of revelation into three "times" according to his threefold form of the Word. Revelation is first Jesus Christ, the logos of God. Second, revelation is scripture, the written witness given by the prophets and apostles. Third, revelation is the witness of the church.[6]

---

[2]Our concern throughout this book has been with Barth's view of scripture found within the fuller articulation of the doctrine of revelation, principally in *CD* I/1. It has been well documented that Barth's earlier view of scripture changed profoundly with his break from liberalism. See especially Richard Burnett's *Karl Barth's Theological Exegesis: The Hermeneutical Principles of the Römerbrief Period* (Grand Rapids: Eerdmans, 2004).

[3]Smith, *Bible Made Impossible,* pp. 121-23.

[4]Robert Gundry provides a good example of the unenthusiastic evangelical response to Smith in Gundry, "Smithereens! Bible-Reading and 'Pervasive Interpretive Pluralism,'" *Books & Culture,* September/October 2011, pp. 9-11. Even Smith's back-cover endorsements (Vanhoozer and Noll), while recommending the book, distance themselves from Smith's position.

[5]Smith, *Bible Made Impossible,* pp. 123-24.

[6]As Barth puts it, preaching is "derivative proclamation related to the words of the prophets and apostles and regulated by them" (*CD* I/1, p. 145 [*KD* I/1, p. 150, "der abgeleiteten, auf die Worte der Propheten und Apostel bezogenen und durch sie normierten Verkündigung"]).

Why does Smith find this positioning of scripture to be so helpful? By placing scripture within the context of a broader notion of divine revelation, Barth discourages an isolated view of scripture, where scripture becomes an object of worship on a par and therefore in competition with God himself for our allegiance and affections. Smith also finds that Barth's view of scripture undercuts some of the critical assumptions that lead to biblicism. But Smith's biblicism is itself a rather complex and varied "constellation of assumptions,"[7] and, by strongly contrasting Barth's view with Smith's explication of biblicism, it is very easy to obscure Barth's view. In fact, if we take a close look, we find that there are certain aspects of Smith's biblicism that could fit comfortably alongside Barth's theology of revelation, and there are certain aspects of Smith's preferred view that do not. The best way to see this is to track the main lines of Smith's thesis. His argument is that—for many evangelicals—problems regarding how scripture is read and its meanings known stem from misunderstanding what scripture is. In other words, the biblicists' ontology of scripture distorts their epistemology of scripture's reception.

With respect to the epistemology of scripture's reception, biblicism affirms that the Bible can be easily understood and interpreted through simple rules and methods and distilled into sets of instructions. It is biblicism's simplistic and overly optimistic view of the obviousness ("perspicuity") of scripture that squares so poorly with pervasive interpretive pluralism. Smith reasons that if the Bible were as transparent and its reception as simplistic, mechanical and self-certain as biblicists believe, then we would find much greater interpretive consensus than actually exists. The reality of interpretive dissonance conflicts with a simplistic view of biblical interpretation. But, in Smith's thought, the simplistic view of biblical interpretation is a consequence of the biblicist's ontology of scripture. The simplistic view of biblical interpretation has to go and so, therefore, must the biblicist's understanding of what scripture is.

With respect to scripture's ontology, the biblicist view, according to Smith, maintains that scripture is, in its entirety, God's inerrant and

[7]A list is given here: Smith, *Bible Made Impossible*, pp. 4-5.

therefore thoroughly internally consistent words. Scripture is also the exclusive and exhaustive communication of God to humanity, concerned primarily with what we should believe and how we should behave. Finally, the words of scripture have distinct, singular and unchanging meanings. In Smith's mind, this view of what scripture is leads to the conclusion that scripture ought to yield simple, singular and uncontroversial readings. The heart of the problem, according to Smith, is assuming that scripture is a neat and tidy collection of perfectly lucid and harmonious assertions. At least some of the ethical and dogmatic propositions that are attributed to scripture, rather than being obvious, are in fact "'underdetermined' by the text."[8] In such cases, scripture cannot adjudicate among the multiple interpretive possibilities. What Smith finds most missing in this view of scripture is an appreciation for scripture's "multivocality" and "polysemy." He maintains that scripture does not present us with distinct, singular and unchanging meanings but rather multiple interpretive possibilities. "It can and does speak to different listeners in different voices that appear to say different things."[9]

Smith's solution is to embrace a view of scripture that makes better sense of a reasonable degree of interpretive dissonance. This brings us back to our main interest, how Barth's view of scripture is supposed to help address the problem by means of those two Barthian moves Smith highlights. To reiterate, the first move is Barth's framing of the Bible as the second form of the Word of God. The second move is the recognition that the Bible has a christological center, which is taken to be an implication of its relationship to Christ, the first form of the Word of God. To be clear, it is not Barth who presents these as Barth's first and second "moves"; it is Smith who orders them according to their helpfulness in addressing the problems he identifies with biblicism.

The critical point to see is that what Smith finds pivotal about Barth's exposition is the degree of separation that Smith understands Barth to introduce between Jesus Christ and scripture. In Smith's articulation,

---

[8]Ibid., p. 51.
[9]Ibid., p. 47.

Jesus Christ is "the highest, truest, most real and authoritative divine revelation."[10] By contrast then, scripture has to be less real, less true, less authentic and therefore less authoritative. The logic of this is transparent in Smith's view. The only revelation of God that is unchanging, entirely inerrant, thoroughly consistent and perfectly lucid is Jesus himself. In Smith's analysis, the biblicist is simply blurring the distinction between the perfect revelation in Christ and the less than perfect revelation in scripture. Smith reads Barth as encouraging biblicists to lower their view of scripture, to recognize that while revelation in scripture is important and authoritative, it is imperfect revelation. The problem with this is that Barth would never speak about scripture and revelation in this way. Smith makes an extremely common, deceptively subtle, but massively consequential mistake in his reading of Barth's view of the relationship between scripture and revelation.[11] And the irony of Smith's misreading is that it is the same misreading that led to such distrust of Barth's theology on the part of the evangelicals in North America that Smith is criticizing.[12]

The common mistake can be explained as separating what Barth always keeps together while holding together what Barth always keeps separate. Barth never separates or stratifies revelation into kinds. There is no such thing in his thinking as a division between a more real, truthful and authentic revelation on the one hand and a less real, truthful and authentic revelation on the other. Barth is emphatic about this. Revelation is always and only God's transforming self-disclosure in the gift of faith. We can distinguish aspects to God's revealing action, but they correspond to the Trinity and are therefore distinguishable but inseparable. God himself is inseparable from his act of self-revelation and from the means of its revealing. The means of the revelation of God is God:

---

[10]Ibid., p. 124.

[11]This misreading of Barth is similar to Wolterstorff's, which I discussed in my defense of the propositional nature of revelation in chapter 8.

[12]Francis Schaeffer is one prominent example. His misreading of Barth is so extreme that he ends up classifying Barth as a theological liberal who anchors revelation on "a peg in midair." "Barth's basic position was this: Of course, the Bible has all kinds of mistakes in it, but it doesn't matter; believe it religiously" (Schaeffer, *The Church Before the Watching World* [Downers Grove, IL: InterVarsity Press, 1971], p. 20).

"He reveals Himself *through Himself*."[13] It is indeed impossible on Barth's view of revelation to suggest that revelation in Christ is in any sense different in quality or content from revelation in scripture. And yet, this is precisely what Smith argues for, saying, "the Bible is not God's only revelation, or ontologically the highest and most authentic."[14] This is the first aspect of Smith's mistaken reading of Barth. Barth keeps divine revelation single and unified. Or, better put, Barth keeps divine revelation triune and unified.

What Barth does distinguish ontologically, as we have seen, is divine revelation from the creaturely medium of revelation. Given our development of this point in the previous chapter, we can move relatively quickly here. The medium on its own has no power to reveal God and should not be confusingly referred to as *itself* revelation. God gives himself *in and through* the creaturely form, not *as* the creaturely form. This explains Barth's reticence to affirm in a direct and unqualified sense that the human words of scripture are equivalent to the Word of God.[15] Whether we are considering the humanity of Christ, the expressions of scripture or the utterances of the preacher, they all share this attribute of being unable to give genuine knowledge of God each strictly on its own. That does not, of course, make them the same in all other respects, but it does mean that there is something significantly misleading in the common ways that many thoughtful Christian theologians and biblical scholars talk about the Bible. The reason Smith conceives of the Bible as delivering a truth that is inferior to Jesus is that he follows a manner of expression whereby the Bible is *a* revelation on its own. He writes, "Scripture thus *speaks* a real truth that mediates knowledge of the Real Truth."[16] This conception seems to turn the medium of revelation into a thing in itself that has revelatory capacity. If Barth and our developing Barth/Plantinga proposal are correct about the revelation of God as

[13]*CD* I/1, p. 296, emphasis original; *KD* I/1, p. 312. The central theme of the introduction to §8, "God in His Revelation," is the inseparability of God from the event of revelation and its effect on human receivers.

[14]Smith, *Bible Made Impossible,* p. 124.

[15]The mediation of scripture becomes, to use John Baillie's expression, a "mediated immediacy" (Baillie, *Our Knowledge of God* [London: Oxford University Press, 1939], pp. 178-200). This is also what Barth has in mind with God's unveiling through the veil (*CD* I/1, pp. 169, 174-79, 315-23).

[16]Smith, *Bible Made Impossible,* p. 124, emphasis added.

always God-enabled self-revealing, then we cannot collapse the distinction between revelation and the medium of revelation. As Barth says, the medium does not become a "third thing between God and man, a reality distinct from God that is as such the subject of revelation."[17] Consequently, it may be a misleading convention to talk of the Bible as an agent of revelation. The Bible might be thought, in some independent sense, to have a capacity to convey propositional knowledge or information about God, but not what would constitute a genuine knowledge of God in the ways that both Barth and Plantinga have in view. That requires warranting divine action proceeding in conjunction with God's truth-aimed design.

I said we would be leaning more heavily on Barth's theology than on Plantinga's epistemology, but it is worth noting that this is another point where Plantinga's model agrees with and augments Barth's theology. For Plantinga, like Barth, the Bible is indispensable. As Plantinga develops his extended A/C model of warranted Christian belief, he describes it as a "three-tiered cognitive process," featuring the Bible as its first element. Plantinga makes several important affirmations about the Bible, but the Bible is not itself the sufficient or even the central warrant-enabling process in his model. What enables warrant is the testimony of the Spirit giving the gift of faith. By the transforming work of the Spirit we are given an understanding of what God is teaching through scripture and we are given a warranted grasp of its goodness, beauty and truth. On Plantinga's model, warranted Christian belief could not be accounted for as merely the result of hearing the testimony of scripture. This hearing must also be accompanied by God's self-witness in the gift of faith, which grows in conjunction with the transformation that it effects in the proper functioning of cognitive capacities and the restoring of faith-conducive environments.

In light of these considerations we can see that Smith's alternative to biblicism, so far as it concerns revelation that yields a genuine knowledge of God, is, like biblicism, too simplistic or not sufficiently nuanced. We can also see that certain aspects of the biblicism that Smith is criticizing

---

[17]*CD* I/1, p. 321; *KD* I/1, p. 339.

could be retained—with some qualifications—coherently in conjunction with Barth's theology of revelation. The example I have in mind is the supposed problem of scripture's inerrancy. Going down this path brings us into a rather polarizing debate, but one where I believe the Barth/Plantinga proposal offers an alternative that maintains many of the core theological convictions shared by those in the debate. My intent here will not be to address the arguments made for and against inerrancy but to clarify further the understanding of scripture and revelation that coheres with our proposal.

Must we affirm that scripture contains errors? Biblicism's commitment to the Bible's being inerrant and thoroughly internally consistent is, in Smith's view, a critical flaw in biblicism's ontology of scripture. Smith seems to think that this flaw motivates a naiveté about the ease of interpretation and encourages turning scripture into an idol. To get the separation Smith wants between scripture and paradigmatic revelation in Christ, he argues that scripture is a less than perfect revelation. Scripture's being a less than perfect revelation offers an acceptable explanation for interpretive dissonance and a sufficient discouragement for bibliolatry. On the Barth/Plantinga proposal, the separation that discourages the worship of scripture is the firm ontological distinction between divine self-revealing and the creaturely medium of revelation. The interpretive dissonance is accounted for first by the fact that divine revelation cannot simply be transmitted by and contained in linguistic expressions. Moreover, the wrestling to understand, articulate and agree about that revelation is both a limitation of the mere creaturely medium and a reality of the complex dynamics of the transformation being effected by God in the coordination of cognitive capacities and environments that are still in the process of being redeemed.[18]

Smith and others suggest that avoiding the positivism and naiveté of

[18]In the judgment of Bruce McCormack, the missing key for evangelicals to understand Barth's view of scripture is to understand Barth's actualism and the way in which scripture has its being in becoming. McCormack very helpfuly clarifies that "becoming" language for Barth secures the grounds for the authority of scripture by anchoring the being of scripture in the determination of God (McCormack, "The Being of Holy Scripture Is in Becoming: Karl Barth in Conversation with American Evangelical Criticism," in *Evangelicals and Scripture: Tradition, Authority and Hermeneutics*, ed. Vincent Bacote, Laura Miguélez and Dennis Okholm [Downers Grove, IL: InterVarsity Press, 2004], pp. 53-75).

biblicism requires a frank admission of errors and inconsistencies in scripture. On the Barth/Plantinga proposal I am advancing, this is neither entailed nor required. In fact, I would argue that a qualified notion of the inerrancy of scripture is the best fit for the Barth/Plantinga view. I say "a qualified notion" because what is meant by *inerrancy* of course depends on what constitutes an error, and what constitutes an error depends in turn on what scripture is and how truth is conveyed through it. If by *error* we mean a flaw of some kind, then determining whether an error is present seems to require comparing scripture against an ideal notion of scripture. If by *error* we mean the affirmation of a false proposition, then detecting an error seems to require that we know how propositions are conveyed by scripture. Either way it will benefit us to expand further our understanding of the ontology of scripture in order to understand what it would mean to affirm that it errs.

Consider what we have affirmed about scripture thus far. The key affirmation has been that scripture is properly understood to be a creaturely medium of revelation, but much more can and should be said to expand this in line with Plantinga and Barth. Scripture is the decisive, authoritative, divinely chosen and orchestrated written medium of revelation. As Plantinga affirms, God "arranged for the production of *Scripture,* the Bible, a library of books or writings each of which has a human author, but each of which is also specially inspired by God in such a way that he himself is its principal author."[19] Crucial for Barth is the affirmation that the relationship between the human and divine with respect to revelation through scripture is like the relationship between God and man in the hypostatic union.

> Holy Scripture is like the unity of God and man in Jesus Christ. It is neither divine only nor human only. Nor is it a mixture of the two nor a *tertium quid* between them. But in its own way and degree it is very God and very man, i.e., a witness of revelation which itself belongs to revelation, and historically a very human literary document.[20]

We want to include, therefore, in our ontology of scripture more than

---

[19] *WCB,* p. 243, emphasis original.

[20] *CD* I/2, p. 501.

merely what this collection of human writings is *outside* of its relationship to divine revelation. The canon of Christian scripture is the medium that God has ordained for his definitive, authoritative self-disclosure. On our model, we want strongly to affirm both the absolute distinction between the human and the divine and an uncompromising unity in the function for which God has ordained it.[21] On the one hand, the human collection of writings does not possess divinity. In all its human attributes it never gains a capacity on its own to transform and transmit revelation to its hearers. Only in the divine-human coordination that God enables is scripture the vehicle for successful revelation of God. On the other hand, we cannot separate this collection of writings at any place from its divine ordination and the reality of its function in God's self-revealing.

Thomas H. McCall argues that Barth should collapse the distinction between the human words and the Word of God because in Barth's two-natures analogy "the Person is directly analogous to the Bible."[22] It is possible to confuse what Barth is saying because he can alternate in his usage of terms. Sometimes, as in the quotation from Barth above, he uses "Holy Scripture" to refer to the whole communicative act of revelation by means of the written witness of the Bible. On Barth's two-natures analogy, the analogue to the Person is the *process* of revelation through the written medium. Nevertheless, the impact for our ontology of scripture is enormously consequential if the human witness finds its true being in relation to its divine determination to serve as the definitive written means of God's self-revealing. God gives himself *in and through* the creaturely form, not *as* the creaturely form.

Ronald Thiemann worries that in Barth's view of scripture Barth is unable to keep the unity of divine revelation and the human medium. He worries that Barth's insistence on the disjunction between the two

---

[21]McCormack suggests that this key feature of Barth's view of scripture and revelation follows from his Reformed Christology. "If there was a constant in Reformed treatments of the person of Christ, it was that the divine and human natures of Christ remain distinct and unimpaired in their original integrity *after* their union in one Person" (McCormack, "Being of Holy Scripture Is in Becoming," p. 70, emphasis original).

[22]Thomas H. McCall, "Understanding Scripture as the Word of God," in *Analytic Theology: New Essays in the Philosophy of Theology*, ed. Oliver D. Crisp and Michael C. Rea (Oxford: Oxford University Press, 2009), p. 184.

leads to Barth's "taking refuge in the miracle of grace."[23] He finds that Barth's division undermines the trustworthiness of the medium. As Thiemann puts it, "Christian faith demands that once God has claimed a piece of creaturely reality as his own and bound himself to it, then we are warranted in accepting the God-forged link between the human and divine."[24] Like Wolterstorff and Smith, Thiemann seems to fail to grasp that the division that Barth demands is necessary to uphold his critical insight that creaturely media are unable (*non capax*) to reveal God on their own. Like Thiemann, Barth is motivated in his theological epistemology to identify the secure and warranted grounds for the knowledge of God. Barth, however, sees that any approach that seeks secure grounding for revelation in the human medium is insufficient and insecure. Thiemann is troubled by the division Barth demands, but he also seems to miss the other side of Barth's two-natures analogy—that is, the positive affirmation that Barth makes of the coordination of divine operations and the human medium that maintains the integrity and instrumentality of the human witness. We will unpack this more in a moment, but in the miracle of grace to which Thiemann refers there is no neglect or trivializing of the human medium.

This brings us to the next question in sequence as we continue to pursue what it would mean for scripture to err. Given this two-natures analogy, what is implied about how propositions are conveyed by scripture? Following the analogy, we affirm the full humanity of scripture. One sensible conclusion drawn from this is that scripture is in an important sense not different from other texts in the way in which propositions are conveyed by human authors. Barth is very clear that, although revelation requires divine action, there is no end-around the human witness. The human witness is not arbitrarily pressed into the service of revelation; rather, the divine revelation comes when—paying careful attention to the human witness—we are enabled to know the God to whom this witness testifies and given an understanding of the meaning of that testimony. Barth demands in our exegesis of scripture a fidelity

[23]Ronald Thiemann, *Revelation and Theology: The Gospel as Narrated Promise* (Notre Dame, IN: University of Notre Dame Press), p. 95.
[24]Ibid.

to all the general hermeneutical principles one applies to texts, but without the limitations they might impose on its object or the assumption that by them *alone* is revelation delivered.[25] What makes these texts different is their object, not their form. Revelation does not violate or happen in spite of the human witness; it happens by divine coordination of that witness in a *thoroughly* though *not merely* human process.

It should be clear that these thoughts on the ontology of scripture affirm traditional doctrines both of *illumination*—pertaining to the enabling of hearers of the Word—and of *inspiration,* by which God coordinates and sufficiently ensures the canon of Christian scripture to be the authoritative written medium of revelation.[26] In conjunction we can distinguish two kinds of divine action in God's determining the Bible to be the definitive and authoritative written medium of revelation. There is God's action pertaining to the coordination of the witness, and there is his action pertaining to the reception of revelation in those encountered by that witness. Through his valuable work in speech-act theory, Kevin Vanhoozer has shown how grasping this twofold nature of divine action in scriptural revelation can help to disentangle misunderstandings about Barth's view of scripture. God's action in the coordination of the witness brings about locutions and illocutions that God uses by the transforming work of the Spirit, who "enables what we might call illocutionary uptake and perlocutionary efficacy."[27] Having said this, we should also recognize that, while categorizing types of divine action

---

[25]See especially *CD* I/2, pp. 726-27.

[26]It is famously argued that "Barth confuses inspiration and illumination" (Carl F. H. Henry, *God, Revelation and Authority* [Waco, TX: Word Books, 1979], 4:266); however, Barth affirms both, even if the intent of his corrective is to recapture the sole theo-foundational grounds of the authority of scripture within the broader action of personally transformative divine self-revealing.

[27]Kevin Vanhoozer, "A Person of the Book? Barth on Biblical Authority and Interpretation," in *Karl Barth and Evangelical Theology,* ed. Sung Wook Chung (Grand Rapids: Baker Academic, 2006), p. 57. Vanhoozer finds in Barth insufficient attention to locutions and illocutions. Similarly, Timothy Ward in his impressive study judges that Barth is guilty of "eliding illocution into perlocution" (Ward, *Word and Supplement: Speech Acts, Biblical Texts, and the Sufficiency of Scripture* [Oxford: Oxford University Press, 2002], p. 112 n. 138). In light of Barth's commitment to the unique authority of scripture and to the importance of careful attention to the human witness, I find myself unpersuaded that Barth has collapsed or neglected locutions and illocutions. On the other hand, Ward seems to leave perlocution to the side when he concludes that "Scripture, as text, is sufficient for that speech act, bearing propositional content and conveying illocutionary force" (Ward, *Word and Supplement,* p. 298).

may serve as a helpful clarification, Barth would resist a dichotomized view of God's action and being. By the same token, while speech-act theory is helpful, we should also be careful not to impose its framework on Barth's own language about revelation. As we discussed in chapter two, Barth is happy to speak of the revealing act and the effect of revelation as one and one with God. This is Barth's way of pushing the notion of revelation to its fullest sense. In revelation God gives us himself through a fellowship of the Spirit that unites us to Christ. Union in the Spirit is the ultimate subjective impartation of the revelation of God.

In concluding our all too brief thoughts on the ontology of scripture, we should also note that there is, of course, some degree of fuzziness about just which precise collection of words constitutes the books of the Bible, not to mention their proper translation into other languages. We will return to this question in the second half of this chapter, only observing here that Barth's view of scripture can tolerate degrees of imprecision of this kind on the grounds of God's ongoing redeeming, inspiring and illuminating action. The end result for Barth is a very high view of both the authority and the humanity of scripture without ever blurring the divine/human lines or suggesting a capacity in the human elements alone to reveal or contain God. Scripture in its human aspects is the definitive, divinely chosen and orchestrated, written medium of divine revelation. It is the outcome of human participation in a divine work through which God reveals himself by human participation in a divine work.

Now we can consider directly our question about errors and imperfections in scripture. Given our discussion of the ontology of scripture as divinely commissioned human witness, what would it mean to affirm that scripture contains errors and imperfections? If scripture and revelation are distinct in the senses we have described on the Barth/Plantinga proposal, it would not be an imperfection of scripture that it lacks *in and of itself* the capacity to reveal God. Rather, an imperfection or error would have to be construed as a breakdown in the coordination between the human witness and the divine intentions for that witness. It would have to be a place at which the human witness of scripture distorts rather than serves as a medium of revelation, a place where the unity of the human and divine is compromised. Notice that this is markedly different from thinking of an error as merely the affirmation of a false proposition. It is likely that the "inerrancy" that Smith associates with biblicism is simply the claim that scripture affirms nothing false. On the ontology of scripture we have argued for, scripture is much more than merely a collection of expressions of true propositions. But is it less? That is, is it possible for scripture in its human witness to express or testify to false propositions without compromising the unity of the divine and human?

Barth appears to have thought that the human authors of the Bible made mistakes *in their witness*.[28] Most of his cautions about the human medium of scripture have to do with the issue of the human form lacking a "capacity" for being revelation in his full sense.[29] Nevertheless, he appears to have affirmed not merely the limitations and fallibility of the authors of scripture, but also the fallen cultural/linguistic frameworks that impinge on all human thought and communication. He also concludes that the prophets and apostles were "in their function as witnesses . . . actually guilty of error in their spoken and written word."[30] Barth's two-natures analogy for the coordination of the divine and human in the formation of scripture and the hearing of God's Word in it does not ensure the perfect obedience of the human form to the divine content. Perfected human obedience is found in the human life of the incarnation exclusively. It seems safe to say that Barth would not have affirmed even a qualified form of inerrancy.[31] I would argue, however, that we are free to disagree with Barth on this point while remaining faithful to the

[28]In my judgment, the evidence suggests this but still leaves room for the possibility that this is a misinterpretation of Barth's comments. For instance, it is oft noted that Barth affirms that the Bible contains "obvious overlappings and contradictions" (*CD* I/2, p. 509), but in this passage it is doubtful that Barth was using *contradiction* in its strict logical sense, which would necessarily involve the affirmation of a false proposition.

[29]"Instead of talking about the 'errors' of the biblical authors in this sphere, if we want to go to the heart of things it is better to speak only about their 'capacity for errors'" (*CD* I/2, p. 508).

[30]*CD* I/2, p. 529. Barth seems to suggest that this follows from the fact that—as the prophets and apostles were called into participation with God in generating the written witness of scripture—the integritiy of their humanity was retained and their freedom was not overriden.

[31]McCormack uses the phrase "dynamic infallibilism" to describe Barth's view of scripture, highlighting his uncompromising commitment to scripture's unique authority as it becomes what it is—what God determines it to be as the definitive written means of actual divine self-revealing (McCormack, "Being of Holy Scripture Is in Becoming," p. 73).

Barth/Plantinga proposal and the ontology of scripture that finds its being in relation to its divine determination to serve as the authoritative written revelation of God. It is certainly not an implication of the two-natures view that the human witness, as witness, is flawed. Nor, I will argue, does anything we have affirmed with Barth or Plantinga about scripture require the belief that the human witness of scripture expresses false propositions.

Many of us are familiar with these debates. Thoughtful and devout scholars of the Bible have suggested examples of false propositions expressed in scripture. These often have to do with historical or geographical details, or they amount to the claim that scripture affirms at various points the truth of contradicting propositions. Other thoughtful and devout scholars of the Bible have contested these examples on historical, archaeological and exegetical grounds. Sometimes the appearance of dubious claims and supposed contradictions amounts to a failure to give careful attention to literary forms.[32] At other times, the testimony of external sources and data is weighed against the testimony of scripture. Without engaging in those debates, we can consider generally whether the view of scripture I have argued for could countenance the affirmation of false propositions in scripture. To be clear, the possibility we are considering here is not that scripture *appears* to assert false propositions but that it really does in certain places assert them. Can we harmonize the claim that false propositions really are affirmed in scripture with the Barth/Plantinga proposal; the personal, verbal, cognitive nature of divine revealing enabled in the transforming gift of faith; and an ontology of scripture that features its being in relation to divine revelation?

The strategies that might be pursued for doing so can be divided into two general kinds depending on how one answers this question: should God be considered the principal author of every propositional affirmation in the human witness of scripture? If the answer is yes to this question, and yet it is accepted that the human witness of scripture af-

---

[32]On more than one occasion, Vanhoozer notes his agreement with James Barr on this point. Barr writes, "Genre-mistakes cause the wrong kind of truth values to be attached to the biblical sentences" (Barr, *The Bible in the Modern World* [London: SCM Press, 1973], p. 125, referenced in Vanhoozer, *First Theology: God, Scripture & Hermeneutics* [Downers Grove, IL: InterVarsity Press, 2002], p. 156).

firms false propositions, then we would have to embrace the rather counterintuitive notion that God at times intentionally presents falsehoods as truths as the means to some greater good in revelation. Perhaps Kenton Sparks's retrieval of Calvin's notion of "accommodation" is an instance of this.[33] On this view, for truth-revealing purposes, God adopts the errant views of the scripture writers. If, however, the idea of God presenting falsehoods as truths is not palatable and yet false propositions are asserted in scripture, then it would seem that God cannot be considered the principal author of every propositional affirmation in scripture. One might hold that false propositions affirmed in scripture are extraneous to but do not detract from God's revelatory purposes, but doing this might be seen to threaten the unity of the divine-and-human-coordinated authorship of scripture.

I think it must be said that on the Barth/Plantinga proposal I am advancing, there is room for a range of attitudes toward inerrancy. There is room for what we might call a more *conservative* affirmation that the divine coordination of the human witness operates such that the freedom and authentic humanity of the witness are not violated as God ensures that every proposition that is affirmed by the human witness is true. But it also allows for the view that God is committed to achieving his revelatory purposes by means of our careful attention to a human witness that he has coordinated without needing to ensure that strictly every proposition affirmed in it is true. Those who embrace the Barth/Plantinga proposal and are convinced by the evidence they have considered that scripture does in fact assert some false-propositions will naturally take the latter view. They may even add that false propositional affirmations were allowed by God to uphold the authentic humanity of the human witness.[34] Those, like me, who find no convincing reason to

---

[33]"In essence, Calvin paradoxically believed in inerrancy but allowed for errant viewpoints in Scripture" (Kenton Sparks, *God's Word in Human Words: An Evangelical Appropriation of Critical Biblical Scholarship* [Grand Rapids: Baker Academic, 2008], p. 256; see pp. 230-59).

[34]Peter Enns is an example of a contemporary Bible scholar and theologian who finds an incarnational model of scripture helpful for explaining how the authority of scripture as divine revelation need not be challenged by the limited perspectives and mistaken views expressed by the human authors. (See especially Enns, *Inspiration and Incarnation: Evangelicals and the Problem of the Old Testament* [Grand Rapids: Baker Academic, 2005].) As Enns puts it, "theological tensions and contradictions reflect the incarnate 'moment' from which those diverse texts arose" (Enns, "Further

think otherwise, are more likely to maintain that the veridical continuity between witness and revelation remains unified.

The Barth/Plantinga proposal does not require a specific construal of inerrancy, but it does discourage some views of scripture that are sometimes associated with simplistic formulations. It would reject any notion of inerrancy that merely equates human texts with the personal, cognitive, transformational self-revelation of God. It would reject any notion of inerrancy that would suggest capacities in human authors or texts that belong to God alone or that would imagine that revelation can be transferred into a human text. It would also reject any mere propositionalism with respect to revelation. Finally, as we turn now to consider the authority of scripture, we will find that the Barth/Plantinga proposal would also strenuously object to grounding the authority of the Bible in the *qualities* of the written medium of revelation. It is possible that some notions of inerrancy—perhaps the biblicism that Christian Smith has in mind—affirm some or all of these views that our proposal emphatically resists. These rejections noted, the Barth/Plantinga proposal is completely at home with our qualified affirmation of inerrancy even in its more conservative form.

We conclude here our articulation of an ontology of scripture informed primarily by the core concerns that Barth contributes to our proposal, and we turn primarily to Plantinga's contributions as we pursue a way of thinking about scripture's normativity. It may be instructive to note that, again in the case of scripture, we continue to respond to human epistemological incapacity not by bolstering our view of human capability but by increasing our view of God's coordinating power and purpose. On the Barth/Plantinga proposal, scripture finds its being in God's action that brings human words and ears to participate in his self-revelation.

WARRANT AND THE AUTHORITY OF SCRIPTURE

The criterion for determining the "altitude" of one's view of scripture is the subject of lively and factious debates. Nevertheless, it is safe to say that a "high" view of scripture would include a commitment to the normativity of scripture for Christian theology and proclamation. While

Thoughts on an Incarnational Model of Scripture," paper presented at the annual Logos Workshop, Center for Philosophy of Religion at the University of Notre Dame, June 2-4, 2011, p. 9).

Barth's view of scripture's ontology removes any reason to place confidence in human works alone, he remains uncompromising in his affirmation of the unique authority of revelation through scripture.[35]

> Scriptural exegesis rests on the assumption that the message which Scripture has to give us, even in its apparently most debatable and least assimilable parts, is in all circumstances truer and more important than the best and most necessary things that we ourselves have said or can say. In that it is the divinely ordained and authorized witness to revelation, it has the claim to be interpreted in this sense.[36]

By divine ordination and authorization, the authority of scripture imposes itself as norm for the church[37] and has the "supremacy" over all present-day proclamation, which depends on and derives from scripture.[38] The special authority that scripture has is not anchored in a property of the human witness itself, but only in the secure authority of the Word of God communicating through the form: he is the church's one foundation.

Our concern in the first part of this chapter was to analyze the implications of the Barth/Plantinga proposal for thinking about the nature of scripture. Now, we want to turn to its usefulness for thinking about the uniquely authoritative role of scripture in the church. We will not be using the Barth/Plantinga theo-foundational epistemology as a means of demonstrating the veracity and trustworthiness of scripture. Instead, we will consider what light is cast by the Barth/Plantinga proposal on this notion that the normativity of scripture imposes itself on us. It is broadly held throughout the church that the unique normative status of Christian scripture flows from the action of God,[39] who commissions and authorizes it to serve as divine revelation or discourse.

---

[35]A common concern about Barth's view of scripture is that it might undermine the authority of scripture by placing the determination of its truthfulness in the subjective hands of the interpreter (e.g., G. K. Beale, *The Erosion of Inerrancy in Evangelicalism: Responding to New Challenges to Biblical Authority* [Wheaton, IL: Crossway, 2008], p. 220). This is certainly not the case for Barth himself, who is interested in identifying the most secure grounds for scripture's authority.

[36]*CD* I/2, p. 719.

[37]*CD* I/1, p. 106; *KD* I/1, p. 109.

[38]*CD* I/1, p. 102 (*KD* I/1, p. 105: "die Überlegenheit").

[39]John Webster refers to this as "purposive divine action in its interaction with an assemblage of creaturely events, communities, agents, practices and attitudes" (Webster, *Holy Scripture: A Dogmatic Sketch* [Cambridge: Cambridge University Press, 2003], p. 5).

In the remainder of this chapter we will tackle two epistemological questions raised by the possibility of knowledge of scripture's authority. Our first question is, how does this sweeping claim about God and the authority of Christian scripture have genuine epistemic warrant? In light of the response to this question, we will turn to a second question about the possibility of warranted reception of divine communication through human words.

The first question: the question of warrant. We begin with the question of how one might have knowledge of the special normativity or divine authority of Christian scripture. Attempts could be made to demonstrate the truth of this claim by means of arguments and appeal to evidences. Many adherents to the divine authority of scripture, however, do not hold their view on the basis of inference from an argument or as a result of calculations based on evidences. We saw in chapter eight that being grasped by revelation involves an epistemic gift of faith. We saw in chapter seven that, while rational arguments and appeals to evidences may be helpful as catalysts for and confirmations of warranted Christian belief, they are neither necessary nor sufficient for it. We will take a similar view of evidences and rational arguments with respect to warrant for belief in scripture's authority as we engage the uniquely helpful resources of the Barth/Plantinga proposal. This means that, strictly speaking, our question is not *whether* it is true that God speaks through scripture. Instead the question is, if it is true that God speaks through scripture, how would it be possible to know that it is true? What is it that might provide the epistemic warrant for this belief?

As described in chapters four and five, Plantinga's analysis of the notion of *warrant* is his key contribution to epistemology. In the discussion that follows we will give particular focus to the helpfulness of his contribution for thinking about warranted recognition of scripture's authority. For those who may have forgotten, we will begin with a reminder of the salient features of Plantinga's warrant.

After a painstaking analysis of competing views of knowledge, Plantinga concludes that our beliefs count as knowledge if they are held firmly enough, if they are in fact true and if they have warrant. Warrant for Plantinga is what provides the connection between the truth of what we believe and the formation of that belief. This connection is ultimately the gift of God, who endows human knowers with their rational capacities, faculties and powers, designed for the production of true beliefs such that when they are functioning properly in a fitting environment, the beliefs they produce, if strong enough, will have warrant sufficient for knowledge. At the heart of Plantinga's system are human noetic processes designed for the production of true beliefs. And yet the conditions are formidable; forming warranted beliefs requires both the proper functioning of complex human noetic equipment and the suitability of the environment for the designed function.

As Plantinga extends his general account of warrant into an explicitly Christian model, he acknowledges that human sin and alienation from God have had a serious impact on both proper function and our cognitive environment. Drawing heavily on Calvin, he develops the notion of faith as one of the designed belief-producing processes—one that yields both cognitive and affective results. But the deliverances of faith begin, external to our noetic equipment, with the special action of God: the internal instigation of the Holy Spirit. This process, though it has a supernatural element, conforms nevertheless to Plantinga's general account of warrant.[40] The operations of faith are designed to produce true beliefs when functioning properly, and this is a process specifically designed to deal with the environmental and noetic effects of sin.

On this view, belief in the reliability and authority of scripture is not based on reasoning from propositional evidence but rather from the evidence provided by the deliverances of faith that immediately recommend belief.[41] Like convictions formed on the basis of phenomenal imagery, the convictions formed on the basis of faith result from being given a view or perception of the truth of what is believed by the illumination of the Spirit. These beliefs therefore have warrant without requiring the support of inferential reasoning. Plantinga quotes Calvin:

---

[40]See especially *WCB*, pp. 258-66.

[41]Plantinga quotes Jonathan Edwards, "This evidence, that they, that are spiritually enlightened, have of the truth of the things of religion, is a kind of intuitive and immediate evidence. They believe the doctrines of God's word to be divine, because they see divinity in them" (*WCB*, p. 259, quoting *A Treatise Concerning Religious Affections*, ed. John E. Smith [1746; New Haven: Yale University Press, 1959], p. 298).

> Illumined by his power, we believe neither by our own nor by anyone else's judgment that Scripture is from God; but above human judgment we affirm with utter certainty that it has flowed to us from the very mouth of God by the ministry of men. We seek no proofs. . . . Such, then, is a conviction that requires no reason.[42]

This does not mean that all ordinary human processes have been supplanted by the supernatural, or that belief is causally determined by God regardless of its conformity to human reason. If it were in fact the case that Plantinga was proposing that human noetic processes were bypassed, then we would be strong-armed into a model of divine communication that trivialized the human elements, which inevitably leads toward a docetic view of scripture. In order to see that this is emphatically not what Plantinga is proposing, we can recall how the belief-producing process of faith interfaces with the rest of the human noetic apparatus and Plantinga's general account of warrant. The key components are human external and internal rationality and the corresponding conditions for warrant that pertain to each.

External rationality is the domain of cognitive processes that apprehend and present experience from all our cognitive inputs.[43] These inputs are not belief neutral. They do not merely acquire data; they recommend belief in accordance with the data they present. In this sense, all cognitive inputs *impel* belief—i.e., they present doxastic experience. This does not mean that they *compel* belief. Actual belief formation happens on the basis of this experience, but not by the experience itself. The instigation of the Holy Spirit is a special instance of a belief-exhorting process functioning primarily in the domain of external rationality. It is an experience of God the Spirit, recommending to us belief.

[42] *WCB,* p. 260, quoting John Calvin, *Institutes of the Christian Religion,* ed. John T. McNeill and trans. Ford Lewis Battles (1559; Philadelphia: Westminster, 1960) 1.7.5, pp. 80-81. It is worth noting that this view has broad support throughout the church. The Dogmatic Constitution *Dei Filius* on the Catholic faith of Vatican I states: "This faith, which is the beginning of human salvation, the Catholic Church professes to be a supernatural virtue, by means of which, with the grace of God inspiring and assisting us, we believe to be true what He has revealed, not because we perceive its intrinsic truth by the natural light of reason, but because of the authority of God himself, who makes the revelation and can neither deceive nor be deceived" (3.2).

[43] *WCB,* p. 257.

This work of the Spirit fulfills several of Plantinga's key conditions for warrant. It is designed to guide us toward true beliefs and is particularly suited to our cognitive environment, affected as it is by sin. We can expand the notion of cognitive environment to include our entire interpretive grid, which is heavily conditioned by environmental factors—social, cultural, linguistic, historical, moral and so forth. While the corruption of our cognitive environment has a distorting and attenuating effect on the doxastic experiences of faith, the proximity of the Spirit, who ministers Christ, has a restorative impact on our cognitive environment. The work of the Spirit drawing us to Christ also helps to rehabilitate proper function of belief-forming processes downstream from external rationality. Of considerable importance in this connection is the Spirit's role in the church, the community of believers. I expanded Plantinga's thought with Barth's to emphasize the role of the Spirit to form and nurture conducive ecclesial cognitive environments. The Spirit uses communities of faith to facilitate proper function in the formation of belief by faith. Moreover, since the cognitive process of faith is driven by the personally loving and omniscient action of the Spirit, these deliverances can be tailored to make best use of otherwise distortive environments, as well as to draw on one's wider network of personal relationships to participate in the generation of true belief.

Internal rationality has first to do with the formation of right belief on the basis of experience but also takes into account all the considerations that come from the rest of our framework of beliefs. This includes consideration of proper fit or coherence and requires that one pursue a connected set of beliefs that is free of internal contradiction. It also extends to the maintenance of good doxastic practices. Plantinga mentions "preferring to believe what is true, looking for further evidence when that is appropriate, and in general being epistemically responsible."[44] This includes, furthermore, a responsibility to investigate other points of view—particularly in regard to highly contentious beliefs—and keeping one's eyes open to potential defeaters. In general, proper function has to

[44]Ibid., p. 112.

do with conformity to design of those processes involved in the formation of belief, including the presentation of doxastic experience, the assimilation of right belief and the responsible management of one's matrix of belief. Warrant requires proper function and the appropriateness of the overall design to the production of true belief given the environmental conditions.

With respect to these conditions of warrant, the cognitive process of faith is no different from any other avenue of human knowing. It does not bypass our creaturely faculties but is itself a thoroughly human cognitive process. The key difference between the cognitive process of faith and other human cognitive faculties or processes is that the formation of doxastic experience is motivated by the internal instigation of the Holy Spirit. I have also suggested that the Spirit's drawing us to Christ begins to restore the noetic structures and processes involved, including the gradual repair of our socially, culturally, linguistically, historically and morally conditioned interpretive grids. Furthermore, Plantinga develops the affective corollaries to the cognitive mechanics so that the role of the will and affections is not overlooked. And as we have already recalled, the Spirit is free to make redemptive use of our wider relational as well as internal cognitive environments. What we end up with is a fairly comprehensive, fully human though Spirit-driven cognitive process with a detailed account of how it is possible that the beliefs it produces have warrant.

Warranted belief in the divine authority of scripture. Now we can return to the motivating question of this part of the chapter: how, according to Plantinga, might it be possible for one to know that scripture has a special divine authority? There are two options, which Plantinga himself acknowledges, for how this might go. First, it might be that belief in the divinely sanctioned normativity of scripture is itself one of the direct deliverances of faith—that when considering a collection of human writings commonly called "the Bible," the Spirit enables one to grasp the truth of the proposition that scripture comes from God and therefore is authoritative. The second option, and the one Plantinga himself endorses, is that "upon reading or hearing a given teaching . . . the Holy Spirit teaches us, causes us to believe that *that* teaching is both true and comes from God."[45] On this view, the Spirit does not establish our confidence in the authority of scripture with a generic endorsement, which then provides by inference the grounds for belief in the normativity of any particular part of scripture. Instead, the Spirit works as a person engages the particularity of scripture within a sufficiently propitious environment, and confidence in its general authority is therefore retrospective on this engagement. Plantinga does not spend much time developing his view, but one could easily imagine other options or variations. Perhaps grasping the truthfulness of scripture involves first grasping something of its central narrative.

In either case, one affirms the authority of Christian scripture by grasping the truthfulness of what it communicates as one is grasped and transformed cognitively and affectively by the Holy Spirit. This cognitive experience does not happen in a vacuum. As I have already indicated, our own complex and externally conditioned interpretive grids and relational networks are not circumvented. The Spirit is simultaneously engendering conducive ecclesial cognitive environments to facilitate proper function.[46]

In Plantinga's view, knowledge of scripture's divinely authorized normativity is *enabled* first by a special belief-producing process designed by God. This process involves the critical work of the Holy Spirit, who sufficiently heals and overcomes the environmental and noetic effects of sin, to motivate cognitive assent and the appropriate affective response to the testimony of scripture. But how do we move from a grace-given apprehension of the central truths or grand narrative revealed through scripture to an affirmation of the comprehensive authority of a particular set of writings as definitively tied to divine communication? This question brings us back to a deceptively difficult though critical question—namely, which texts count as scripture, and in what way? This is not only the concern of canon composition but also the question of which manuscripts, editions and translations count as authoritative.

[45]Ibid., p. 260, emphasis original; also see p. 248 n. 15. "Comes from God" might sound too direct for Barth, who would be happier with the language of the Westminster Confession of Faith, "the Holy Spirit speaking in the Scripture" (10.1).

[46]As is often the case, our original hearings of scripture will come not from personally reading the text but from the communication of the testimony of scripture by family or church community.

Without becoming mired in these important but protracted considerations, it may be sufficient here to note four interesting options for extending Plantinga's model to address these issues.

What constitutes scripture? The first option would be to suggest that the same testimony of the Holy Spirit, in the cognitive process of faith, is also the way that we arrive at warranted judgments about the textual composition of scripture. In this view it is not just the central teachings or primary narrative of scripture that we are enabled to grasp but all that is communicated through scripture, such that the specific authoritative texts are only those specially marked out for us by the Holy Spirit. But this approach would not yield the kind of unified affirmation of the church's scripture that is entailed in a traditional affirmation of scripture's authority. One might worry that, instead, individuals would begin to assemble their own Bibles on the basis of numerous subjective judgments.

I have already mentioned a second option for how an affirmation of the authority of specific writings might have warrant. This was the alternative considered above where the Holy Spirit allows us a theoretical grasp of the truth of the authority of scripture. Perhaps it could be argued that *scripture,* which is grasped as authoritative, must indicate concrete texts rather than a pure abstraction.[47] If this view were acceptable, we would have an answer to the question. I argued along with Plantinga that in actual Christian experience authority is grasped retrospectively on an encounter with the content and truthfulness of the primary narrative—which comes in fact together in an encounter with the One to whom scripture testifies. But this does not rule out the possibility that there could be a simultaneous or even retrospective role for the Spirit's affirmation of the authority of the particular Bible we engage—the modern translation read or heard in Christian worship.

A third option would emphasize the noetic role of the being-healed ecclesial cognitive environment in affirming which writings constitute scripture. There might even be a thoroughgoing alternative ecclesial account in which the Spirit enables us first to grasp the trustworthiness of

---

[47]It does not necessarily follow that on this view there is a single concrete and definitive set of texts. The Holy Spirit could be affirming the authority of a number of different texts and translations in various ecclesial environments.

those proclaiming or explaining to us the primary narrative of scripture and on that basis to infer the truth of what is being conveyed. But again here it seems much more likely that the trustworthiness of the messenger is being confirmed simultaneously by a perception of the truth and goodness of that to which they are testifying rather than the other way around.

A final option would reach a conclusion on the basis of inference. An argument might be built from the primary narrative already affirmed to the conclusion that God would remain involved in the rulings of the church, the preservation of manuscripts, the editorial decisions and modern translations to such an extent that the product of these would be adequate texts for God's revelatory purposes. It might also be the case that warrant for affirming the divine authority of concrete Christian scripture is delivered in multiple or mutually supporting ways. For our purposes here it is not necessary that we decide, so long as we see that what enables a warranted conclusion for scripture's divine authority is first the proper functioning of the cognitive process of faith, which critically involves the illumination of the Spirit, who, ministering Christ to us, begins the healing of ecclesial cognitive environments to bring a transformed apprehension of the truth of what God is communicating through scripture.

The second question: warranted reception of divine address. Leveraging the work of Plantinga, I have just sketched an answer to the first question regarding how we might possess legitimate human knowledge of the divine authority of scripture. We are now ready to engage our second epistemological question, regarding the possibility of warranted reception of divine communication through the human medium of scripture.

We might do well to note that in answering the first epistemological question we have already significantly encroached on the turf of the second. In fact, what is implied in the account we have given is that our reception of divine communication with real cognitive content comes before or simultaneous with our growing acceptance of the authority of scripture. Following Plantinga, we find that at the core of the cognitive process of faith is the Spirit enabling us to grasp the truth of some of the primary narrative of scripture.[48] But this, in one motion, involves each of the epistemological issues with which we are interested. Grasping the truth of the primary narrative of scripture in terms of logical priority requires that we be given first adequate authentic human understanding of what is being revealed and second the experience of perceiving the truth of that which has been revealed. We might say that the first concern is hermeneutical (pertaining to interpretation) while the second is alethiological (pertaining to truth). In the model presented, these aspects appear to occur simultaneously. It is not merely grasping the truth of what is being revealed; it is grasping both what is being revealed and its truth. Two questions spring to mind. First, is it possible not merely to distinguish a logical priority to these two aspects of a single event but also to distinguish them temporally as separate events? And second, to the heart of the issue, what else can be said about the roles of the Spirit and the human knower in the hermeneutical aspect of belief formation through the cognitive process of faith?

Belief and the hermeneutical role of the Spirit. Is it possible to separate the hermeneutical and the alethiological in the process of human knowing by faith? By *hermeneutical* we are not here referring to a science of hermeneutics, at least not yet. We are simply considering what is involved in an adequate human conceptual grasp of what it is that is revealed to be true by the Spirit in the belief-engendering process described above. In chapter eight we gave some thought to what it means to have an adequate human conceptual grasp of a proposition. We saw that human conceiving transcends the formulation of its concepts in human language. The fact of the need for the interpretation of texts implies that despite the indispensable role of language and texts in the shaping and communication of meaning, meaning remains distinct from language.[49] In what Plantinga describes as the cognitive process of faith, human beings are given some grasp of the primary narrative of scripture

[48]Plantinga adopts from Jonathan Edwards the notion of the "great things of the Gospel" (*WCB*, pp. 80, 101). "It is therefore a knowledge of the main lines of the Christian gospel. The content of faith is just the central teachings of the gospel; it is contained in the intersection of the great Christian creeds" (ibid., p. 248).

[49]We need not be committed to a particular theory of language or meaning to make this modest though significant claim.

together with a confirmation of its truth. Just as the humanity and freedom of the original authors and editors was not overridden in the formation of the text, so also, on this model, reception in readers and hearers is achieved not by an overriding divine implantation but through an interaction with some human expression of what it is that God is communicating through scripture.

Whatever that expression is, its interpretation depends not least on the broader narrative, history, culture, language and communities within which it is situated and operates. Healing and using this broader framework, or wider cognitive environment, the Spirit grants human ears to grasp the meaning that these expressions intend—that is, what God intends to reveal or say by them. In this way the Spirit breathes life into our conceptual frameworks to allow an adequate human conceptual grasp of divine communication. The Spirit does this by ministering Christ to us, Christ who is the Revelation of God. We can go even further to suggest that the most central and significant communication that we are enabled to grasp involves personal knowledge of God himself. This is the natural consequence of the fact that the mission of the Spirit is to lead us into personal relationship with Jesus Christ and a participation in the God-knowing of the human Jesus.

The question is, can we have a kind of *theoretical* knowledge of this communication, without yet being persuaded that it presents the truth about reality? Can we, so to speak, from a distance have an adequate cognitive grasp of the ultimate referent without embracing it? In chapter eight we answered a similar question vis-à-vis the personal nature of a genuine knowledge of God by means of the free grace of God's own self-disclosure. The question here is broader in scope, but there are reasons once again to be qualifiedly doubtful that a merely theoretical understanding constitutes adequate cognitive grasp.

We could start with the more traditional answer. Because of the darkening of our minds and cognitive environments that results from our alienation from God, we cannot, without divine assistance and repair, adequately grasp what God is saying through scripture. Our interpretive grids distort the message, our corrupt wills impose our own desires, and our fallen imaginations fail to reach the heights to which they are called.

Still, we would have to grant that from an agnostic perspective one could correctly grasp a great deal that is being taught in scripture and even agree on the best way to describe it. The closer to the center one moves, however, the less and less likely it becomes that unbelief itself will not begin to eclipse the divine voice. Could such cognition ever adequately penetrate the reality?

One line of thinking would suggest that any theoretical cognitive grasp that remains agnostic about truth is by definition not an adequate cognitive grasp of *reality*. It is a cognitive grasp of a *theory* and nothing more. There is an interesting parallel here to the renowned ontological argument for the existence of God. One of the most important facts about God is the actuality of his existence. There is, therefore, a decisive difference between a conception of God that does not affirm his existence and one that does. Only the latter is an adequate conception of God. In the same way, only a grasp of the message conveyed by scripture that affirms its truth is an adequate grasp of that true message.

Another response would appeal to the comprehensive nature of human knowing and the difficulty of detaching only the cognitive portion without thereby significantly altering it. A thoroughgoing view of human knowing involves not merely cognitive but also supracognitive elements. This is particularly true of personal knowing with its affective and relational aspects. To know God and his core message through scripture is to be in personal relationship with God and to love the truth that he discloses. Clearly, the supracognitive aspects of human knowing cannot be agnostic about truth—cannot remain purely theoretical. The argument then is that the supracognitive, while it may be distinguished from the cognitive, cannot in fact be separated from the cognitive without doing severe violence to the integrity of human knowing. On this view, the supracognitive and the cognitive are so interdependent that it is impossible to allow one to remain agnostic without forcing the other to do the same. But if adequate supracognitive knowing of what God is communicating through scripture cannot remain purely theoretical, then neither can adequate cognitive knowledge.

Finally, a teleological argument can be given. One slippery notion in our analysis is that of *adequacy*. What are the necessary and sufficient conditions for an adequate human cognitive grasp? One compelling suggestion notes that adequacy is often determined in light of purpose. We might then ask, for what purpose does the Spirit enable a cognitive grasp of the primary narrative of scripture? If the internal instigation of the Holy Spirit is part of the Spirit drawing us into relationship with Jesus Christ, the Truth, the Revelation of God, then cognitive grasp is part of the broader personal relationship. Cognitive grasp helps to enable us to fully and rightly respond to and embrace this relationship. The obvious conclusion of this is that purely theoretical knowledge is inadequate to this purpose. The proper conclusion given the weight of these responses, I would maintain, is that while theoretical grasp of the message of scripture is clearly possible, there are good reasons to think of it as a less than adequate human cognitive grasp of the realities being taught.

What does this mean for the Christian exegesis of scripture? It is difficult to imagine how determinations at the higher levels of exegesis and theology could have warrant sufficient for knowledge and conviction without the deliverances of the cognitive process of faith. We should acknowledge that the likelihood of having a warranted grasp of the right theological conclusions is quite low without the transformation of our minds that comes as the Spirit ministers Christ. The deliverances of faith are part and parcel of that transformation. A grasp of and commitment to the narrative of scripture is critical to the reconstituting of our interpretive frameworks, which so strongly influence exegetical decisions. And so we conclude that growing in a knowledge of what God communicates through scripture is a thoroughly human though divinely enabled process whereby our being grasped by divine communication through scripture serves at some level our advancement into every exegetical truth.

If we cannot separate an adequate human cognitive grasp of the message of scripture from seeing and believing it to be true, then we must conclude that indeed both are aspects of the deliverances of faith requiring the special activity of the Holy Spirit. From this we can conclude with a few significant implications for the hermeneutical role of the Spirit. First, as with the alethiological role of the Spirit in the proposed model, human noetic functions are neither displaced nor overridden. While the Spirit provides decisive human interpretive grasp, none of the dynamics of human communication and interpretation are *spiritually* bypassed. The means by which one comes to a grasp of the core message that God intends to communicate through scripture may vary greatly in terms of context and manner, but in each instance it will be an irreducibly and indispensably human process. Our background experience, our interpretive frameworks, our ecclesial and nonecclesial cognitive environments, along with the expression of the narrative itself, are each taken up by the Spirit to be used and healed through the ministry and self-revelation of Christ to play its part in the illumination of human cognition to grasp both what is being communicated and the fact that it corresponds to the one who is Truth.

In addition, as with all human noetic processes, the strength of the beliefs they engender comes in degrees. Warrant itself, on Plantinga's model, is something that comes in degrees, and only when warrant for a belief is strong enough is it sufficient to count as knowledge. So also with the cognitive process of faith, due to the interconnected problems of improper function, unconducive cognitive environments and relational distance from God, the hermeneutical deliverances of faith may be distorted and ineffective. There is a sweeping range of human error and resistance that can weaken and cloud the results, whether this is mistakenly applying the wrong historical interpretive framework to a biblical narrative, preferring not to be challenged in one's attitude toward poverty or sexual ethics or some other obstruction. We might despair that an essential element in the success of the process is dependent on our fallible participation, yet our confidence rests in the ministry of the triune God, who is simultaneously the ground of our warrant and the one who grows and enables our participation through gracious gifts of relational epistemic transformation.

CONCLUSION

At every stage of this chapter we have returned to questions and affirmations about the participation of the fully human in the ontologically determinative action of the fully divine. This relationship, and its radical asymmetry, is at the core of the Barth/Plantinga proposal and its response to the fundamental epistemological dilemma confronting theology. Extending the Barth/Plantinga proposal, I argued that a proper ontology of scripture maintains the uncompromised humanity of authors and texts but is finally dependent on God's ordination, intention and ongoing action. I suggested that the being of scripture cannot be separated from divine action in inspiration and illumination while at the same time the humanity of the witness cannot be confused with the divinity of the Revealer.

Then I affirmed that our knowledge both of scripture's authority and of the inspired content God communicates through it can have genuine epistemic warrant through a united but not confused participation of human noetic processes in transforming and warrant-infusing divine action. The central theme of the Barth/Plantinga proposal is its theo-foundational epistemology, in which the triune God is the ground of the warrant for our knowledge of him. In his self-revelation we are grasped and given acquaintance with the real referent, by means of the transforming gift of faith. Without neglecting or overriding human processes and conditions, God remains the ground for our warrant in our engagement with scripture as the definitive written means of that self-revelation.

CONCLUDING POSTSCRIPT

Fallibility and Assurance

◆

I am mindful and quite at ease with the possibility that, for some busy readers, this may be the first and perhaps the only part of this book that you read. Anxious as I am not to undermine your attempt to avoid reading, what I provide here is much less than a synopsis, and yet something more than a summary. For my dutiful sequentialist companions, I will consider the fruit of our engagement and make some closing comments in light of what I think will be lingering epistemic concerns.

In the introduction, I identified what I take to be a central epistemological dilemma facing Christian theology and, for that matter, Christian belief altogether. It is a dilemma created by two competing assertions. The first affirms with confidence that theological knowledge—not mere theological *belief*—is a real human possibility. The second threatens that confidence with a recognition of human fallibility. Christian theology cannot dispense with its acknowledgment that we are humanly unable to self-secure the grounds of theological knowledge, yet Christian theology must affirm with conviction that God makes himself humanly known. As I said at the beginning, Christian theology must acknowledge itself an impoverished earthen vessel while daring not to diminish the value of the treasure it confesses.

I then made the suggestion that Christian theology points to a solution to this dilemma and that one theologically and philosophically robust tag-team approach can be found by bringing together the insights of Karl Barth and Alvin Plantinga.

In the details of the Barth/Plantinga proposal I fleshed out a theo-foundational epistemology, rooted in the self-revealing action of the Trinity, who, by drawing us to himself, makes possible a human participation in a warranted, cognitive and personally transforming knowledge of God. As I applied this proposal to concrete issues in the epistemology of revelation, I sought in each instance to maintain the primacy and indispensability of divine action without confusing it with or transferring its efficacy to human capacities. The result was not a reduction or overriding of full human engagement but a restoring and bolstering of human faculties, media and environments to serve in the divine purposes of revelation. In the discussion on natural theology I argued that human reason, while wrongly conceived if providing the grounds for theological knowledge, retains an active and significant role in its acquisition and maintenance. In the discussion on faith and knowledge we saw that the gift of faith enables genuine human cognitive knowledge of the real referent of revelation. And, in the discussion of the nature of scripture and warrant, we affirmed the full humanity of its composition and reception without reducing the ground of revelation to a text or a human competence.

Another way to view this proposal is to see that the fundamental epistemological problem we have had in view is a facet of the problem of the possibility of human fellowship or reconciliation with God. When faced with Jesus' strong words about the impossibility of making ourselves righteous, the earnest question came: who then can be saved? At its core, the solution to the epistemological problem given in the Barth/Plantinga proposal follows Jesus' response: "What is impossible with man is possible with God" (Lk 18:27). Despite my efforts to defend this proposal in considerable detail, I suspect that some readers will be left unsatisfied by the simplicity of this basic response. Theological knowledge is a human possibility because it is given and received, not because it is humanly established and demonstrated. The dissatisfaction with this as a solution to our epistemic problems may come with very practical concerns, and I would like to consider two of them in closing.

The first is the *self-deception concern*—that the epistemic dependency inherent in the Barth/Plantinga proposal leaves us with no way of ruling out the possibility of self-deception. That is of course correct. The proposal leaves us with no way of ruling out the possibility of self-deception. But being unable to rule out this possibility is just a feature of being human and follows from our acknowledgment that we are humanly unable to self-secure the grounds of knowledge. It should be noted that this difficulty, if it should even be considered a difficulty, is a challenge to all claims to human knowledge and not just theological knowledge. It is true that the epistemic situation we face is not one where it is possible to apply a fail-safe test or criteria that can rule out the kinds of epistemic failure described in chapter one. If a solution like this were available, then we could dispense with rather than affirm human fallibility, and there would be no need to remain dependent on God for knowledge of God. But our situation is not as bleak as might seem to be implied by this concern. It is not as if we have been left with no grounds for confidence in what we believe we know.

It seems to me that we could distinguish healthy and unhealthy versions of the self-deception concern. The unhealthy version requires an unattainable degree of certainty for knowledge. The healthy version is in line with what Plantinga conceives of as the proper functioning of our internal rationality. Internal rationality is that region of our epistemic equipment that is responsible for the proper formation of belief downstream from experience. Among other things, its provinces include the applying of critical scrutiny, the maintaining of healthy skepticism and attention to doubts. When performing well, it finds that all-things-considered, elusive balance between maximizing true beliefs and minimizing false ones. Of course we can press on all these notions and find difficult questions. The point is that the epistemic situation conceived of in the Barth/Plantinga proposal presents us with avenues for scrutinizing beliefs without suggesting that they can provide for us the grounds of certainty.

The self-deception concern might be followed up with a *practicality concern*. This concern has to do with the apparent uselessness of this proposal for determining whose view is the right view on a number of debated questions in contemporary theology. In fact, this proposal fails even to offer an argument to settle the most basic questions in theological epistemology (e.g., is there a God to know?). How could an epistemological proposal be helpful in the slightest if it fails to offer good reasons for thinking that it is true? You may recall that similar complaints have been frequently voiced in response to Plantinga's model for warranted Christian belief. My proposal in Barth's terms is indeed without weapons. If this proposal conceives of the truth correctly, the weaponry and demonstrative power reside on God's side of revelatory action and are not simply at our disposal. But that does not mean that we should be willing to grant either that this proposal is useless or that it has nothing to say to important debates in contemporary theology.

The usefulness of the Barth-Plantinga proposal I have advanced arises from its ability to provide a nuanced and coherent way of thinking about the knowledge of God that is deeply informed by Christian theological reflection while remaining in conversation with analytic philosophical critique. It demonstrates the rich resources of the Christian doctrines of Trinity and incarnation for painting a comprehensive vision of revelation in connection with human transformation. In so doing I have clearly affirmed the truth of theological convictions that strongly inform important debates in contemporary theology. At the heart of my thesis lies the conviction that self-certainty and triumphalism have no place in the Christian faith, and yet a properly fallibilist view of human knowing is consistent with confident assurance. Even if the proposal does not settle certain matters of debate, it nevertheless gives us reason to engage differences with generous humility and still full conviction. It gives us reason to persevere in the search for unity of mind by positing a unity of action in God. And it removes the fears that improperly intensify our disagreements when we see ourselves as responsible for securing the ground of our own knowledge. If things are roughly as the proposal suggests, the resolution to our epistemological troubles comes as the ground of our knowledge is secured for us in Jesus Christ.

At this point some readers may want to return to the self-deception concern since our response to the practicality concern depends on finding a God-given assurance. But how do we know that our assurance is God-given and not merely a manufactured self-assurance? To the extent that this is the same concern as above, looking for verification to self-secure our knowledge of God, then the same response given above applies. Or maybe the question is looking for the kinds of confirmations that we discussed in chapter seven, which provide not the real grounds of faith but rather catalysts used by God to advance us in the intellectual satisfaction of faith. And yet, this may be a slightly different question. Perhaps this is a question about the nature of the experience of receiving God-given assurance. Perhaps the question is seeking a kind of phenomenological description of what it is like to receive the gift of faith. On this question the proposal gives us reason to believe that that experience may be quite unique to each individual. The proposal argues that this assurance is grown in us by the mediation of revelation in a process of whole-person transformation, influencing our unique noetic structures and environments, taking into account our particular historical, psychological, social, cultural and linguistic frameworks. In this light we can see why it would be important not to give an oversimplified answer. The immense variety of testimonies of personal experience underscores this point.

There are many other specific epistemic concerns that the Barth-Plantinga proposal does not seek to answer. In every case, however, the proposal points to God as the source and reasonable ground for epistemic hope and encouragement. We are reminded that God has revealed himself to be one who goes to great lengths to make himself known, patiently enduring our own resistance to the kinds of changes that need to be made in us for the fullness of that knowledge to be achieved. He is revealed to be the God who in the incarnation takes on our humanity so that he can be our priest-of-knowing. Not only does he stand in our place to effect for us what we could never effect for ourselves, but he also gives us a participation in his perfect human knowledge of God. As Alan Torrance puts it, "Participation in the sole priesthood of Christ is participation in Christ's epistemic, noetic and semantic communion with the Father."[1] Whether it is wrestling with vexing doubts, with the extreme limitations of our own knowledge or with the massive array of

[1]Alan J. Torrance, "Reclaiming the Continuing Priesthood of Christ: Implications and Challenges," paper presented at the First Annual Los Angeles Theology Conference, Biola University, January 18, 2013, p. 20.

diversity and disagreement in contemporary theology, the proposal of this book intends to point us to a profound and reasonable hope: "What is impossible with man is possible with God" (Lk 18:27).

BIBLIOGRAPHY

Abraham, William J. *Canon and Criterion in Christian Theology: From the Fathers to Feminism.* Oxford: Oxford University Press, 1998.

———. *Crossing the Threshold of Divine Revelation.* Grand Rapids: Eerdmans, 2006.

———. "Revelation and Natural Theology." In *Alister E. McGrath and Evangelical Theology: A Dynamic Engagement,* edited by Sung Wook Chung, pp. 264-79. Carlisle, UK: Paternoster, 2003.

Adams, Edward. "Calvin's View of Natural Knowledge of God." *International Journal of Systematic Theology* 3, no. 3 (2001): 280-92.

Alston, William P. "Christian Experience and Christian Belief." In Plantinga and Wolterstorff, *Faith and Rationality,* pp. 103-34.

———. *Epistemic Justification: Essays in the Theory of Knowledge.* Ithaca, NY: Cornell University Press, 1989.

———. "Epistemology and Metaphysics." In *Knowledge and Reality: Essays in Honor of Alvin Plantinga,* edited by Thomas Crisp, Matthew Davidson and David Vander Laan, pp. 81-109. Dordrecht: Kluwer Academic, 2006.

———. *Perceiving God: The Epistemology of Religious Experience.* Ithaca, NY: Cornell University Press, 1991.

———. *A Realist Conception of Truth.* Ithaca, NY: Cornell University Press, 1996.

———. "Two Types of Foundationalism." *Journal of Philosophy* 73, no. 7 (1976): 165-85.

Andrews, Isolde. *Deconstructing Barth: A Study of the Complementary Methods in Karl Barth and Jacques Derrida.* Frankfurt am Main: Lang, 1996.

Aquinas, Thomas. *Summa Contra Gentiles.* Translated by Anton C. Pegis, James F. Anderson, Vernon J. Bourke and Charles J. O'Neil. New York: Hanover House, 1955-57.

———. *Summa Theologica.* Translated by Fathers of the English Dominican Province. New York: Benziger, 1947.

Audi, Robert. *The Architecture of Reason: The Structure and Substance of Rationality.* Oxford: Oxford University Press, 2001.

———. "Direct Justification, Evidential Dependence, and Theistic Belief." In Audi and Wainwright, *Rationality, Religious Belief, and Moral Commitment,* pp. 139-66.

———. *Epistemology: A Contemporary Introduction to the Theory of Knowledge.* 3rd ed. New York: Routledge, 2010.

———. *The Structure of Justification.* Cambridge: Cambridge University Press, 1993.

Audi, Robert, and William J. Wainwright, eds. *Rationality, Religious Belief, and Moral*

Commitment: New Essays in the Philosophy of Religion. Ithaca, NY: Cornell University Press, 1986.

Baillie, John. *Our Knowledge of God.* London: Oxford University Press, 1939.

Baker, Deane-Peter, ed. *Alvin Plantinga.* Cambridge: Cambridge University Press, 2007.

———. "Plantinga's Reformed Epistemology: What's the Question?" *International Journal for Philosophy of Religion* 57 (2005): 77-103.

Balthasar, Hans Urs von. *Karl Barth: Darstellung und Deutung seiner Theologie.* Cologne: J. Hegner, 1951. Translated by Edward T. Oakes as *The Theology of Karl Barth: Exposition and Interpretation.* San Francisco: Ignatius Press, 1992.

Barr, James. *The Bible in the Modern World.* London: SCM Press, 1973.

———. *Biblical Faith and Natural Theology: The Gifford Lectures for 1991, Delivered in the University of Edinburgh.* Oxford: Oxford University Press, 1993.

Barth, Karl. *Anselm, Fides Quaerens Intellectum: Anselm's Proof of the Existence of God in the Context of His Theological Scheme.* 2nd ed. Library of Philosophy and Theology. London: SCM Press, 1960.

———. "Antwort an Erwin Reisner." *Evangelische Theologie* 2 (1935): 51-66.

———. "Ein Briefwechsel mit Adolf von Harnack." In Barth, *Theologische Fragen und Antworten,* pp. 7-31.

———. "Church and Culture." In Barth, *Theology and Church,* pp. 334-54.

———. *Church Dogmatics.* Translated by Geoffrey W. Bromiley. Edited by Geoffrey W. Bromiley and Thomas F. Torrance. 4 vols. Edinburgh: T & T Clark, 1956–1975.

———. *Credo: A Presentation of the Chief Problems of Dogmatics with Reference to the Apostles' Creed.* Translated by J. Strathearn McNab. London: Hodder & Stoughton, 1936.

———. *Credo die Hauptprobleme der Dogmatik dargestellt im Anschluss an das Apostolische Glaubensbekenntnis. 16 Vorlesungen, gehalten an der Universität Utrecht im Februar und März 1935.* 3rd ed. Munich: Kaiser, 1935.

———. "Die dogmatische Prinzipienlehre bei Wilhelm Herrmann." In *Vorträge und Kleinere Arbeiten 1922–1925,* edited by Holger Finze, pp. 545-603. Zurich: Theologischer Verlag, 1990.

———. *Ethics.* Translated by Geoffrey W. Bromiley. Edited by Dietrich Braun. Edinburgh: T & T Clark, 1981.

———. *Ethik I: Vorlesung Münster, Sommersemester 1928.* Edited by Dietrich Braun. Complete works 2, part 2, vol. 1. Zurich: Theologischer Verlag, 1973.

———. *Ethik II: Vorlesung Münster, Wintersemester 1928/29.* Edited by Dietrich Braun. Complete works 2, part 2, vol. 2. Zurich: Theologischer Verlag, 1978.

———. *Evangelical Theology: An Introduction.* Translated by Grover Foley. London: Weidenfeld & Nicolson, 1963.

———. "Fate and Idea in Theology." In Barth, *Way of Theology in Karl Barth,* pp. 25-61.

———. *Fides Quaerens Intellectum: Anselms Beweis der Existenz Gottes im Zusammenhang*

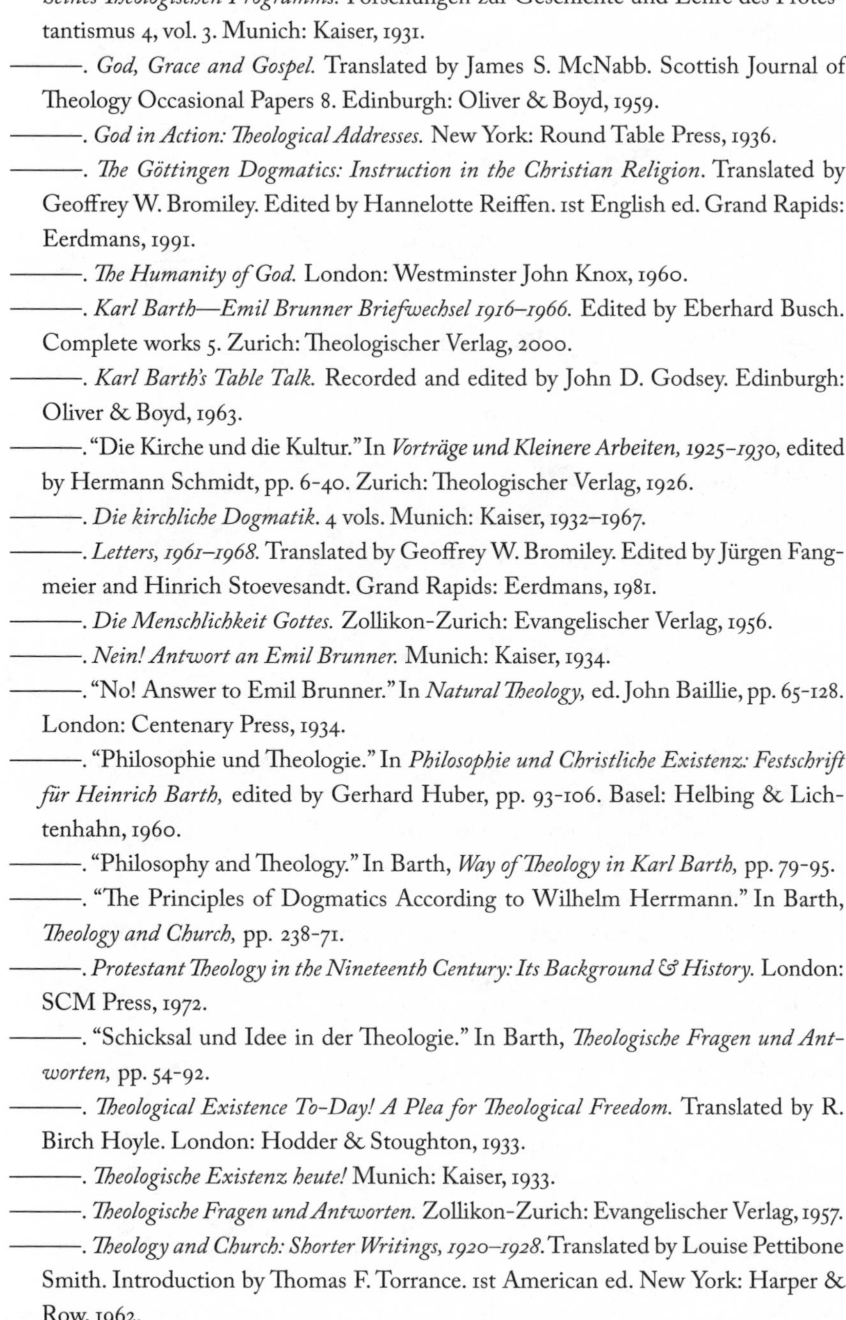

Seines Theologischen Programms. Forschungen zur Geschichte und Lehre des Protestantismus 4, vol. 3. Munich: Kaiser, 1931.

———. *God, Grace and Gospel.* Translated by James S. McNabb. Scottish Journal of Theology Occasional Papers 8. Edinburgh: Oliver & Boyd, 1959.

———. *God in Action: Theological Addresses.* New York: Round Table Press, 1936.

———. *The Göttingen Dogmatics: Instruction in the Christian Religion*. Translated by Geoffrey W. Bromiley. Edited by Hannelotte Reiffen. 1st English ed. Grand Rapids: Eerdmans, 1991.

———. *The Humanity of God.* London: Westminster John Knox, 1960.

———. *Karl Barth—Emil Brunner Briefwechsel 1916–1966.* Edited by Eberhard Busch. Complete works 5. Zurich: Theologischer Verlag, 2000.

———. *Karl Barth's Table Talk.* Recorded and edited by John D. Godsey. Edinburgh: Oliver & Boyd, 1963.

———. "Die Kirche und die Kultur." In *Vorträge und Kleinere Arbeiten, 1925–1930,* edited by Hermann Schmidt, pp. 6-40. Zurich: Theologischer Verlag, 1926.

———. *Die kirchliche Dogmatik*. 4 vols. Munich: Kaiser, 1932–1967.

———. *Letters, 1961–1968.* Translated by Geoffrey W. Bromiley. Edited by Jürgen Fangmeier and Hinrich Stoevesandt. Grand Rapids: Eerdmans, 1981.

———. *Die Menschlichkeit Gottes.* Zollikon-Zurich: Evangelischer Verlag, 1956.

———. *Nein! Antwort an Emil Brunner.* Munich: Kaiser, 1934.

———. "No! Answer to Emil Brunner." In *Natural Theology,* ed. John Baillie, pp. 65-128. London: Centenary Press, 1934.

———. "Philosophie und Theologie." In *Philosophie und Christliche Existenz: Festschrift für Heinrich Barth,* edited by Gerhard Huber, pp. 93-106. Basel: Helbing & Lichtenhahn, 1960.

———. "Philosophy and Theology." In Barth, *Way of Theology in Karl Barth,* pp. 79-95.

———. "The Principles of Dogmatics According to Wilhelm Herrmann." In Barth, *Theology and Church,* pp. 238-71.

———. *Protestant Theology in the Nineteenth Century: Its Background & History.* London: SCM Press, 1972.

———. "Schicksal und Idee in der Theologie." In Barth, *Theologische Fragen und Antworten,* pp. 54-92.

———. *Theological Existence To-Day! A Plea for Theological Freedom.* Translated by R. Birch Hoyle. London: Hodder & Stoughton, 1933.

———. *Theologische Existenz heute!* Munich: Kaiser, 1933.

———. *Theologische Fragen und Antworten.* Zollikon-Zurich: Evangelischer Verlag, 1957.

———. *Theology and Church: Shorter Writings, 1920–1928.* Translated by Louise Pettibone Smith. Introduction by Thomas F. Torrance. 1st American ed. New York: Harper & Row, 1962.

———. *The Theology of Schleiermacher: Lectures at Göttingen, Winter Semester of 1923–24.*

Translated by Geoffrey W. Bromiley. Edited by Dietrich Ritschl. Grand Rapids: Eerdmans, 1982.

———. *The Way of Theology in Karl Barth: Essays and Comments.* Edited by H. Martin Rumscheidt. Princeton Theological Monograph 8. Allison Park, PA: Pickwick, 1986.

Beale, G. K. *The Erosion of Inerrancy in Evangelicalism: Responding to New Challenges to Biblical Authority.* Wheaton, IL: Crossway, 2008.

Beilby, James K., ed. *Epistemology as Theology: An Evaluation of Alvin Plantinga's Religious Epistemology.* Aldershot, UK: Ashgate, 2005.

———, ed. *Naturalism Defeated? Essays on Plantinga's Evolutionary Argument Against Naturalism.* Ithaca, NY: Cornell University Press, 2002.

———. "Plantinga's Model of Warranted Christian Belief." In Baker, *Alvin Plantinga,* pp. 125-59.

Bender, John W., ed. *The Current State of the Coherence Theory: Critical Essays on the Epistemic Theories of Keith Lehrer and Laurence BonJour, with Replies.* Philosophical Studies 44. Dordrecht: Kluwer Academic, 1989.

Bergmann, Michael. "A Dilemma for Internalism." In Crisp, Davidson and Vander Laan, *Knowledge and Reality,* pp. 137-77.

———. "Evidentialism and the Great Pumpkin Objection." In Dougherty, *Evidentialism and Its Discontents,* pp. 123-33.

———. "Externalism and Skepticism." *The Philosophical Review* 109, no. 2 (2000): 159-94.

———. "Internalism, Externalism and the No-Defeater Condition." *Synthese* 110 (1997): 399-417.

———. *Justification Without Awareness: A Defense of Epistemic Externalism.* Oxford: Oxford University Press, 2006.

Berkhof, Louis. *Systematic Theology.* 4th rev. ed. Grand Rapids: Eerdmans, 1969.

Bernstein, Richard J. *Beyond Objectivism and Relativism: Science, Hermeneutics, and Praxis.* Philadelphia: University of Pennsylvania Press, 1983.

Beversluis, John. "Reforming the 'Reformed' Objection to Natural Theology." *Faith and Philosophy* 12, no. 2 (1995): 189-206.

Blanshard, Brand. "Critical Reflections on Karl Barth." In Hick, *Faith and the Philosophers,* pp. 159-200.

Bockmuehl, Markus, and Alan J. Torrance, eds. *Scripture's Doctrine and Theology's Bible: How the New Testament Shapes Christian Dogmatics.* Grand Rapids: Baker Academic, 2008.

Bonhoeffer, Dietrich. *Gesammelte Schriften.* 4 vols. Munich: Kaiser, 1958.

———. *Letters and Papers from Prison.* Edited by Eberhard Bethge. Enlarged ed. London: SCM Press, 1971.

BonJour, Laurence. "Can Empirical Knowledge Have a Foundation?" *American Philosophical Quarterly* 15, no. 1 (1978): 1-14.

———. "Externalism/Internalism." In Dancy and Sosa, *Companion to Epistemology,* pp. 132-36.

———. *In Defense of Pure Reason: A Rationalist Account of a Priori Justification.* Cambridge Studies in Philosophy. Cambridge: Cambridge University Press, 1998.

———. *The Structure of Empirical Knowledge.* Cambridge, MA: Harvard University Press, 1985.

Bouillard, Henri. *The Knowledge of God.* Translated by Samuel D. Femiano. London: Burns & Oates, 1969.

Brazier, Paul. "Barth's First Commentary on Romans (1919): An Exercise in Apophatic Theology?" *International Journal of Systematic Theology* 6, no. 4 (2004): 387-403.

Bromiley, Geoffrey W. "Karl Barth." In *Creative Minds in Contemporary Theology,* edited by Philip Edgcumbe Hughes, pp. 27-59. Grand Rapids: Eerdmans, 1966.

Brown, David. *Tradition and Imagination: Revelation and Change.* Oxford: Oxford University Press, 1999.

Brown, Hunter. "Plantinga and Natural Theology." *International Journal for Philosophy of Religion* 30 (1991): 1-19.

Brunner, Emil. "Die andere Aufgabe der Theologie." *Zwischen den Zeiten* 7 (1929): 255-76.

———. *Natur und Gnade: Zum Gespräch mit Karl Barth.* Tübingen: Mohr, 1934.

———. "Nature and Grace." In *Natural Theology,* edited by John Baillie, pp. 15-64. London: Centenary, 1934.

Burnett, Richard. *Karl Barth's Theological Exegesis: The Hermeneutical Principles of the Römerbrief Period.* Grand Rapids: Eerdmans, 2004.

Busch, Eberhard. *The Great Passion: An Introduction to Karl Barth's Theology.* Edited by Darrell L. Guder and Judith J. Guder. Translated by Geoffrey W. Bromiley. Grand Rapids: Eerdmans, 2004.

———. *Karl Barths Lebenslauf: Nach seinen Briefen und autobiographischen Texten.* 2nd rev. ed. Munich: Kaiser, 1976.

Calvin, John. *Institutes of the Christian Religion.* Edited by John T. McNeill. Translated by Ford Lewis Battles. 2 vols. Library of Christian Classics 20-21. London: SCM Press, 1961.

Chavannes, Henry. *L'Analogie entre Dieu et le monde selon Saint Thomas d'Aquin et selon Karl Barth.* Cogitatio Fidei 42. Paris: Éditions du Cerf, 1969.

Chignell, Andrew. "Epistemology for Saints." *Books & Culture* 8, no. 2 (2002): 20-21.

Chisholm, Roderick M. *The Foundations of Knowing.* Brighton, UK: Harvester Press, 1982.

———. *The Problem of the Criterion.* Aquinas Lecture. Milwaukee: Marquette University Press, 1973.

———. *Theory of Knowledge.* Foundations of Philosophy. Englewood Cliffs, NJ: Prentice-Hall, 1966.

Clark, David K. "Faith and Foundationalism." In Moser and Copan, *Rationality of Theism,* pp. 35-54.

Clark, Kelly J. "Plantinga vs. Oliphint: And the Winner Is . . ." *Calvin Theological Journal* 33 (1998): 160-69.

Conee, Earl. "The Basic Nature of Epistemic Justification." *Monist* 71, no. 3 (1988): 389-404.

Conee, Earl, and Richard Feldman. "Evidentialism." *Philosophical Studies* 48, no. 1 (1985): 15-34.

Crisp, Oliver D. "*Ad* Hector." *Journal of Analytic Theology* 1, no. 1 (2013): 133-39.

———. *Divinity and Humanity: The Incarnation Reconsidered.* Cambridge: Cambridge University Press, 2007.

Crisp, Oliver D., and Michael C. Rea, eds. *Analytic Theology: New Essays in the Philosophy of Theology*. Oxford: Oxford University Press, 2009.

Crisp, Thomas M., Matthew Davidson and David Vander Laan, eds. *Knowledge and Reality: Essays in Honor of Alvin Plantinga.* Dordrecht: Kluwer Academic, 2006.

Cupitt, Don. "Anti-Realist Faith." In *Is God Real?* edited by Joseph Runzo, pp. 44-55. London: Palgrave Macmillan, 1993.

Dancy, Jonathan, and Ernest Sosa, eds. *A Companion to Epistemology.* Blackwell Companions to Philosophy. Cambridge, MA: Blackwell Reference, 1992.

Davidson, Donald. "Truth Rehabilitated." In *Rorty and His Critics,* edited by Robert Brandom, pp. 65-74. Oxford: Blackwell, 2000.

Davies, Brian. *An Introduction to the Philosophy of Religion.* 2nd ed. Oxford: Oxford University Press, 1993.

Davis, Stephen T. *Christian Philosophical Theology.* Oxford: Oxford University Press, 2006.

Deddo, Gary W. *Karl Barth's Theology of Relations: Trinitarian, Christological, and Human; Towards an Ethic of the Family.* Issues in Systematic Theology 4. New York: Lang, 1999.

Descartes, René. *Meditations on First Philosophy.* Translated by John Cottingham. Rev. ed. Cambridge: Cambridge University Press, 1996.

Diller, Kevin. "Does Contemporary Theology Require a Postfoundationalist Way of Knowing?" *Scottish Journal of Theology* 60, no. 3 (2007): 1-23.

Dole, Andrew. "Cognitive Faculties, Cognitive Processes, and the Holy Spirit in Plantinga's Warrant Series." Review of *Warrant and Proper Function* and *Warranted Christian Belief,* by Alvin Plantinga. *Faith and Philosophy* 19 (2002): 32-46.

Dougherty, Trent, ed. *Evidentialism and Its Discontents.* Oxford: Oxford University Press, 2011.

Dowey, Edward A. *The Knowledge of God in Calvin's Theology.* New York: Columbia University Press, 1952.

Duhem, Pierre. *The Aim and Structure of Physical Theory.* Princeton, NJ: Princeton University Press, 1954.

Dulles, Avery Robert. *Models of Revelation.* Garden City, NY: Doubleday, 1983.

Dupré, Louis. "Reflections on the Truth of Religion." *Faith and Philosophy* 6, no. 3 (1989): 260-74.

Enns, Peter. "Further Thoughts on an Incarnational Model of Scripture." Paper presented at the annual Logos Workshop, Center for Philosophy of Religion at the University of Notre Dame, June 2-4, 2011.

———. *Inspiration and Incarnation: Evangelicals and the Problem of the Old Testament.* Grand Rapids: Baker Academic, 2005.

Evans, C. Stephen. "Faith and Reason." In *The Oxford Handbook of Philosophy of Religion*, edited by William J. Wainwright, pp. 323-43. New York: Oxford University Press, 2005.

———. *Faith Beyond Reason: A Kierkegaardian Account.* Grand Rapids: Eerdmans, 1998.

———. *The Historical Christ and the Jesus of Faith: The Incarnational Narrative as History.* Oxford: Oxford University Press, 1996.

Evans, C. Stephen, and Merold Westphal, eds. *Christian Perspectives on Religious Knowledge.* Grand Rapids: Eerdmans, 1993.

Fales, Evan. Review of *Warranted Christian Belief,* by Alvin Plantinga. *Noûs* 37, no. 2 (2003): 353-70.

Feldman, Richard. "Proper Functionalism." *Noûs* 27, no. 1 (1993): 34-50.

Feuerbach, Ludwig. *The Essence of Christianity.* Translated by George Eliot. New York: Harper, 1957.

Fisher, Simon. *Revelatory Positivism? Barth's Earliest Theology and the Marburg School.* Oxford Theological Monographs. Oxford: Oxford University Press, 1988.

Flew, Antony. *The Presumption of Atheism and Other Philosophical Essays on God, Freedom, and Immortality.* New York: Barnes & Noble, 1976.

Fogelin, Robert J. *Pyrrhonian Reflections on Knowledge and Justification.* Oxford: Oxford University Press, 1994.

Franke, John R. "Barth *Redivivus:* Karl Barth, Postmodernity, and Evangelical Theology." Paper presented at the annual meeting of the Evangelical Theological Society, Toronto, November 20, 2002.

———. "The Postfoundationalist Task of Theology: Wolfhart Pannenberg and the New Theological Rationality." *Interpretation* 55 (2001): 214.

———. "Postmodern and Reformed? A Response to Professors Trueman and Gaffin." *Westminster Theological Journal* 65 (2003): 331-43.

———. "Postmodern Evangelical Theology: A Nonfoundationalist Approach to the Christian Faith." In *Alister E. McGrath and Evangelical Theology: A Dynamic Engagement,* edited by Sung Wook Chung, pp. 280-309. Carlisle, UK: Paternoster, 2003.

———. "Reforming Theology: Toward a Postmodern Reformed Dogmatics." *Westminster Theological Journal* 65 (2003): 1-26.

Fumerton, Richard A. *Metaepistemology and Skepticism.* Lanham, MD: Rowman & Littlefield, 1995.

———. "Plantinga, Warrant, and Christian Belief." *Philosophia Christi* 3, no. 2 (2001): 341-52.

Garcia, Laura L. "Natural Theology and the Reformed Objection." In Evans and Westphal, *Christian Perspectives on Religious Knowledge,* pp. 112-33.

Geivett, R. Douglas, and Greg Jesson. "Plantinga's Externalism and the Terminus of Warrant-Based Epistemology." *Philosophia Christi* 3, no. 2 (2001): 329-40.

Gettier, Edmund. "Is Justified True Belief Knowledge?" *Analysis* 23, no. 6 (1963): 121-23.

Goetz, Stan. "Belief in God Is Not Properly Basic." *Religious Studies* 19 (1983): 475-84.

Goldman, Alvin. "Internalism Exposed." *Journal of Philosophy* 96 (1999): 271-93.

Graham, Gordon. "The Philosopher: A Christian Philosopher in a Theological Seminary." In *The Long Shadow of Emile Cailliet: Faith, Philosophy, and Theological Education,* edited by Abigail Rian Evans and Clemens Bartollas, pp. 123-38. Eugene, OR: Wipf & Stock, 2011.

Greene, Richard, and N. A. Balmert. "Two Notions of Warrant and Plantinga's Solution to the Gettier Problem." *Analysis* 57, no. 2 (1997): 132-39.

Grene, Marjorie. *The Knower and the Known.* London: Faber & Faber, 1966.

Grenz, Stanley, and John R. Franke. *Beyond Foundationalism: Shaping Theology in a Postmodern Context.* Louisville, KY: Westminster John Knox, 2001.

Grigg, Richard. "The Crucial Disanalogies Between Properly Basic Belief and Belief in God." *Religious Studies* 26 (1990): 389-401.

Groothuis, Douglas R. "Warranted Christian Belief." Review of *Warranted Christian Belief,* by Alvin Plantinga. *Journal of the Evangelical Theological Society* 45 (2002): 178-82.

Gundry, Robert. "Smithereens! Bible-Reading and 'Pervasive Interpretive Pluralism.'" *Books & Culture,* September/October 2011, pp. 9-11.

Gunton, Colin E. *Act and Being: Towards a Theology of the Divine Attributes.* Grand Rapids: Eerdmans, 2003.

———. *A Brief Theology of Revelation.* Edinburgh: T & T Clark, 1995.

Guretzki, David. "Barth, Derrida and *Différance:* Is There a Difference?" *Didaskalia* 13, no. 2 (2002): 51-71.

Haack, Susan. *Evidence and Inquiry: Towards Reconstruction in Epistemology.* Oxford: Blackwell, 1993.

Harris, Harriet A. "Does Analytical Philosophy Clip Our Wings? Reformed Theology as a Test Case." In Harris and Insole, *Faith and Philosophical Analysis,* pp. 100-118.

Harris, Harriet A., and Christopher J. Insole, eds. *Faith and Philosophical Analysis: The Impact of Analytical Philosophy on the Philosophy of Religion.* Aldershot, UK: Ashgate, 2005.

Hart, John W. "The Barth-Brunner Correspondence." In Hunsinger, *For the Sake of the World,* pp. 19-43.

Hart, Kevin. "The Experience of God." In *The Religious,* edited by John D. Caputo, pp. 159-74. Blackwell Readings in Continental Philosophy. Malden, MA: Blackwell, 2002.

Hart, Trevor A. "Karl Barth, the Trinity, and Pluralism." In *The Trinity in a Pluralistic Age: Theological Essays on Culture and Religion,* edited by Kevin J. Vanhoozer, pp. 124-42. Grand Rapids: Eerdmans, 1997.

———. *Regarding Karl Barth: Essays Toward a Reading of His Theology.* Carlisle, UK: Paternoster, 1999.

———. "Revelation." In Webster, *Cambridge Companion to Karl Barth,* pp. 37-56.

Hebblethwaite, Brian. *Philosophical Theology and Christian Doctrine.* Oxford: Blackwell, 2005.

Hector, Kevin. "Responses to *JAT*'s Symposium on *Theology Without Metaphysics." Journal of Analytic Theology* 1, no. 1 (2013): 140-47.

———. *Theology Without Metaphysics: God, Language and the Spirit of Recognition.* New York: Cambridge University Press, 2011.

Helm, Paul. *Belief Policies.* Cambridge Studies in Philosophy. Cambridge: Cambridge University Press, 1994.

———. *The Divine Revelation: The Basic Issues.* Foundations for Faith. Westchester, IL: Crossway, 1982.

———. *Faith and Understanding.* Reason and Religion. Edinburgh: Edinburgh University Press, 1997.

———. *Faith with Reason.* Oxford: Oxford University Press, 2003.

———. Review of *Warrant: The Current Debate* and *Warrant and Proper Function,* by Alvin Plantinga. *Religious Studies* 31 (1995): 129-33.

———. Review of *Warranted Christian Belief,* by Alvin Plantinga. *Mind* 110, no. 440 (2001): 1110-15.

Henry, Carl F. H. *God, Revelation, and Authority.* Vol. 4. Waco, TX: Word Books, 1979.

Heron, Alasdair I. C. "Homoousios with the Father." In Torrance, *Incarnation,* pp. 58-87.

Herrmann, Wilhelm. *Die Gewissheit des Glaubens und die Freiheit der Theologie.* 2nd rev. ed. Freiburg im Breisgau: Mohr, 1889.

———. *Der Verkehr des Christen mit Gott: Im Anschluss an Luther dargestellt.* 2nd completely rev. ed. Stuttgart: Cotta, 1892.

———. *Warum bedarf unser Glaube geschichtlicher Thatsachen? Vortrag zur Feier des 22. März 1884 in Marburg gehalten.* 2nd ed. Halle: Niemeyer, 1891.

Hick, John, ed. *Faith and the Philosophers.* London: Macmillan, 1964.

Hilpinen, Risto. "Knowing That One Knows and the Classical Definition of Knowledge." *Synthese* 21, no. 2 (1970): 109-32.

Hintikka, Jaakko. *Knowledge and Belief: An Introduction to the Logic of the Two Notions.* Contemporary Philosophy. Ithaca, NY: Cornell University Press, 1962.

Hoitenga, Dewey J., Jr. "Christian Theism: Ultimate Reality and Meaning in the Philosophy of Alvin Plantinga." *Ultimate Reality and Meaning* 23, no. 3 (2000): 211-37.

———. *Faith and Reason from Plato to Plantinga: An Introduction to Reformed Epistemology.* Albany: State University of New York Press, 1991.

Hunsinger, George. *Disruptive Grace: Studies in the Theology of Karl Barth.* Grand Rapids: Eerdmans, 2000.

———, ed. *For the Sake of the World: Karl Barth and the Future of Ecclesial Theology.* Grand Rapids: Eerdmans, 2004.

———. *How to Read Karl Barth: The Shape of His Theology.* New York: Oxford University Press, 1991.

———. "The Mediator of Communion: Karl Barth's Doctrine of the Holy Spirit." In Webster, *Cambridge Companion to Karl Barth,* pp. 177-94.

Insole, Christopher J. "Political Liberalism, Analytical Philosophy of Religion and the Forgetting of History." In Harris and Insole, *Faith and Philosophical Analysis,* pp. 158-70.

———. *The Realist Hope: A Critique of Anti-Realist Approaches in Contemporary Philosophical Theology.* Aldershot, UK: Ashgate, 2006.

Jäger, Christoph. "Warrant, Defeaters, and the Epistemic Basis of Religious Belief." In *Scientific Explanation and Religious Belief,* edited by Michael Parker and Thomas Schmidt. Tübingen: Mohr Siebeck, 2005.

Jantzen, Grace M. *Becoming Divine: Towards a Feminist Philosophy of Religion.* Manchester: Manchester University Press, 1998.

Janz, Paul D. *God, the Mind's Desire: Reference, Reason and Christian Thinking.* Cambridge Studies in Christian Doctrine. Cambridge: Cambridge University Press, 2004.

Jaspert, Bernd, and Geoffrey W. Bromiley, eds. *Karl Barth-Rudolf Bultmann Letters, 1922–1966.* Grand Rapids: Eerdmans, 1981.

Jeffreys, Derek S. "How Reformed Is Reformed Epistemology? Alvin Plantinga and Calvin's 'Sensus Divinitatis.'" *Religious Studies* 33 (1997): 419-31.

Jenson, Robert W. "What If It Were True?" *CTI Reflections* 4 (2001): 2-21.

Johannesson, Karin. *God Pro Nobis: On Non-Metaphysical Realism and the Philosophy of Religion.* Leuven: Peeters, 2007.

Johnson, Keith L. *Karl Barth and the* Analogia Entis. London: T & T Clark, 2012.

Johnson, William Stacy. *The Mystery of God: Karl Barth and the Postmodern Foundations of Theology.* Louisville, KY: Westminster John Knox, 1997.

Jüngel, Eberhard. "Die Möglichkeit theologischer Anthropologie auf dem Grunde der Analogie." In *Barth-Studien,* pp. 210-32. Gütersloh: Mohn, 1982.

———. *Theological Essays II.* Edited by John B. Webster. Translated by Arnold Neufeldt-Fast and John B. Webster. Edinburgh: T & T Clark, 1995.

Kant, Immanuel. *Critique of Pure Reason.* Translated by Norman Kemp Smith. Rev. 2nd ed. New York: Palgrave Macmillan, 2003. Originally published as *Kritik der reinen Vernunft* (1st ed., 1781; 2nd ed., 1787).

Kasper, Walter. *The God of Jesus Christ.* Translated by Matthew J. O'Connell. New York: Crossroad, 1984.

———. *Der Gott Jesu Christi.* Glaubensbekenntnis der Kirche 1. Mainz: Matthias-Grünewald-Verlag, 1982.

Kerr, Fergus. *After Aquinas: Versions of Thomism.* Malden, MA: Blackwell, 2002.

Kierkegaard, Søren. *Philosophical Fragments by Johannes Climacus.* Translated by Howard V. Hong and Edna H. Hong. Princeton, NJ: Princeton University Press, 1985. Originally published as *Philosophiske Smuler eller Smule Philosophi* under the pseudonym Johannes Climacus in 1844.

King, Rolfe. *Obstacles to Divine Revelation: God and the Reorientation of Human Reason.* New York: Continuum, 2008.

Klein, Peter D. *Certainty: A Refutation of Scepticism.* Minneapolis: University of Minnesota Press, 1981.

Kretzmann, Norman. *The Metaphysics of Theism: Aquinas's Natural Theology in Summa Contra Gentiles I.* Oxford: Oxford University Press, 1997.

Kuhn, Thomas. *The Structure of Scientific Revolutions.* Chicago: University of Chicago Press, 1962.

Kuyper, Abraham. *Encyclopedia of Sacred Theology: Its Principles.* London: Hodder & Stoughton, 1899.

Kvanvig, Jonathan L. "The Evidentialist Objection." *American Philosophical Quarterly* 20 (1983): 47-55.

———. "In Defense of Coherentism." *Journal of Philosophical Research* 22 (1997): 299-306.

———. *The Value of Knowledge and the Pursuit of Understanding.* Cambridge Studies in Philosophy. Cambridge: Cambridge University Press, 2003.

———, ed. *Warrant in Contemporary Epistemology: Essays in Honor of Plantinga's Theory of Knowledge.* Lanham, MD: Rowman & Littlefield, 1996.

Le Morvan, Pierre, and Dana Radcliffe. "Notes on Warranted Christian Belief." *Heythrop Journal* 44, no. 3 (2003): 345-51.

Lindbeck, George A. *The Nature of Doctrine: Religion and Theology in a Postliberal Age.* Philadelphia: Westminster, 1984.

Lubac, Henri de. *The Mystery of the Supernatural.* Translated by Rosemary Sheed. London: Chapman, 1967.

Lyotard, Jean-François. *The Postmodern Condition: A Report on Knowledge.* Minneapolis: University of Minnesota Press, 1979.

MacDonald, Neil B. *Karl Barth and the Strange New World Within the Bible: Barth, Wittgenstein, and the Metadilemmas of the Enlightenment.* Carlisle, UK: Paternoster, 2000.

Macquarrie, John. *Principles of Christian Theology.* 2nd ed. New York: Scribner, 1977.

Markham, Ian. Review of *Warranted Christian Belief,* by Alvin Plantinga. *Expository Times* 112 (2001): 244.

Marsh, James L. *Post-Cartesian Meditations: An Essay in Dialectical Phenomenology.* New York: Fordham University Press, 1988.

Marshall, Bruce. *Trinity and Truth.* Cambridge Studies in Christian Doctrine. Cambridge: Cambridge University Press, 2000.

Mascord, Keith A. *Alvin Plantinga and Christian Apologetics.* Milton Keynes, UK: Paternoster, 2006.

McCall, Thomas H. "Understanding Scripture as the Word of God." In Crisp and Rea, *Analytic Theology,* pp. 171-86.

McCormack, Bruce L. "The Being of Holy Scripture Is in Becoming: Karl Barth in Conversation with American Evangelical Criticism." In *Evangelicals and Scripture: Tradition, Authority and Hermeneutics,* edited by Vincent Bacote, Laura Miguélez and Dennis Okholm, pp. 53-75. Downers Grove, IL: InterVarsity Press, 2004.

———. "Graham Ward's Barth, Derrida and the Language of Theology." *Scottish Journal of Theology* 49, no. 1 (1996): 97-109.

———. *Karl Barth's Critically Realistic Dialectical Theology: Its Genesis and Development, 1909–1936.* Oxford: Oxford University Press, 1995.

———. "Revelation and History in Transfoundationalist Perspective: Karl Barth's Theological Epistemology in Conversation with a Schleiermacherian Tradition." *Journal of Religion* 78 (1998): 18-37.

McFarlane, Andrew. "Sense and Spontaneity: A Critical Study of Barth's Kantian Model of Human Cognition in *CD* II/1." Paper presented at the Scottish Barth Colloquium, St Andrews University, St Mary's College, March 6, 2006.

McGrew, Timothy, and Lydia McGrew. "On the Historical Argument: A Rejoinder to Plantinga." *Philosophia Christi* 8, no. 1 (2006): 23-38.

———. "Strong Foundationalism and Bayesianism." Paper presented at the Formal Epistemology Workshop, UC-Berkeley, May 25-28, 2006.

Meek, Esther L. *Longing to Know.* Grand Rapids: Brazos Press, 2003.

———. "Michael Polanyi and Alvin Plantinga." *Philosophia Christi* 14, no. 1 (2012): 57-77.

Migliore, Daniel L. "Response to the Barth-Brunner Correspondence." In Hunsinger, *For the Sake of the World,* pp. 44-51.

Milbank, John, Catherine Pickstock and Graham Ward, eds. *Radical Orthodoxy: A New Theology.* London: Routledge, 1999.

Moltmann, Jürgen. *The Trinity and the Kingdom: The Doctrine of God.* San Francisco: Harper & Row, 1981.

Mondin, Battista. *The Principle of Analogy in Protestant and Catholic Theology.* The Hague: Nijhoff, 1963.

Moore, G. E. *Philosophical Papers.* New York: Collier Books, 1967.

———. *Some Main Problems of Philosophy.* New York: Humanities Press, 1953.

Moreland, James P., and William Lane Craig. *Philosophical Foundations for a Christian Worldview.* Downers Grove, IL: InterVarsity Press, 2003.

Morrison, John D. "Thomas Torrance's Reformulation of Karl Barth's Christological Rejection of Natural Theology." *Evangelical Quarterly* 72 (2000): 59-75.

Moser, Paul K. *The Elusive God.* New York: Cambridge University Press, 2008.

———. *Empirical Justification.* Philosophical Studies Series in Philosophy 34. Dordrecht: D. Reidel, 1985.

———. *Knowledge and Evidence.* Cambridge Studies in Philosophy. Cambridge: Cambridge University Press, 1989.

———. "Man to Man with *Warranted Christian Belief* and Alvin Plantinga." *Philosophia Christi* 3, no. 2 (2001): 369-78.

Moser, Paul K., and Paul Copan, eds. *The Rationality of Theism.* London: Routledge, 2003.

Mourad, Ronney B. "Review: Proper Function and Justified Christian Belief." *Journal of Religion* 81, no. 4 (2001): 615-27.

Murphy, Nancey. *Beyond Liberalism and Fundamentalism: How Modern and Postmodern Philosophy Set the Theological Agenda.* Rockwell Lecture Series. Valley Forge, PA: Trinity Press International, 1996.

———. "Theology and Scientific Methodology." In *Philosophy of Religion: Selected Readings,* edited by Michael Peterson, William Hasker, Bruce Reichenbach and David Basinger, pp. 513-30. Oxford: Oxford University Press, 2001.

Nichols, Aidan. *The Shape of Catholic Theology: An Introduction to Its Sources, Principles, and History.* Collegeville, MN: Liturgical Press, 1991.

Niebuhr, H. Richard. *The Meaning of Revelation.* New York: Macmillan, 1941.

Nietzsche, Friedrich. *Will to Power.* Translated by Walter Kaufmann and R. J. Hollingdale. New York: Random House, 1967.

Oakes, Kenneth. *Karl Barth on Theology and Philosophy.* Oxford: Oxford University Press, 2012.

Olson, Roger E. *Reformed and Always Reforming.* Grand Rapids: Baker Academic, 2007.

Oppy, Graham. "Natural Theology." In Baker, *Alvin Plantinga,* pp. 15-47.

Pannenberg, Wolfhart. *Basic Questions in Theology: Collected Essays.* Translated by George H. Kehm. 2 vols. Philadelphia: Fortress, 1970–1971.

———, ed. *Offenbarung als Geschichte.* Göttingen: Vandenhoeck & Ruprecht, 1965.

———. "Die Subjectivität Gottes und die Trinitätslehre: Ein Beitrag zur Beziehen zwischen Karl Barth und der Philosophie Hegels." In *Grundfragen systematischer Theologie: Gesammelte Aufsätze,* 2:96-111. Göttingen: Vandenhoeck & Ruprecht, 1980.

———. *Theology and the Philosophy of Science.* Philadelphia: Westminster, 1976.

Parker, T. H. L. *The Doctrine of the Knowledge of God: A Study in the Theology of John Calvin.* Edinburgh: Oliver & Boyd, 1952.

Patfoort, Albert. "Vers une réconciliation entre saint Thomas et Karl Barth." *Angelicum* 48 (1971): 226-32.

Penelhum, Terence. *God and Skepticism: A Study in Skepticism and Fideism.* Philosophical Studies Series in Philosophy 28. Dordrecht: D. Reidel, 1983.

Phillips, D. Z. "Advice to Philosophers Who Are Christians." *New Blackfriars* 69, no. 820 (1988): 416-30.

Pironet, Fabienne, and Christine Tappolet. "Faiblesse de la raison ou faiblesse de volonté: Peut-on choisir?" *Dialogue* 42 (2003): 627-44.

Plantinga, Alvin. "Advice to Christian Philosophers." *Faith and Philosophy* 1, no. 3 (1984): 253-71.

———. "Augustinian Christian Philosophy." *Monist* 75, no. 3 (1992): 291-320.

———. "The Boethian Compromise." *American Philosophical Quarterly* 15, no. 2 (1978): pp. 129-138.
———. "A Christian Life Partly Lived." In *Philosophers Who Believe: The Spiritual Journeys of 11 Leading Thinkers,* edited by Kelly James Clark, pp. 45-82. Downers Grove, IL: InterVarsity Press, 1993.
———. "Christian Philosophy at the End of the Twentieth Century." In *Christian Philosophy at the Close of the Twentieth Century: Assessment and Perspective,* edited by Sander Griffioen and Bert M. Balk, pp. 29-53. Kampen, Netherlands: Uitgeverij Kok, 1995.
———. "De re et de dicto." *Noûs* 3, no. 3 (1969): 235-58.
———. "Divine Knowledge." In Evans and Westphal, *Christian Perspectives on Religious Knowledge,* pp. 40-65.
———. *Does God Have a Nature?* Aquinas Lecture, 1980. Milwaukee: Marquette University Press, 1980.
———. "Epistemic Justification." *Noûs* 20, no. 1 (1986): 3-18.
———. "Epistemic Probability and Evil." *Archivio di Filosofia* 56 (1988): 557-84.
———. "Faith & Reason: A Response to Pope John Paul II's Encyclical Letter, *Fides et Ratio.*" *Books & Culture* 5, no. 4 (1999): 20-32.
———. "The Foundations of Theism: A Reply." *Faith and Philosophy* 3, no. 3 (1986): 298-313.
———. *God and Other Minds: A Study of the Rational Justification of Belief in God.* Contemporary Philosophy. Ithaca, NY: Cornell University Press, 1967.
———. "How to Be an Anti-Realist." *Proceedings and Addresses of the American Philosophical Association* 56, no. 1 (1982): 47-70.
———. "Internalism, Externalism, Defeaters and Arguments for Christian Belief." *Philosophia Christi* 3, no. 2 (2001): 379-402.
———. "Is Belief in God Properly Basic?" *Noûs* 15 (1981): 41-51.
———. "Is Belief in God Rational?" In *Rationality and Religious Belief,* edited by C. F. Delaney, pp. 7-27. Notre Dame, IN: University of Notre Dame Press, 1979.
———. "Justification and Theism." *Faith and Philosophy* 4, no. 4 (1987): 403-26.
———. "Justification in the 20th Century." *Philosophy and Phenomenological Research* 50, supplement (1990): 45-71.
———. "Natural Theology." In *A Companion to Metaphysics,* edited by Jaegwon Kim and Ernest Sosa, pp. 346-49. Oxford: Blackwell, 1995.
———. *The Nature of Necessity.* Clarendon Library of Logic and Philosophy. Oxford: Oxford University Press, 1974.
———. "On Christian Scholarship." In *The Challenge and Promise of a Catholic University,* edited by Theodore Hesburgh, pp. 267-95. Notre Dame, IN: University of Notre Dame Press, 1994.
———. "On Heresy, Mind, and Truth." *Faith and Philosophy* 16, no. 2 (1999): 182-93.
———. *"Our Vision": Calvin College Commencement Address, May 20, 2000.* DVD. Grand Rapids: Calvin College, 2000.

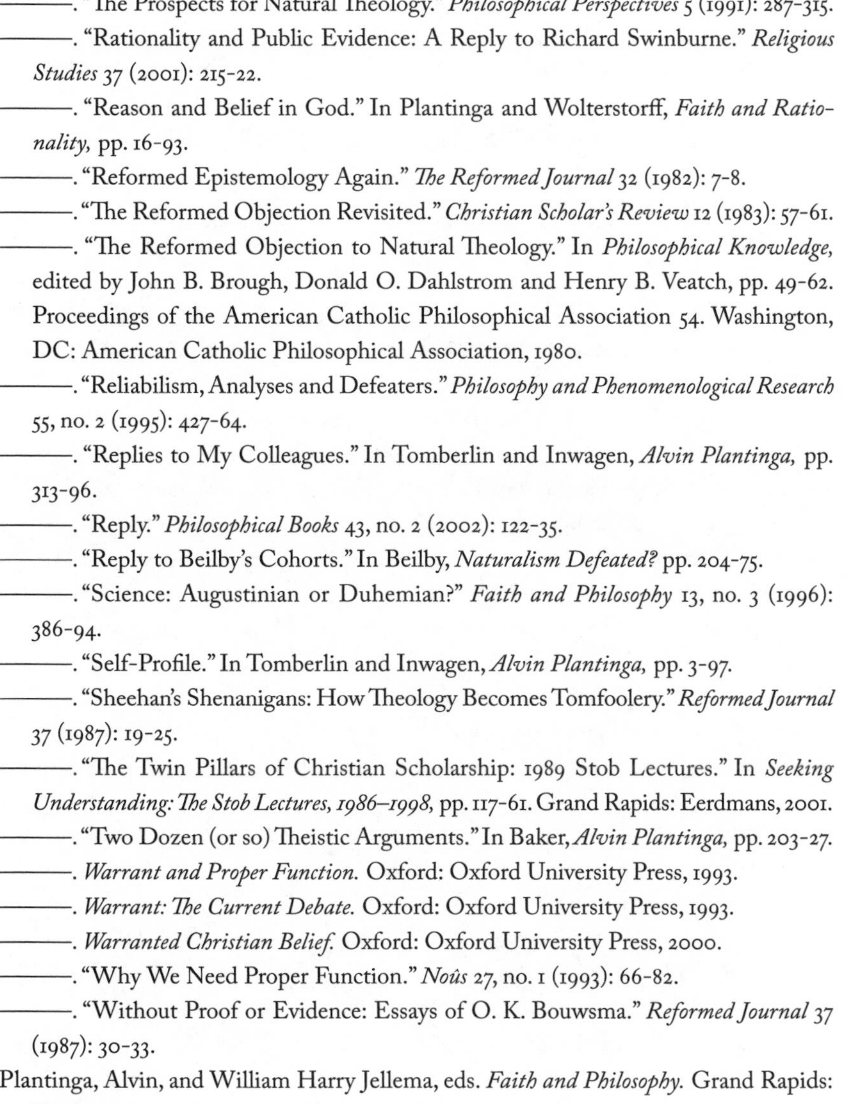

———. "The Prospects for Natural Theology." *Philosophical Perspectives* 5 (1991): 287-315.

———. "Rationality and Public Evidence: A Reply to Richard Swinburne." *Religious Studies* 37 (2001): 215-22.

———. "Reason and Belief in God." In Plantinga and Wolterstorff, *Faith and Rationality*, pp. 16-93.

———. "Reformed Epistemology Again." *The Reformed Journal* 32 (1982): 7-8.

———. "The Reformed Objection Revisited." *Christian Scholar's Review* 12 (1983): 57-61.

———. "The Reformed Objection to Natural Theology." In *Philosophical Knowledge*, edited by John B. Brough, Donald O. Dahlstrom and Henry B. Veatch, pp. 49-62. Proceedings of the American Catholic Philosophical Association 54. Washington, DC: American Catholic Philosophical Association, 1980.

———. "Reliabilism, Analyses and Defeaters." *Philosophy and Phenomenological Research* 55, no. 2 (1995): 427-64.

———. "Replies to My Colleagues." In Tomberlin and Inwagen, *Alvin Plantinga*, pp. 313-96.

———. "Reply." *Philosophical Books* 43, no. 2 (2002): 122-35.

———. "Reply to Beilby's Cohorts." In Beilby, *Naturalism Defeated?* pp. 204-75.

———. "Science: Augustinian or Duhemian?" *Faith and Philosophy* 13, no. 3 (1996): 386-94.

———. "Self-Profile." In Tomberlin and Inwagen, *Alvin Plantinga*, pp. 3-97.

———. "Sheehan's Shenanigans: How Theology Becomes Tomfoolery." *Reformed Journal* 37 (1987): 19-25.

———. "The Twin Pillars of Christian Scholarship: 1989 Stob Lectures." In *Seeking Understanding: The Stob Lectures, 1986–1998*, pp. 117-61. Grand Rapids: Eerdmans, 2001.

———. "Two Dozen (or so) Theistic Arguments." In Baker, *Alvin Plantinga*, pp. 203-27.

———. *Warrant and Proper Function.* Oxford: Oxford University Press, 1993.

———. *Warrant: The Current Debate.* Oxford: Oxford University Press, 1993.

———. *Warranted Christian Belief.* Oxford: Oxford University Press, 2000.

———. "Why We Need Proper Function." *Noûs* 27, no. 1 (1993): 66-82.

———. "Without Proof or Evidence: Essays of O. K. Bouwsma." *Reformed Journal* 37 (1987): 30-33.

Plantinga, Alvin, and William Harry Jellema, eds. *Faith and Philosophy.* Grand Rapids: Eerdmans, 1964.

Plantinga, Alvin, and Nicholas Wolterstorff, eds. *Faith and Rationality: Reason and Belief in God.* Notre Dame, IN: University of Notre Dame Press, 1983.

Plato. *Meno.* Translated by R. W. Sharples. Warminster, UK: Aris & Phillips, 1985.

Polanyi, Michael. *Knowing and Being: Essays.* Edited by Marjorie Glicksman Grene. London: Routledge & Kegan Paul, 1969.

———. *Personal Knowledge: Towards a Post-Critical Philosophy.* London: Routledge & Kegan Paul, 1958.

———. *The Tacit Dimension.* Gloucester, MA: Peter Smith, 1983.

Pollock, John L. *Contemporary Theories of Knowledge.* Rowman & Littlefield Texts in Philosophy. Totowa, NJ: Rowman & Littlefield, 1986.

———. "The Structure of Epistemic Justification." *American Philosophical Quarterly* monograph series 4 (1970): 62-78.

Pollock, John L., and Joseph Cruz. *Contemporary Theories of Knowledge.* 2nd ed. Lanham, MD: Rowman & Littlefield, 1999.

Popper, Karl. *Conjectures and Refutations: The Growth of Scientific Knowledge.* New York: Harper & Row, 1962.

Putnam, Hilary. "The Depths and Shadows of Experience." In *Science, Religion, and the Human Experience,* edited by James D. Proctor, pp. 89-114. Oxford: Oxford University Press, 2005.

Quine, W. V. O. "Epistemology Naturalized." In *Ontological Relativity and Other Essays,* pp. 69-90. New York: Columbia University Press, 1969.

Quinn, Philip. "The Foundations of Theism Again: A Rejoinder to Plantinga." In Zagzebski, *Rational Faith,* pp. 14-47.

———. "In Search of the Foundations of Theism." *Faith and Philosophy* 2, no. 4 (1985): 469-86.

Quinn, Philip L., and Charles Taliaferro. *A Companion to Philosophy of Religion.* Blackwell Companions to Philosophy 8. Cambridge, MA: Blackwell, 1997.

Rae, Murray. *Kierkegaard's Vision of the Incarnation: By Faith Transformed.* Oxford: Oxford University Press, 1997.

Ratzinger, Joseph. *Introduction to Christianity.* Communio Books. San Francisco: Ignatius Press, 2004.

Reed, Thomas McHugh. "Christianity and Agnosticism." *International Journal for Philosophy of Religion* 52 (2002): 81-95.

Reid, Thomas. *Essays on the Active Powers of the Human Mind: An Inquiry into the Human Mind on the Principles of Common Sense.* Edited by Dugald Stewart and G. N. Wright. London: T. Tegg, 1843.

Reno, R. R. "Theology's Continental Captivity." *First Things* 162 (2006): 26-33.

Richards, Jay Wesley. *The Untamed God: A Philosophical Exploration of Divine Perfection, Immutability and Simplicity.* Downers Grove, IL: InterVarsity Press, 2003.

Ricoeur, Paul. "Toward a Hermeneutic of the Idea of Revelation." In *Essays on Biblical Interpretation,* edited by Paul Ricoeur and Lewis Seymour Mudge, pp. 73-118. Philadelphia: Fortress, 1980.

Ritschl, Albrecht. *Three Essays.* Philadelphia: Fortress, 1972.

Robbins, J. Wesley. "Belief in God, Proper Basicality, and Rationality." *Journal of the American Academy of Religion* 61, no. 2 (1993): 339-41.

———. "Is Belief in God Properly Basic?" *International Journal for Philosophy of Religion* 14, no. 4 (1983): 241-48.

Roberts, Robert Campbell. *Faith, Reason, and History: Rethinking Kierkegaard's Philosophical Fragments.* Macon, GA: Mercer University Press, 1986.

Robinson, James McConkey, and Jürgen Moltmann, eds. *The Beginnings of Dialectic Theology.* Richmond, VA: John Knox, 1968.

Rogers, Eugene F., Jr. *Thomas Aquinas and Karl Barth: Sacred Doctrine and the Natural Knowledge of God.* Notre Dame, IN: University of Notre Dame Press, 1995.

Rumscheidt, H. Martin, ed. *Revelation and Theology: An Analysis of the Barth-Harnack Correspondence of 1923.* Cambridge: Cambridge University Press, 1972.

Russell, Bertrand. *Human Knowledge, Its Scope and Limits.* London: Allen & Unwin, 1948.

Russman, Thomas A. "'Reformed' Epistemology." In *Thomistic Papers,* edited by Leonard A. Kennedy, 4:185-205. Houston: Center for Thomistic Studies, 1988.

Schaeffer, Francis A. *The Church Before the Watching World.* Downers Grove, IL: InterVarsity Press, 1971.

Schellenberg, J. L. *Will to Imagine: A Justification of Skeptical Religion.* Ithaca, NY: Cornell University Press, 2009.

Schubert, Frank. "Is Ancestral Testimony Foundational Evidence for God's Existence?" *Religious Studies* 27 (1991): 499-510.

Schwöbel, Christoph. "Theology." In Webster, *Cambridge Companion to Karl Barth,* pp. 17-36.

Shogenji, Tomoji. "The Role of Coherence in Epistemic Justification." *Australasian Journal of Philosophy* 79, no. 1 (2001): 90-106.

Shults, F. LeRon. *The Postfoundationalist Task of Theology: Wolfhart Pannenberg and the New Theological Rationality.* Grand Rapids: Eerdmans, 1999.

Smith, Christian. *The Bible Made Impossible: Why Biblicism Is Not a Truly Evangelical Reading of Scripture.* Grand Rapids: Brazos Press, 2011.

Smith, John Edwin. "Experience and Its Religious Dimension: Response to Vincent G. Potter." In *Reason, Experience, and God: John E. Smith in Dialogue,* edited by Vincent Michael Colapietro, pp. 85-103. American Philosophy Series 7. New York: Fordham University Press, 1997.

Sosa, Ernest, ed. *Knowledge and Justification.* 2 vols. Brookfield, VT: Dartmouth, 1994.

Soskice, Janet Martin. "The Ends of Man and the Future of God." In *The End of the World and the Ends of God: Science and Theology on Eschatology,* edited by John Polkinghorne and Michael Welker, pp. 78-87. Harrisburg, PA: Trinity Press International, 2000.

Sparks, Kenton. *God's Word in Human Words: An Evangelical Appropriation of Critical Biblical Scholarship.* Grand Rapids: Baker Academic, 2008.

Spiegelberg, Herbert. *The Phenomenological Movement: A Historical Introduction.* With the collaboration of Karl Schuhmann. 3rd rev. and enlarged ed. Phaenomenologica 5-6. The Hague: Nijhoff, 1982.

Stadtland, Tjarko. *Eschatologie und Geschichte in der Theologie des jungen Karl Barth.* Neukirchen-Vluyn: Neukirchener Verlag, 1966.

Steup, Matthias, ed. *Knowledge, Truth, and Duty: Essays on Epistemic Justification, Responsibility, and Virtue.* Oxford: Oxford University Press, 2001.

———. "Proper and Improper Use of Cognitive Faculties: A Counterexample to Plantinga's Proper Functioning Theory." *Philosophy and Phenomenological Research* 55, no. 2 (1995): 409-13.

Stewart, H. L. "The 'Reverent Agnosticism' of Karl Barth." *Harvard Theological Review* 43, no. 3 (1950): 215-32.

Stout, Jeffrey. *Ethics After Babel: The Languages of Morals and Their Discontents.* Princeton, NJ: Princeton University Press, 1988.

Sudduth, Michael L. Czapkay. "The Internalist Character and Evidentialist Implications of Plantingian Defeaters." *International Journal for Philosophy of Religion* 45 (1999): 167-87.

———. "Plantinga's Revision of the Reformed Tradition: Rethinking Our Natural Knowledge of God." *Philosophical Books* 42, no. 2 (2002): 81-91.

———. "Reformed Epistemology and Christian Apologetics." *Religious Studies* 39, no. 3 (2003): 299-321.

Swinburne, Richard G. *Epistemic Justification.* Oxford: Oxford University Press, 2001.

———. *Faith and Reason.* Oxford: Oxford University Press, 1981.

———. "Plantinga on Warrant." Review of *Warranted Christian Belief,* by Alvin Plantinga. *Religious Studies* 37 (2001): 203-14.

———. *The Resurrection of God Incarnate.* Oxford: Oxford University Press, 2003.

———. *Revelation: From Metaphor to Analogy.* 2nd ed. Oxford: Oxford University Press, 2007.

———. "The Value and Christian Roots of Analytical Philosophy of Religion." In Harris and Insole, *Faith and Philosophical Analysis,* pp. 33-45.

Swinburne, Richard G., and Alvin C. Plantinga. "Swinburne and Plantinga on Internal Rationality." *Religious Studies* 37 (2001): 357-58.

Taliaferro, Charles. *Evidence and Faith: Philosophy and Religion Since the Seventeenth Century.* Evolution of Modern Philosophy. Cambridge: Cambridge University Press, 2005.

Taylor, Charles. "Overcoming Epistemology." In *After Philosophy: End or Transformation?* edited by Kenneth Baynes, James Bohman and Thomas McCarthy, pp. 464-88. Cambridge, MA: MIT Press, 1987.

Thiel, John E. *Nonfoundationalism.* Minneapolis: Fortress, 1994.

Thiemann, Ronald F. "Revelation and Imaginative Construction." *Journal of Religion* 61 (1981): 242-63.

———. *Revelation and Theology: The Gospel as Narrated Promise.* Notre Dame, IN: University of Notre Dame Press, 1985.

Thiselton, Anthony C. *A Concise Encyclopedia of the Philosophy of Religion.* Oxford: Oneworld, 2002.

Tilley, Terrence W. "Reformed Epistemology and Religious Fundamentalism: How

Basic Are Our Basic Beliefs?" *Modern Theology* 6, no. 3 (1990): 237-57.

———. Review of *Warranted Christian Belief,* by Alvin Plantinga. *Theological Studies* 62 (2001): 388-90.

Tomberlin, James E., and Peter van Inwagen, eds. *Alvin Plantinga.* Dordrecht: D. Reidel, 1985.

Torrance, Alan J. "Is Love the Essence of God?" In *Nothing Greater, Nothing Better: Theological Essays on the Love of God,* edited by Kevin J. Vanhoozer, pp. 114-37. Grand Rapids: Eerdmans, 2001.

———. *Persons in Communion: An Essay on Trinitarian Description and Human Participation, with Special Reference to Volume One of Karl Barth's Church Dogmatics.* Edinburgh: T & T Clark, 1996.

———. "Reclaiming the Continuing Priesthood of Christ: Implications and Challenges." Paper presented at the First Annual Los Angeles Theology Conference, Biola University, January 18, 2013.

Torrance, James B. "The Vicarious Humanity of Christ." In Torrance, *Incarnation,* pp. 127-47.

Torrance, Thomas F. *The Christian Frame of Mind.* Edinburgh: Handsel Press, 1985.

———. *God and Rationality.* London: Oxford University Press, 1971.

———, ed. *The Incarnation: Ecumenical Studies in the Nicene-Constantinopolitan Creed A.D. 381.* Edinburgh: Handsel Press, 1981.

———. *Karl Barth: An Introduction to His Early Theology, 1910–1931.* London: SCM Press, 1962.

———. *Karl Barth, Biblical and Evangelical Theologian.* Edinburgh: T & T Clark, 1990.

———. "The Problem of Natural Theology in the Thought of Karl Barth." *Religious Studies* 6 (1970): 121-35.

———. *Reality and Scientific Theology.* Theology and Science at the Frontiers of Knowledge 1. Edinburgh: Scottish Academic Press, 1985.

———. "Revelation, Creation and Law." *Heythrop Journal* 37 (1996): 273-83.

———. *Theological Science.* London: Oxford University Press, 1969.

Trigg, Roger. Review of *Warranted Christian Belief,* by Alvin Plantinga. *Faith and Philosophy* 19 (2002): 123-26.

Van Huyssteen, J. Wentzel. *Essays in Postfoundationalist Theology.* Grand Rapids: Eerdmans, 1997.

———. *The Shaping of Rationality: Toward Interdisciplinarity in Theology and Science.* Grand Rapids: Eerdmans, 1999.

Van Ness, Peter H. Review of *Philosophers Who Believe: The Spiritual Journeys of 11 Leading Thinkers,* edited by Kelly James Clark. *Journal of the American Academy of Religion* 64, no. 4, thematic issue on Religion and American Popular Culture (1996): 886-89.

Vanhoozer, Kevin J. "The Apostolic Discourse and Its Developments." In Bockmuehl and Torrance, *Scripture's Doctrine and Theology's Bible,* pp. 191-207.

———. *First Theology: God, Scripture & Hermeneutics*. Downers Grove, IL: InterVarsity Press, 2002.

———. "God's Mighty Speech-Acts: The Doctrine of Scripture Today" In *A Pathway into the Holy Scripture,* edited by P. E. Satterthwaite and David F. Wright, pp. 143-81. Grand Rapids: Eerdmans, 1994.

———. *Is There a Meaning in This Text? The Bible, the Reader, and the Morality of Literary Knowledge.* Grand Rapids: Zondervan, 1998.

———. "A Person of the Book? Barth on Biblical Authority and Interpretation." In *Karl Barth and Evangelical Theology,* edited by Sung Wook Chung, pp. 26-59. Grand Rapids: Baker Academic, 2006.

Vanhoozer, Kevin J., and Martin Warner, eds. *Transcending Boundaries in Philosophy and Theology: Reason, Meaning and Experience.* Aldershot, UK: Ashgate, 2007.

Veitch, James A. "Revelation and Religion in Karl Barth." *Scottish Journal of Theology* 24, no. 1 (1971): 1-22.

Vlastos, Gregory. "Socrates' Disavowal of Knowledge." *Philosophical Quarterly* 35, no. 138 (1985): 1-31.

Volf, Miroslav. "Theology, Meaning, and Power." In *The Future of Theology: Essays in Honor of Jürgen Moltmann,* ed. Miroslav Volf, Carmen Krieg and Thomas Kucharz. Grand Rapids: Eerdmans, 1996.

Wainwright, William J., ed. *God, Philosophy, and Academic Culture: A Discussion Between Scholars in the AAR and the APA.* Reflection and Theory in the Study of Religion 11. Atlanta: Scholars Press, 1996.

Wallace, Mark I. "Ricoeur, Rorty, and the Question of Revelation." In *Meanings in Texts and Actions: Questioning Paul Ricoeur,* edited by David E. Klemm and William Schweiker, pp. 235-53. Charlottesville: University Press of Virginia, 1993.

Ward, Graham. *Barth, Derrida and the Language of Theology.* Cambridge: Cambridge University Press, 1995.

———. "Barth, Modernity and Postmodernity." In Webster, *Cambridge Companion to Karl Barth,* pp. 274-95.

Ward, Keith. *Religion and Revelation: A Theology of Revelation in the World's Religions.* Oxford: Oxford University Press, 1994.

Ward, Timothy. *Word and Supplement: Speech Acts, Biblical Texts, and the Sufficiency of Scripture.* Oxford: Oxford University Press, 2002.

Webb, Stephen H. *Re-Figuring Theology: The Rhetoric of Karl Barth.* SUNY Series in Rhetoric and Theology. Albany: State University of New York Press, 1991.

Webster, John B., ed. *The Cambridge Companion to Karl Barth.* Cambridge: Cambridge University Press, 2000.

———. *Holy Scripture: A Dogmatic Sketch.* Cambridge: Cambridge University Press, 2003.

———. "Introducing Barth." In Webster, *Cambridge Companion to Karl Barth,* pp. 1-16.

Westphal, Merold. Review of *Warranted Christian Belief,* by Alvin Plantinga. *Modern Theology* 17 (2001): 99-100.

Willard, Dallas. *Knowing Christ Today: How We Can Trust Spiritual Knowledge.* New York: HarperCollins, 2009.

Wittgenstein, Ludwig. *Tractatus Logico-Philosophicus.* New York: Harcourt, Brace, 1922.

Wood, Jay W. *Epistemology: Becoming Intellectually Virtuous.* Downers Grove, IL: InterVarsity Press, 1998.

Wood, Laurence W. "Defining the Modern Concept of Self-Revelation: Toward a Synthesis of Barth and Pannenberg." *Asbury Theological Journal* 41, no. 2 (1986): 85-105.

Wolterstorff, Nicholas. *Divine Discourse: Philosophical Reflections on the Claim That God Speaks.* Cambridge: Cambridge University Press, 1995.

———. "The Migration of Theistic Arguments: From Natural Theology to Evidentialist Apologetics." In Audi and Wainwright, *Rationality, Religious Belief, and Moral Commitment,* pp. 38-81.

———. "The Reformed Tradition." In Quinn and Taliaferro, *Companion to Philosophy of Religion,* pp. 165-70.

———. "What New Haven and Grand Rapids Have to Say to Each Other: 1992 Stob Lectures." In *Seeking Understanding: The Stob Lectures, 1986–1998,* pp. 251-93. Grand Rapids: Eerdmans, 2001.

Wright, N. T. *New Testament and the People of God.* Christian Origins and the Question of God 1. London: SPCK, 1992.

Wykstra, Stephen J. "Externalism, Proper Inferentiality and Sensible Evidentialism." *Topoi* 14, no. 2 (1995): 107-21.

———. "'Not Done in a Corner': How to Be a Sensible Evidentialist About Jesus." *Philosophical Books* 42, no. 2 (2002): 92-116.

Yandell, Keith E. "Is Contemporary Naturalism Self-Referentially Irrational?" *Philosophia Christi* 3, no. 2 (2001): 353-68.

Zagzebski, Linda. "The Inescapability of Gettier Problems." *Philosophical Quarterly* 44, no. 174 (1994): 65-73.

———, ed. *Rational Faith: Catholic Responses to Reformed Epistemology.* Notre Dame, IN: University of Notre Dame Press, 1993.

———. "Religious Knowledge and the Virtues of the Mind." In Zagzebski, *Rational Faith,* pp. 199-225.

Zeis, John. "A Critique of Plantinga's Theological Foundationalism." *Philosophy of Religion* 28 (1990): 173-89.

AUTHOR INDEX

SUBJECT INDEX

Strategic Initiatives in Evangelical Theology

IVP Academic presents a series of seminal works of scholarship with significan relevance for both evangelical scholarship and the church. Strategic Initiatives in Evangelical Theology (SIET) aims to foster interaction within the broader evangelical community and advance discussion in the wider academy around emerging, current, groundbreaking or controversial topics. The series provides a unique publishing venue for both more senior and younger promising scholars.

While SIET volumes demonstrate a depth of appreciation for evangelical theology and the current challenges and issues facing it, the series will welcome books that engage the full range of academic disciplines from theology and biblical studies, to history, literature, philosophy, the natural and social sciences, and the arts.

Published Volumes

Addiction and Virtue, Kent Dunnington
The God of the Gospel, Scott R. Swain
Incarnational Humanism, Jens Zimmerman
Rethinking the Trinity & Religious Pluralism, Keith E. Johnson
Theology's Epistemological Dilemma, Kevin Diller
The Triumph of God Over Evil, William Hasker

An imprint of InterVarsity Press
Downers Grove, Illinois

Assumes the very dilemma: natural kn. is indep. of God. But it can't get us kn. of God so... why not deny ①?

45-46 - God makes first move. But why? Could say same for knowing external reality. God gives us capacity for knowing...

54 - Knowledge of God as "participatory"

56 - Why do we lack capacity for divine knowledge "on our own"? Why not generally true?
p. 57 - one side is uncreated?
* 58 - finitude means no bridge, no analogy?
62 - fallenness is barrier too, overcome by revelation

72 - worry about fideism

75 - Why is "unassisted" human reason starting point for anything?

93 truth from below indep. of revelation
- again, why Xn accept this for anything? need new metaphysics, not more epist.

122 - Nice Pl. evolution summary

130-3 - Argument is not required though might still be possible, fruitful, etc.

134 - GAP!

146 - Role of defeaters

179 - But Xns deny this for natural law!

244 - Analogia as antichrist

246* Key idea is that analogy of being is meant to ground epistemic claims. But not metaphysics!